Mullaghmore harbour c. 1914 showing Zulu lugger leaving, and a Greencastle yawl entering the harbour.

Note "lodges" showing location of entrance doors to four separate apartments.

(Sketch: courtesy of M. Bussman)

W9-DBG-308

CHICAGO PUBLIC LIBRARY
BEVERLY BRANCH
1962 W. 95th STREET
CHICAGO, IL   60643

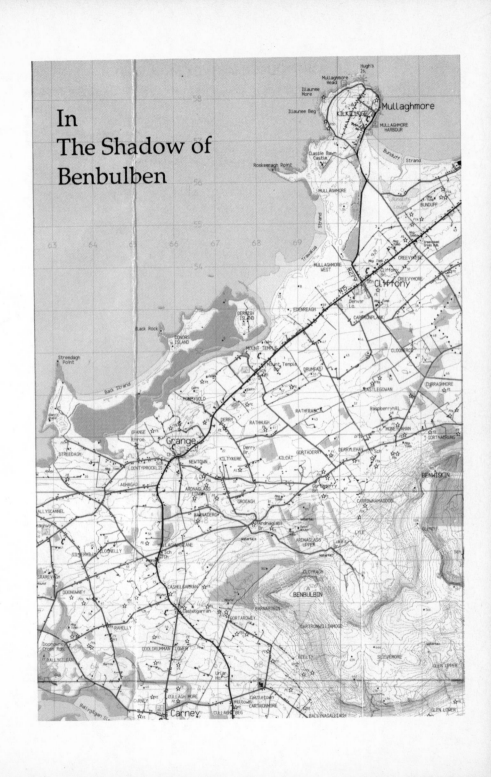

In The Shadow of Benbulben

ORDNANCE SURVEY MAP C.1910
Shows old family names in Mullaghmore after turn of the century

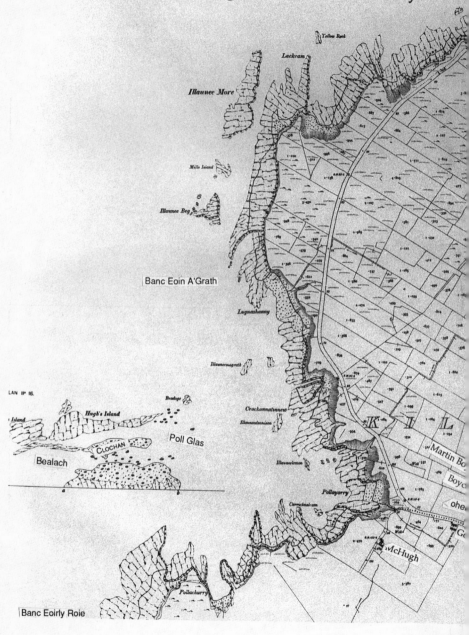

Published by Aeolus 1993
© Joe Mc Gowan

DA
990
.S6
M24
1993

Cp. 1

Cover photographs of Jim Coen drawing hay and
Mick Brennan in his forge by the author.

ISBN   0 9521334 0 7
In The Shadow of Benbulben: Anecdotes & history of North
    Sligo (Hardback)

ISBN   0 9521334 1 5   (Paperback)
In The Shadow of Benbulben: Anecdotes & history of North Sligo

Production Co-Ordination and Typesetting
DRUMLIN PUBLICATIONS, NURE, MANORHAMILTON, CO. LEITRIM.
TEL: 072 - 55237
Printed by: Colour Books, Dublin

R07122 97864

2424

A Dedication

To you who have gone before us, who have blessed the soil of the centuries with your sweat and life's blood; who have fought and died; suffered starvation, hardship and oppression, but nevertheless endured so that we might enjoy what you have won.

"O Benbulben,
At thine feet Classiebawn
At dawn is a bauble.
Through dark night

Thine great eye
Penetrates An Mullac Mor;
Then thou silently smile
To the challenge of David"

(Photo J. Mc G)

In The Shadow of Benbulben

Joe McGowan

Foreword

Sligo is surprising! And Mullaghmore is a gem in its crown, tucked away on a beautiful peninsula to the northwest of the country.

The magic of Mullaghmore must indeed have enthralled me, as I have been coming here on holidays for over thirty years. I am captivated by its charm and beauty, the freshness of its air, and its unpolluted seas. In that time I have seen the changing face of Mullaghmore and applauded the timely decision to establish the Mullaghmore Development Council in order to protect the uniqueness of the area.

It was with great pleasure that I learned that Joe McGowan had decided to chronicle the history of North Sligo, the lore and legend of this beautiful place. He is well fitted for the job – a local man, whose roots go deep into the soil of his native Sligo. He paints a memorable portrait of growing up in this little seaside village; memoirs of a simple way of life of a hardy seafaring people, which is rapidly disappearing.

Anecdotes of the famine years, the land League, the War of Independence and how those momentous events affected the lives of the ordinary people of North Sligo, then and to the present day, are here too.

The stories of the fabled men and women who marched across history's pages are related also, from Balor of the Evil Eye, "who lived at Dun Balra near Mullaghmore", to the decline of the great Irish chieftains, the O'Connor Sligoe, followed by the rise of the Cromwellian planters, Gore, Hamilton, and the Palmerston line. The rise and decline of these settlers is traced from Palmerston, Prime Minister of England (1855-65), who changed the face of North Sligo on his arrival in 1808, to the assassination of Mountbatten of Burma in his fishing boat of Mullaghmore, in August 1979.

This is the story of a troubled and a happy land, with an introduction in the first chapter which reflects the transformation and momentous changes that have taken place in rural Ireland in the past half century.

I hope that all those who love Mullaghmore, as I and my family do will read and treasure this book.

Alderman Sean Dublin Bay-Rockall Loftus.

Contents

1. MEMORABILIA   15

2. FROM BALOR TO THE FRENCH   31
    The Spanish Armada   35
    The Sacking of Sligo town & 'Fryery'   37
    Grange...O'Hart...Soden   43
    Mass Rocks & hedge schoolmasters   46
    The French at Mullaghmore   50

3   OF COFFIN SHIPS AND FAMINE   53
    The Pomano   55
    Letter From Fr. Noone of Grange   58
    Coffin Ships   59

4   GUN RUNNERS AND LAND LEAGUERS   67
    The Erins Hope   67
    The 'Red Fox'   69
    Land Leaguers   72
    Living Conditions at Ballyconnell   75
    Pat Donlevy, Land Leaguer   79
    The Land League Ass   85

5   PROLOGUE TO CONFLICT   85
    United Irish Leagues   87
    Irish Volunteers   88
    Arrival of Father Michael O'Flanagan   91
    The Easter Rising and its consequences   96

6. FREEDOM'S STRUGGLE   101
    Cliffoney Land Fight   101
    Bernie Conway & the Cookstown Barracks   102
    Drowning of the Dogs   106
    Burning of Coastguard station   110
    The Moneygold Ambush   113

7   THE CIVIL WAR AND AFTER   113

    Capture of the Ballinalee   132
    Sligo's Noble Six   134
    Prison Life   135
    Tarring the roads   141
    I.R.A., Volunteers and Blueshirts   144
    The Coastwatchers   148

8   LAND OWNERSHIP & DEVELOPMENT   157

    Succession of Ahamlish   159
    'Squaring the Land'   162
    1826 roadworks   164
    John Hannon's Report   167

9   SCHOOLS, CHURCHES AND COMMERCE   171

    Schools   172
    Churches   176
    The Lodges   183
    Lime & Lime Kilns   186
    A Directory   190

10   'CLASHYBAAN' HARBOUR TO THE BARYTES RUSH   197

    Mullaghmore Harbour   198
    Shipwreck   200
    Cross inscribed slab & Palmerston trees   202
    Classiebawn Castle   203
    1895; the way we were   206
    Cliffoney Lace   215
    Kelp: Loading the Ships   217
    Mullaghmore Barytes Rush   223

11   'THE LAST OF THE WINDJAMMERS'   229

    Mullaghmore Regatta   233
    Returns From fishing   234
    Greencastle yawls   236
    Conditions of fisheries in 1896   237
    Witches & enchanted rats   242
    Zulu Luggers   244

12   OF SIGNAL STATIONS, SEA FENCIBLES & COASTGUARDS   249

    Signal Stations   250
    Sea Fencibles   251
    Coastguards   253

Appendix A
THE ENVIRONMENTAL SETTING   259
by Don Cotton

Appendix B
MINERAL WATER WEALTH &
THE SCENERY OF SLIGO   268

Appendix C
CLIFFONEY'S REBEL PRIEST   273

Appendix D
THE REBEL COUNTESS   279

Appendix E
MULLAGHMORE HARBOUR 1826   282

Appendix F
PLACENAME TRANSLATIONS   288

POETS CORNER   293

BIBLIOGRAPHY   310

GRIFFITH'S VALUATIONS OF TENEMENTS   312

NOTE: SUB-HEADINGS ARE INCLUDED ONLY AS A GUIDE FOR EASE OF REFERENCE TO CONTENTS.

Acknowledgements

Acknowledgements, like charity, should begin at home so on that note I will begin by thanking my wife Antoinette for suggesting the title and for her interest and encouragement during the course of the work, also Janet, my daughter, for doing the groundwork at the Public Records Office in Kew, London, and familiarizing me with the intricacies of accessing information there; to Tara who spent many long hours seeking out information in the Public Records Office and National Museum in Dublin; to Kathleen who sat patiently for hours listening to and transcribing taped interviews and information; lastly to Peter who patiently guided this member of a gentler, ass and cart oriented generation, through the complexities of the word processor. This guidance involved, on occasion, the restraining of the frustrated user from wreaking vengeance on a recalcitrant machine with a lump hammer!

The lists of people who helped this book to become a reality by tendering support, advice and information would fill a book in itself. I will try to mention a few of these here, who are not mentioned elsewhere in this book:- Finbarr Hegarty, Sligo; John McTernan and staff of Sligo County Library; Bernie Barry, Lower Bunduff; Thomas Boyce, Mullaghmore; Eileen Coyne, Carns; the Devins family, Aughaged; Pakie Connolly, Castlegal; Bernie Kelly, Mullaghmore; Henry Conway, Carns; Dan Gilmartin, Ballintrillick; Francis Crean, Ballintrillick; Michael Leonard, Bunduff; Moore family, Drumfad; Josie Harrison, Lower Bunduff; John Harrison, Cliffoney; James Gallagher, Cliffoney, Jimmy McGann, Drumfad; Aidan McGowan, Carns; Joyce Enright; John Crean, Ballintrillick; Kathleen Clancy, Cliffoney; Mary Deery, Mullaghmore; Beatrice McLaughlin, Bunduff; Ann O'Dare, Cliffoney.

A very special "thank you"

I also wish to thank the sponsors named on this page who helped to overcome the cost of printing. Without their very real commitment, generosity, moral and financial support, this book might naver have got beyond the manuscript stage. Go raibh mile maith agat.

CONNOLLY, MAY & JOHN JOE
DONLEVY, JOHN & SHEILA
ANONYMOUS
HEGARTY, FINBARR & ELEANOR
JONES, TED & KIT
LIM, DR. JOE & PAULINE
LOUGHRIN, PETER & BRIDIE
McHUGH, JACKIE & DOROTHY
TREACEY, RICHARD & ROSEMARY

CONWAY, BRIAN & EMER
FARREL, SEAMUS & SIOBHAN
GORMLEY, JAY & RITA
HAZLETTE, OLIVER & JOAN
KEENAN, DES & ANNE
LOFTUS, SEAN & UNA
MAGUIRE, TOMMY & PAULINE
PHOENIX, NOEL & MARGARET
ANONYMOUS

BOYLE, DANNY & ATTRACTA
DEERY, MARY
GILMORE, LARRY & MONICA
LOMAX, RODNEY & TRUDY
McLOUGHLIN, JOHN & BEATRICE
O'SULLIVAN, EITHNE

BURKE, THOMAS & SHEILA
DEVINS FAMILY
HAWKSHAW, MICHAEL & MARY
McHUGH, LIAM
O'DOWD, DAITHI & FRANCES
QUINN, KEVIN

"Even now the devastation is begun,
And half the business of destruction done:
Even now, methinks, as pondering here I stand,
I see the rural virtues leave the land.

Ill fares the land, to hastening ills a prey,
Where wealth accumulates, and men decay;
Princes and lords may flourish, or may fade;
A breath can make them, as a breath has made:
But a bold peasantry, their country's pride,
When once destroyed, can never be supplied"

(O. Goldsmith)

CHAPTER 1

*M*emorabilia

High above, a small cigar shaped, silver object moved urgently across a lazy blue Summer sky. Behind it, apparently being towed, could just be seen a smaller dot."Targets for the fighter planes", my Father said, and sure enough the Spitfires wheeled and dived in mock attacks behind.

It was the closing years of the second World War and as a child of five the conflict being fought in Europe and beyond was totally incomprehensible to me. Still, now, they form my earliest memories of a distant past, made more distant by the tremendous changes that have taken place in Mullaghmore (the village that a happy fate deigned I would be born in); changes that are microcosmic of the transitions that have taken place all over rural Ireland in the past fifty years.

For some, the war years and Globo coffee will bring a bitter memory and an even more bitter taste to mind. With rationing, we quite often couldn't get tea, only the bitter tasting Globo coffee dispensed with tight lips and a dismissive flourish of the hand by Mylie Doyle, our Postmaster, grocer, and dictator absolute of the one telephone line in and out of Mullaghmore.

My Mother, in common with all the older folk, complained long and hard about the unavailability of white flour and the black bread and flour available in the shops. Tobacco too, was in short supply, and some of the men tried drying tealeaves and smoking them, that is of course when the same method of drying the tealeaves had not already been used to recycle the tea for the pot. Paraffin oil for the lamps was in short supply too, but man is at his best in adversity. I remember Dan Kelly and my father melting tallow which had been washed in on the shore, pouring it into the casing of a bicycle pump with a string drawn through and using the resulting candle for light at night.

At this time, in the early 40's, much effort was expended by the local men along the seashore searching for "eadaills". These "eadaills" were the result of shipwrecks and sinkings at sea and were washed ashore in the form of logs, planks of timber, rafts, barrels of oil, and sometimes whiskey, butter and bales of raw rubber. The men were on the move with lanterns before daybreak and especially keen after an Atlantic storm. Men vied with each other for flotsam coming ashore and quite often the man with the longest throw with a grapnel beat the man who was there first, to the prize. Stories of close calls were many; my Father with his foot caught between two boulders, chest deep in water with a flood tide and unable to reach his boot to unlace it, finally wrenching his foot free when all seemed lost, leaving the boot behind; on another occasion surrounded by a multitude of rats attracted to the light of the cart lamp; Johnny Barry, daring to go further in to secure a plank of timber only to be washed out to sea by a freak wave and when drowning seemed inevitable, being re-deposited on the shore by another more benevolent wave, breathless and dazed.

Frank Sweeney of Grange was giving five pounds for a bale of rubber then. This was a kings ransom for these desperately poor people and many a bale of rubber was brought to Frank, but secretly, as technically and in law, any items being washed ashore were the property of the State. If the men of the area were diligent and assiduous in attending the seashore then the Gardai of the day were just as diligent in pursuing the men and goods to recover what they considered to be State property. Many a fearful day was spent in the village as the "Guards" probed turf stacks and hay ricks and dug up gardens to recover items from these poor people. My mother still recalls the day when the excise men accompanied by Garda Burns came to Mullaghmore to confiscate any contraband they could find. The excise man, refusing to believe my father's protestations of innocence regarding possession of a bale of rubber, plunged his steel probe into the hayrick, "Ye have the rubber, I know it and I'm going to find it."

"You're wrong," my father replied.

"Ye fooled me about the dog before," Burns chipped in.

"Never mind the dog," my father replied, "it's rubber you're after now."

The bale of rubber was not included in their seizures that day, being safely cradled in the bosom of a friendly neighbours stack of turf. Centuries of hiding from and eluding the English invader had moulded a resourceful people, and many were the planks and logs brought by circuitous routes by these hardy coast dwellers, to be cut and sawn into boards by Johnny Mc Cann of Milk Harbour and made into horse and ass carts and sturdy wheelbarrows. Many a nocturnal trip too was made to Frank Sweeney and many a deal done by candle light.

One grey stormy day, through the roars of an Atlantic gale, we heard the sound of an airplane circling. My Father and the older men looked to sea with their craggy weatherbeaten faces, etched by many a Winter gale, shaking their heads as they watched from behind stone and sod fences as the plane circled and searched for a safe landing. Peaked caps turned to the backs of their heads in their way, a surer indicator than any barometer of the severity of the storm, they watched helplessly as the plane fell into the sea about two miles off Mullagh Head. A sadness fell over the watchers as we stood there and prayed while these strangers fought for their lives in the angry ocean. After awhile, the men broke up into little groups and moved silently homewards.

In relative terms, war or world events, generally speaking, seemed to have as little effect on our little village as our power to control them. Typical of North Sligo, Mullaghmore was a busy farming community which included a fair number of fishermen; many of these were farmers who supplemented their income by part time fishing. (It is said that when Palmerston "squared" the land, that he moved the majority of the people to the western half of the peninsula, in the hope that the severe conditions there would cause them to abandon their holdings and the area. What is certain is that the farmers were installed to the west of the Hill road and the fishermen with their small plots on the other side.)

The average home would have eight or so in the family; plenty of help for tending the cattle and working the fields. Every home was practically self sufficent with fields given over to meadow for Winter hay and more fields kept for pasture for herds of three or four dairy cows. An acre or two would be kept for potatoes; Aran Banners for the livestock and the early Epicures, and later on floury Kerrs Pinks for the household table. The "poheens" or little potatoes would be picked out of the household store, put along with the Banners and kept for the livestock. A portion of the tilled area was kept for rye and oats; the rye and oat grain crushed and used for cattle fodder, the straw used as a rich golden thatch for the homes, byres and stables. The oaten straw was not always considered to be suitable for thatching and was often grown to be used as fodder, a special favourite with the family horse or ass.

Still more of this tilled area was given over to turnip swedes, mangels, "Early York" cabbage, "Flat Dutch" cabbage, carrots and parsnips. The swedes and mangels were sliced by hand and fed with a sprinkling of "injun" meal to the cattle along with armfuls of hay in the Winter. Swedes were a tasty vegetable for the kitchen too along with the carrots and parsnips. "Flat Dutch" was a good table cabbage and was also fed to the cattle in the late harvest.

Average farm holdings consisted of 15 to 20 acres of good land. The homes, most of which were built in the early years of the 19th century, were solidly constructed of stone with a kitchen/livingroom in the middle and a bedroom on either end. The front entrance would often have a half door which served well to let in the light whilst keeping out the hens, chickens and turkeys that were constantly on the mooch, looking for food. Years ago the half door was a very practical alternative to enlarging a window or putting in a new one as these improvements would result in increased rents to the landlord. A huge open fireplace was the dominant feature of the kitchen, its cheery turf fire providing the heat for cooking and warming; it was here that soda bread was made in cast iron ovens hanging from a "crane" or "crook" over the open fire; it was here that the potbellied, three legged, blackened pot huffed and puffed and boiled the poheens for the hens or the "Kerrs Pinks" for the dinner or the nettles and comfrey that had been gathered (painfully) in big bags for the guldering turkeys.

The blazing fire was a social focal point too as in the long Winter nights the flames danced and shadows leaped and flickered on the wall as the older men and women told and retold their stories of ghosts and fairies and haunted houses; stories that had been passed on to them by previous generations and added to by their own experiences. Ghosts were fought and lucky escapes recounted; stories of being "put astray" by the fairies, and banshees that wailed at night to foretell a death. By the flickering firelight and later in the night by the pallid glow of the oil lamp, anything was possible and the spirit-peopled other world became a real thing. Later in the night grim possibilities lurked in every shadow as they leered and leaped at you as you made your way to bed in the "upper" room and God help you if you had to make your way home in the dark night having heard these stories in a neighbour's house. Today's television soap operas, like Neighbours and Coronation Street, are poor substitutes indeed for thrills like these.

School days came dramatically when, one day, having received an extra good scrubbing, I was taken by the hand by Mary Dowdican and in short-trousered bewilderment, escorted past the boundaries of my familiar world, up the road and down the little narrow lane, past Bruens old house to arrive eventually at an awesome grey building where I was deposited into the care of Miss Moffit, warden and teacher of the infant classes. It seems rather strange now, but in those days knee length short trousers were worn by young boys until they reached the age of ten or twelve; my generation was fortunate to escape the indignity inflicted on previous generations of small boys, who were dressed in petticoats during these tender years. There can be no nostalgic yearning to re-live these years by anyone who experienced them, as these short corduroys were absolutely no defence against angry, sally rod wielding parents or teachers who with very little effort could leave painful, angry red welts on those defenceless, unprotected tender legs in an age when to, "spare the rod and spoil the child," was dogma. The transition to long trousers was a much welcomed defence, a merciful benefaction which signified too, an important step forward into the adult world.

Miss Moffit taught the infant classes, a diminutive figure but nevertheless a staunch one, who instilled fear into her even more diminutive charges. Here you learned your A B C's earnestly, although sometimes with a false gusto, whether you liked it or not. I don't ever remember Miss Moffit, or Mrs. Hunt as she later became, using the "stick." A rigid forefinger armoured with half an inch of manicured, pointed fingernail at the end, when poked stiffly at the nearest available exposed part of the anatomy, usually the forehead, was punishment enough and provoked many a pained, if shallow promise of model behaviour in the future.

Strangely enough it was here, in Miss Moffit's room, that my first skirmish with the nether regions of the opposite sex came unexpectedly and uninvited when K——, one roasting Summers day, jumped up on my school desk to open the window to let the cool Summer breezes flow through the hot classroom. It was not the only place the cool Summer breezes were blowing; a slight billowing of skirts, an almost imperceptible and involuntary (I believe) inclination of my inquisitive young neck and K——'s orbs like two plump, pimple cratered, half moons, unobscured by either lace or cotton, leered at me from the shadowy recesses of the forbidden zone. Education indeed covers more than the three R's and experiences like this must surely be considered in more ways than one as being part of a well rounded education.

The turf fire was a focal point of life in the cold months, in the infants room as well as in the senior's. These fires were fed sometimes by the parents of the pupils delivering the occasional cart of turf, or more often, by a clod or two carried under the arm into school each morning by the students. The smallest pupils were in the desks closest to the fire. Graduating to the long high desk at the back of the room, where the smug, self satisfied older students sat, gave a feeling of having made it; of having taken a major step on that long road towards maturity and the grown-up world. Growing up brings responsibilities and it was here that I first experienced that uneasy feeling in the pit of the stomach — a tangible sense of fear that first manifested itself when I was called on to produce some evidence of homework having been attended to the previous night. My bluff was called and with nothing to show for my time except a long winter's night spent dallying over books and listening to Dan Kelly and Johnny Cummins and the older people telling ghost stories, my stomach churned as I made my faltering way to the end of that big desk and the long walk to face Miss Moffit's beetling brow and armour plated fingernail.

With the basics learned, the next major move was into the outer senior's room where Sr. de Pazzi held sway. Our childhood behind us, here we felt a new sense of importance and purpose. The days of the puddle under the desk were now left behind us as we took another important step towards the adult world. Still, despite a grim determination the more unfortunate ones sat over the very occasional salty trickle before a fevered, tremulous, "cead agam dul amach," brought a watery and welcome relief; the telltale spot on the short trousers soon fading away.

At this age, one doesn't appreciate the importance of a good sound education so our progress had to be nurtured and encouraged more by a healthy respect for Sr. de Pazzi's cane, wielded at the end of a strong right arm than any intrinsic appreciation of the three R's. Sr. de Pazzi's unfortunate discovery that my father owned a thicket of sally bushes which were used for scollop thatching resulted in my reluctant participation in a scheme of replenishment for her store of sally rods. This reluctant co-operation was punctuated only very occasionally by a hestitant defiance when I would deliver a faulty set of rods, nicked halfway through so that they would snap on being used. I had no confidence in the much discussed theory, held at the time, that on placing a hair across the palm of the hand immediately before being slapped, the offending rod would break in half. This theory lasted all through my school years as obviously there were some practical difficulties and obstacles in the way of carrying out a test. For myself, I never could figure out how to get the hair in place before being slapped, as Sr. de Pazzi was quite unpredictable in matters like this.

Colm Watters was our hero as he seemed to have an infinite capacity to absorb any amount of hard slaps with the rod, with no outward show or change of expression except, maybe a slight reddening of the face and perhaps, if you really looked closely, just a hint of moisture behind the eyes. However damaged, he always managed a swagger and at least a weak smile for us on the way back to his desk. He was our man out there in front, our ambassador and representative; being weaker creatures ourselves, we all shared in his idomitable spirit, proof to the tyrant nuns that we might be beaten but never broken.

One of the strongest memories of my days spent in this room is of being gathered with the other pupils in a big semi-circle around a roaring winter fire learning page after page of poetry; the Bridge of Athlone, Song of Victory and Song of Defeat come to mind. It was through the medium of poetry that we learned one day the meaning of the word "paradox":

> *O'Brien, Mitchell and Meagher;*
> *Aye, and of newer note*
> *Names that Eire will not forget,*
> *Though some have faded in far off lands,*
> *And some have passed by the hangmans hands,*
> *And some — are breathing yet....*

> *...And their memories green and sweet,*
> *On every hillside and every mart*
> *In every cabin, in every street,*
> *Of a land, where to fail is more than to triumph,*
> *And victory less than defeat.*

illustrating that in our national struggle for freedom, paradoxically, we gained more of a sense of determination from our defeats than from our victories. Our teacher exuded a sense of love of life and national pride as she taught us lessons which are just as relevant today as they were then; lessons which we would do well to apply on a personal level in our daily lives too, in the years ahead.

Short lived rebellions we had then too! One of these flared spontaneously when a group of us left the school yard and went down the road about a hundred yards to Mc Hughs shed during the lunchtime break. When Sr. de Pazzi rang the school bell at the end of lunch hour, some kind of madness took hold and we made an instant and poorly thought out decision not to return. Once the decision was made one could not be branded a coward and risk ostracisation by having second thoughts when a second and more insistent ringing of the bell was heard. There could be no going back! Besides, it was a lovely day, this was great fun really when you thought about it, and who knows where it might end? The mob ruled anyway and we held fast even when the nun's threat of, "If ye don't come back, I'll flake ye." rang out on the autumn air. The impasse was broken when the nun, armed with a stout stick, routed us after chasing us for several circuits of the shed, eventually driving a chastened bunch of rebels before her up to the school. We were lined up for punishment at the door and he was a lucky boy that was first in the line and didn't have to endure the lingering dread of those in the back

21

who watched anxiously as their comrades submitted one by one to the whizz, splat, of the cane as it landed with deadly accuracy on out-stretched palms. Our hero, Colm, took it on the chin with his usual air of nonchalance, even though I'm sure his warm, pulsating palms felt just as sore as anyone elses.

Even though the old schoolhouse stands silent and empty now, it seems to me it has a sense of stateliness about it; a sense of past glories and achievements; and why not? This humble building has sheltered in it's day the fostering of the noblest ambitions of mankind, the enlighten-ment that has helped to bring him in a relatively short space of time from stone axe to his first step on the moon.

If you are very quiet and listen hard enough, you can still hear the shouts of laughing children echo around it's now lonely walls; listen and you will hear it — but only if you believe, as I do, that these sounds never die completely away.

This, too, was the era of the twilight of the country house dances. The Parish hall had yet to replace the kitchen as a social centre and despite Fr. Shannon's dire warnings of the "divil being in the house that there was a dance in", young and old would, on special occasions, gath-er into the kitchen and dance "round the house and mind the dresser". Thomas Wymbs and George McClure, Petie McGowan or Henry Gallagher and Peter Mullaney or the Rabbit and the Boar would play fiddle and "melojin" for half sets and Lancers, Stacks o' Barley and Stacks o' Whate. The dancers would whirl and beat out the rythm "heel and toe" on the white scrubbed flagstone floor. After a particularly good night it wasn't unusual for some local poet to write a song about the event:

> "There was dances in the houses and dances in the hall
> But the dance in Mick the Newman's was the dandy of
>   them all.
> Here comes the boys from Cliffoney with their pockets
>   full of pride,
> Thomas Hargadon and Jimmy Barry to dance
>   the Polly Clyde.   •
>
> Johnny Newman and Mick Burns got out to dance a reel
> And no mistake about it, they gave it toe and heel.
> Jack Kelly was heard to whisper, "By jingoes, boys,
>   they're good"
> "Quite right", says Paddy Keagans, "It's natural that they should"

The last dance in our house was held around 1948 on a wild, stormy Winter's night, a hand wound gramaphone providing the music. The thatched roof creaked and shivered with the weight of the Winter gale and under it, oblivious to the storm, the dancers revelled and swung and cheered. We all felt secure, but outside, my Father fought the gale as he checked and tied scollop and thatch and readjusted the "slingers" on the hayricks. We didn't feel as secure the next day as he grumbled loudly about the lack of helping hands in the crisis the night before!

In the Springtime, when the lengthening evenings came, the new years crop of calves would arrive, one by one. This was a very important event and crucial to the survival and well being of the family, and while we may not have realised it at the time, to the welfare of the village and country as well. When calving time was near, there were days of anxious waiting and watching and profound observations by my father and sometimes visiting neighbours, experts in these matters, on whether the "bones" were up or down (the bones were an indicator of how soon the cow would calve). There were all night vigils too and when, at last, the new arrival was imminent, a neighbour or two would be required to help with a difficult "calving".

The slithery newcomer would be carried upside down by the legs from the byre into the kitchen and deposited on a fresh bed of hay. After a few hours, when he had been rubbed dry and was already standing up, albeit on shaky legs, he would be fed with beestings, the first milk of the cow. Shortly after, he would be tied with a length of rope to an iron peg in the floor and a "ponger", with holes for breathing, secured over his snout to prevent him from choking on wisps of hay. This new arrival may have been the pride of the family and a status symbol in the community — partcularly if he was a black bull calf— but my strongest memory is of breakfasts ruined by the indelicate odour emanating from the friendly calf as he stared curiosly at us while unembarrassedly performing his bodily functions

Bungalow blight had yet to stalk the land, and in my mind's eye I can still see the sturdy three-roomed thatched and whitewashed homes; the front windows and doors outlined with lamp black and with brightly painted front doors, a latch always ready for the lifting and no need to knock. As I grew older, I joined the rest of the farming community in their daily bustle as the brightly painted orange and black ass and horse carts rattled and trotted to and fro; to the bog or with five or six creamery cans to the creamery, or to Jimmy Barry's well for a barrel of water. In between trips to Jimmy Barry's with the barrel, the water was brought from Tobair Leice in sturdy two gallon tin cans made by the tinkers, or tinsmiths as those travelling men with the trade preferred to be known. A trip to the well was a social event too and as we met the neighbours, cans were left down, news exchanged, weather discussed and arms rested before picking up the cans and going on another bit.

The Winter supply of turf was carted home from Cloonerco or other bogland areas along the mountain after a tedious season of hard work, from the cutting in the Spring to the footing, reckling and later on the clamping. Each cart had an individual and unmistakeable sound of its own and on a clear evening, long before you could see the cart, you could tell whether it was the tight and lively tip of Johnny Gallagher's cart or the more measured stroke of James Rourke's or the more ponderous sound of Boyce's jennet and cart.

While these beasts of burden were dependable ninety eight percent of the time and presented no more problem than a lively chase through the fields in the morning to capture and put the "winkers" on them, occasionaly there would be a "runaway". These runaways could be quite dangerous, particularly when a horse cart was involved, as the panic stricken beast with heavy cart in tow, tore out of control for miles along narrow country roads.

One pleasant Autumn evening as I was coming home from Cloonerco bog with a full "crivening" of turf, succumbing only now and again to temptation and picking the odd blackberry, I walked along side Belle, the donkey, driving and monitoring her progress, as we proceeded at a leisurely pace towards home. Suddenly, at the top of Carnduff hill, she took fright at something real or imagined in the ditch at the side of the road, leaped sideways and then catapulted forward down the hill. She was gone before I could react and I raced after her, watching helplessly, while she galloped headlong down the hill. I was only sixteen at the time as with a cotton dry mouth and rising fear, I sped, tripping and running over the turf that were now spilling in all directions off the careening cart. She stopped, finally, lathered in sweat and shaking at the crossroads. I was shaking too as I looked back and saw the trail of black turf and bits of the cart that were scattered back for a mile of the road. "Oh, God, I'll be killed when I get home," I thought as I went back and gathered as much as I could of what was left of my neat load of turf.

Eventually, on arriving home, I stuttered my story to my father, a stern man at the best of times. "Are ye alright", he said, and that was all. Relieved, I unloaded what was left of the turf, unharnessed the ass and watched her as she tumbled and rolled, as asses do, in her favourite spot. Finished, she stood, staring defiantly and snorting through flared nostrils at me; she would not have been so "chan" had she sensed my hardening resolve to be a much more stern taskmaster in the future. The day of the horse and ass drawn carts are gone; no busy asses hooves now stir up the dust of winding country roads. These squat, raucous monsters, the noisy, exhaust belching tractors and trailers which have replaced them may not present as picturesque and romantic an image as those easy going days of long ago but we cannot deny that they are much more efficient and attuned to the times we now live in.

With the advent of the hot Summer days, it was time to apply a fresh coat of whitewash to the house. My father showed me how to mix the lime and water and add the secret ingredient that made our house that bit whiter than the others; a ball of Reckitts blue, normally used for bleaching clothes. As I wielded the long handled wooden brush, I thought idly and with a sense of dread and inevitability and with no hope of escape that the hay season could not be far off. On a really bad run of luck, Petie Watters or Luke Leydon would arrive seated on their horse-drawn mowing machine before the whitewashing was finished; their sturdy team of bay horses drawing the machine up the road, its cast iron wheels muffled and protected from the rough road by an encirclement of cast-off car tyres (a scarce commodity in those days). My father would have made an "opening" in the entrance to the field with the scythe; this was to prevent the horse team and machine from trampling the meadow as they entered the field. More often than not, the blades would have to be sharpened before commencing to mow and this was an opening ceremony that required much care and deliberation, reminiscent of the pomp and flourish attached to the fiddlers tuning of his fiddle prior to the music commencing. To the uninitiated, it seemed more like a ceremonial rite that had to be performed, rather than a necessary part of the days work.

Saving the hay took all Summer; picking the weeds, shaking, making "lappings" and rucks in bad weather, hand shakings and eventually when the hay was dry enough, trampcocks. My father was of the old school and making a trampcock was not something to be taken lightly. It had to be considered and approached with due care and deliberation; the field of hay viewed and appraised with the same critical gaze with which, surely, the sculptor viewed his uncut block of stone.

When it was time for the making of the trampcocks, the ass was hooked up to the handshakings and they were drawn one by one into a circle around the site chosen. While this was going on, the builder would have a foundation built of about four to five feet in height, at which point he would climb on and tramp and build and shape it.

Another person was then required to fork the hay to the builder and it was then built and shaped as systematically and carefully as any round tower; layer after layer, the outside wads of hay were laid clockwise in a circle and "tied" on the inside with forkfuls of hay and tramped solid. The sides had to be carefully "let out" at the right time and just as carefully "taken in" when the cock was high enough. The foundation was pulled around and the sides combed and shaped with the rake, further layers of hay were added with more raking and scraping until a final "lapping" of hay was chosen for the top. For my father just any bit of hay would not do for this and I would have to go looking for a green bit which he then shaped carefully and put under his knees, as the cock was by then too tall and shaky to stand up on. All that was left then was to tie it down with the hayropes which had been twisted earlier; a final rake and then the builder would slide down and survey with a cocked eye, his handiwork, as he slowly walked around it.

It was hard work and for me the two best and most sought after times of the day were, one, when my Mother came out with the tea in a sweet can, or in a five naggin bottle, with a sock pulled up over it to keep the tea hot. The sweet smell of the hay was all around as we sat down then and ate thick slices of home-made bread with thick gobs of home-made butter melting into the warm, freshly baked bread.

The most favourite time of all, I must admit, was when the rain threatened from "Innismorra" or swept around the corner of Benbulben and slowly advanced on us until my father said, "Gather up, we'll go home". It was pure joy to have a valid excuse to sit down in the middle of a working day, dig out whatever books we might have and follow Hopalong Cassidy or Kit Carson as they galloped across the prairie and fought the "baddies" to a standstill; or read about our own heroes, Dan Breen and Tom Barry and their romantic sounding Flying Columns, as they attacked and destroyed and fought their baddies, the R.I.C. and Black and Tans, to a standstill. The rain outside provided a re-assuring background melody as it dripped and splashed from the thatched eaves to form puddles and little rivulets on the cobbled street; streamlets which fussed and sped along to make their way eventually, no doubt, to play their part in the greater scheme of things. Dowdicans barrel, which sat dourly under the downspout during the good weather, now took on a new life, and seemed to dance as the water bubbled and streamed rhythmically into it's empty depth, the barrel resonating at a different pitch, as it filled up, until eventually it overflowed with a proud splash, dashing the water over the rim and on to the ground. When this happened, I was sent across the road to carry the surplus to our barrel at the back of the house; you see, the Dowdicans had an advantage over us in that the water could be gathered from their slated roof, whereas it was impossible to do this with our thatched eaves.

The financial reward to be gained at the end of a year's hard work would hopefully be gained through the sale of a few marketable cattle, fat yearlings or two year old stirks for the fairs of Grange or Kinlough in the spring or autumn. If Francie Joe showed up in his pony and trap, accompanied by Tim Gonigle or Michael Mc Gowan, prior to the fair day, it boded well for a good fair with brisk demand. They walked the fields, these shrewd cattle jobbers, slapping their Wellingtons authoritively with their ash plants, as they strode purposefully across the farmers lands, stopping to poke and evaluate the stirk or calves before making an offer.

A price was asked for and a counter-offer made which of course was flatly refused by the seller at this early stage of the deal, no matter how good he might think it was. A battle of wits then ensued as each side fought for the advantage. Open hands were proffered, spat on and slapped as both parties manouevered for the best price. One side or the other would walk away to illustrate his disgust at the stubborness of the other, only to be called back by Michael or some other neutral go-between for a reconciliation and renewed handslapping and bargaining. The rules for these encounters were never written down but they were there all the same and observed as carefully as any prizefight in a ring.

Sometimes a bargain was made in the field, saving a tiresome walk of many miles on the fairday. As often as not, the farmer would take his chances at the fair where, hopefully, there would be more buyers in competition for the cattle. These were bad times and it was not unusual to stand all day at the fair, not reach the offer that was made in the field and have to walk the ten or more miles back home again. On a good day, my father would come home in a good humour, slightly tipsy and with a good fistful of money which he then counted out to my mother. Those were the days when you could "keep a book" in the local grocery shop and cattle in the field were guarantors that the bill would be paid some day. A good fair meant a clean sheet for another year.

The signs of the end of our way of life were all about us then if we could but see them. Some years earlier, Pat Charlie, a man who said his own Mass and communed with the fairies, foretold the changes that were to come. He predicted that the Green Road, where he lived, would come to be known, one day, as Orangemans Row and that King Billy's horses would again jump through the farmers fields. He foretold that the day would come when cows would wear earrings; he spoke about

Hitler long before anyone even heard of the name; looking down at the sandy banks at the beach he declared that he could see people that looked like magpies, long before the Sisters of Mercy built their convent at Mullaghmore. The neighbours found this amusing at the time, but his predictions proved to be as accurate as any that Nostradamus ever made!

Johnny Barry was the first innovator to make a fork cock; it needed no man on top to tramp. In a house where six boys were reared, now there was only Johnny. Every other house was the same, help was getting scarce and Johnny had to make do. Young men and women filtered off to Australia, England and America to make a new and hopefully a better life. My own discontent was growing and one day I would follow them. The men of marriageable age that were left in the village, went to Cliffoney Hall to the dances and sometimes further afield, but time crept on and they didn't get married — others emigrated. There would be no new generation. In time the wolves would gather to prey where there was no heir; property speculators and cheap bargain hunters with no interest in what was best for Mullaghmore.

> *Lost in the passion that never needs a wife —*
> *The pricks that pricked were the pointed pins of harrows.*
> *Children scream so loud that the crows could bring*
> *The seed of an acre away with crow-rude jeers.*
> *Patrick Maguire, he called his dog and he flung a stone*
> *   in the air*
> *And halloed the birds away that were the birds*
> *   of the years.*

The new God, that great destroyer, and maker of the uni-culture, the T.V. set, came to our village, making its first snowy screened appearance to a wondering audience in the Pier Head House in the late fifties. It was the beginning of the end of many things, not least the rambling house and the handing down of the old lore and culture to the next generation. All was about to change and change utterly and absolutely.

O'Rourke in his History of Sligo, written in the last century criticised Palmerston for having developed Mullaghmore as a "watering hole for the rich". This monopoly was broken with the advent of independence in the early '20's and a "bold peasantry" became dominant for some time. The wheel has turned full circle and Mullaghmore once again serves the wealthy who have speculated and exploited and scarred its fair face with the destruction of its woodlands, tasteless housing developments and holiday homes for the rich, that for most of the year stand in empty silence; sepulchral memorials to the rich tapestry of life that was once woven in this fair land:

> *"And then my heart hath told me:*
> *These will pass,*
> *Will pass and change, will die and be no more,*
> *Things bright and green, things young and happy;*
> *And I have gone upon my way*
> *Sorrowful"*

BUNDUFF SOUTERRAIN

Seamus Moore In Smaller inner chamber CREEVYKEEL COURT CAIRN. *stone built into wall near*

A magnificent example of a late stone age court tomb; it has a full court, a two chambered gallery with one corbel stone still in position and three lateral chambers towards the west of the cairn

(Photo J. Mc G)

CHAPTER 2

From Balor To The French

O Donovan in his letters relative to the ordinance survey taken in 1836 gives us some information on the first recorded and as it turns out very famous resident of Ahamlish:

"I am informed that there was a Caiseal at Mullaghmore in the Parish of Ahamlish at the seashore, called Dun Balra where Balor resided for some time. It is said by the people there that he was perfectly skilled in the Magic Art, that he always kept a cover on his eye, which he took off whenever he intended to do an injury by his look."

Balor was a warrior leader of the Firbolgs some two thousand years before Christianity. The Tuatha de Danaan, under the leadership of King Nuada, eventually defeated the Firbolgs and our distinguished resident, at the battle of Moyturra. Balors fate was to have his eye put out, "the blood from which gushed forth to form the lake of Lochaun na Sule near Moyturra in the Parish of Kilmactranny."

Kilkilloge, or as it is more commonly known, Mullaghmore is in the Parish of Ahamlish or Ath-Iomlaisi. Ath-Iomlaisi may have referred to a ford which at one time existed near Ahamlish cemetery. Ahamlish is in turn in the Barony of Carbury which takes its name from Cairbre na Cartragh, the third son of Niall of the Nine Hostages. Niall was a High King of Ireland and son to King Eochaid Mughmedon, High King of Ireland c. 400 A.D. Niall got his nickname from his habit of taking hostages from each of the five regional Kings of Ireland; this worked so well that he took four more hostages from the Welsh chieftains; the name translates leterally as "the giving of hostages". Another son of Niall's, Brian, was ancestor to the O'Connor Sligo, one time chieftains of Sligo, town and county.

It is interesting to note here that Niall was great-great grandfather to St Colmcille who was granted family lands at Drumcliffe to build a monastery in the sixth century. Colmcille's sister was Cumenia, mother to St. Molaise of Inishmurray and patron saint of Ahamlish.

If we are to look for the earliest surviving signs of habitation or civilisation in this area, then we must go to Creevykeel court tomb which, I believe, we can safely say was the first place of worship in these parts. It dates to the Stone age, two thousand to four thousand years B.C. and was surely the focal point of this early community; a place of ceremony and worship which fulfilled most of the functions of the Christian churches of today. Ashes and bone fragments indicate burials and cremation, fulfilling a ceremonial rite of passage to the after life then, as our present day churches do now.

These ancestors of ours probably came from Brittany and show a settlement pattern of small communities based on agriculture and stock raising. Direct evidence of the way of life of these people is provided by the discovery of the bones of cattle, sheep, goats and pigs in excavations of tombs from the period; grain remnants on pottery fragments show that they also cropped the land. We may well speculate that this represents the lifestyle and times of our friend Balor and the Firbolgs.

It is to be expected that if we are to look back further than the last three to four hundred years for enlightenment on local history and happenings, then the pickings are very slim indeed. No anecdotes have been handed down by the local storytellers from this dim distant past but we can be sure that our ancestors were forged in the white heat of history and would have been severely affected by incidents that we know of, such as the Viking landing of 5,000 men in North Sligo in 807 A.D. While no anecdotes of local interest come down to us from this event, we know that the countryside was devastated, villages burned and even the monastery on Inishmurray destroyed and the monks murdered. The Viking grip on Ireland was eventually broken forever at Glenmama in Wicklow in 999 A.D. and Irish control re-asserted by Brian Boru at the Battle of Clontarf in 1014.

The O'Connors, a sept of the Uí Briúin, descendants of Brian, son of NIall of the Nine Hostages, first come to notice in this area in the 12th century when they are known to have settled in Carbury. They were hotly contested for ownership by O'Donnell of Tirconaill and in the battle of Crich Cairbre in 1181, O'Donnell gained the upper hand. The O'Connor never accepted their dominance but it would be two centuries before O'Connor regained Carbury absolutely and struck deep into Tirconaill.

The Norman invasion of Ireland in 1169 was to have a lasting effect on Irish history, its consequences still affecting Ireland nationally and locally to this day. Dermot Mc Murrough, King of Leinster, a man with few friends and many enemies had gone too far when he took Dervogilla, the wife of Tiernan O' Rourke of Breifne. (Some accounts say she went willingly, possibly eloped) Attacked on all sides by his enemies,

Mc Murrough fled to Wales and sought the assistance of Henry the 2nd, Norman ruler of England.

There followed the Anglo Norman invasion of 1169, Strongbow himself arriving in Waterford with a huge army in 1170. In 1239, the Anglo Norman, Maurice Fitzgerald and by then Lord Deputy and Chief Justice of Ireland, gained the upper hand of the Irish chieftains, O'Donnell and Felim O'Connor, who were then in possession of much of all of the parish of Ahamlish, North Sligo and indeed much of North Connaught. In 1245 Fitzgerald built a castle in Sligo on the site of the present City Hall feeling that Sligo town was the gateway to the North. Some historians believe that the 1245 castle built by Maurice Fitzgerald was probably the usual standard 100 metres from the abbey on the river bank – about halfway between the two lanes from O'Connell and Castle St. – and that the Red Earl's castle of 1305, destroyed in 1310 was probably the one on the site of the Town Hall. His intention was to consolidate control in this area and push further into O'Donnell territory. King Henry had long been worried at the successes of the Norman invasion and afraid of being left out of the picture came over to Ireland in 1171, declaring himself to be King of Ireland and demanding submission from all the chiefs, Norman, Irish and Viking. Sligo, town and the six baronies, including Carbury, which was ruled by O'Connor, were now in the possesion of the foreigner and the Irish chieftains subject and beaten, physically at least.

The success of the foreigner could then as well as at other times down through the centuries to the present day be attributed as much to the disunity of the Irish as to the superiority of arms of the invader. In the 14th century there was a Gaelic revival and in 1333 the invader was expelled by a great union of the O'Haras, O'Dowds, O'Connors and O'Donnells. Now comes the golden era of the O'Connor as the English or Anglo-Norman fade from the picture and the battle for supremacy begins among the Irish chieftains again. In 1356 Cathail Oge O'Connors victory over the O'Donnells at Ballyshannon was so decisive that he became by it chief of Tirconaill for a period of time.

By 1396, despite the destructive feuding and attacks on the O'Connors, Sligo town had advanced from the "collection of rude and fragile huts" of the Fitzgeralds to "splendid buildings of wood and stone". The O'Connors, O'Donnells, McDonaghs and Burkes shared in the prosperous times of the middle and late 15th century. However, as we move into the 16th century, we see power and advantage along with the possession of Sligo castle once more see-sawing back and forth between the O'Donnells and the O'Connors. In 1533, Teige Óg O Connor seized Sligo castle from the O'Donnells and in 1536 assumed for the first time the title of O' Connor Sligo.

We can be sure that all of these events had a profound effect on the residents of this area as now, the O'Donnells demanded allegiance from the people and again, the O'Connors, when they were dominant. When attacking Sligo, the O'Donnells traversed through Bundoran across the Drowes through Bunduff, Cliffoney and Grange hugging the coast through Breaghy, Lissadell, Ballygilgan and Carney and in reverse order when the O'Connors drove the attackers back. It is hard for us to imagine today what the countryside looked like then. There were no bridges over the rivers, only fords; roads didn't exist so the coastal route proved the easiest passage, free of dense woodland and boggy ground further inland. It is probable too that the mountain route by Glenade and Ballintrillick and on to Sligo would have been used, as this passage too, would have been relatively free.

In 1522 O'Neill captured the castles of Belleek, Ballyshannon and Bundrowes but in a counter attack at night was completely routed by O'Donnell. O'Donnell marched victoriously through Bunduff and Cliffoney encamping at Carnamada, two miles East of Grange. In 1526 O'Donnell demolished the castle of Grange, the mansion seat of the descendants of Bryan O'Connor. O'Donovan in 1836 relates that, "there is an old castle in Grange called Caisleán na Grainsigh, which was built by the O'Harts, whose descendants claim Grange as their hereditary right and are called by the people Muintir Airt Eiridhe na Grainsigh. It was used as a malt house a few years ago". There is nothing at this time to indicate where this castle stood but local sources say that it may have been sited on a hill outside of Grange, called Caiseal. The O.S. map of 1837 shows a castle in Grange (see map) which may have been Caislean na Grainsigh or a newer castle built in 1604, where we are told that, "a new castle and seven cottages were built by Hugh O'Hart in the town of Grange, Co. Sligo." Grange at that time was known as "Grange Muintir Hart", as it had been assigned to this family by the O'Connors, long before that.

In the middle of the 16th century, the English under Queen Elizabeth, after an absence of three centuries now reappear and reassert themselves. Sir Henry Sydney marched through Ulster and on to Sligo. By bribes, threat and coercion the Irish chieftains were now forced to abandon the Brehon ways. They were coerced into the infamous "surrender and regrant" whereby they surrendered their lands, possessions and titles to the Queen and were then re-granted these, on condition that they pay rent and offer allegiance. In return the Queen offered "protection" and an English title. Another course adopted at the time was to have "all minors, brothers or near relations of the Irish chiefs, educated in England, thus to imbibe English ideas".

The O'Connor Sligo was taken to England by Sydney in 1567 and confined to the Tower of London until he submitted. He returned to Ireland as Sir Donald O'Connor but while gaining from the English a measure of protection against O'Donnell, he had no intention of paying rent or honouring an agreement which was imposed by force. Eventually however, on Sir Richard Bingham's arrival with a huge force in 1584, O'Connor was forced to submit fully. Bingham increased the rents to a punitive level and at this time the O'Hart family of Grange were forced to make payments to him which had been traditionally due to O'Connor. The lands of Grange belonged to the Cistercians of Boyle Abbey and the O'Harts made land rent payments to them but now these rents also had to be paid to Bingham. Bingham, by all accounts a cruel and ruthless man, was vengeful as he believed that the people of Grange were hoarding wealth washed in from the Spanish galleons wrecked at Streedagh. He ill treated, imprisoned and tortured the natives when he suspected them of hiding or giving succour to survivors.

The condition of the Irish at this time can hardly be imagined! A description by Spencer of the condition of parts of Ireland at this time after years of warfare said that:

"They (the people) were brought to such wretchedness as that any strong heart would have rued the same. Out of every corner of the woods and glens they came creeping forth upon their hands for their legs would not bear them.They looked like anatomies of death; they spake like ghosts crying out of their graves. They did eat of the dead carrions ..... and if they found a plot of watercress or shamrock, there they flocked as to a feast for the time, yet not able long to continue therewithal, so that in short space there were none left and a most populous and plentiful country suddenly left void of men and beast."

We have no reason to believe that things were any different about North Sligo at this time!

The wrecking of three ships of the Spanish Armada off Streedagh, in 1588, was the most awful tragedy to happen in the maritime history of this area. One of the survivors, Francesco de Cuellar, relates that the ships anchored half a league from the shore, where they remained

"four days without being able to make provision or do anything. On the fifth day there sprang up such a great storm on our beam with a sea up to the heavens, so that the cables could not hold nor the sails serve us, and we were driven ashore upon a beach shut in on one side and the other by great rocks. Such a thing was never seen; for within the space of an hour all three ships were broken in pieces, so that there did not escape three hundred men and more than a thousand were drowned, and amongst them many persons of importance – captains, gentlemen and other officials".

De Cuellar was one of the lucky ones to make it to the shore, but when he reached Staad Abbey he found that Binghams men had been about their evil work. He found the Abbey deserted "and the Churches and the images of the saints burned and completely ruined, and twelve Spaniards hanging within the Church by the act of the English Lutherans who went about searching for us to make an end to us who had escaped from the perils of the sea". It seems that the arrival of the Spaniards provided the perfect opportunity for the English to destroy churches and church property. It is said that they "left neither place of worship nor hermitage standing for they had demolished them all and made them drinking places for cows and swine."

Others of de Cuellars companions, evidently attempting to make their escape by the mountain route, were hanged at Keeloges church at Ballintrillick; there may be some debate about the hanging but it is certain that the church was set on fire and destroyed. It is said that some of the survivors may have met a similar fate at a little church or abbey which existed at that time on the site of the present ruin in Ahamlish cemetery. The saga of the adventures and misadventures of de Cuellar and his unfortunate countrymen is already well told in all its horrific detail in other publications so we need not go into it in detail here.

From de Cuellars descriptions though, we have an opportunity to get some idea of how our people lived at that time, their clothes and diet. At Grange he refers to cabins with thatched roofs which seemed to differ little from those in use in the late 19th century and even later.

"The men are all large bodied and of handsome features and limbs, active as the roe deer. They do not eat oftener than once a day, and this is at night and that which they usually eat is oaten bread. They drink buttermilk for they have no other drink; they don't drink water though it is the best in the world. On special days they eat some flesh, half cooked without bread or salt, for that is their custom. (We can be sure that this diet was supplemented by fish in coastal areas.) They clothe themselves according to their habit with tight trousers and short loose coats of very coarse goats hair (homespun woolen frieze). They cover themselves with blankets and wear their hair down to their eyes". ..."The head dress of the women is a linen cloth doubled over the head and tied in front....... the women are great workers and housekeepers after their fashion".

Speaking of the Churches etc. he says,

"most of them have been demolished by the hands of the English and by these natives who have joined them, who are as bad as they". He concludes, "In this country there is neither justice nor right, and everyone does what he pleases".

The Spanish Armada came to an inglorious end as all along the west coast Spanish seamen were rounded up, shot and hanged on Sir Richard Binghams instructions. The Irish chieftains who harboured them received a similar fate and Mac Clancy who had sheltered de Cuellar and his men a year earlier, was eventually shot and beheaded on the lake shore beside his castle in 1589, and his head sent to be hung outside Dublin Castle.

Brian O'Ruairc, Prince of Breffni, was executed at Tyburn in England on 3rd. November 1591. The following verses, written by T. D. Sullivan were inspired by O'Ruairc's speech from the dock.

You ask me what defence is mine. Here midst your armed bands!
You only mock the prisoner who is helpless in your hands.
What would defence avail to me though good it be and true,
Here! in the heart of London town, with judges such as you?

On that wild day when near our coast the stately ships of Spain
Caught in a fierce and sudden storm, for safety sought in vain;
When wrenched and torn 'midst mountain waves some foundered in
*   the deep,*
And others broke on sunken reefs and headlands rough and steep—
I heard the cry that off my land where breakers rise and roar
The sailors from a wrecking ship were striving for the shore.
I hurried to the frightful scene, my generous people too,
Men, women, even children, came, some kindly deed to do.
We saw them clutching spars and planks that soon were washed away,
Saw others bleeding on the rocks, low moaning where they lay;
Some cast ashore and back again dragged by the refluent wave,
Whom one grip from a friendly hand would have sufficed to save.
We rushed into the raging surf, watched every chance, and when
They rose and rolled within our reach we grasped the drowning men.

We took them to our hearths and homes and bade them there remain
Till they might leave with hope to reach their native land again.
This is the 'treason' you have charged! Well, treason let it be,
One word of sorrow for such fault you'll never hear from me.
I'll only say although you hate my race, and creed, and name,
Were your folk in that dreadful plight I would have done the same.

In the following years the Elizabethan wars were fought and the Irish chieftains slowly ground down, their lands confiscated and given, on one pretext or another, to English and Scotch settlers. In 1603, Irish music was outlawed because of the part taken by harpers, pipers and poets in this last great uprising of Gaelic Ireland against the invader. The Gaelic aristocratic order which had encouraged and fostered music was destroyed, Queen Elizabeth herself ordering the extermination by martial law of: "all manner of bards, harpers etc, later ordering her liutenants, "to hang all the harpers wherever found."

Sir William Strafford confiscated and took title for the King, of the county of Sligo, as a prelude to the granting of these lands to Scottish and English adventurers. In Donegal, the Flight of the Earls took place from Lough Swilly in 1607 and was followed by the confiscation of their properties and the Plantation of Ulster.

The great chiefs of Sligo, including in their armies men from this area of Ahamlish; the O'Harts of Grange, O'Connor, Sligo and many others rose up against the injustices and atrocities perpetrated in this area by English soldiers, adventurers and land grabbers. In 1641 they attacked and took the town of Sligo. The killing of some of the English settlers in Sligo jail gave Sir Frederick Hamilton, that "ruthless monster", the pretext for one of the most notorious massacres ever to happen in this area.

Sir Frederick, who was based at Manorhamilton and from whom the town gets its name, descended on Sligo town on the night of 1st July 1642. The following excerpt is from a diary which was kept at the time by one of his soldiers.

"Our Colonel with his horse falling on many good houses full with people upon this side of the bridge, where he burned and destroyed all, appointing his rendezvous with the foote at the Southwest end of the Towne , where he crossed a forge which brought him close to the Fryery, where the foote met and fired their brave Mass house and Fryery where it is said we burnt many good things which people had given for safety to the fryers and all their superstitious trumperies belonging to the Mass. It was thought some of the Fryers themselves were burnt; two of them running out were killed in their habits; we finished this work giving God the praise for our success".

He encounters the Irish again that night on his way back to Manorhamilton,

"notwithstanding our wearisome march and hot service that night in burning the Towne of Sligo where it is confessed by themselves we destroyed that night near three hundred souls by fire, sword and drowning, to Gods everlasting great honour and glory for our comforts".

This diary also gives an interesting account of the many activities of Hamilton and his men and the horrors inflicted on the native Irish at that time:

> "A party sent towards Sligo where we met with a party of rogues, (his usual name for the Irish) hurt divers, killed three, brought home their heads to our Colonel, with a lusty prisoner who was hanged the next day......killed about thirty in three cabins, hanged our guide, who died a most obdurate villian......chased the people like dogs with horse and foote from hill to hill, killing a number......sent a party of horse and foote upon them where we had good sport in killing nearly sixty of them with all their three captains and Captain Teige O'Connors wife......we killed forty of their best men, stript them all, divers of their best gentry, as the O'Connors and O'Harts beng thus killed......marched towards the Rosse (Rosses Point ?) where we killed neere sixty of their ablest men with two of their famous priests, Connor O'Hart and Donnell O'Lynch, bringing home seven prisoners, five whereof were hanged the next day, one of them called Captain Con O'Connor and the other Cormac O'Hoy".

The following incident regarding the return to barracks of Hamiltons men after the burning of the Friary is recorded in the Folklore Collection of 1937; it is recalled too in remarkable detail and colour in the oral folklore of the area. It is told that a party of cavalry went astray in the region of Glencar and commandeered a local man to show them the way. They put one of the monk's cloaks on him and followed him along a rough path. Eventually he signalled the horsemen that the way was straight on from there and they galloped forward, not knowing that there was a steep precipice just ahead. They tumbled over it except for one of the men who got entangled in a bush at the edge of the cliff. When their "guide" went to see if his plan had been successful, he found the entangled soldier who pleaded with him to be saved. "If I free you, you'll kill me," the guide replied. The soldier swore not to harm the man and allowed him to take his sword to cut him free. When the guide got the sword he cut loose the bush and the soldier saying, "Alright, away you with the rest of them." The place is called Lug-na-Gall or the Protestant Leap; even in recent years, items have been found there, such as rusted horseshoes and bits of harness, which give credibility to the story.

A local historian, Bernie Barry often told that during these times a man called Swiney was chief of the Mullaghmore peninsula. Because of Hamilton's raids, men were posted day and night to keep watch and give ample warning if any attack seemed imminent. One night the sentries saw a mass movement on Mullaghmore beach but couldn't make out if it was cattle or cavalry. It is more than likely that the area between Mulaghmore and Bunduff/Cliffoney was at this time a region of shifting sands as some time before that Mullaghmore was an island and accessible by foot from the mainland only at low water. Swiney told his sentries to go back and watch, if it was cattle they would stop to graze when they reached the grass. They didn't stop and it became clear that it was soldiers. Swiney then sent his people to hide in coves along the shore or any other hiding place they could find. As the soldiers searched for the people the child of one of the women hidden in a cave began to cry. One of the soldiers passing by heard this and began to sing,

"Old woman, old woman be aisy,
Old woman, old woman rocking the cradle",

thus covering the sound of the childs crying and saving the lives of both the child and the Mother. The child's name was Owen or Donal Donlevy; he was later smuggled to France and eventually returned to Ireland and married Eliza Crean. Until recently their headstone could be seen in Ahamlish cemetery. They would have been the forebears of Pat Donlevy who played a part in the later history of the area and about whom we shall read much more in this book. The inhabitants of Mullaghmore either fled or were banished at this time. Swiney was removed to a site in lower Bunduff, between the sea and where Hugh Currid lives now and a McAndrew family given control of the area. In the early 1800s the Swiney's were moved again by Palmerston, this time to the townland of Derry about two miles North of Grange. We don't know for sure why they were moved again; the following little anecdote, told to me by Bernie, probably had nothing to do with it:

Swiney was attending Palmerston while shooting on Ben Bulben. Palmerston went to the edge of the cliff, put his foot out over it and said to Swiney, "There's not a man in Ireland would do that". Swiney took off his cap, placed it at the edge of the cliff and stood on his head on it. "There's not a man in England would do that", he said.

Kate Swiney, mother of Bernie Kelly of Mullaghmore was descended from the Swiney of these stories. For more information on the Swiney and Mullaghmore see Chapter 9.

The rebellion of 1641 by the Sligo chieftains was eventually suppressed, Sir Charles Coote delivering the coup-de-grace in this area in Summer '45 when he assaulted Sligo town with a force of six thousand foot and five hundred horse plus artillery. The town was taken after a fierce fight. O'Connor Sligo negotiated the terms of surrender and marched out of Crean's castle; the terms of surrender were immediately broken and two hundred men along with a number of women and children were disarmed, stripped and massacred. Two men and two women were the only survivors.

O'Rourke, in his history of Sligo, tells us that the Cromwellian epoch which opened in 1641 opened a new era of evil on the country:

"The aim of the State during the period was to aggrandize the few; the descendants of Cromwell's settlers, at the cost of the mass of the people; and the means employed for the accomplishment of this gigantic injustice being, first, the sword, and after the disuse of the sword, the law, and the tyranny practised under the law, by Cromwellian landlords, magistrates and country gentlemen."

This was the time of the catchcry, "To Hell or to Connaught"; it was no idle threat, and the people had no more rights than the animal in the field as they were driven from their homes to the province of Connaught. South of the county of Sligo, neither were they allowed to settle within three miles of the sea for fear of their supporting any invasion from that direction. Sixty three thousand acres of native land in Sligo was handed over to Cromwellian soldiers and adventurers while the O'Connors, O'Dowds, O'Harts and other old Irish families were driven across the sea. Sir John Temple's denunciations of the "atrocities" commited by the Irish during the rebellion of 1641 were widely used to justify Cromwell's savage reprisals some years later. Predecessor of the Palmerston line, he was Master of the Rolls in Ireland and a member of the Privy Council in England; when the Irish Catholic chieftains were dispossessed and deported, he was granted the parish of Ahamlish, much of Sligo town and large tracts of the city of Dublin. Following is a list of 'Papist Proprietors' of the Barony of Carbury, Co. Sligo, who had forfeited their lands by 1657:

ANDREW CREAN	MARTIN DARCY
BRYAN O'CONNOR	OWEN O'HAIRTT
BRYAN O'HART	PHELIM O'CONNOR
CAHELL O'CONNOR	LORD OF CLANRICKARDE
CARBRY O'HELY	ROGER BALLAGH O'CONNOR
DONELL O'CONNOR	ROGER O'CONNOR
GARRET BAXTER	TERLOGH O'CONNOR
DON. O'CONNOR	THOMAS O'CONNOR
GARRETT BAXTER (2)	JAM. FFRENCH AND HIS HEIRS
MANUS O'CONNOR	

TOTAL: 19 CONFISCATIONS IN THE BARONY OF CARBURY

Many more of these vast properties acquired at this time can still be seen locally and all over Ireland, although now much reduced in size, while others, with the passage of time, have passed back into Irish hands through being "cut up" and redistributed. The following piece, taken from "Prendergast's Cromwellian Settlement" and written by a contemporary observer of the time makes grim reading and is not for the faint hearted but necessary for an understanding of the conditions of this period:

"Ireland, in the language of the Scripture, now lay void as a wilderness. Five sixths of her people had perished; women and children were found daily perishing in ditches, starved. The bodies of many wandering orphans, whose fathers had been forced to embark for Spain and whose mothers had died of famine, were preyed upon by wolves (wolves were common in Ireland at that time). In the years 1652 and '53 the plague and famine had swept away whole counties, that a man might travel twenty or thirty miles and not see a living creature; man, beast and bird were all dead or had quit these desolate places. If two or three cabins were met with there were found there none but aged men with women and children and they 'become as a bottle in the smoke, their skin black like an oven' because of the terrible famine. They were seen to pluck stinking carrion out of a ditch, black and rotten, and were said to have even taken corpses out of the grave to eat".

Stories of this era with a local interest can still be heard and the following story was told to me by the aforementioned Bernie Barry of Lower Bunduff, a remarkable man who held a great lore of stories handed down to him by his grandparents: A group of Cromwell's men were terrorizing and killing people near the Aughaged bogs. Two women of the area were fleeing and being pursued by a soldier who was sent to kill them. On being caught they pleaded with him to save their lives on which he told them to lie down flat in the heather. He then fired two shots, pretending to have killed them and rejoined his company. The women lay there until dark, not daring to move, and then made their way home to where they lived at Munianeane.

Years afterwards a beggar came by their house begging for food. They offered him some potatoes and as he opened his bag to receive the offering one of the women noticed a scar on his hand similar to a scar she had noticed on the soldier's hand years earlier. In reply to her questions it transpired that he had deserted from the army, having no stomach for the work he was required to do and now feared for his life, as if he was discovered, he would be shot. The women took him in, out of gratitude for having saved their lives years earlier, and he stayed with them until his death, many years later.

Before we leave this period of the history of this area, it is rather gratifying to note that the Irish had some successes too. The end of Sir Frederick Hamilton and his reign of terror comes down to us in song; three of these verses go like this:

"The night was wild and windy,
But the rebels lasted on.
Bold Frederick's men are seated
With women, wine and song.

What light flares on the casement?
Loud shriek the startled dames!
The Mayo men have gained the walls
The castle's wrapped in flame.

The lead ran down like molten wine
And bubbling blue and red.
That night saw Frederick fleed afar
From Castle Hamilton"

Despite a valiant struggle, the O'Connors, O'Harts and most of the old Irish family names, dispossessed and banished, disappear forever at this time from any place of importance in later history, and are replaced by Gore, Wynne, Soden, Temple (Palmerston's predecessor) and other planter names.

Local lore has it that after the Cromwellian wars the title deeds of the Moneygold estate were bestowed in Athlone on an English officer as payment for his active services during the war. On his arrival in Sligo he chanced to meet Soden who offered to show him where his newly acquired lands were. When the two men arrived at Munianeane hill, Soden stopped and pointing across to the dunes at Streedaghh said, 'There lies Moneygold" "So," said the officer, sorely disappointed, "this is my share, the home of the snipe."

Soden never told him that further north lay a fertile plain of rich land which was also his, so the soldier never saw the Moneygold lands.

Sore at heart at the view before him and longing for his home the Cromwellian soldier confided to Soden that he would part with the deeds if only he could find someone to provide him with enough money to take him back to his native England, Soden then told him that he had at home thirty shillings in good English coins that he was willing to part with for the deeds. Journeying back to Sligo, the money and deeds changed hands and Soden became the owner of Moneygold.

The following story entitled 'The Last of the O'Hartes of Moneygold' was told to the Folklore Commission by John Gilmartn of Grange in 1938:

"In the townland of Cashel, near the village of Grange, in the parish of Ahamlish, may be seen the ruins of an ancient castle from which the townland derives its name. This was the homeland of the O'Hartes, overlords of Moneygold. When the new Protestant overlord took over the lands after the Cromwellian plantation, he built a dwelling further north in the present townland of Moneygold. His name was Soden, greatgrandfather of Mrs. Eccles, wife of Major Eccles, the present owner of Moneygold house.

When Soden took up his abode in Moneygold, he found the people hostile and willing to pay allegiance only to their old, Gaelic, Catholic overlord, Harte. Filled with rage and hatred towards O'Harte he tried by many means to make him quit his home, but O'Harte could not be removed. At last, Soden got some of his hirelings to bring one of his horses to Cashel and by bribery have it placed under lock and key in O'Harte's stable so that he might charge O'Harte with theft, the penalty for which then, was death by hanging.

Early in the morning, in company with his yeomaen, Soden paid a visit to the home of "Harte, found his horse in the stable and thereupon arrested O'Harte, bringing him to Sligo where he was bound in irons and lodged in Sligo jail. A sham trial followed at which O'Harte was convicted and sentenced to death. On the height known as Gallows Hill he was publicly hanged and so passed the last of the O'Hartes, Lords of Moneygold in North Sligo."

Attempts were made to exterminate the Catholic religion and priests were shot on sight. Twenty pounds reward was given for their discovery and if anyone was found to have given shelter to a priest, it meant certain death.

Around this time there lived a priest in Moneygold who was well liked in the district and was friendly with many of his protestant neighbours. Invitations were sent out to this Fr. Rynn and all the prominent people of the area to attend dinner at the house of a man named Allen in the village of Grange. Soden, who had by now gained a reputation as a notorious tyrant and priest hunter, was also invited. As the dinner went on, a catholic servant in Allen's household who waited on the tables became aware of a plot orchestrated by Soden to capture and kill the priest on that night. When Fr. Rynn became aware of the plot he quietly made his escape from Allen's and returned to his own house in Moneygold. The following is written down as it was told to the commission which collected this local lore in 1937

"The priest gathered some of his people and told them to listen and report any noise they might hear. They listened at a short distance from the priest's house which is now called the "Farmstead". After a time they came back and told the priest that they could hear shot after shot being fired by Soden and his group who were now aware of the priests escape and out to capture him. He then sent them out again to listen a little further down the road and they came back this time and told him that they could hear nothing. He sent them out a third time and this time they came back and told him they could hear wild roars like a lion. "Now", he said to them, "you and I are safe." Next day there was great excitement in the area as the events of the night before became known. It transpired also that Soden, who had attempted to kill the priest, on arriving at his house that night, had gone mad, he ate his own flesh and nothing could be done with him. A steel jacket was procured and he was placed in it where he had to be kept until he died".

He had such a terrible death that the people of the area were frightened to pass near where he lived for many years. Passers by had also reported that they had seen a huge dog with fire coming out of its mouth on land owned by Soden. Some years later when reports of this ghostly apparition persisted, the local curate who lived in Grange exorcised and banished this spirit to Bomore island. It is told that this strange creature has been seen in quite recent times as it returns once every seven years from it's exile at sea; it is claimed that during these visitations it can be seen at a gateway near the old Eccles estate between Derry and Carns.

For a while in the close of the 17th century, the accession of King James to the throne of England gave some hope to the Catholics and native Irish for a relief of their condition. The Protestants gathered and armed themselves; fearing the loss of their new found status and privelege, they secured Sligo town. In 1689, the Jacobites, under Patrick Sarsfield routed their forces and drove them in disarray along Benbulben and into Ballyshannon where he camped for some time at the Bundrowse. Following reversals in the Jacobite fortunes of war, Sarsfield retreated to Sligo where he and his supporters held out for some time while the war was being lost to the Williamites at the Boyne and elsewhere. Eventually, Sligo was re-taken and the war ended with the "Flight of the Wild Geese" when Sarsfield, and many thousands of his followers were forced, as had happened so many times before in our history, into exile. The defeat of James sealed the fate of the Catholic merchants of Sligo who sided with him and Sarsfield and most of these now also disappear. By the beginning of the 18th century, Sligo town was in the firm control of British Protestant merchants.

PENAL TIMES

As we go into the 18th century we find that the mis-use of the law now replaces the sword as the method to keep the Irish in subjection. The Penal Laws were a blatant violation of the Articles of Surrender of the Treaty of Limerick and were designed to degrade and emasculate the tattered remnants of the Irish landed gentry. Among a long list of provisions, they declared that:

CATHOLICS WERE NOT ALLOWED TO SIT IN THE IRISH PARLIAMENT.

NO CATHOLIC COULD BE A SOLICITOR, GAMEKEEPER OR CONSTABLE.

CATHOLICS COULD NOT POSSESS A HORSE OF GREATER VALUE THAN £5.

ANY PROTESTANT OFFERING THAT SUM COULD TAKE POSSESSION OF THE ANIMAL.

CATHOLICS WERE NOT ALLOWED TO ATTEND A UNIVERSITY, KEEP A SCHOOL,OR SEND HIS CHILDREN TO BE EDUCATED ABROAD.

TEN POUNDS REWARD WAS OFFERED FOR THE DISCOVERY OF A ROMAN CATHOLIC SCHOOLMASTER.

CATHOLICS COULD NOT BUY LAND OR RECEIVE IT AS A GIFT FROM A PROTESTANT.

NO CATHOLIC MAY BEQUEATH HIS LAND AS A WHOLE, HE MUST DIVIDE IT AMONG ALL HIS SONS, UNLESS ONE OF THEM BECOMES A PROTESTANT, IN WHICH CASE HE WILL INHERIT THE WHOLE ESTATE.

THE ORPHAN CHILDREN OF CATHOLICS MUST BE BROUGHT UP AS PROTESTANTS.

While some Catholic lands were saved by transferring them to friendly Protestant neighbours until better times, the result of these laws was that only 5% of land ownership in Ireland remained in Catholic hands. By the last quarter of the eighteenth century the Catholics were almost completely detached from the land and trade of the country and reduced to mere occupiers, artisans or day labourers. The following measures, directed exclusively at the Catholic clergy became law in 1703:

1. Every clergyman of the popish religion that shall come into this kingdom any time after the first of January 1704 shall be liable to such penalties, forfeitures and punishments as by the Act 9 Will III,c.26, is imposed on popish bishops etc. or any other papists exercising ecclesiastical jurisdiction who shall come into this kingdom contrary to the Act (that is to say imprisonment and transportation for the first offence, death for the second).

2 Any person who shall knowingly harbour, relieve, conceal or entertain any such clergyman of the popish religion shall be liable to such penalties and forfeitures as by the said Act is imposed on the harbourers and con-

cealers of any popish bishop etc. or regualr popish clergyman, to be levied in the same manner as by the said Act is directed.

All justices of the peace, sheriffs, high and petty constables and all other subjects are required to use their utmost diligence in apprehending all such regular or other popish priest who shall come into this Kingdom contrary to this Act.

These then became the times of the Mass rocks and the hedge schoolmaster as the Irish clung to their religion and attempted to educate their children by any means possible. In secluded places in every town-land, the people gathered around the fugitive priest as he said the Mass under a tree or in the open field while others kept watch lest they be discovered by soldiers or the police. Protected and sheltered by the whole population the priests were hidden in dugouts, lanes, sheds and wood-lands in defiance of the law. The price on the head of a priest in those days was the same as that of a wolf. Major Morgan complained to the Westminster Parliament of the heavy charge for public rewards:

'We have three beasts to destroy that lay burthen upon us. The first is the wolf, on whom we lay five pounds a head if a dog, and ten pounds if a bitch. The second beast is a priest, on whose head we lay ten pounds,... if he be eminent, more...'

Still, no one could generally be found to take the bribe. While these repressive codes were successful in their intent to pauperise and degrade, they were a complete failure in their main purpose of Protes-tantising the mass of the people. In fact it had the opposite effect for by the end of the nineteeth century the Irish had become the staunchest Catholics in Northern Europe.

Mass is still said, at a restored Mass rock, in Tawley, on the anniversary of the execution of Blessed Oliver Plunkett on the first of July 1681. This mass rock, one of three such rocks to be found in Tawley was restored by the local priest and parishioners in 1975. It is said that Blessed Oliver, appointed Archbishop of Armagh in 1669, ordained priests during visits to this area, until his arrest in 1679. This connection may be borne out by the date of 1671 which is etched on the holy water font at the Mass rock. The rock is considered to be the genuine article as the rock itself is inscribed with the initials I.H.S. The stone candlesticks which went with the original altar cannot be found.

Another very well preserved cross inscribed Mass rock, can be found on the land of Hugh Pat Gallagher in the townland of Gorteen in Ballintrillick and another one at McGonigles bridge in Gortnahowla. Another one at Lecklasser in Ballintrillick in the shape of a heart with a cross inscribed on it has been lost as it was unfortunately used to fill in a drain. It is quite probable and reasonable to suppose that Blessed Oliver visited these Mass rocks too, during his visits to the area. Another such Mass rock can be found at Carns in a field called Lug na hAbhann, but these sites are in abundance everywhere and no townland can be visited without some of these places being pointed out, a visible link and tangible proof that these terrible events and times did actually happen.

Hedge schools too were plentiful, although their locations are not as well marked today, as the places where Mass was said. We are told that Hugh Walters taught in the hedge school tradition in the upper room of a house belonging to a man called Johnny McGowan in the townland of Drumfad. Another of these schools was situated in Carnamadow where Pat Foley lived. Terry McGowan taught here and also in the kitchen of his own little thatched dwelling house. The last hedge schoolmaster in this area was James Costello who taught in Newtownward; he was greatgrandfather of the Costello's of Moneygold. Other teachers of hedge schools were John Gallagher who was grandfather to John Gallagher who lived next door to Mount Temple N.S. and a Mr. Bernard Hart who taught in Maugherow. Another hedge school was situated in Grange where the remains of Flanagan's house stood in 1938. Teachers here were Brian Hart, Paddy Gillen, Master Currid and Miss Currid.

For an insight into the hedge schools we will draw on a story told to the Folklore Commision in 1937 by William Mc Gloin of Grellagh who was 80 years old at the time:

"Paddy Mc Nulty, sometimes called the pedagogue, was going around here teaching as a hedge schoolmaster; he had no school and no home whatsoever. He depended on those he taught for his food, clothes etc. He was not native to this area and moved around through Grellagh, Castlegal, Cliffoney, Mullaghmore and Bunduff. He taught in sheltered places in the open air so as not to endanger the people of the area although in very bad weather he would go to the pupil's houses. Here he would stay as long as was necessary; he would receive food and clothes, depending on the circumstances of the family; if the family were well off, they might give him money. Paddy spoke Irish and encouraged its use; the subjects he taught were the three R's, reading writing and arithmetic. The reader he used was called 'Reading made Easy', another was the 'Goff' and another the 'Voster'. The 'Voster'was both an arithmetic and a dictionary. Great care was given to these books and it was wonderful how many words the people knew the explanation of. The writing was done on slates and by quills on paper. Each pupil had to bring his own quill and the teacher supplied the paper. Very little writing was done on paper as the slate was the most popular way of taking down lessons."

William also related that many decades later, when Palmerston built a school in Cliffoney, the first master there, a Mr. Clarke, discouraged the use of Irish. He had no choice in the matter as that was official policy at the time; secretly he encouraged it, but if this became known, he would lose his job. The method used to discourage Irish was to tie a stick around the pupils neck; each time he spoke a word of Irish a notch was made on the stick. In the evening before going home, the notches were counted and as many slaps given to the pupil as there were notches on the stick. The system was totally effective, as in most parts of Ireland, Gaelic rapidly became a dead language. Many efforts have been made since the turn of the century to revive the language but with little or no success. Much effort and much discussion has gone into efforts to find methods to revive the language but they have all failed as Irish by and large is rarely spoken outside the classroom in Ireland today. It is even under threat in the Gaeltacht areas. The tally stick was totally effective in eliminating the language but no such simple device has been found that would restore it.

Padraig McGowan was another one of these hedge schoolmasters, the first in a long line of schoolteachers who to this day, still impart their knowledge to the rising generations. Padraig taught in the Rossinver area in the early 1700's wherever he could find shelter; under a hedge, in a shed or in a friendly house; that is, when the owners were prepared to take a chance, as discovery meant instant retribution. One of his descendants, Martin Bernard McGowan, a schoolmaster also, in the parish of Glenade in Leitrim, was well known all over North Sligo in the formative years of the Freestate and is mentioned elsewhere in this book. Another descendant, Aidan Mc Gowan, carries on this proud, unbroken, 300 year old link as headmaster of Grange N.S.

Following is an excerpt from a poem that was penned in tribute to the hedge schoolmaster by the Donegal writer, Seamus Mc Manus:

"Their lore was not the brightest, nor their store, maybe the best,
But they fostered love, undying, in each young Irish breast;
And through the dread, dread, night and long, that steeped our
island then,
The lamps of hope and fires of faith were fed by these brave men.

The grass waves green above them; soft sleep is theirs for aye;
The hunt is over and the cold; the hunger passed away.
O hold them high and holy! and their memory proudly pledge,
Who gathered their ragged classes behind a friendly hedge

THE FRENCH

As the 18th century wore on many of the Protestant merchants became disenchanted with restrictive trade laws which they felt were inflicted on them. Across the Atlantic, the American colonists became restless too and their move to independence was bannered with a cry of "No taxation without representation". In Ulster, the Protestant Irish Volunteer Movement could muster 100,000 armed men at the peak of its power in 1782, representing a formidable threat to all who opposed it. Henry Grattan declared the Irish Parliament to be independent of Britain, but in effect this independence was in name only. In 1789 the French Revolution started with the attack on the Bastille in Paris. There was a new spirit abroad in Ireland and for a time, Presbyterian, Catholic and Dissenter found common cause. This resulted in the formation of the United Irishmen in 1791, its leaders to be found among men like Tone, Henry Joy Mc Cracken and Napper Tandy, whose cannon had played a great, if silent part in the earlier Volunteers. England feared nothing as much as the prospect of Catholic and Protestant united and so encouraged the formation of the Orange Order with the intention of applying the old maxim of "Divide and Conquer". The Orange Society was established in the village of Loughgall, Co. Armagh in 1795 with the sworn intention of supporting the King and "exterminating all Catholics".

In America, the War of Independence had been fought successfully. The Tories, the American equivelant of the Irish Planters, locked up in prison ships on the Hudson, their properties confiscated if they insisted on supporting the English cause and huge numbers of them expelled to Novia Scotia or England. War was brewing between England and France. Could it be long until the United Irishmen took on the English Oppressor?

In May 1798, despite Lord Edward Fitzgerald and other leaders being arrested, the people could wait no longer and struck out in many parts of the country. The most famous and well recorded of these engagements through the years have been the battles fought in Wexford, with Vinegar Hill and Father Murphy being well remembered in song and story. Major General Humbert commanding three warships, the Francine, the Medee and the Concorde landed in August at Killala.

In Mullaghmore, another French munitions boat, part of a fleet commanded by Admiral Bonaparte, came with soldiers and supplies to link up with the invasion at Killala. However, some time previously the English, fearing just such an eventuality, had rounded up all the horses and asses in this area. Three Mullaghmore men were sent out in a small boat to the frigate to explain that there was no way to transport the munitions because of the seizures. After some discussion the captain decided to sail for Killala with the three men as pilots. As they passed Inishmurray an English cutter coming from the direction of Donegal intercepted, and after a fierce fight, captured the French frigate. When recounting their adventures later on, one of the Mullaghmore men recalled that, early in the battle, one of the ships officers tried to fly a white flag and was immediately shot dead by a superior officer. In another incident during the battle, the top of a French marine's head was blown off and landed in the hold where the three Mullaghmore men were kept. They recalled that it looked like a bloody red bowl.

On arrival in London, the Frenchmen were given passage to France but our three friends were tried, sentenced to be executed and kept in the Tower of London. They met with the Governor of the Jail on the eve of their execution and during the conversation discovered that he was a good friend and old schoolmate of Dickson, the Tawley landlord. The Governor granted the men a stay of execution to give them time to contact Dickson telling them that if he would give them a reference, they could go free. Dickson replied with a recommendation that the men be released, on which they were given passage to Derry, from where they walked home to Mullaghmore where they told and retold their adventure for many a year. The names of the three men were Barry, McCannon and Kelly.

Like so many hopes of freedom cherished by the Irish nation, this rising too, was doomed to failure. Wolfe Tone and the United Irishmen were defeated. Once again Irish soil was drenched in the blood of young Irishmen who had thought to struggle one more time for freedom; those that lived kept the torturer and the hangman busy for many a day. The Frenchmen were given an honourable surrender, feted in Dublin and shipped back to France; the French being classified by the British as prisoners of war but the Irish as mere traitors to the crown. Wolfe Tone's ship, the "Hoche" was smashed and captured in Lough Swilly; later he was recognised among the French officers who sat at breakfast in Letterkenny, clapped into chains immediately and sentenced to death. In Enniscorthy, the hospital where the wounded were kept, went on fire "by accident", the bedclothes being set on fire by the wadding of the soldier's guns, who were shooting the injured in their beds.

Another shining light of the campaign fought in the Northwest was young Bartholomew Teeling, a brave and able soldier, who was captured, refused prisoner of war status and hung publicly like a common criminal. An elegant monument to his sacrifice overlooks the battlefield at Carricknagat on the Dublin road south of Sligo town.

Weary men, what reap ye? Golden corn for the stranger."
What sow ye? "Human corpses that await for the avenger."
Fainting forms, all hunger stricken, what see you in the offing?
"Stately ships to bear our food away amid the stranger's scoffing"
There's a proud array of soldiers, what do they 'round your door?
"They guard our masters granaries from the thin hands of the poor."
Pale mothers, wherefore weeping?
"Would to God that we were dead,
Our children waste before us, and we cannot give them bread!"

"No; the blood is dead within our veins; we care not now for life;
Let us die hid in the ditches, far from children and from wife;
We cannot stay to listen to their raving famished cries,
Bread! Bread! Bread! — and none to still their agonies.
We left an infant playing with her dead mother's hand:
We left a maiden maddened by the fever's scorching brand:"
Better, maiden, thou were strangled in thy own dark twisted tresses!
Better, infant, thou were smothered in thy mother's first caresses.

"We are fainting in our misery, but God will hear our groan;
Yea, if fellow men desert us, He will hearken from His throne!
Accursed are we in our own land, yet toil we still and toil;
But the stranger reaps our harvest, the alien owns our soil.
Oh Christ, how have we sinned, that on our native plains
We perish, houseless, naked, starved, with branded brow, like Cain's?
Dying, dying wearily, with a torture sure and slow,
Dying as a dog would die, by the wayside as we go.

We are wretches, famished, scorned, human tools to build your pride,
But God will yet take vengeance for the souls for whom Christ died.
Now is your hour of pleasure, bask ye in the world's caress;
But our whitening bones against ye will arise as witnesses,
From the cabins and the ditches, in their charred, uncoffined masses,
For the Angel of the Trumpet will know them as he passes.
A ghastly spectral army before great God we'll stand
And arraign ye as our murderers, O spoilers of our land."

Lady Wilde (1826-96)

CHAPTER 3

Of Coffin Ships and Famine

In 1800 the Act of Union was passed nullifying what little power Grattan's Parliament had. 1803 saw another abortive rising with Thomas Addis Emmet and his brother Robert as chief players. What Irishman has not heard of Emmet's speech from the dock?: –

"Let no man write my epitaph; for as no man who knows my motives dare now vindicate them, let not prejudice or ignorance asperse them. Let them and me rest in obscurity and peace; and my tomb remain uninscribed, and my memory in oblivion, until other times and other men can do justice to my character. When my country takes her place among the nations of the earth, then and not till then, let my epitaph be written".

The complete speech is compulsory reading and one of the great works of English literature; who can read it and not feel regret that such a great mind should perish in such a foul manner. He was publicly beheaded on a Dublin Street. His words are remembered and his tomb uninscribed to this day.

Famine struck around 1820 and an epidemic of cholera in 1832. Around this time also, the Tithe Applotment Book was drawn up as an aid to assessing the hated tithes which tenants had to pay to the Church of Ireland pastor in addition to what they had to pay to the landlord. There are many reports in the newspapers of 1838, of reaction to threats by Dickson, the Tawley landlord, to evict tenants who refused to give a tenth of their labours or wages to the parson even though in some cases they were not required to do so being that they held their leases from year to year. Catholic Emancipation in 1829 brought only a small measure of relief. Poverty and destitution were widespread in Sligo and elsewhere in the first half of the 19th century; housing was poor with "the brute and human beings inhabiting the same huts, the walls of the poor huts are made of sods, roofed with some rubbish of sticks and thatched with some rubbish of straw or rushes".

Food was almost entirely of poatoes with some oaten bread, flummery, milk, eggs, butter and along the sea, dried fish. The dependence on potatoes was to be responsible for the greatest natural disaster that ever occurred in Irish history.

Famine had occurred at earlier times, notably in 1839, but paled into insignificance when compared with the hardship, starvation, dispossession, evictions and forced emigration of the middle of the 19th century, reaching a peak in 1847. In 1845, the local papers carried numerous reports of failures of the potato crop, attacking the authorities for refusing to allow American corn into the Port of Sligo. The Sligo Champion accuses the landlords of plundering and impoverishing the people and "keeping them on the brink of starvation while they revel in all the luxuries of life regardless of all the heartbreaking wretchedness around them." The great-grandfathers of these poor tenants had died, unnoticed, in the great famines of the 18th century; in 1739, 15 to 20 percent of the population were wiped out in a famine which lasted until 1741. Unbelievably, the port of Sligo had one of it's best years in 1739, exporting large amounts of beef, butter, barley, oats, pork, etc. to foreign parts. It must have been quite a feat to export so much foodstuff past a starving population! Humanitarianism had begun to be a more important factor in the world of 1847; the power of the press too, was beginning to make itself felt; in this area the Sligo Champion proved itself a dauntless defender of the people holding every action of the landlords up to public scrutiny.

Some years before "Black '47", in 1839, Sir Robert Gore-Booth took possession of 800 acres of land at Ballygilgan in North Sligo. The Seven Cartrons, as it was known, had been acquired by Sir Robert Gore-Booth, along with some other properties, in a deal over the dinner table, from Lord Orkney some years earlier, in 1833. Having decided to make clearances on the property, he secured the services of Capt. Dodswell, who was even then notorious in Sligo for his ruthless evictions. The evictions and forced emigrations that followed are still etched in local minds and inextricably intertwined with stories of the Famine which occurred a few years later. In the relative security and comfort in which we live today, the horror of these evictions can hardly be imagined. The following describes an eviction of the time:

> "Houses were demolished, roofs torn off, walls thrown down. The scene was frightful; women running wailing with pieces of their property and clinging to door posts from which they had to be forcibly torn; men cursing, children screaming with fright. That night the people slept in the ruins; next day they were driven out, the foundations of the house were torn up and razed."

Refusing the emigrant ship, it was quite common for people to seek refuge in what was called a scalp. A hole was dug in the earth, two to three feet deep, roofed over with pieces of sticks and turf and in this burrow a family existed. Slightly superior was a scalpeen, a rather larger hole, often made within the ruins of a tumbled house. Both from scalps and scalpeens, the evicted, when discovered, were remorselessly hunted out.

A local woman from Lissadell, remembers seeing a family still living in one of these scalpeens at the turn of the century. It was dug into a bank of earth and had no windows. A "shakedown" of straw and rushes was used as they had no beds. Mrs. McGowan, who now lives in Teesan, near Sligo town recalls that a man named Jack McLean lived in a sod house, similar to this, in Ballygilgan, somewhere between Cooper's and Frank Mc Gowan's.

There is to this day, a place near Ballygilgan known as "Cats Corner". It has had this name since the time of the evictions, when it is said, the cats of the area gathered, also homeless, crying with hunger and looking for something to eat or someone to feed them.

The existence of the coffin ship, the Pomano, which it is said carried the evicted families to a watery grave, is still the subject of controversy to this day. There is evidence to show that a ship called the Pomana took the tenants overseas, made the return voyage, and plied the seas for many years afterwards. On the other hand, etched into the folk memory and popularised in a forbidden ballad of the time, the story of this infamous coffin ship still survives. The song was banned and sung only in private houses, never publicly; to be heard singing it, or gathered in a home or rambling place where it was sung, meant instant reprisal, eviction or worse:

"Many's the pleasant summer day I spent in Maugherow,
 And many a cold hard Winter's day at the handling of a plough.
Our rent was paid, we were not afraid,
but still we were forced to go
When they banished the Seven Cartrons on board of the Pomano.

Many's the lad and pretty lass, that evening on the shore,
Lamenting for their own sweethearts, they'd never see them more.
They're sailing on the ocean to a place they do not know,
 And they'll mourn tonight for their hearts delight
on board the Pomano

The ship she was a rotten one, the truth to you I'll tell
And they struck her on the Corraun rock, right under Lissadell...."

and so it goes on. Stories are still told by the older inhabitants of

Maugherow of the cries of drowning men and women being heard on the shore. An incident was told to me of two women washed ashore who were found to be alive and nursed back to health by two families, Feeney and McLoughlin, at nearby Knocklane. John Kelly of Maugherow recalled that many years later when he worked as a ploughman on the Lissadell estate, he often ploughed up crooks and other household goods, and on one occasion a crowbar which more than likely had been used to knock down the houses.

Between 54 to 63 families comprising at least 328 and probably closer to 400 individuals were dispossessed at this time. According to the Report from the Select Committee of the House of Lords of 1848, 'Twenty one families got land and some of them Residences, as follows:

JAMES MC LEAN, HOUSE AND LAND.
THADY CURRID, LAND, IN LISADELL.
MICHAEL BURNS, LAND, IN LISADELL.
MARTIN FEENEY, HOUSE AND LAND, CLOONACHINE.
TERENCE MC SHANY, LAND, IN BALLINTULLICK.
JAMES MC SHANY, LAND IN BALLINTULLICK.
ANTHONY MULLARKEY, LAND IN BALLINTULLICK.
MICHAEL MC GLONE, LAND, IN CARTRON WILLINMOGUE.
PATRICK FEENEY, LAND IN   "   "   "
MICHAEL MC GOWAN, LAND IN   "   "
JOHN CONEY, LAND IN   "   "   "
WILLIAM LINDSEY, LAND IN COOLADRUMMOND.
THOMAS EWING, LAND IN CULLAGHMORE.
JAMES CURREY,   "   "
PATRICK O'BRIEN, LAND IN BALLINAFULL.
REVEREND MALACHAI BRENNAN, HOUSE AND LAND, IN CULLAGHMORE.
PATRICK M.O'BRIEN, HOUSE AND LAND IN BALLYGILGAN.
JACK O'BRIEN, HOUSE AND LAND, IN BALLYGILGAN.
JAMES ARMSTRONG, HOUSE AND LAND, IN BALLYGILGAN.
FRANCIS FEENEY, REMAINS IN BALLYGILGAN.
BARTH GILLEN, HOUSE AND LAND, IN CLOONACOOL,
WHICH HE SOLD FOR 80 POUNDS."

The following is an extract from the same record, which consisted of questions and answers:

"2640. Even anterior to the failure of the potato crop, did you find it necessary, in certain cases where the population was in excess, to assist the people to emigrate, in order to place that land on a proper footing?
Yes; in very many cases.

2641. Do you think you could have done it without that resource consistently with the peace of the country or with the interests of humanity?

Certainly not; I should have been throwing them on the world and leaving them to beg.

2642. At present, confining the whole of the questions to a period anterior to the failure of the potato crop, did you then find any disinclination or the reverse on the part of the people to emigrate?

I think usually they were very willing to emigrate when absolutely obliged to quit the land; but they have a very strong affection for the ground they have resided upon, and would, in many instances, prefer existing upon it to getting rich elsewhere. They are an uncertain people; they sometimes take a dislike to move, but when forced to do so by circumstances, they preferred emigration to the holding of an indifferent farm which required much labour."

After a partial failure of the potato crop in 1845, there were some hopes of an improvement in 1846, but this was not to be. The Sligo Champion reports in August '46 that the people were in absolute despair as no matter where you went "nothing but withered stalks and leaves meet the eye... what should be green is black.. such a universal and overwhelming calamity never before fell upon a nation". In response to pressure from the landlord classes, who feared reprisals from the people, a Coercion Bill was passed imposing, what was in effect, martial law. A curfew was imposed between sunset and sunrise, arrests could be made on suspicion, magistrates could sentence to transportation for seven years on a whim. William Smith O'Brien was the only objector to the passing of the Bill in the House of Lords, accusing the Government of sending soldiers instead of food, as starvation was threatening Ireland.

Unscrupulous landlords lost no time in taking the opportunity to clear their land and in September Sir Robert Gore-Booth is reported as having evicted thirty families. A few of the families returned for shelter to the broken down walls and were promptly brought before the Magistrate at Teesan Petty Sessions "where on consenting to leave their lands, they were released". Cattle, pigs, corn and even the very butter and eggs had to be sold to meet the landlords rent demands. Non-payment of rent meant eviction while selling of goods to pay rent meant starvation; "they had nothing to call their own but the potato and this had now disappeared," the Sligo Champion reports.

Public works were undertaken to relieve the situation but these were hopelessly inadequate. People fell down dead from want on these schemes as there was a ten day waiting period before they were paid.

Among the deaths reported in the Parish of Ahamlish in December 1846 was that of a man named James Gonigle of Derrylehan, a tenant of Lord Palmerston. The inquest was presided over by Coroner Burrowes and Dr. Hamilton of the Carney dispensary. Gonigle's widow told the jury: that her husband

> " did not eat one morsel on Saturday the 28th nor on the 27th but two spoons of Indian meal gruel, nor on the 26th but boiled cabbage without butter, gruel or anything else but salt, and they lived in that way for five weeks before, during which weeks she got turnips from Lord Palmerston's herd at one penny per stone."

Following a proclamation by the Lord Lieutenant, a special session was held in the County Courthouse under the supervision of magistrates Sir Robert Gore Booth, John Wynne and Sir William Parke. Fr. Brennan submitted that out of 10,000 souls in the Parish, 8,000 were utterly destitute; it would take £12,000 to feed that number for a whole year. Fr. Brennan was told that as Palmerston's Poor Law valuation was little over £3,000 for a whole year, works would be undertaken but not for any amount over £3,000. In Sligo town, people were dying of typhus fever and dysentery; cemeteries were filled over and over again with "coffins piled upon each other to the very surface of the earth, the very air being infected by foul and pestilent vapours issuing from this revolting abode of the dead."

The following letter was written to the Sligo Champion in February 1847 by Fr. Noone of Grange:

> Sir,
> From the sympathy you have shown for our suffering and starving people and your indefatigable exertions on their behalf, I feel that no excuse is necessary for furnishing you with the following list of persons who have been victims of starvation in the past ten days in the Parish of Ahamlish;-

John Hoy, Silverhill	age 12
John Doherty, Breaghey	„ 64
Frank Finan	„ 64
Pat Mullen	„ 59
John Watters, Mt. Edward	„ 18
James Finan, Silverhill	„ 58
John Quinn, Mt. Edward	„ 63
Honor Kivlehan, Streedagh	„ 61
James Leydon, Bunduff	„ 66
Anne Kerrigan, Castlegal	„ 68
John Gillen, Gortnaleck	„ 15
Mary Gillen, sister	„ 13
James Feeney	„ 40
Mary Gilmartin	„ 56

Owen Haran and his son, both of whom had to be put into one coffin for want of funds. William Hooks, Grange, age 50 and for the last month we had fifty other cases of which no mention was made.

signed,

Dominick Noone, R.C.C.

By contrast, an editorial in the Champion gives vent to outrage at the

" Balls and parties" hosted by public officials where "all the markets of Sligo could not furnish sufficent articles for their groaning supper table, so that expressses were sent to the city for wines and fruits and other luxuries......showing the gross vulgarity of underbred people making ostentatious displays of their wealth while not subscribing a single sixpence to thr relief of the poor."

In 1847, the Poor Law was changed, requiring the destitute population to be maintained out of local rates at the expense of owners of property. Emigration now became a more popular alternative than eviction, the landlord feeling that the two pounds it would cost him was money well spent to be rid of many of his tenants and many tenants doubtless jumping at any opportunity for relief of their desperate condition. For most, this escape proved no relief, for even of the sea voyage itself it was said:

"Before the emigrant is at sea a week, he is an altered man. How can it be otherwise; hundreds of poor people, men ,women and children of all ages, from the drivelling idiot of ninety to the babe just born, huddled together without light, without air, wallowing in filth and breathing a fetid atmosphere, sick in body, dispirited in heart, the fevered patients lying between the sound, in sleeping places so narrow as almost to deny them the power of indulging, by a change of position, the natural restlessness of the disease; by their agonised ravings disturbing those around; living without food or medicine except as administered by the casual hand of charity, dying without the voice of spiritual consolation, and buried in the deep without the last rites of the Church."

During the summer and autumn of 1847, nine vessels, carrying over 2,000 persons, left Sligo with tenants evicted and "shovelled out" from Lord Palmerstons Sligo estates, arriving in Canada half naked and totally destitute. The Canadians were shocked at the condition of the immigrants, who arrived in a state of complete destitution. The middlemen who had arranged the transport had transported them in very overcrowded conditions and made no provision for clothing. Palmerston had promised these poor unfortunates £2 to £5 on arrival in Canada but for those who managed to make it alive, there was no one there to meet them or give them any assistance; they were forced to beg in the snow, barefoot and in rags, during their first Canadian winter.

The "Carrick of Whitehaven" was the first of the ships chartered by Palmerston to leave the port of Sligo. Bound for Quebec and loaded with emigrants she had reached the Gulf of St. Lawrence on the 28th April 1847, when a fierce northerly gale sprang up. The crew were unable to control the ship as battered by wind and mighty waves she was relentlessly driven ashore, hitting the rocks near the village of Cap-de-Rosiers. Passengers and crew were pitched into the boiling tide as mountainous seas broke over the wreck, pounding her to bits. Local fishermen managed to save 48 of these unfortunate individuals while 87 bodies were washed ashore in the following days; some of those lost in this tragedy were never found. Most of the survivors settled in the area where many of their descendents still live today; a huge cross marks the mass grave where the bodies of those washed ashore were buried.

The "Eliza Liddell" was the first vessel to arrive at St. Johns in New Brunswick in July of 1847. The "Lord Ashburton" arrived at Quebec on Oct. 30th with 477 passengers; 107 persons had died on the voyage of fever and dysentery, on landing 174 of the passengers, widows with young children, the aged, destitute and decrepit were found to be almost naked; 87 had to be clothed by charity before they could leave the ship. The Sligo Champion of Sept. 11 reported the deplorable condition of Palmerston's tenants board the "Richard Watts" waiting to be shipped out from Sligo Harbour. It described them as being half-naked and completely destitute, placing the blame on Palmerston's agents, the Dublin firm of Messrs. Stewart and Kincaid, for their condition. It seems that Palmerston had become a subscriber to the paper and received it every week so the editor, knowing this, implored him as a reader of the Champion not to allow these people "to face the ruthless whims and tempests of the fierce Atlantic without clothes, without money, without food". Despite the pleas of the Champion the "Richard Watts" sailed and arrived at Quebec with these desperate creatures of Palmerston's in November '47.

Worse was yet to come with the arrival, later in November, of the "Aeolus" with a cargo of widows with helpless young families, decrepit old women and men riddled with disease. The St. Lawrence was icebound, the streets of Quebec filled with snow and the poor passengers in a state of nudity. The city of St. John would have to take them in care, and outraged, sent a letter to Lord Palmerston expressing regret and fury that he or his agents "should have exposed such a numerous and distressed portion of his tenantry to the severity and privation of a New Brunswick Winter......unprovided with the common means of support,

with broken-down constitutions and almost in a state of nudity ......
without regard to humanity or even common decency". Palmerston
passed on the criticism to his agents in Ireland; Kincaid replied,
defending his actions, maintaining that he was quite correct in sending
out the worst off of his tenants. This Kincaid was well known in
Mullaghmore, the older people still telling of his having spent his
Summers there in the "Lodges".He kept a large yacht in the harbour
which was moored Winter and Summer at what was later known as the
"Lugger Quay", the remains of which can still be seen at the claddagh
across from the new quay. The huge anchor, which was imbedded in the
green for use as a mooring post, can be seen in the front garden of
Lomax Boats.

While some records are available, it is not possible in the majority of
cases, to pinpoint which townlands these poor unfortunate creatures
that were shipped out, came from, as the passenger lists of these ships,
while obtainable, unfortunately listed only the name of the passenger
and their occupation, no record was made of the townland of origin.

In 1847, the first of Sir Robert Gore-Booth's ships for that year, left
the port of Sligo with 500 of his tenants. As usual, the landlords agents
and the Sligo Journal, very much an ascendancy newspaper and a voice
for the landlords, gave glowing accounts of the wonderful vessel and the
luxurious accomodation:

> "Never have I seen a vessel fitted out so painstakingly for the comfort
> of the passengers. The sleeping berths are most spacious and
> provisions plentiful.... Beds and bedding is also provided, including a
> pair of comfortable warm blankets."

On arrival at the port of St. John, no such luxuries were in evidence;
the authorities were appalled at the condition of the passengers,
accusing Sir Robert of clearing out his estates so as to avoid the new Poor
Law charges. Again these poor unfortunate emigrants had become
public charges in a foreign land; having to be housed by the local
authorities they survived by begging in the streets for food to support
themselves and their families. The local newspaper, the "Courier"
continued:

> "Many have been sent to the Alms House and Infirmary and a large
> portion of these will, in all probability, become a permanent charge
> upon this community".

Two other ships, the "Yeoman" and the "Lady Sale" followed later in the
season, bringing the numbers of emigrants shipped out by Sir Robert in
that year, to a total of 1,300.

Indian meal porridge was given out at several locations in this district. One of these distribution points was at Eddie Mc Garrigle's at Castlegal, opposite the old boy's school. McGarrigle was appointed to cook and dispense the porridge once a day. To get some of this gruel you had to go first to the Parish Priest or schoolmaster and get a ticket, this then allowed you to get one porringerful of the mixture for each person in the house. There were three other meal distribution centres located at Mullaghmore, Cliffoney and at Mc Gowan's in Bunduff. After the famine, Mc Garrigle's house was given for use as a school to the schoolmaster, Edward Mc Gloin, who until then had only a mud cabin. Mc Garrigle was moved to Carns by the landlord and later again to Mullaghmore. Later a Mrs McIntyre came into possession of Mc Garrigles old house and, according to the Folklore Collection, from her are descended the present McIntyres who lived at Bunduff Bridge, owning the salmon fishery rights.

One might have expected help or at least sympathy at this desperate time in our history, but no, the English papers and particularly the Times generated a lot of anti-Irish feeling. The Sligo Champion, a true champion and defender of the people at this time, in an editorial on May 8th '47 responded with,

> "one argument which we would advocate against the Times and all the other railers at the Irish, which we think has some force in it. They assert we are a worthless idle race, an annoyance to their country......now, if this be the case, why not cast us off, and give us back our independence. We love not the connection; we hate it. Let them set us free from it and we will trouble them no more; but no, they dream of no such thing......"

By August there was hope that the worst of the famine was over as healthy crops were reported with good harvest weather and indeed there was some improvement, but not enough, as when the crops were harvested there was just enough to provide seed for the following Spring. The people's Champion states the situation,

> "There's enough food to support the population 'till a new harvest but the landlords must get their rent and their arrears of rent, so to meet their demands, the grain must be sold. The grain will be sent out of Ireland to feed English horses......every shilling will go into the landlords pocket and the tenant will have to make out provision for his family without money, without grain or the potato to fall back on"

> *Where oppression is law from age to age,*
> *Where the death plague and hunger and misery rage*
> *And tyrants a Godless warfare wage*
> *'Gainst the holiest rights of an ancient land.*

Where the corn waves green on the fair hillside,
With each sheaf by the serfs and slavelings tied
And taken to pamper a foreigners pride!
There is our suffering Fatherland.
Where broad rivers flow 'neath the glorious sky
And valleys, like gems of emerald lie;
Yet the young men and strong men starve and die
For want of bread in their own rich land.

The story is told that, locally, there were three farms that were not affected by blight. One of these lucky farmers was Michael Langan of Carns who managed to save some small potatoes to plant in the Spring of '48. As he was setting them, the Parish Priest, Fr. Crofton passed by and seeing Langan at work, enquired of him what he was doing. "Setting potatoes", says he. "You're wasting your time", replied the priest, "Eat them or leave them there". Langan replied that he would plant them in the name of God and in spite of the devil and that they would grow. He planted them; they did grow and the following Autumn he had a good crop.

While it is reported that some seaside places suffered horribly during the famine years, there is no great store of famine stories locally and despite many enquiries I have not unearthed any significant amount of local lore, even about Palmerston's coffin ships. It's as if the horrible memories of these years have been shut completely out of peoples consciousness. Some older people tell of farmers from the surrounding villages, such as Cliffoney, Ballintrillick and Tawley travelling in convoys of asses and carts or with ass and creels, to the seashore along the Circular road at the back of Mullaghmore. They would gather edible sea-weeds, molluscs and shellfish, light fires along the road to cook these, eat as much as they could and carry the remainder home. It is said that so many "winkles" were eaten by some of the people that their eyes had taken on the colour of these creatures. This may be the time when the following now almost forgotten taunt originated, "The mountainy clebs, their eyes are red,blowing the fire to the boxty bread". The retort to this insult was, "The seaside hawks, their fingers are wore, picking the crannac along the shore".

On the humourous side, a story told to the Folklore Commission relates that:

A man named Paddy Cullen lived near the village of Cliffoney. One day as he was digging potatoes in his field, the Parish Priest who was walking along the road came into the field and asked him what kind of potatoes he had,

"Raw ones", Paddy replied. The priest, naturally enough, was not pleased with this answer and retorted. "I wonder do you know your catechism as well".

"Try me, says Paddy. The priest then asked him, "what is Baptism?." Paddy replied,"It was two shillings and sixpence in my father's time but it's five shillings since you came into the Parish".

As black '47 came to a close sixteen landlords had been shot dead throughout Ireland; in Sligo-Leitrim the police could give the names of ten landlords who were marked men, "their lives not being worth a sheet of paper". There were 15,000 extra troops in the country waging a campaign of terror, workhouses being enlarged, people dying of starvation, inside and outside of them, no employment, fever still raging and the people as pauperized and wretched as ever before.

According to his biographer, Joseph Ridley, Palmerston had hoped that the famine would make revolution less likely in Ireland, "as men must eat in order to be able to fight." For some time, John Mitchell, Gavan Duffy, William Smith O'Brien and Thomas Francis Meagher had been advocating armed rebellion. After an abortive attempt at an insurrection in 1848 the noble gesture was, as so many times before, crushed and the leaders sentenced to transportation for life to Van Diemen's Land. The Irish in America had planned to rescue Mitchell when his ship reached Bermuda but the British embassy in Washington discovered the plot and Palmerston passed on the information to the authorities in Bermuda. Six years later, in 1854, Palmerston persuaded the Cabinet to pardon O'Brien and some others on condition that they did not return to Britain or Ireland.

As the blight bit hard again in 1848, evictions and forced emigrations continued apace. People being admitted to the workhouse were forced to surrender their land to the landlord before obtaining relief; this method of dispossesion was called "passing paupers through the workhouse", a man went in, a pauper came out. This was to change when in May the quarter acre clause of the Poor Law which had forbidden relief to any individual owning a quarter acre of land or more was not enforced and despite fierce opposition from Trevelyan, head of the Treasury, and others, these small landowners could now receive assistance. This, however, provided no relief but resulted only in an increase of landlord clearances and evictions as landlords attempted to be rid of these classes of people.

Failures of the potato crop continued on and off in later years but never again reached the crisis proportions of black '47. The fungus which caused the potato blight (fungus phytophthora infestans) was not finally conquered until 1885 when a French botanist in Bordeaux came up with a concoction of bluestone and lime which inhibited the fungal growth on the potato stalk. For any reader with a farming background, mention of bluestone will bring to mind visions of huge, pot-bellied wooden barrels in a corner of the potato field at spraying time. In use until recently, these barrels were filled with water and a mixture of bluestone crystals and washing soda placed in a jute bag, which was suspended in the water and left overnight. The resultant watery blue solution was then filled into the old copper knapsack "spraying machine" which deposited the liquid in two fine, misty jets onto the green stalks, thus giving protection against the dreaded blight.

The failure of an English government to act effectively during the famine, has, down through the years, been seen as an act of genocide, an opportunity for greedy landlords to increase their holdings; an attempt to finally obliterate the Irish race. It left a bleak and desolate countryside shorn of over two million of its inhabitants and a legacy of hatred and resentment which lasted for many generations and has shadowy repercussions even today. About one million people or twelve per cent of the population of Ireland died of starvation in these years; another one million emigrated. Emigration from the port of Sligo was higher for it's size than any other port in Ireland; the number of emigrants leaving here were twice that of Limerick and four times that of the port of Galway. It is estimated that in the twenty year period ending in 1851, more than 60,000 sailed from Sligo harbour to ports in New York, Boston, Quebec and St. John in New Brunswick. Many of those who survived the coffin ships did gain employment and a foothold on the other side; for too many of those who were forced out and fled overseas, a monument at Grosse Isle, the receiving station near Quebec, tells the story:

> *In this secluded spot lie the mortal*
> *remains of 5,424 persons who*
> *flying from Pestilence and Famine in*
> *Ireland in the year 1847 found in*
> *America but a Grave.*

THE BREEZE IN THE THISTLES

Benbulben wakes, sweet sunlight ceases sleeping,
And stands aloft over the green and grey.
Dewdrops fall from flowers quietly weeping;
History's scars lie bedded deep in clay.
In fields, invasions shadows have etched their mark;
Cool earth has drunk the blood of culture dying.
Rising to the sky's face through the dark
The seas immortal echoes have heaved her sighing.
Dawns bright light has melted the shadows cast,
The sea's breast swells and roars out it's refrain:
Though deep the cuts emblazoned on our past,
The breeze in the thistles is free to roam again!

Paul Cunningham

CHAPTER 4

Gun Runners and Land Leaguers

The Irish people were now impoverished and debased. Ireland was to all human appearances dead and buried at last. The English rulers had finally subjected a pauperised people and need never again fear the uprising of a hostile Irish Nation. But men pass through terror into courage; the quarry at bay forgets fear, and fights for his life. His anger is the black tragedy of history.

The wellspring of Irish nationalism was irrepressible, and sprang forth again with the formation of the Fenians by Luby, Stephens, Kickham and O'Leary in 1858.

> *"That rake up near the rafters, why leave it there so long?*
> *It's handle of the best of ash is smooth and straight and strong;*
> *And, Mother, will you tell me, why did my father frown*
> *When to make the hay in Summertime, I climbed to take it down?"*
> *She looked into her husband's eyes, while her own with light did fill,*
> *"You'll shortly know the reason, boy!" said Rory of the Hill.*

An insurrection planned for 1867 was defeated, before a blow could be struck, by the arrest and jailing of the leaders on information, as has too often been the case in our history, given by informers. Theirs was a noble failure but not quite as fruitless as it might seem as these brave men fanned and kept alive the spark of Irish freedom and passed it on through our darkest days.

One of the most remarkable sagas of this period was the cruise in May 1867 of the 'Jacknell', renamed in mid Atlantic, the "Erin's Hope". Crewed by forty Irishmen who had distinguished themselves in the recently concluded American Civil War, she left New York with a cargo of 5,000 rifles, three batteries of artillery, 1,000 sabres and 5,000,000 rounds of ammunition. She arrived in Donegal Bay on the 10th of May and for six days sailed within a couple of miles of the coast, sending signals to these shores which remained unanswered, nor was there any sign of the insurrection they had come to help. They were visited by local fishing boats anxious to know why they were there but these fishermen knew nothing of a Fenian rising. As the days went by signals were sent from the coastguards on shore demanding that they identify themselves and state their business. They were boarded eventually by the authorities off Mullaghmore Head, but they, apparently finding nothing suspicious, made no attempt at an arrest.

Near this time some of the crew were injured by the "accidental" discharge of a weapon by a man named Buckley who, later on, was to betray his shipmates. The injured men were put ashore near Streedagh and were found suffering of gunshot wounds by the Coastguard patrol stationed at that time at Streedagh. The men were eventually brought before Ormsby-Jones J.P. and sent to prison.

Captain Kavanagh, after two weeks of waiting, landed two of his men, Colonel O'Doherty and Lieut. O'Shea at Sligo town with the intention of linking up with the local Fenians. He had high hopes that the men of the North-west would rally to his call and strike a blow for freeedom, as the men of Mayo did when the French boats came to Killala. As the ship glided stealthily into Sligo harbour a message came from Col. Kelly, chief organiser in Dublin of the I.R.B., telling the captain that the insurrection was in disorder and ordering him to proceed to Skibereen. A search party was sent ashore to recall O'Doherty and O'Shea, but failed to find them. The Erins Hope had been too long in the bay so the Captain reluctantly hoisted sail and sped south, narrowly avoiding a confrontation with an English gunboat which had been summoned to the area from Blacksod Bay Station, more than likely as a result of the boarding incident at Mullaghmore.

The subsequent adventures of the Erin's Hope took place out of this area and therefore do not concern us in this book, except briefly. After many more adventures and attempted landings along the Irish coast and the eventual loss of thirty two of her crew, Captain Kavanagh set sail for New York grieving for his crew members held in British dungeons because of the aforementioned informer, Buckley. The Erin's Hope may not have rendezvoused with the Fenians but her proud captain had made fools of the best of the English navy in Ireland for over three weeks, evading capture, landing men, exchanging communications and after a voyage of over 9,000 miles, finally returning safely with his ship and cargo to New York. In his wake, three boats which had attempted to capture him were sent to the bottom of the sea; the gunboat 'Lapwing' lost in Killala Bay, the 'Revenge', wrecked on Daunt's Rock and another gunboat which foundered in a gale off Cape Clear.

According to the Irish Folklore collection. Canavaun lounge in

Cliffoney was in 1867 owned by Ned Foley; it was a stopover place used twice daily by Bianconi cars travelling between Sligo and Bundoran. Tom Hickey was the stableboy there whose job it was to have the two horses ready when the car arrived. Tom was also charged with the task of hiding and protecting Pat Hayes during his stay in Cliffoney.

Pat Hayes' or the Red Fox as he was known was on the run from the authorities, having shot dead a landlord in Dobbin's Hotel in Tipperary town. The landlord, a Captain Bell, demanded his rent which Hayes did not have. When the landlord insisted on payment, Michael pulled out a pistol saying, "This will have to do", taking aim and shooting the landlord dead. Forced to flee immediately, he eventually came to this area and was put in touch with the local "Steel Boys" who decided to hide him in Foleys, considering that it was such a busy place and so close to the barracks that it was probably the last place the police would look. There was an old hayloft that was used for the horses and this is where he was kept for over six months. According to Owen Donlevy, the story was handed down in his family that Hayes spent much of his time concealed in a secret hiding place on the Donlevy premises during his stay in Cliffoney.

The police knew or suspected that he was in the area and this made it very difficult to smuggle him away. On one occasion they were on the point of smuggling Hayes out, but were given a timely warning, so when the police patrol appeared everything seemed normal. Success finally crowned their efforts and he was smuggled out of Cliffoney in the middle of a crib of turf to Rosses Point and from there to Raughley harbour where he was brought out on a ship to America by a Capt. Conway.

This Capt. Conway's grandnephew, Seamus Conway, still lives in Cliffoney and can verify the accuracy of the story. Capt. Conway learned the principles of navigation from a man named Celier who taught for a time in Cliffoney school. The massive beams that we see in Cliffoney chapel today were brought in on Conway's ship to the port of Sligo and transported to Cliffoney. The iron bindings on the beams were made at McGarrigle's forge that stood on the street of Cliffoney where Pat Gallagher lived until recently. Peter Mc Garrigle and Owen Donlevy's grandfather were instrumental in the organisation of Hayes safekeeping and eventual escape. The ownership of Ned Foleys changed to Brennans when Henry Brennan, nephew of Fr. Malachai Brennan, returned from Australia and married Ned's daughter Brigid. The present owners of this historic building are Harrisons.

Prior to Hayes' arrival at Cliffoney he had made his way to

Ballintrillick where he was kept at a house that is presently owned by Petie Gillespie of Gortnadrung. For security reasons, he was moved after a time to the house of James Foley in Drinaghan where only the walls stand now. While in Foley's the house was visited by a neighbour who offered Hayes his pipe for a smoke. When this man left, Foley warned Hayes that he must go immediately as the fellow could not be trusted. It was a timely warning as some hours later Foley's house was surrounded by soldiers and the area searched thoroughly; but Hayes was safe, he had crossed over from there to McCormacks in Tawley; shortly thereafter the local Steel Boys brought him to Cliffoney.

It is said that by one of these strange twists of fate, Captain Bell's son, unknowingly, became Hayes' employer in America. The following verse has survived down through the years:

A dollar a day, it is my pay,
My master likes me well;
But little he knows that I'm the man,
Who shot old Captain Bell.

"THE BATTERING RAM HAS DONE ITS WORK". 1772. W.L.

"Oh, heaven ne'er looked on a sadder scene
Earth Shuddered to hear that such woe had been
Then we prayed in despair to a foreign Queen
For leave to live in our own fair land"

70
(Photo Courtesy of the Nat Library of Ireland)

THE LANDLORD'S SONG

I sit like a king in my lordly tower
And all that I see is mine,
And reign supreme and I wield a power
By virtue of right divine;
And the farmer ploughs and the farmer sows
And he toils with care and pain.
'Tis for me he ploughs and reaps and mows
And gathers the golden grain.

And the miners dig in the darksome caves
Where the sun does never shine;
Though they work and toil like the galley slaves
The fruit of their toil is mine.
And I eat the fat and I drink the sweet
And I neither toil nor spin
And I pass the time with companions meet
And ever the rent comes in.

And the markets may rise
or prices may fall
And men may be discontent
But though ruin should overwhelm them all
yet still I must have my rent.
For I make the laws which hedge me around
That none my right assail
And I've built them up with a skill profound
And a cunning that must prevail.

(WRITTEN IN 1887 BY AN UNKNOWN AUTHOR; TAKEN FROM THE LAND
WAR AND THE FALL OF PARNELL BY PROINNSÍOS Ó DUIGNEAIN.)

LAND LEAGUE

In the following years the English Courts in Ireland were kept busy with the trials, imprisonment and deportations of Fenian prisoners. In 1870 Isaac Butt, a Tory lawyer and M.P., who had come to admire the sacrifices and dedication of the Fenians, formed the Home Rule League.

Their aim was to agitate for Home Rule by parliamentary methods. The physical force people persisted too, continuing to believe then, as now, that the manipulation of moderate men was one of Englands chief devices for consolidation of its power in Ireland. Parnell took over the chairmanship of the Home Rule League in 1877. He, too, had a limited belief in the effectiveness of parliamentarianism and conciliation. "We will never gain anything from England," he said, "unless we step on her toes".

Michael Davitt, whose name was to become synonymous with that of the Land League, was released from prison in December 1877 after serving almost eight years for Fenianism. He had good reason to know the condition of the Irish peasant as at the age of five, together with his parents and two sisters, he was evicted, their little home in Straide, Co. Mayo razed to the ground and their plot of land taken over by the landlord. On making their way to Lancashire, Michael was sent to work in a mill. At the age of twelve his arm became entangled in one of the machines and was so badly injured that it had to be amputated. Despite his injury, while still young, he joined the I.R.B. and was tried and sentenced for smuggling arms in 1870.

The blight which caused the potato to rot had still not been conquered. In 1879, famine loomed again, rack-renting and evictions were the order of the day, "the landlord owned his tenant, his tenants land and quite often even his tenants women folk"; sometimes the poor farmer had to make a choice between eviction or sending his daughter up to the manor house, whether his rent was paid or not. The landlord's rights in these matters were notorious and no mention of these times would be complete without recording this reality which, difficult as it is to comprehend now, was a fact of life then. These stories were rarely written down but were passed from generation to generation in the rambling houses; the following story while being humorous has a grim side to it. To avoid giving offence to descendants of the parties involved, the names have been changed:

Andrew was a driver for Sir G. who was a notorious womanizer. Andrew often had to drive him to collect a farmer's daughter and bring her to the manor house when the rent was not paid. One day Sir G., on picking up a young girl, decided to get down to it before he actually got home. He dismounted, got Andrew to hold the horses reins and proceeded, to put it delicately, to engage this girls attentions on the verge of the roadside. Andrew, the quintessential lackey, was observing the action while holding the horses and dissatisfied with the degree of the girls co-operation, shouts over to her, "Will ye get yer arse off the ground there and keep the dacent mans b——s out of the gutter". We are not told if the driver's admonition was heard or heeded!

Michael Davitt formed the Land League in 1879 at Castlebar. At mass meetings in Sligo county and all over the West of Ireland he declared that it was time to rid Ireland once and for all of the evils of landlordism and rackrenting, advocating civil resistance on a massive scale. At a great meeting in Gurteen on November 2nd he was arrested and immediately lodged in Sligo jail. The high profile trial that followed made a mockery of the law and gained national and international attention for the cause.

The trial was moved to Dublin and the charges eventually dropped, making a huge propaganda victory and a resounding success for the Land League. Now, thousands of people took to the streets; process servers and landlords agents could not travel without drawing a crowd; if a farmer was evicted there was no-one to take his house or land. The agitations on Captain Boycott's estates gave a new word to the English language and landlords were ostracised and boycotted up and down the land. The Irishman may have been conquered but he was never beaten!

> Hold the rents and hold the crops, boys
> Pass the word from town to town
> Pull away the props, boys
> So you'll pull coercion down.

In 1881, Pat and James McGowan waited patiently, outside of Inishmurray Island, for three days, in their fishing boat, the "Charmin' Molly", eventually taking on and landing a shipment of arms. Within days they were arrested, but had to be released as there was by this time, no shred of evidence to support a conviction. Shortly after, in Feb 1881 the Sligo Chronicle carried an article announcing the arrival of the gunboat "Goshawk" in the bay, reporting that a Yankee Irishman cutter had been seen in the area having, "in all probability landed arms in the Northwest."

The Sligo Champion, still very firmly on the side of the people, describes the justices of the court as "just-asses" and "doughty and gouty dispensers of the law". In September, a large crowd had gathered at Grange Petty Sessions as Patrick Boyce of Mullaghmore, a tenant of Lord Ashley's of Classiebawn, was brought before one of these "just-asses" and charged with assault. It was alleged that he attacked a party of shooters headed by Ashley, the local landlord, who tried to cross his land. Charles Barker, on behalf of Ashley, told the court that Boyce was mowing in the field, that he confronted Lord Ashley's party when they attempted to pass and attacked them with a scythe. Boyce denied the charge, saying that he had just tried, in a peaceful manner, to prevent the party from crossing the field as he was afraid they would trample and ruin his potato crop. The "doughty and gouty" dispenser of the law presumably didn't believe Boyce and handed him a six week prison sentence. There was a large number of police outside the court in the event of trouble but the crowd dispersed and went home peacefully.

In Lisadell, Sir Henry Gore-Booth, son of Robert seemed to be as immune to the sufferings of his people as was his father. In March 1882 he received a letter:

"My dear Lucifer,

I must inform you that you have the poorest tenants in Ireland and all owing to your bad treatment......the time has come that by God we don't care for man or the divil is that you are stuck in Lisadell like the divil in hell but I'll meet you like Captain Bell."

Maud Gonne reported in her autobiography a conversation which took place at the dinner table. It reveals the contempt in which the tenant was held by the landlord:

"That damned Land League is ruining the country......they would stop us hunting, would they, the so and so's. As I was coming home this evening I saw Paddy Ward and his family lying out in a ditch. His wife doesn't look as if she will live until morning. I stopped and told him he would be responsible for her death. I had warned him as to what would happen if he joined the Land League. Now he has no roof to shelter his family and the woman will be dead before tomorrow." On expressing concern, Maude Gonne was told, "Let her die. These people must be taught a lesson."

Gore-Booths agent, Michael Boyle, had also come to the attention of the Land Leaguers, receiving the following letter:

"Michael Boyle, when you are takin beyond Carney or in Sligo you may have your coffin along with you......you will be treated like a mad dog that is quartered and buried underground and that is the death you must get......the crew that was with you if they can be knowing they will get bad treatment but not half as bad as you will get......we are the lads that does not fear to do you. Be sure of the words I have said......"

A visit by a reporter from the Times to this area, reported in the Sligo Chronicle of March 12 1881, gives us a glimpse of the living conditions of the inhabitants of the area at this time:

"Ballyconnell belongs to Mr. Gethin and Mr. Huddlestone, both absentee. About the famine time the land was enclosed and squared; families of five or six in each one roomed house, built of mud or rough stone, usually low and dark and innocent of lath and plaster; the thatch held on by straw ropes at 9" intervals over the roof. The furniture consists of one, occasionally two beds, a rough table and a few benches. The donkey and any cattle, pigs or poultry of course, are housed with their master. Many of the older people, especially the women, cannot speak English. The children, seldom shod, are not very good Winter attenders at school. Those able to keep a cow do fairly well. The milk greatly helps the potatoes and Indian meal which are their staple dietary. Potatoes and a little home grown oatmeal are fairly plentiful from harvest until about March, when Indian meal generally has to be got, usually on credit, and is paid for in Summer by an extra take of fish, by the produce of the cow or by the crop of oats.

Some of the land is charged at 40 shillings an Irish acre; the general complaint is that rates have been repeatedly raised. Another grievance is the 4s.2d imposed 16 years ago for the privelege of cutting and gathering seaweed. One old woman, reputed the matriarch of the village, has about four acres and a one room cottage, pays about £7.13s.0d of rent for these. She grows about three quarters of an acre of potatoes, a little piece of oats, and is master of a cow and donkey."

The previously mentioned and "properly" titled Hon. Evelyn Ashley was Secretary to the Board of Trade and came to reside, in 1881, on more or less of a semi-permanent basis in the newly completed Classiebawn Castle. In response to mass protests and threat of boycott he made peace with his tenants by writing off one half years rent and reducing all rents by 40%. One can imagine the rack-rents that had been extracted beforehand! The Sligo Chronicle reported that the local Land League was satisfied with the arrangement but it's doubtful if this is completely true as disturbances continued.

Ashley's agent, George Barker, considered locally to be a cruel and vindictive man, was constantly at loggerheads with the tenants, sometimes for petty reasons, as evidenced by the incident concerning Boyce. In another incident a boycott was placed on him as a result of having summonsed a man for allowing his ass to graze near Classiebawn. A crowd of over 1,000 people led by Henry Brennan, who lived where Canavaun pub in Cliffoney is now, gathered on a Sunday near Classiebawn demanding his dismissal.

Ashley defended his agent and shortly afterwards, on 22nd Oct. 1881, Henry Brennan was arrested, taken to Galway and lodged in jail. The charge was "Unlawful assembly with others to the terror of his Majesty's subjects for the purpose of disturbing the public peace." The confidential police report went on to say that on,

> " 4th Sept. 1881, Brennan headed an assembly which passed the house of George Barker and intimidated him and his family by shouting. Threatening notices were posted the same day, boycotting Barker. Brennan is the leading land league agent in his district and the disaffected meet at his house."

His arrest provoked further mass protests by the people who gathered together to save Brennans crops. Fr. Commins is reported in the papers as having led large numbers of people in prayer on the Sunday following his arrest. Following the prayers the crowd gathered at Brennans public house but were warned by a large contingent of police, who had arrived from Sligo to reinforce the local constabulary, that if the public house was opened on a Sunday there would be arrests. They proceeded to take the names of those present "on which the crowd drifted away." Brennan was eventually released from jail on the 24th March 1882. Barker, however, was not dismissed and continued to be feared and hated by the people as, "a tyrant of the worst description."

The following correspondence is from the Broadlands Records held at the Hartley Library:

Cliffoney, Sligo,
Sept. 30th 1881

Dear Sir,

We have seen the list of charges drawn up by your tenantry against your keeper, Barker. From our intercourse with the people, we are in a position to say that they are not at all exaggerated. We regret to say that he has, and not on a few occasions, wounded, and wantonly so, the feelings of a very sensitive people. We trust as you value the esteem and affection of your tenantry, you will accede to their request and remove from their midst, a man who has given them so much just cause of offence and occasioned so much disturbance in the parish.

Hoping that the kindly relations that hitherto existed between you and those poor honest people will not now be disturbed or severed by the retention of *this man*.

We are, dear Sir, Faithfully Yours

Malachai Brennan P.P., John Cummins C.C.

Robert ? C.C.

8 Oct. '81

Dear Sir,

I take the liberty of writing to you to say that your wishes as regards the protection of your gamekeeper, George Barker, have been carried out. You are already, I presume, aware that two policemen now constantly reside with Wm. Barker and accompany him everywhere, and also any member of his family leaving home. Five policemen are also stationed in your gate lodge at Classiebawn, and their duties are altogether devoted to the protection of Barker and your property in the neighbourhood.

Today, 12 police were considered necessary to escort him to Grange Petty Sessions where he had some evidence to give. He has in his employment a man named Gilmartin and the people are bitter against him too, insomuch that they threaten to boycott Gilmartin's father-in-law, if he doesn't turn out his daughter who is married to Gilmartin.

Boycotting is getting much more rife in the portions of this county north of Sligo than formerly and I share with the magistrates I met at Grange today the opinion that much trouble is in store for all hands here this Winter....... I need not say that I will always be happy to afford you every information in my power, you may require and I regret I was on leave when the trouble arose at Classiebawn, otherwise I should have had the honour of waiting upon you.

I remain, Your obedient Servant,
T. Reeves, Sub. Insp. R.I.C.

Moneygold
Oct. 3rd 1881

Mr. Barker,

I am sorry to say that I am forced against my will to give up my situation by these Land League fellows and I am sorry for it. I was fairly boycotted for the last three months especially since last Saturday evening I am sorry from my heart that we must part and I hope its not forever. I'll tell you for a fact, Mr. Barker I could not stand it longer I was hung with lies saying I was talking to you in backward places so now I fear I cannot speak to you for the future.

I am informed that James Christal gave up all and like myself he could not stand it longer for there was a notices in the Chappele wall last sunday about yourself and you staff I suffered a deal of abuse from the rubbish of this place lately my hay was knocked several times and my garden wall knocked .... Mr Barker I asked you will write to me shortly agan and let me know what is best to do James Christal did not call for the bags yet will I send them down I declined sending down the pigs as I was afraid my living would be far worse then.

I remain yours
truly Michael Commins
write soon, Good Bye

Cliffoney Dec. 26th 81

To the Hon. A. E. Ashley,

Hon. Sir,

At a meeting of your tenantry at Cliffoney, it was resolved and carried by the more reasonable portion of your tenantry that we again make a second and final appeal to you for a reasonable reduction in our rents, which we find that we are unable to pay for this year, after passing through three years of adversity. Notwithstanding the substantial reductions given by you for the past two years, the majority of us would inevitably have perished of hunger were it not for the charitable subscriptions of foreign countries, which the books of the relief committee can show. It cannot be reasonably expected that we are on our legs again after passing through such an ordeal, nor do we think that heaping ruinous costs on a reduced people will much assist us to pay what rent we are able or to be of any profit to you. If you consider it expedient to resort to extreme measures, it will only tend to make us the more suitable subjects for charity next year for no process of law can make us pay what we have not.

Trusting that if we had been chastised with whips in times gone by that you will not now beat us with scorpions.

Joseph Lockhart	Jim Feeney
Francis Rooney	Patrick Timoney
John Feeney	Martin Moffit
Chas. Higgins	Thomas Kearins
John Gilmartin	

Ashley stood by Barker and in a letter to Ashley dated Nov. 14 he feels that things "is near at an end I have succeeded in getting some men I have set four on to plant and I am more than happy to tell you that I have got them quite independently of one person so now if you have not wrote do not for it is you that must be firm now.....". He goes on to say that he is playing off the men who are coming to work against each other and relates that Mr Ross and his Mrs. were to see him and told him that, " it is likely that Henry Brennan will be sent to gaol again." The letter continues, "if he is sent to gaol they will take the license from the house and that will tame him now Mr. Ashley you need not be afraid of not being comfortable for a little shooting now as I have a nice lot of game and plenty of beaters I see a nice lot of woodcocks all ready I hope you will be over soon the weather is nice and frosty ......" He goes on to discuss the business of the estate and signs himself "George T. Barker"

Earlier that same year, on 7th March 1881, a secret police report stated that:

"At about 4.30 in the morning, the house of Andrew Mc Loughlin, farmer, was attacked and fired into by a party of about 20 men. Two revolver shots were fired through the back door and a gunshot through the front window of the kitchen. The back door was forced open and five or six of the party entered and it is alleged, fired more shots into the house. Intention, evidently was to intimidate, not to take life."

It seems that Mc Loughlin, known locally as "Dutchman", had supplied two carts of turf to Dolan, a local R.I.C. constable. In addition to being a member of the R.I.C., his wife had incurred further disfavour in the community by taking the post as teacher in Cliffoney school over the preference of the community for a local teacher. Patrick Gilgar, Francis Commins, Patrick Dunleavey, Patrick Gonigle and Thomas Gallagher were arrested and subsequently discharged.

The Patrick Donlevy (Dunleavey) mentioned in this report was one of the controversial figures who played an important and central role in the events which took place around this time. Now almost forgotten, he died a tragic and untimely death, but nevertheless in his young life, left an indelible mark on events of the time. A song which was written in his memory has survived and was recalled for me one winter's night by Henry Conway of Carns:

> "He was a grand and bold young man,
> As all around do know.
> He was beloved in Sligo town
> In Leitrim and Sligo."

He was born in July 1861 to Eugene Donlevy and Elizabeth Clancy. Eugene had made a fortune in America as a trader supplying goods to the forces engaged at that time in the Civil War. He returned to Cliffoney and opened a pub and shop which still stand today although, as a private residence at this time.

Pat joined the Land League while still young and many stories are told of his exploits as he took on the local constabulary and landlords both by civil resistance and by force of arms. It is certain that he was instrumental in gaining the previously mentioned concessions from Ashley. Stories are told too of his having mounted attacks on Cliffoney barracks from the roof of what is now Ena's Pub, formerly the residence of Palmerston on his visits to Cliffoney. It seems he fell into conflict with some of his fellow Land Leaguers who much preferred talking to acting and were partial to the occasional hunt with the hound as well as running with the hare. Pat was warned by his family to tend his shop and lands, advising him that if the authorities didn't get him, some of his associates would. The warning was prophetic.

79

A routine mission had been organised to go to Dernish Island, some say to reprimand an informer while others say their errand was to take a gun off Petie Mulligan. Pat and his accomplices approached the channel surrounding the island on a wild, stormy night and proceeded to board a boat which his comrades had secured for the job.

This was a treacherous stretch of water from which Willie Devins, N.T. and James Currid of Grange, had secured a very narrow escape from drowning some time before, when their boat sprung a board. Some time before that a man named Higgins of Rosses Point had actually been drowned.

It is said that when Pat got on board the boat, the men with him pushed the boat out from the shore without oars, knowing that it was holed. We can only imagine the struggles of this young man fighting for his life in the treacherous channel, without oars to bring the boat ashore and water rushing in through the hole in her bottom; his murderers who watched from the shore would never reveal the secrets of that dark and awful night. Some days later the boat was found washed ashore at the back of Dernish island. The song continues:

> 'Twas on the 18th of September
> Bellashanny Harvest day,
> That this young man was missed from home
> The public papers say.

> He was searched both near and far
> But could nowhere be found
> 'Till days went past and then at last
> Lord save us, he was drowned

> 'Twas at Killybegs broad harbour
> And there in broad daylight
> His body was found floating,
> Heart rending was the sight........

> .....His friends arrived from Cliffoney
> And bore the corpse away.
> Sorrowful hearts did follow it
> Upon that mournful day.

According to his death certificate, his body was found on 7th of Oct. 1881 at St. Johns Point and brought ashore at Killybegs, so ending the career of one of the most daring young men of his time. His Land League uniform can be seen on display in Sligo Museum; stories of his deeds are still told quietly by the old men of the parish. The names of the men who accompanied him on that night cannot be written here; it is said that the ghost of Pat Donlevy haunted one of these men, giving him no peace until the day he died.

> God help his poor aged father
> His loss he deeply mourned
> Lamenting for his loving son
> That never would return......

> ....He has left a lovely wife to mourn
> His loss she does deplore.
> The Lord on high may comfort her
> She'll ne'er see him no more.

On the other side of the divide and just down the road from Donlevy's, lived Tom William Higgins, landlords agent, and leader of the "Crowbar Brigade", a "walking divil" who showed no mercy whatsoever. Adjacent to his house and beside the bridge that spans the little river which flows through Cliffoney there is a pound, built during Palmerstons time, which can still be seen; this was used as an enclosure to hold cattle which had been seized for rent arrears. The cattle could be released on payment of one shilling and a promise to pay the amount due shortly after. This treatment was only for his favourites though, as most of the time he showed no mercy and the cattle would be confiscated and sold forthwith. For people who fell behind badly with the rent there was eviction and the crowbar brigade. If the tenants wouldn't leave when Higgins demanded it he would throw them out, burn the house and throw down the walls with crowbars. Two families who received this treatment were Mary Gibbons of Grellagh and a house in Cliffoney village now owned by Patsy Harrison.

It is said that after Higgins' death, a terrible noise like thunder and the rattling of chains was heard in the house every night. Higgins sister, who survived him, went to the parish priest and he is said to have "fought the devil out of it." Until recently the place was regarded as "unearthly, something evil or sinister hangs around it". An upstairs room was unusable and considered to be haunted as the priest had isolated the evil spirit in this room. Whatever the reason, it is said that this room was always kept locked. In my childhood, this house was owned by the local midwife, Nurse Bennet; it is presently owned by a Burns family, roofless and in disrepair.

The incident of the Cliffoney land fight comes to us from a story told to the Folklore Commision by Pat Kennedy of Cliffoney in 1937.

There were twelve farmers living in Edenreagh on the South side of Cliffoney whose farmlands ran down towards the sea from the main Sligo Bundoran road. Between the foot of their land and the sea ran a grazing common and through it a right of way which from time immemorial had been used by the farmers to cart wrack and famluc from the shore to their farms. It was spread to dry on the common before being brought home. This seaweed was a very nutrient rich manure and much prized by the farmers. In the Winter of 1887 when this valuable fertilizer had been cast up by the storms the Cliffoney men started to cart it home as was their custom. Barker, the landlords agent, attempted to stop them but they insisted they had a perfect right to use the cartway and continued with their work. He summonsed them and all had to appear at Grange court. The case aroused tremendous local interest and Grange courthouse was crowded on the day of the trial.

At that time the landlord and his agent had the full support of English law, but nevertheless in this particular case the resident magistrate took a very lenient view of the matter and fined each of the twelve defendants the sum of one penny or alternatively one night in Sligo jail. I'm sure he believed in his heart that the poor farmers were justified in doing what they did but the law required that he bring in a guilty verdict. The sidecar being the mode of transportation in those days, four cars were ordered to convey the men to Sligo jail as they had decided not to pay the fine of one penny. The men now refused to go in the cars as well, and insisted on walking to Sligo. This was done for the purpose of attracting peoples attention to the matter and it worked well as propaganda.

Four policemen were picked to escort the men to Sligo jail. As they moved off from Grange R.I.C. barracks they were followed by a large crowd of people who conveyed them for miles and kept up a continuos din and cheering all the time. The four policemen walking alongside twelve strong powerful men who refused to pay a penny fine was a never to be forgotten sight and one the police would rue for a long time.

Eventually they reached Sligo town where a huge concourse of people awaited their arrival, word having been sent ahead from Grange before their departure. In Sligo they were followed by large numbers of the people of Sligo who sympathised with them and approved of their action in not paying the fine. The local papers took up the matter and altogether it got widespread publicity. The following night when the prisoners arrived in Cliffoney they were met by all the people of the parish with bands and banners.

After that time they continued their work as usual but they were confined to a small area for spreading the weed and they had to use a cartway which was then built by Barker along the bottom of their lands. Pat Gilgar, John Timoney and Roger Currid were the names of some of the farmers involved and since that time no person has interfered with the rights of the farmers of Edenreagh.

At this time, the people of Ireland had been made strangers in their own country, their lands confiscated and then rented out to them or worse still, sent out on coffin ships, beaten and subdued by force of arms and the misuse of the law. With nothing left to them but their wits, they now proceeded to make a mockery of authority and the law. Another similar incident which happened about this time was triggered by the seizure by the police of an ass belonging to Andrew Murtagh of Bunduff for non payment of rent:

> *The Land League ass went out one day*
> *To walk in Bunduff town.*
> *He was arrested by the police*
> *And brought to Cliffoney pound*

By law the ass could be sold for the sum of twopence if they found someone prepared to pay this but of course no-one in this area would come forward.

> *There wasn't a man in Cliffoney town*
> *Would give a silver, gold or brass*
> *So they locked him into jail*
> *Because he was a Cliffoney Land League ass.*

The police were then required to bring the ass into Sligo town to the public auction. On the night before the police were to take the ass into town, some locals got into the pound, painted the ass green and wrote on his side, "LAND LEAGUE ASS". Next day the unfortunate police attracted a big crowd again as they walked into Sligo. Henry Conway tells me that his father often recalled the ridiculous sight of the two policemen driving the painted ass up the road to Sligo with a crowd of people following behind.

At the crown auction the next day the most that was bid for the ass was a penny ha'penny as nobody would bid the required tuppence knowing that if this sum was reached the peelers were off the hook.

> *He roared a meela murther*
> *And lay down on the floor.*
> *"I'll give five bob to any man*
> *Who'll take this damned ould ass away".*

The police had to walk all the way back to Cliffoney with the ass and eventually had to return him to Bunduff where they found him.

DUBLIN METROPOLITAN POLICE C 1890
Top Right Denny Cummins, Mullaghmore; *(family photo)*

CHAPTER 5

*P*rologue to Conflict

With smiling gay faces, we'll go to the races,
Our lads and our lassies are coming all o'er.
We'll dance and we'll sing and we'll make the town ring,
And enjoy the grand races in famed Mullaghmore.

For generations, Mullaghmore Horse Races had been the highlight of the North Sligo social season, well attended by both rich and poor. During my childhood, they continued under the auspices of Fr. Gallagher, but unfortunately, were discontinued after his retirement in the 60's. Despite the unrest and political upheavals leading up to the end of the 19th century, Mullaghmore Hurdle Races carried on with P.A. Mc Hugh as chief steward. Patrick Mc Hugh championed the rights of the people in print from the time he acquired the Sligo Champion in 1885 to his untimely death at the age of fifty one in 1909, caused in large measure, no doubt, as a result of his efforts on behalf of the people and his many terms spent in English jails. A prime mover in support of the United Irish League and a constant striver for unity among the Irish parties, he was M.P. for North Leitrim at first, eventually being elected for and representing North Sligo. A measure of this mans popularity must have been his election as Mayor of Sligo for five consecutive terms. He had just been released from a six month sentence in Derry jail for supposed inflammatory remarks in articles in his newspaper when he was listed as chief steward of the Mullaghmore Races in August 1893.

It is an interesting window on the past to read the names of the people involved in this event just one hundred years ago. Fellow stewards to Mr. Mc Hugh were Bernard Collery, also an M.P. for Sligo, Thomas Scanlon, Mayor of Sligo, J.L. Tottenham J.P., Col. J Dickson J.P., F. Kenny Esq. M.D., B.G. Lowe Esq., Henry Brennan, Joseph Lockhart, Edward Foley, Patrick Gilgar, Michael Clancy. Starters were Col. Dickson and the Right Hon. St. George Roe, M.P. Hon. Secs. were C.F. Allen of Grange and J. Crumbie of Cliffoney.

£4.19s was the first prize in the Cliffoney Plate for working farmers horses. It was run over two miles and was won by Mr. J. Young's "Whirl", second was Michael Clancy's "Black Prince" and third, Mrs. Allen's "Lady of the Glen". The Grange Plate was won by Mr. C. Bree's "Red Light" while Mr. G.B. Lowe's "Bunduff" came second.

With a large population of young men in every village, there were plenty of volunteers for other sports. Handball was one of the most popular of these with every village having a team, the most popular venue for matches being the gable of Hannon's Pub in Mullaghmore and Tommy Hannon's (now Gorevan's) at Cliffoney. Football, too, was very popular with matches being played at the race track, as they are today. In September 1895, Creevykeel Celtic played a match against Sligo town at this venue.

Players were:-

CREEVYKEEL C.	SLIGO A.
P. GALLAGHER (CAP.)	A. KILFEATHER
C. McGARRIGLE	T. HOWLEY
THOMAS HANNON	P. KEARINS
J. McGLOIN	WILLIAM BURNS
J. GALLAGHER (FORWARDS)	J. O'ROURKE
F. GALLAGHER	T. GILLEN
T. McGARRIGLE	W. TUOHY
A. MURTAGH (HALF-BACKS)	J. ROBERTS
T. McLOUGHLIN	J. McCARRICK
M. LEONARD (FULL-BACKS)	T. McGUIRE
P. HANNON (GOAL)	JAMES LAMBERT

Sadly, the days when you could gather a football team in Creevykeel are long gone! Combat on the playing field then was, perhaps unwittingly, but surely, practice for more serious things to come; we know that many of these young men who strove on these playing fields, played their part in the freedom struggle in the years ahead, as a restless spirit and a longing for freedom was ever abroad among the young men of Ireland at this time:

> *Oh brave young men, my love, my pride, my promise,*
> *'Tis on you my hopes are set,*
> *In manliness, in kindness, in justice,*
> *To make Erin a nation yet"*

Disheartened and confused by the failure of the Parnell movement at the close of the 19th century, a new life was breathed into the people again by the formation of the Gaelic League in 1893. Stories were retold of the forgotten glory of the Gael; Gaelic song, music and writing was revived, and captured the imagination of the country. A resurgence of nationalistic fervour followed. Prompted too by famine conditions in the West of Ireland, the United Irish League was launched at Westport, Co. Mayo in January 1898. This organisation was eventually to become the constituency organisation of the Home Rule, Irish Parliamentary Party.

In May, 1901, the R.I.C. reported that, "in Sligo, owing to the pernicious influence of the United Irish League, and the fact of the resolutions, real or imaginary, passed at their meetings, being widely circulated in the columns of "The Sligo Champion", there is considerable intimidation and boycotting....." In July, 1901, the Inspector Generals report reads: "This state of things (activities of the U.I.L.) is largely due, I consider, to the baneful influence of "The Sligo Champion" newspaper,....... its influence for evil cannot easily be exaggerated...... "Referring to other organisations, they go on to say that in some places, "members of the G.A.A. and I.R.B. have joined the U.I.L., and endeavour to dominate it. As a rule, however, the I.R.B. members are strongly opposed to it." Much of the Inspector's Confidential Reports at this time are taken up with the activities of the U.I.L. considering it to be the "most important political organisation in the country, the Central Executive of which is busy utilizing it's machinery in collecting money and by creating new branches by means of it's paid organizers, who continue to roam about the country."

Branches of the U.I.L. florished in this area until around the time of the Easter Rising. On Feb. 6th 1915 at a meeting held in Cliffoney under the chairmanship of Fr. Michael O'Flanagan, support was pledged to the Irish Parliamentary Party and Redmond. Francis Mc Gowan was elected vice-chairman; Treasurer, Neil Rooney and secretary was P. Gilgar. Other members included Charles Mc Garrigle D.C., P. Gilgar D.C., R. Currid, P. Conway, A. Coleman, B. Kennedy, J. Gallagher, M. Mc Gowan, R. Moore, P. Rooney, A. Harrison, J. Kennedy, N. Rooney, P. Mc Gann, P. Feeney.

Thirty four branches existed in the county at this time, these included Grange, Ballintrillick and Maugherow.

Another organisation which emerged in the early years of this century was the National Council which was founded in 1903 to protest the upcoming visit of Edward the Seventh of England; this organisation was eventually to become Sinn Féin under his leadership in 1907. The Ancient Order of Hibernians was re-activated at this time too, having roughly the same aims as the U.I.L. Meetings of the Mullaghmore division were held in one of "the cottages" (recently owned by John Callery) under the chairmanship of James Mc Gowan who lived there at the time; other branches existed at this time in Ballintrillick, Cliffoney and Grange with a total of about twenty seven in the county at large. Fr. P.J. Scott C.C. seems to have been very much involved with the the A.O.H. and their military branch, the Hibernian Rifles. Local scources say that he was "out 'till all hours shooting with the Hibernian Rifles in Cliffoney!" Made in the same mould as Fr. O'Flanagan, he seems to have been active too in the organisation of the Volunteers and "went to Kinlough to assemble for the Rising." He was later transferred to Ballyrush and served on Sinn Féin courts in the Riverstown district. He was arrested many times by the police and had his house and furniture broken on more than one occasion by the Black and Tans.

An organisation known as the Irish Unionist Alliance, whose members were opposed to Home Rule, existed in Sligo town under the chairmanship of Col. Perceval. No Unionist organisation existed in North Sligo.

In January 1913, men were recruited in England, Ireland and Scotland by Sir Edward Carson for his Ulster Volunteer Force with the support and blessing of Bonar Law, leader of the Tory Party in England. His purpose was to levy war on the Nationalists of Ireland, as the slow but persistent progress of the Home Rule movement seemed to threaten their cherished power. In October of the same year, Padraig Pearse wrote,

"Ireland unarmed will attain just as much freedom as it is convenient for England to give her; Ireland armed will attain ultimately just as much freedom as she wants...... the nation which regards it (bloodshed) as the final horror has lost its manhood. There are many things more horrible than bloodshed and slavery is one of them."

On the 25th of November, with heavy I.R.B. involvement, the Irish Volunteers were formed as a direct response to Carson's Volunteers and to make sure that Home Rule would not be prevented from coming into operation. Their numbers increased rapidly to over 150,000 men nationwide. Events now moved swiftly onward with the landing by the U.V.F. of 35,000 rifles and five million rounds of ammunition at Larne in April 1914. Pearse, never a sectarian, when he heard of this said, "Personally, I think the

88

Orangeman with a rifle is a much less ridiculous figure than the nationalist without a rifle."

The April landing by the U.V.F. was followed in July with the landing by Erskine Childers of 1500 guns for the Irish Volunteers at Howth in the yacht Asgard. While the landing of twenty times that amount went smoothly for the U.V.F. at Larne, the nationalist community had no such immunity as a company of Scottish Borderers, having failed to impound the weapons, fired on the crowd, killing four and wounding thirty seven.

Fr. Brian Crehan of North Sligo attended the inaugural meeting of the Irish Volunteers in Sligo town in February 1914. By the end of April, branches had been formed in Cliffoney, Grange and Ballintrillick. While some of the U.I.L. membership may have supported the Volunteers, the organisation gave it no official endorsement, probably as a result of Irish Party scepticism. Cliffoney branch of the Volunteers would have drawn members from a two to three mile radius to include Bunduff, Mullaghmore, Castlegal, Creevykeel, Drumfad and so on.

Drilling was done openly on the "green" near the harbour in Mullaghmore, under the supervision of Paddy "Beag" Barry. Paddy was a retired Chief Petty Officer of the American Navy and a veteran of the Spanish American war. For drilling purposes, his recruits used mock rifles, with carved wooden stocks attached to rails, taken from the old iron beds of the day, as barrels, making very realistic weapons indeed. His brother, Mattie Joe recalled that Paddy took to his duties with enthusiasm, sternly ordering his charges to, "Hold your rifle in this position — don't be holding it like you were presenting a bunch of flowers to a young lady." Drilling was sometimes done on the racecourse near the sandbanks, and when times demanded it, secretly at the back of Mullagh.

Another of these men who drilled the early Volunteers "came into Sligo with a circus, driving a pair of horses. Jim Gilgan, ex British army soldier, said to have been a native of Manorhamilton, came to live in a house belonging to Cummins in Cliffoney; when his abilities became known, he was put in charge of drilling the Cliffoney Volunteers. He quickly gained a reputation as a well drilled man, an eyewitness recalling, "mind ye, he gave the word of command in style." Through time he moved to Aughaged near Grange and eventually to Streedagh, where his descendants live yet. Bernie Harrison was another one of these early drillmasters, drilling his men in groups of seventy or eighty on the sand flats behind his house in lower Bunduff.

Willie Devins was among the numbers of young men drilling with the Irish Volunteers in Grange Hall. Their drill instructor was John Armstrong, a native of Dromahair and a Protestant. John had served for twenty one years with the British army and was now putting that experience to good use to break that same army's grip on Ireland. The north-west was now truly awake; any of Carson's Volunteers coming within the proverbial asses roar of north Sligo was in for a very rough time of it indeed!

British gunboats roamed the coast amid speculation that arms were about to be landed somewhere on the coast of North Sligo. Conlon's coal boat, on a regularly scheduled run to Mullaghmore with coal, was stopped and searched but nothing was found. An American yacht was stopped and searched off the coast of Donegal on the other side of the bay; some reports stated that nothing was found, others claimed that the Mayor of Sligo now had at his disposal 300 rifles which were landed from another boat and which were to be dispersed among the local Volunteers. The Maugherow Volunteers claimed that they were custodians of the arms, stating that they were safe, having been removed from Ardgoran Wood in Lissadell, "carefully oiled and placed under lock and key awaiting further orders."

On the fourth of August 1914, Britain declared war on Germany; on the eighteenth of September Home Rule was dead, as the Act was suspended; on the twentieth of Sept. John Redmond called on the Irish Volunteers to fight for Britain and on the 24th of Sept. Eoin Mc Neill and the executive repudiated Redmond. A split resulted, with one group of Volunteers becoming the National Volunteers and Mac Neills followers, many of them also members of the I.R.B., retaining the title, Irish Volunteers.

After the outbreak of the war, much effort was put into recruiting young Irishmen for the British regiments nationwide and locally; their efforts met with limited success in this area. The Volunteers were addressed in Grange, at the drill hall, by John Jinks and a man named Howley who exhorted them to "see a bit of the world, boys, ye'd make fine soldiers on the battlefields of France and Flanders." In no time at all, according to an eyewitness, they discovered in no uncertain manner that they were in the wrong place as they were heckled and jeered and pulled down off the stage. These recruiters for Redmond and John Bull had to make a hurried and undignified exit from Grange Hall as with tall hats and swallow tail coats in disarray, they fled to their waiting carriage. A hail of stones and "scraws" rained on their coach as they beat a hasty retreat from Grange village and these local stalwarts, some of whom, though they couldn't have known it then, had much work to do and hardship and privation to suffer in the years ahead.

In Maugherow, Sir Josslyn Goore Booth didn't fare any better. When he advised the young men of the area to "join the Army and fight the Hun" he too, was put to flight in a hail of stones; for those who had eyes to see, the Hun had been in Ireland for many centuries now. To the cry of "Neither King nor Kaiser, but Ireland", Redmond's Volunteers melted away to organisations which were once again, as in ages past, prepared to strike a blow for Ireland.

In Cliffoney, there was a gradual change from a pacifist viewpoint to a more militant one. In January 1915 the last reported meeting of the A.O.H. was held with P. Gilgar in the chair and E. Gillespie Sec., discussing nothing more important than a motion giving support to the people of Cliffoney to change the old boy's school into a Parish Hall. Shortly after this, in February, Fr. Michael O' Flanagan is reported as having chaired a meeting of the United Irish League which had been inactive for some time; collections were organised and the branch affiliated to the national executive. From 1914 on, others were secretly drilling and training with the I.R.B. and Irish Volunteers in the open fields and occasionally in the old Boys School.

Not everyone supported the uprising of nationalism which was gaining momentum and some of these provided a fifth column for the authorities. The following is an extract from a letter dated Cliffoney, Aug. 26th 1914:

"To give you, Mr. Ashley, a rough sketch of our village at present, I'll try. There are subscriptions for arming the volunteers and I must pay through fear and having no protection. Last night I lent my shawl to a little girl going to the "crossroads", you know the distance Mr. Ashley. This morning I got it back cut in several places with a knife and unfit to be seen again. I have it hidden. I am ill from the effect which the sight took on me. The conclusion I can draw from it is that myself would be treated likewise.

I am afraid to post your letter in Clancy's P.O. and has to go to the pillar at the crossroads with them after mail car passes. I would have posted this last night but was afraid to go as Gillespie (a tailor) next door and a relation of the P.O. Clancy's and likewise a relation of the post boy (Mc Cannon) delivering our letters daily was watching. There are suspicious characters going around the country (as I believe spys to our enemy) ....."

Late in 1914, Cliffoney was distinguished by the arrival of the aforementioned Fr. Michael O'Flanagan as Parish Priest, a man later to be described by Cathal Brugha as "the staunchest priest that ever lived". Immediately on his arrival he became involved in organising the people, openly in committees such as the U.I.L. and secretly in the Volunteers. Johnny Barry often told me of visits made to his father, Paddy Beag, by Fr O'Flanagan asking Paddy to continue as drill instructor for the Volunteers after the split.

North Sligo's rebel priest had his first major confrontation with the authorities in what became known as the "Cloonerco Bog Fight". This was initiated by the Congested Districts Board's acquisition of the Hippsley and Sullivan estate and their consequent refusal to allow the local people who had been cutting the bog there from time immemorial, to continue to do so. This was a major blow to the people of the area as turf was the only fuel then in use for cooking and heating. Despite intensive correspondence by Fr. O'Flanagan to have the turbary rights restored, the C.D.B. were determined to reserve these rights for other purchasers. By June the people were in a desperate position as no turf had been cut and they seemed to be facing a Winter without fuel. Despite being warned by Bishop Coyne not to get involved, Fr. O'Flanagan asked his congregation to wait outside for him after Mass on June 29 1915; here he instructed them to meet the next morning with their turf cutting implements, telling them that he would lead them to the bogs where he himself would cut the first of the forbidden turf.

The people took his advice and followed Fr. Michael to the bogs where he cut the first turf, advising his followers to do likewise, despite the presence of a large body of R.I.C. who ordered the people to stop. There were arrests and legal action but the turf were cut and saved and eventually brought down from the bogs, where they were built in a large stack close to the R.I.C. baracks and directly in front of Cliffoney Hall. A banner was erected on top declaring, "OUR OWN TURF FOR OUR OWN PEOPLE; FOREIGNERS HAVE NO RIGHTS HERE". Fr. O'Flanagan requested that the turf be divided among the people and that a cart of turf be left at the door of each one of the older people in the neighbourhood and also for those who had no transportation, as there were many poor people in the area at that time who had no carts. O'Flanagan survived the actions brought against him by the authorities but Bishop Coyne was furious at this flouting of his authority and shortly afterwards transferred him from Cliffoney to another parish.

Bishop Coyne now found himself in confrontation with the people of Cliffoney, Bunduff, Mullaghmore and surrounding areas as they barricaded the Church, nailing the doors and windows shut, thus preventing the Bishop sending a replacement and demanding that Fr. O' Flanagan be re-appointed to Cliffoney. They mounted a guard, day and night and assembled on Sundays outside the Church to recite the rosary. Not content with this and much to the Bishops dismay, hundreds of the congregation made their way in procession to the Bishop's palace in Sligo, walking and travelling in ass and horse carts they pleaded for the return of their Fr. O' Flanagan. The stalemate continued until Christmas 1915 when the Bishop agreed to provide someone "who would be a good Irishman and a patriot" to replace Fr. O' Flanagan.

As a sequel to this incident, some months later in deference to the appeals made by Canon Doorly, P.P. Cliffoney on behalf of Patrick Gilgar, Charles Mc Garrigle, Andrew Harrison and Francis Higgins, against whom injunction proceedings were obtained in connection with the bog incident, the Congested Districts Board decided to drop the case in return for a fine of £5 being paid by the defendants.

Fr, O'Flanagan was again to be the subject of the Bishop's ire some years later and this time, he was suspended. Again, in Crossna, the people locked the doors of the Church to prevent a replacement being sent. They gathered on Sundays to say the rosary until Fr. O' Flanagan returned to say that he wished to leave quietly and the protest ended. Many years afterwards a collection was taken up in Cliffoney by Thomas Hargadon and a group of local people with the intention of installing a holy water font at the front entrance of Cliffoney Church as a memorial to their beloved priest. The font was accepted and installed by Bishop Doorly but no inscription or mention of Fr. O'Flanagan was allowed. (For more on Fr. O'Flanagan, see Appendices)

On Feb. 4th 1915, at Sexton's P.O. in Cashelgarron, Willie Devins and fifteen others were sworn into the Irish Volunteers by Seamus Devins. Seamus was later to become a Brigadier and is remembered as one of "Sligo's Noble Six" who were shot dead on Glencar mountain by Freestate forces during the Civil War. Others who joined at the time were:

MICK MC GARRIGLE	PADDY GILLEN
PATRICK HARGADON	TOM MC DONAGH
JOHNNY MC DONAGH	TOM "THE SOLDIER" WATTERS

MICK OATES	"BIG" PAT FARREL
JOHN FRIEL	THOMAS GOREVAN
JOHN HARAN	"BIG" DOMINICK FEENEY
PADDY HARAN	EUGENE BRADY
TOM SMITH	

One of these men was a brother of Fr. Feeneys, a man who claimed many of the short hairs from the back of my neck in later years when he taught religious instruction at Grange Tech. Many of the above listed men were also in the I.R.B at the same time. They wore armbands with the letters I.V. when marching and drilling; their duties also included doing police duty at gatherings and fairs and later arresting and guarding prisoners at the Sinn Féin courts when they were set up.

Around the same time a unit of the I.R.B. was formed in Cliffoney. Its membership included Eddie Harkin, Thady Conway, Charlie Gilmartin, Petie Mc Gowan, Petie "Red" Gilmartin, John Gilmartin, Andrew Conway, Bernie Meehan, Charlie Foley and George Gardiner. The leaders in Cliffoney were Charlie Gilmartin and Andrew Conway. Although poorly armed at this time, some of the men of the Cliffoney and Grange units were to see action with Pearse and Connolly in Dublin at the Easter Rising.

Meanwhile, the descendants of the planters and their followers had other priorities as they continued to induce the young men of the area to join the British Army. The papers were full of their stories of derring-do and pictures of decorated heroes wounded in action. The Sligo Champion of May 4th 1915 reported that

"cars belonging to the following conveyed the men of the Irish Guards to Lissadell and Grange on a recruitment drive: Georgina Lady Gore-Booth, Jocelyn Gore-Booth, Miss Holliet, Messrs. Harper Campbell Ltd., W.E. Fenton, Major Eccles, C.A. Fowler, Dr. Flannery, H. G. Le Strange, G.E. Martin, P.W. O' Hara, F.W. O' Hara and Basil Phibbs."

At a meeting held on the street of Grange, Mr. W. Devins N.T. and Mr. Bernard Harte, chairman of the Rural District Council told those assembled that they were there to do homage to the Irish Guards "one of the greatest regiments on the face of the earth." Speakers told the stony faced crowd that they hoped and "trusted the people present would volunteer to join and bring the war to a speedy close, it being the "duty of every able bodied man to go."

These meetings were a regular occurrence all over the county and nation but in North Sligo, at least, they met with little success

94

and more often than not, with open hostility. In June, Cliffoney was the object of attention of a detachment of the Connaught Rangers who were touring Sligo; Mayor Jinks, Mr. B. Harte, Mr. B. Clancy, Postmaster, Mr. J. Cummins, J.P. were on the platform as Dr. Mc Dowd related some of the atrocities committed by the Germans. Lieut. Kettle and Pvt Clancy told the crowd how they "enjoyed the life of a soldier." Pvt. Harrison, a native of Cliffoney, emphasised the necessity for farmers sons to join the army and created "general laughter" in the crowd when he declared that "life in the Army was better than clamping turf on the bogs." Shortly after this, on returning to duty, young Harrison was killed in action.

Forty-nine thousand Irish citizens died in action in the British Army. Out of a population of ten thousand in Sligo town, one thousand joined up; in North Sligo takers were few and far between, most of the listeners no doubt considering "clamping turf on the bogs" a much safer and more appropriate occupation for an Irishman than providing cannon fodder for the English on the battlefields of Europe. The Connaught Ranger's visit to Cliffoney may not have resulted in many recruits to fight in Flanders but the U.I.L. were flourishing in North Sligo with an executive committee of fifteen in Cliffoney alone and meetings in the Hall being attended by overflow crowds. They and Fr. O' Flanagan opposed recruitment, advising young men to stay at home and work the land; this advice doubtless saving many young Irish lives. In Cliffoney alone, one hundred or more could be depended on to turn out for Volunteer parades.

Meanwhile, insulated from all of this, life continued on pretty much as usual for the ruling classes as the "nobility" and "gentry" with their retinues of servants, horses and carriages took up residence for the Summer season in Palmerston's Lodges in Mullaghmore. In August, Col. Ashley with his family were in residence in Classiebawn. The Colonel was quite contemptuous of the rebels reporting in the House of Commons that "these were not such formidable rebels after all as seventy of them found drilling recently on my grounds, moved off peacably when discovered by my gamekeeper."

Visitors at the Lodges included Mr. & Mrs. le Strange and family, Mr. & Mrs. Maude & family, Mr. D. O' Hara, His Majesty's Lieutenant for the County, Mr. & Mrs. F. O' Hara, Mr. A. O' Hara, Dublin, Miss D. Wynne, Miss Richardson, Mr. & Miss Perceval, Templehouse, Mr. & Mrs. Hosie, Castledargan and Mrs. A. Cooke and family, Sligo. We are not told if the sun shone high in the

Mullaghmore sky in this Summer of 1915 for these men and women of privelege and power but we do know that it was the twilight of the influence and control of these ascendancy families, if they could but see it, all was to change and "change utterly."

On St. Patricks Day, according to police reports, the newly formed Cliffoney branch of the Irish Volunteers had held a parade in the village after attending Mass. Some weapons were said to be on display with the leaders reported to be carrying revolvers.

"Beware of the thing that is coming, beware of the risen people,
Who shall take what ye would not give. Did ye think to conquer the
people,
Or that Law is stronger than life and than men's desire to be free?
We will try it out with you, ye that have harried and held,
Ye that have bullied and bribed; tyrants, hypocrites, liars!

The rising planned for Easter Sunday, 1916, went ahead on Easter Monday April 24 despite the arrest of Roger Casement and the destruction of 20,000 rifles aboard the Aud. The countermanding order issued by Eoin Mac Neill was another major setback but despite this and with no real chance of success, Pearse, Connolly and their comrades went out to lay down a marker for their generation, "to redeem the claim to Ireland's nationhood".

The Rising ended in apparent failure with the general surrender ordered by Pearse. Pearse and the other leaders were executed, one by one; sixty four of the fifteen hundred rebels who participated in the Rising died and one hundred and thirty four of the Crown Forces; about two hundred and twenty civilians lost their lives.

In North Sligo there was confusion; all units were on alert and ready for action but plans to take Grange and Cliffoney barracks were dropped on orders from Headquarters. Sixty five of the Cliffoney Volunteers who had assembled at the Fr. O'Flanagan Hall on Easter Saturday night disbanded and went home on the Sunday when word of Mac Neill's countermanding order came through. Some Volunteers such as Pat Rooney and Petie "Red" Gilmartin of Carnduff had already travelled to Dublin for the Rising and were afterwards imprisoned.

Early in May strong forces of military and R.I.C., members of the North Staffordshire regiment stationed in Sligo, raided homes in the area, searching for arms and Volunteers. Our house was one of many raided but although my father escaped, he was now one of large numbers on the run. Fifteen were arrested and taken to Sligo

PAT DONLEVY
Land Leaguer c 1880

Courtesy of John Donlevy

THIRD VISCOUNT PALMERSTON

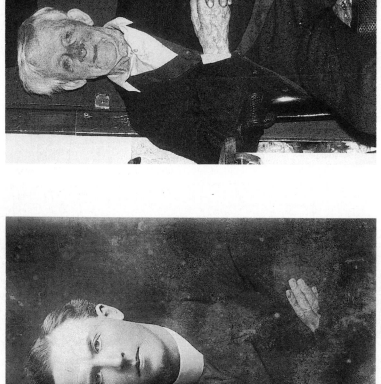

FR. MICHEÁL Ó FLANAGÁIN 1919

Photo: courtesy Beatrice Mc Gowan

WILLIE DEVINS (1992) AUGHAGED

Veteran of the War of Independence & The Moneygold Ambush

(Photo: J. Mc G)

MARTIN BERNARD McGOWAN T.D
O/C No. 1 Brigade Western Division, I.R.A.
Photo: Courtesy of Aidan McGowan

Photo: Courtesy of Aidan McGowan

Members of Third Western Division I.R.A. with the famed 'Ballinalee' armoured car
Front Row: L to R: Harry Young, Todd Burns, Fred Pilkington, John Johnston, Jim Keaveney, Willie Hand
Back Row: Tom McEvilly, Martin Mc Goldrick, Eddie Gunning, Joe Banks, Harry Sheridan, Brigadier
Seamus Devins, Martin Bernard McGowan, Joe Mc Lynn, Jim Keaveney, Jack Pilkington, Peter Burns
(Photo: Courtesy of Donal McLynn)

GROUP OF LOCAL MEN IN FRONT OF 'LODGES'
(now 'Star of the Sea' convent and chapel) at Mullaghmore c1912.
Back Row, right: Dan McGowan; Front Row, right: Tommy McGowan
Photo: Courtesy of Robin Montgomery

GROUP OF OF RESIDENTS AT 'LODGES'
Taken on Mullaghmore Green, Summer 1915
Back Row, L to R: Gerard Eccles, Stella L'Estrange, Donal O'Hara, Jan Eccles, Kathleen Maude
Front Row, L to R: Frank O'Hara, Venetia Maude, Charlie O'Hara, Elizabeth L'Estrange,
Christopher L'Estrange, Dorothy Perceval (mother was Muriel Wynne)
Photo: Courtesy of Lady Durand

THE AUTHOR AND SEAMUS MOORE

at a memorial cross on the mountain marking the spot where two of "Sligo's Noble Six', Benson and Langan were shot dead during the Civil War. Sidhe Hill can be seen in the background

Photo: courtesy of Robert Moore

DEV'S VOLUNTEERS C1934

Outside Left, standing, second from left, Sgt. Curran, (killed by explosion in Glen of Imaal)
Outside Right, standing, L to R, Corporal Hayes, Corporal Cusack,
Back, far left, Tim Gonigle, Far Right, Dan Heraughty
Middle, L to R: Thomas McGowan, Maugherow, John Darcy, Tullaghan,
Danny Foley, ? 'Big' Owen McGowan, Kinlough, Dan Gallagher, Uragh.
Front Row:, far right: Josie Harrison

Photo: Courtesy Josie Harrison

REMEMBRANCE OF PENAL TIMES 1922

Mass is still celebrated annually at this Mass Rock in our neighbouring county at Tawley, Co. Leitrim

Photo: J. McG

'FR. O'FLANAGAN HALL

(Now the Parish hall in Cliffoney) after a visit by the Black and Tans
following the Moneygold Ambush, 1920

Photo: Courtesy of Sligo Library

BERNIE CONWAY'S HOME IN CLIFFONEY

Shortly after being burned by Black and Tans and Auxillaries. Mrs
Brigid Conway and her daughter Brigid shown in picture

Photo: Courtesy of Vivian & Maeve Conway

PRAYER SERVICE
*Group gathered at Mullaghmore Harbour for Prayer Service shortly after
Mountbatten assassination, 1979*

Photo: Courtesy of Sligo Champion

*Gardai carrying remains of Margaret Perry to a hearse near
Mullaghmore, Co. Sligo, June 1992*

Photo: Courtesy of Irish Press

Jail:- Laurence Gonigle, Robert Gonigle, Charlie Gilmartin, John Gilmartin, William Gilmartin, John F. Hannon, Hugh Fowley, Hugh Chrystal, Bernard Meehan, Charles Mc Garrigle, George Gardiner, Patrick Burke, Andrew Conway, Eddie Hannon and Patrick Rooney. Three thousand of these arrests were made countrywide, although it is estimated that only fifteen hundred participated in the Rising. There was a public outcry about the detentions but although protests were made and the matter brought up in the House of Commons by Scanlon, M.P. for North Sligo, the men were transferred to Dublin and then deported to Wandsworth detention barracks in England. Countess Markievicz participated in the Rising with the Citizen Army, as second in command to Michael Mallon. She was arrested at the surrender, sentenced to death with the other leaders, but had this commuted to life imprisonment and was sent to Aylesbury jail in England.

Six of the Cliffoney prisoners were released within the month, C. Gilmartin, E. Hannon, J. Hannon, J. Gilmartin, C. Mc Garrigle and L. Gonigle. The rest of the men were moved to Frongoch in Wales and Lewes where they remained until their release later in the year. Shortly after his release, Charlie Mc Garrigle addressed a meeting of the Board of Guardians in Sligo where the arrests and internments were condemned by Mayor Jinks, who welcomed the released prisoner and called for the release of the rest of the Cliffoney internees. Some more of the Cliffoney men were released later in July and the remainder in the following month. They received a rapturous welcome in Sligo town and were escorted to Cliffoney by neighbours and well wishers where a huge crowd had gathered to welcome them home. Other prominent prisoners, among them, Eoin Mac Neill, Eamonn de Valera and Countess Markievicz were not released until June 1917.

Generally speaking there was little support for the Easter Rebellion, the prisoners were spat on and stoned as they were marched out of Dublin. R.I.C. intellegence reports concluded that there was no support for the Rising among the mass of the people. Pearse was "a man of ill balanced mind" readers of the Irish Catholic were told, the rebels an "extraordinary combination of rogues and fools"; Catholics had "no reason to lament that its perpetrators have met the fate universally reserved for traitors."

Most people believed that they deserved to be jailed but almost no one thought that they deserved to be shot. Public opinion changed as the English spread the fifteen executions over a number of days;

Plunkett was dying of cancer but they shot him anyway; the wounded Connolly couldn't stand up so they shot him strapped to a chair; Willie Pearse was shot only because he was Padraig's brother; Sean Heuston and Con Colbert were barely twenty.

The mood of the people changed; Sinn Féin, a small and ineffective organisation at a national level at this time, benefitted immediately by a massive influx of numbers as a result of this surge of sympathy for nationalism and the feeling of national outrage that followed the Rising and executions. Survivors such as Collins, Lynch, Cathal Brugha, Breen and Barry were now to adopt guerilla tactics and organise a more ruthless and successful war against a ruthless and pitiless enemy.

> "We know their dream; enough
> To know they dreamed and are dead.
> And what if excess of love
> Bewildered them till they died?
> I write it out in a verse –
> MacDonagh and MacBride
> And Connolly and Pearse
> Now and in time to be,
> Wherever green is worn,
> Are changed, changed utterly:
> A terrible beauty is born.

Parades were held and flags flown on the first anniversary of the Easter Rising. Constance Markievicz was released from Aylesbury Prison on June 17th 1917; on July 23rd, with the exception of an attack by Army wives on the parade, she was given a rapturous welcome to Sligo and was bestowed with the freedom of the town by Mayor Hanly, the first and only woman to receive this honour. The Seamus Devins Pipe Band from Grange, under the direction of Master Burke, travelled to Sligo to take part in the celebrations.

Even though her family disapproved of her activities, many saw her as the redeemer of the family name; there's no doubt she was revered by the vast majority of the people of the county and nation. Shortly after her victorious return to Sligo the Countess Markievicz Sinn Féin Club was formed in the newly named Fr. O' Flanagan Hall in Cliffoney. Released prisoners, J.J. Reid and Patrick Fogarty were presented to the meeting and the policies and working of Sinn Féin explained. James Mc Gloin served as Chairman and Willie Gilmartin as Hon. Sec.

Earlier, in April, a Sinn Féin National Council had been established to "deny the right of any foreign Parliament to make laws for Ireland;" Sinn Féin committees were now springing up all over the country, replacing the old United Irish Leagues. The Major Mc Bride S.F. Club had its inaugural meeting in Grange Hall on 10 July with J. Hennigan, County Councillor, presiding and P. Connolly as Secretary. The chairman moved and J. Kearins seconded congratulations to Lt. De Valera on his victory in East Clare and declared their support for the majority of the nation in their intention to break from England. They considered that Ireland should be represented at the peace conference with other nations of the world and be granted its claim for independence.

Sinn Féin delegates from many centres in the county, including Cliffoney and Grange, participated at a meeting in the Town Hall, Sligo for the purpose of forming a North Sligo Sinn Féin Executive. J.J. Clancy was appointed as president and it was agreed to form Volunteer units in conjunction with each Sinn Féin club.

The death of Thomas Ashe on hunger strike on the 25th September 1917, shocked the nation. The newspapers were full of the details but only those passed by the censor were read as the authorities at this time had imposed censorship on all the newspapers, national and local. The Sligo Champion, defender of the people, could now only print that which was approved by the censor.

Earlier, in July, the Irish poet Francis Ledwidge, only thirty years old, was killed in action near Ypres. Even though in service with the English, he was touched by the executions after the Easter Rising. The poem he wrote for Mc Donagh would now be apt for him even though the two men died on very different battlefields. Neither of them would ever again:

> "hear the bittern cry
> In the wild sky where he is lain,
> Nor voices of the sweeter birds,
> Above the wailing of the rain.
>
> But when the Dark Cow leaves the moor
> And pastures poor with greedy weeds,
> Perhaps he'll hear her low at morn
> Lifting her horn in pleasant meads."

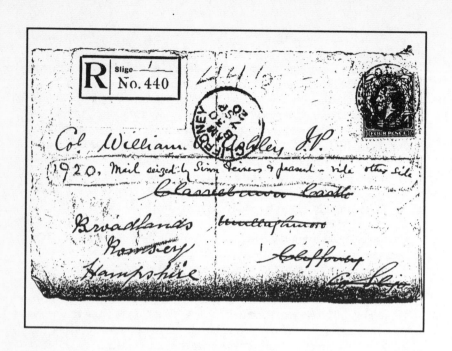

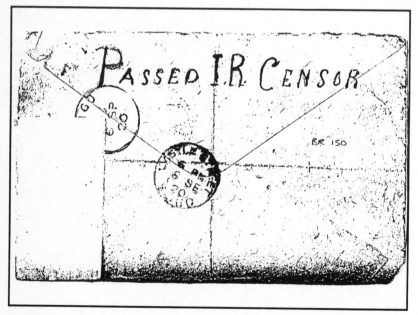

CHAPTER 6

Freedom's Struggle

A major confrontation with the authorities in this area became known as the Cliffoney Land Fight. In Spring 1918, a party of local people under the leadership of Sinn Féin took over a section of Ashley's grazing farm at Cliffoney. They ploughed and cultivated it by day and when the soldiers and R.I.C. came, they returned by night and continued to plough, sometimes pulling the plough themselves when horses weren't available. Their endeavours resulted in five men, Patrick McHugh, Creevymore, Charlie Mc Garrigle, D.C., Andrew Conway, P. Gilmartin and Owen Leonard, all of Cliffoney, being brought to Grange Court by Robert Bracken, Ashley's agent, and charged with unlawful assembly. Sgt. Perry and Constable Casey gave evidence against the men.

On the morning the men were being brought to court, the main road was strewn with broken bottles and barbed wire. On their arrival at the court, Sgt. Perry gave evidence that on the date in question:

" there was about eighty people opposite the Sinn Féin Hall with spades and ploughs, approximately five ploughs and ten horses. The crowd headed by the Bunduff band marched on to the public road, on to Col. Ashley's farm and went in there. One of the crowd cried 'Halt'. This man then said, 'Now, men, we take over this land in the name of the Irish Republic from W.W. Ashley at £1 per acre or five shillings per rood.' The crowd cheered and witness then spoke to the crowd telling them that they were breaking the law and advising them to clear out. A man in the crowd whom witness recognised said they did not recognise the authority of the law and the crowd then proceeded to dig and plough the farm." The case was put forward.

After the court hearing, a mass meeting was held at the Fr. O' Flanagan Hall protesting the arrest of the five men and demanding that they be released. It was decided to hold a fundraising dance and admissions were fixed at one shilling and sixpence for the men and one shilling for the ladies. When the case came to court again Andrew Conway as spokesman would give no evidence saying, "As a soldier of the Irish Republican Army I refuse to recognise the court." Captain

Fitzpatrick said that they would have to be punished and a sentence of two months at hard labour was handed down to Mc Hugh and Conway.

A huge crowd greeted the men's return from Sligo jail some months later.

Countrywide, the R.I.C. had by this time come to be regarded as traitors by the people, being looked upon as Irishmen carrying arms against and spying on their own countrymen. North Sligo was no different as the R.I.C. were ostracized, receiving no co-operation from most of the people around. A boycott was enforced by Sinn Féin clubs and anyone found collaborating with the police or assisting them in any way were likely to be punished. There were numerous instances of individuals being beaten or kneecapped who did not heed earlier warnings. Women who associated with the police or Army were beaten and had their heads shaved. Understandably, there were numerous resignations from R.I.C. ranks throughout the country; many of the men, no doubt, re-evaluating their position in the light of events; some reaching the conclusion that they were on the wrong side and others, doubtless, realising that the threat of escalating violence to the force was a very real one. The authorities took a most serious view of resignations and in some cases arrested and held in custody those resigning.

Some stayed out of conviction while others like Constable Jeremiah Mee, who served for a time in Grange, resigned and fought with the I.R.A. Mee resigned in protest at his Divisional Commanders instruction that they were to shoot down I.R.A. suspects, ensuring them that they would not get into trouble for shooting an innocent person. Const. Mee, during his stay in Grange, was well acquainted with Sgt Perry of Cliffoney, who was later to die in the Moneygold ambush, thus paying a high price, as did so many more of his comrades, for their loyalty to the Crown. In his memoirs, Mee recalled being instructed, along with another constable, Boylan, to attend a meeting in the parish hall in Grange. The meeting was addressed by Mrs. Hannah Sheehy Skeffington and attended by a large number of local people, which included a large contingent of the local Volunteer force. Mee was directed to attend this meeting by his sergeant and recollected having to sit through a speech, much of which "was given over to making unflattering comments about the R.I.C. in general and Boylan and me in particular".

Bernie Conway of Cliffoney joined the R.I.C. in February 1913 serving at several towns in the Northern counties. Constable Bernie Conway, brother of Andrew, who was leader of the Volunteers in Cliffoney, had received an award for dedication to duty during the

Easter Rebellion. As hostilities increased nationally and in his native village of Cliffoney, Bernie found his sympathies to lie more and more with Sinn Féin and the Republican side. While most of the comrades he served with were staunch Orangemen and Loyalists, he was not alone in his sympathies, as he discovered that three other policemen that he served with, who were originally from the West of Ireland, shared his views. The four men came more and more into conflict with the rest of the garrison. As hostility increased, Bernie and the other three decided to make contact with the local unit of the I.R.A. with a view to facilitating a raid on Cookstown R.I.C. barracks where they were stationed.

An I.R.A. scout, pretending to be a tradesman, was shown around the barracks by Bernie and plans were subsequently made for the raid. On the night planned, the men waited in the barracks but no one showed and the raid did not go ahead as arranged. This was possibly as a result of fears by the I.R.A. unit that they were being lured into a trap by what they saw as four uniformed, serving members of the R.I.C. Undeterred, Conway and his comrades made contact with the I.R.A. again and once again new plans were laid. The transfer of Conway and another one of the four from Cookstown was an added complication but this time the I.R.A. were determined to go ahead with the attack as soon as possible. On the night appointed, June 17 1920, Hargadon was barracks orderly, the other conspirator, Leonard, unlocked the back door allowing I.R.A. units from Dungannon and Keady into the barracks. They proceeded immediately to remove rifles, ammunition, grenades and anything else they could find, from the barracks. The raiders had to make a quick escape following an exchange of gunfire after they were discovered by the head constable and some of his men. One of the men injured during the escape died later of his injuries. Constable Leonard, suspected of collusion with the raiders was dismissed from the force and Conway, Hargadon and O' Boyle, feeling their position to be untenable resigned shortly after.

Following the Cliffoney Land Fight, Volunteers in North Sligo drilled openly, Sinn Féin meetings were attended by overflow audiences, informers were arrested and held prisoner. Units from Ballintrillick, Cliffoney, Grange and Maugherow attended a meeting of the North Sligo Comhairle Ceanntair of Sinn Féin held on the 11th of May under the chairmanship of J.J. Clancy. R.I.C. Intelligence was of the opinion that the Cliffoney Volunteers were in possesion of one shotgun and five revolvers early in 1917.

The Sligo Champion of July 6, 1918 reported the appearance in court of Willie Gilmartin, Thady Harrison and James Lambert on charges of "gathering together to disturb the public peace." Sgt. P. Kelly of Cliffoney reported that 120 people had gathered at Cliffoney Sinn Féin Hall on Sunday July 1st 1918. At 7.40 p.m. people started to leave the Hall and gather on the road. When Willie Gilmartin shouted, "All that's for Grange, now fall in", twenty people stepped out from the crowd and formed two ranks. Responding to military orders they moved off in the direction of Grange with Gilmartin in charge and the R.I.C. following. They unfurled a S.F. flag and marched to Moneygold where more military commands were given and the men dismissed.

Sgt. Kelly went on to say that the men in court were then arrested and returned for trial as drilling was illegal. Gilmartin, who was secretary of the Sinn Féin club at the time, had been arrested on his way to Mass and was taken into custody only after a chase and struggle which resulted in his having to be subdued by six policemen. The men refused to accept bail or to recognise the court as they were "soldiers and members of the I.R.A. "They were sentenced and removed from the court to cheering and singing of "Wrap the Green Flag 'round me Boys", from the huge crowd which had gathered outside.

The men were given two months at hard labour and lodged in Belfast jail. In cases like this it was common for the Sinn Féin Club to organise teams of neighbours to take care of the farm work while their members were in jail. Representatives from each townland gathered together to save the men's hay and cut and harvest their wheat. When they returned to Cliffoney from Belfast in September it was to bonfires in the streets and a heroes welcome.

In May 1918, the Freedom of the town of Sligo was conferred on Fr. Michael O'Flanagan in recognition of his work in organising the Volunteers and I.R.B. in Cliffoney and his work in achieving election successes in North Roscommon and East Cavan. An illuminated scroll (which still hangs in the courthouse) was presented to him by the Mayor of Sligo on behalf of the Corporation and people of Sligo.

Meetings were held all over Ireland in August to protest against the recent banning of Sinn Féin by the authorities. At a meeting in Cliffoney, a statement from the National Executive was read by the County Councillor, John Hennigan. Fr. Crehan spoke at similar meetings in Grange and Ballintrillick. In December 1918, a General election which was held throughout the U.K., brought a resounding victory to the S.F. party in Ireland. In the lead-up to the election, meetings were held all over North Sligo; Fr. Mc Hugh, C.C. Cliffoney, Billy Pilkington and Seamus Mc Gowan addressed a meeting at Mullaghmore following the formation of a new Sinn Féin club there. Fr. Michael O'Flanagan returned to Sligo to help with the campaign addresssing a meeting at the Town Hall in Sligo. Fr. Crehan addressed meetings at Grange and Maugherow. The country was carried away on a wave of enthusiasm such as had never been seen before; orations were given after Mass, at fairs, Sinn Féin meetings and anywhere a crowd would gather to listen.

J.J. Clancy who was later to serve many terms in jail, for unlawful assembly, refusal to recognise the court and other offences, was elected as M.P. for North Sligo gaining 9,000 votes over his opponent Scanlon's 4,000. Sinn Féin secured 73 of Ireland's 105 seats, Unionists, 25; Home Rule Party, 6 and Independent Unionist, 1. Out of the 73 S.F. candidates, 46 were in jail. The remaining 27 refused to go to London, drew up a Declaration of Independence, took the title Dáil Eireann and elected the imprisoned De Valera as Taoiseach. The new "Teachtai Dala" started setting up Republican councils and local Sinn Féin arbitration courts.

Grange Sinn Féin court was the first in this area to be established in a house on the street of Grange just across from the vacated R.I.C. barracks. Officers of the court were Denis Leonard, Aughaged, Petie Gillen of the Lower Wood, Francis Feeney of Breaghey; Willie Devins did police duty. The Dail had declared that "where possible, clergymen were to be ex-officio justices on the courts"; Fr. Crehan was the chief officer of the court in Cliffoney with Andrew Conway, Tommy Mc Cann, Willie "Edwards" Gilmartin as officers and Petie Mc Gowan doing police duty. The officers in Ballintrillick court were Fr. T. Mc Gibney, T.F.Hunt, P.J. Rooney and P. Ferguson.

The Volunteers, or Irish Republican Army, as they were now being called, were being formed at the end of 1919, into Battalions. Cliffoney and Grange, under the leadership of Andrew Conway and Seamus Devins were attached to the South Donegal Brigade for a period of time before eventually becoming part of the Sligo Brigade. The R.I.C., alarmed at the rise in hostility towards the police decided to close some of the police stations in the county. Grange was abandoned in November 1919 and the numbers of police in remaining barracks increased so as to successfully withstand any attacks that might be made.

The British Government were now in a quandary as they realised that the shutting down of the new Dail assembly and the taking of firm action against Sinn Féin would only bring more popular support. They were forced into taking action by the military wing of Sinn Féin, the I.R.A., which had started staging raids on police barracks and stores throughout the country, in search of arms. The first casualties of this new phase of the war were suffered at Soloheadbeg in Tipperary when on 21st of January 1919 an I.R.A. unit led by Dan Breen and Sean Treacey shot dead two R.I.C. during a raid for arms. The time for talking was over; Parnell had talked and was dead; Redmond had talked and was dead; what had been taken with the sword would now be taken back with the sword; the axiom that "power comes from the barrel of a gun" was to be put to the test over the next two and a half years as the Irish people fought a bitter guerilla campaign to drive the English out and achieve the old dream of Independence that had been nurtured through the centuries.

One of the most unbelievable and macabre occurences of these times was the drowning by their owners of hundreds of dogs, innocent victims of a peculiar dilemna faced by their owners. How could such a thing be?

The predicament was created by demands from the R.I.C. for payment of dog licences and a counter claim from agents of the new Republic that the payment should be made to them, who now claimed to be the legitimate government of the country. Anyone found guilty of paying the dog license to the R.I.C. was brought before the Republican courts and fined five shillings; if they had no money, payment had to be made in kind. Further, payment to the R.I.C. was seen as non-support of the new order. Anyone paying the licence to the Republicans was still obligated to pay to the R.I.C.; if they refused they were brought to the courts and fined. Also, payment to the terrorists would be viewed as being seditious. The result was that the unfortunate dogs were put down by drowning, to avoid trouble and to resolve the dilemna faced by the owners.

The grouping known as the Irish Volunteers were now coming to be accepted as the I.R.A. or Irish Republican Army. On the 20th of August Dail Éireann resolved on a motion proposed by Cathal Brugha that all its members and officials and the Irish Volunteers must swear allegiance to the Dail and the Irish Republic; the Volunteers thereby became the standing army of the Irish Republic (I.R.A.). Raids for arms on the "big houses" in North Sligo as in the rest of the country were now common as the I.R.A. tried to arm its members.

Willie Devins participated in these actions with the Grange unit and tells about one of these raids:

"The order was given to raid Eccles for arms and a meeting held at the back of Mc Garrigles to finalise plans. Whether you liked it or not, you had to be there! Mc Garrigle couldn't go on this job as he shoed horses for Eccles and was afraid of being recognised. He informed us though that Eccles would be away at the funeral of his sister-in-law, Miss Le Strange, the following evening and that we'd want to be waiting for him when he got back as the house was heavily secured with bolts and locks and bars.

The following evening the three of us, Eugene Gilbride, Seamus Devins and meself met on the avenue for the raid. We rushed the house as Mc Garrigle had advised us, seized a double barrelled shotgun, a Brooks rifle, a revolver and some ammunition and made our escape across the fields. The next day, the boyo next door, Parkes, went out on his bicycle with a rifle and some other stuff concealed in a bag and handed it over to the police. It was a bad mistake the two houses weren't done at the same time."

The Sligo Independent was as pro-British as the Sligo Champion was nationalistic and its issue of Jan. 24th 1920 expressed indignation with the heading: "OUTRAGE AT MONEYGOLD, MAJOR ECCLES HOUSE RAIDED AND ARMS TAKEN. Major Eccles L.G.B., Auditor, was away at the funeral of his sister in law, Miss Le Strange...... a party of 25 men raided his residence," and goes on to explain how, "his little daughter answered the door to a knock," when these "armed ruffians" broke in. A major raid for arms was carried out on an Ulster Volunteer arms dump in Belleek by the Cliffoney company of Volunteers. The building was well manned and was taken only after a lengthy exchange of gunfire.

The Sligo Independent carried a report of Mullaghmore P.O. being raided and money, held for the payment of old age pensions, being taken; an extra £11 of her own money was also taken from Mary Barry, who was postmistress at the time. Mary was an Aunt of Mylie Doyle, the last postmaster at this location. The report went on to say that the raiders went next door to Mrs. Gilmartin but when attempting to gain entry this plucky lady attacked them with a knife, driving them off. (This was well known locally to be a petty theft and unrelated to the political events of the time.) This Mrs. Gilmartin or "Nancy Neddy" as she was known locally had a sister Mary "Neddy" who lived in Markeys in Bunduff next door to my mother's home. My mother, as a child, often heard Nancy telling and re-telling about the incident to her sister Mary when visiting, and remembers Nancy revealing that the raiders would never have found her money even if they did get in, as she had it hidden in a turf bag by the fire.

Local I.R.A. units participated in a raid on one of the "big houses" in Tullaghan. R.I.C. Intelligence reports for that period read that the "house's of Miss V. Tynte and Captain Barton of Tullaghan were raided and one shotgun and one Winchester magazine rifle taken." It went on to say that the Sinn Féiners in the Connaught district had gained for the month, by such methods, 11 military rifles, 6 Schneider and other rifles and 12 shotguns.

R.I.C. patrols regularly visited Bracken's in Mullaghmore or "White House" as it is now known, as it had a commanding view of a large area of Mullaghmore and surrounding area. Observation of these patrols led eventually to plans being laid for an ambush and this was eventually mounted from Anthony Roger's, a little house that stood at that time across the road from Bracken's where now stand two rows of holiday homes. A local man recalls the incident,

"They'd stand up there above at Brackens – they had a whole view of the country 'round with spyglasses they used to get off Watty. The fella's were all in position in Anthony's but badly armed as they had only a revolver and a shotgun between them; I brought them down a feed of praties and mackerel – Anthony was there too. My job was to give the signal and I kept watch from Doherty's Brae. A bigger patrol than usual showed up and immediately seemed to sense that something was afoot or else they spotted the boys. Being badly outgunned the unit withdrew across the fields."

The R.I.C. didn't follow them, possibly fearing a trap and no other effort was made in this immediate area to mount another attack.

The country was now at a fever pitch of activity, raids for arms, ambushes, policemen killed, reprisals and burnings; the first I.R.A. casualty in Sligo was twenty one year old Martin Savage of Ballisodare who was killed in an ambush on Lord French in Dublin. A schedule of activity culled from records of the local I.R.A. unit reads like this:-

"Raids for arms in local Battalion area's Grange, Maugherow, Lisadell, Mullaghmore and Tullaghan; arms and ammunition taken; big raid for arms at Belleek, shots exchanged; doing duty at Sinn Féin courts; enforcing boycott on police; burning of Coastguard station at Mullaghmore; arrest, detention and guarding of prisoners from Bundoran who were a menace to the Republic; waiting in ambush on two occasions for military at Bundoran; attempted ambush at Mullaghmore; taking part in attack on Kinlough R.I.C. barracks; engaged enemy in ambush at Moneygold, casualties inflicted; waiting in ambush for police and military at Creevykeel; assisted in rescue of prisoners from Sligo jail; raiding for dog licenses; participation in burning of blockhouse at Tullaghan and destruction of Bunduff bridge; raiding for Belfast goods; blockading of roads; most of us are now on the run."

Thomas Lynch (not his real name) of Ballinfull had earned the enmity of many people; a process server and suspected spy, he was held responsible for the arrest and detention of scores of local men. In the opening months of 1920 the house was raided by a party of eight armed I.R.A. men; Lynch was seized, taken outside and shot dead. One of the firing party later related to me that during the raid, Lynch's wife pulled the mask off his face. Later, in court, in a case of mistaken identity, she swore that Patrick Cunningham was the man she had unmasked causing the wrong man to be convicted of the offence. Each member of the firing party had a rifle but only one had a live round, the rest being blank; in this way, no one knew who had actually fired the fatal shot. Lynch's son, a prison warder in Belfast, "was going to get it that night too" but he was not at home. He was shot dead some months later in Belfast.

In 1920, English forces, stretched to the limit in Ireland, resorted to the recruitment in England as reinforcements for the R.I.C., of a motley collection of former English army troops and released criminals, the notorious Black and Tans. Not since Cromwell's time had such barbarians been unleashed upon the Irish people as they sped along the roads in their Crossley tenders with apparent carte blanche to intimidate and terrorise the population at will. They fired at random at men working in the fields, searched and beat people for no reason, burned houses and businesses in reprisal; it was they who fired into the crowd at Croke Park on Bloody Sunday killing and wounding seventy people. Their lorries could arrive unexpectedly, day or night, and God help anyone who crossed their path.

One eyewitness of the time told me of their arrival at a rambling house at Drumfad,

"The Tans came into the house after him (Willie Lambert), he ran out of the house again and they followed him, putting bullets in through the bushes where he was lying. Roger Moore was rambling here and they took him out and beat and battered him and told him he should be in his own house. They beat him outa' here to that ditch across the road. Poor Roger, he never came rambling again"

The Inspector General's Report for Sligo for the month of June 1920 reported that the condition of the county was worse at that time than ever before, "by intimidation and outrage, Sinn Féin have put the whole country in a state of terror and men of loyal or moderate opinion have no chance but to submit." It went on to say that the police stations were too few and the force too small to cope with the state of affairs then prevailing. It reports a strike of 140 men at Jossyln Gore-Booth's estate; petty Session Courts being boycotted and "even loyalists forced to submit to Sinn Féin courts". It concluded that intimidation was widespread with nobody attempting to oppose Sinn Féin, "which ruled the country through the armed terrorism of the Irish Volunteers."

The Union Jack which flew across the road from the Coastguard station in Mullaghmore was a constant scource of friction and a target for locals, I.R.A. and civilians alike. The Union Jack was frequently taken down by locals and the Tricolour hoisted. On one such occasion, three soldiers were sent from Finner with instructions to restore the English flag and on arrival in Mullaghmore entered Hannon's shop where a group of locals were gathered. Hannons was at that time a pub, hotel and grocery shop and is now the Beach Hotel. An eyewitness at the time tells it:

"They inquired about the taking down and burning of their flag and demanded that the Tricolour be taken down at once. One of the fella's in the crowd finished his whiskey, walked up to the soldier and broke the glass on his jaw. The soldier fell and was carried out to Hannon's yard by his mates; one of them drew a revolver but the crowd jumped on him, took the gun off him and gave it to the I.R.A. later when they got a chance. The soldiers left after a while, everyone was waiting for reprisals but none came. Afterwards it was discovered that the soldier was a trained boxer that no one in Finner could touch."

Later, when the coastguards were withdrawn for service in the British Navy, an English gunboat would send a detachment of men ashore to restore the flag when it was removed by the local people. Of course, as soon as they were out of sight the Union Jack was taken down again. After one of these visits locals raised the Irish flag, cut the halyard, and then greased the pole. When the gunboat came again, much amusement was provided for the local people by the sailors efforts to climb the greased flagpole.

Eventually they managed to climb it and restore the Union Jack but this time, on the departure of the gunboat, a more permanent solution was reached when the flagpole was sawn down.

Shortly after this it was rumoured that a unit of Black and Tans were to be garrisoned at Mullaghmore. In June 1920, a crowd of forty or fifty people gathered, some local, some from Bunduff, Cliffoney and Grange, with the intention of finishing off the Coastguard station, hated symbol of British occupation, once and for all. The families of the vacated coastguard men were still in the cottages attached to the stations. Prior to the burning, they were removed together with their possesions to the Lodges where the convent now stands. There was a single coastguard left as caretaker for the station and he was on watch in the duty room when the men arrived to destroy the station.

One of these men remembers confiscating a revolver and a new Raleigh bicycle from Ransome, the Chief Boatman on duty, before setting the building alight. A paraffin oil tank was kept at Hannon's, one of two in the village which supplied the oil lamps that were then the only scource of light; it would be many years before electricity was to come to the area. The paraffin oil was emptied into buckets, carried over to the stations and along with as much petrol as could be found, was poured onto the buildings. A huge crowd had by this time gathered to watch as yet another symbol of Britain's empire blazed and burned and collapsed to the ground. Many years after that, as children, we played cowboys and Indians among the ruins, little knowing or caring about its storied past or that historic time when the pages of history were written and it lit up the night sky over Mullaghmore in a spectacular demise. Now, I carry with me a memento of these stations in a knee injury sustained in a dive off one of the ruined walls to the concrete floor below, in a desperate attempt to avoid an arrow from the bow of one of my "red Indian" adversaries.

At this time the Coastguard station at Pullendeva in south Sligo was burned also, and shortly after this, fearing a similar fate for Rosses Point, a British navy vessel landed a contingent of soldiers there, to guard this station. Breaghwy R.I.C. barracks was evacuated in July and burned to the ground shortly thereafter.

Numbers 8, 9, 10 and 11 Lodges, now the convent and Chapel were burned some time later in somewhat more mysterious and suspicious circumstances which were not tied in with any political agitation of the time. When the fire was discovered, Ashley's agent, Bracken, on arriving and realising that the building was going to be a complete loss told the onlookers to salvage what they could. Immediately after this members of Sinn Féin, on instructions from the court recovered much of the furniture and stored it for safe-keping in the Fr. O' Flanagan Hall in Cliffoney

Around this time there was intense pressure at Battalion level to raze Classiebawn, it being seen as a prominent symbol of English landlordism in this area. Strangely enough, it was saved when strenuous opposition by local active serving members caused the plan to be dropped. In more recent times, particularly at the time of the H-Blocks crisis of 1981, when buildings with prominent British connections were being attacked, Classiebawn was once again singled out for attention. As so often happens, history repeated itself, and once again local intervention helped to save the castle.

in 1920, with so many of the R.I.C. barracks closing down the responsibility of peace keeping fell more and more to the Sinn Féin courts who arbitrated on civil disputes and carried the rule of law, as the police became increasingly isolated. Volunteers wearing armbands marked I.V. patrolled fairs and public gatherings and did police duty at Sinn Féin courts.

Anyone guilty of collaborating with the police was warned and if they persisted, action was taken. Notices were posted warning businessmen against supplying goods or providing services to the R.I.C. People who had worked at cutting turf for the police were visited and warned of the consequences if they didn't stop. A "Sculloge" car carrying a policeman and travelling under an English permit was intercepted near Munianeane. The occupants were allowed to go free but the car was completely destroyed. A local man, noted for his collaboration with the police and Tans, was taken from a concealed position in his house, arrested and brought to the Sinn Féin court in Grange where he was warned, sentenced and an R.I.C. revolver found in his possession confiscated.

HAMPION, SATURDAY, OCTOBER 30, 1920.

DEADLY AMBUSH.

FOUR POLICEMEN KILLED. TWO WOUNDED.

REPRISALS IN CLIFFONEY & GRANGE

A sensation was created in Sligo on Monday when the news reached here that a police patrol had been ambushed a short distance outside Grange. At first the details were meagre, and, as occasionally occurs, people were inclined to regard the story as an exaggerated one. Subsequent inquiry proved, unfortunately, that the story was not without its elements of truth. The ambush was a most determined and daring one, occurring as it did at noon. It would appear that a patrol of nine men, in charge of Sergeant Perry, left Cliffoney barracks in or about 11 o'clock. They cycled in the

side them. The wounded were attended to and were removed to the County Infirmary, and the bodies of Sergeant Perry and Constables Laffey and M'Keown were taken to Cliffoney.

From the first it was not anticipated that Constable Lynch could live. His wounds were deadly, and he appeared to have lost consciousness for some hours before he died, which was about seven o'clock on the same evening. Constable Clarke was also in great pain, and Constable O'Rourke was the least dangerously wounded of the lot.

On Wednesday military inquiries were held and verdicts of murder returned against some persons unknown.

Subsequently the remains of Constable

THE MONEYGOLD AMBUSH

The arrival of the Black and Tans had sharpened animosities already existing between the population and the R.I.C. as they worked hand in glove with the forces of occupation providing the local knowledge essential to the military. House searches and harrassment on the streets continued. While raiding a house near Ballintrillick the Tans wantonly shot dead James Connolly, an old man of seventy, while accompanying the R.I.C. in the arrest of his son.

Grange barracks had been closed early in the War of Independence so it was inevitable that the R.I.C. in Cliffoney would become an increasing focus of attention. An ambush had been laid for them at the wooded area near the entrance to Ahamlish cemetery. Ten men lay in wait here for two days but the mission was aborted when the patrol didn't show up.

One of the ambushers was scarcely home when the patrol passed up the road by his house. Their luck was not to last though as shortly after this Seamus Devins and Billy Pilkington scouted the area again, looking for the most suitable ambush site, finally choosing Druim-a-Crusha hill near Moneygold.

Plans were now laid for one of the best planned and most successful ambushes in Ireland. All local units met in a byre and barn in Barnadearg belonging to Alfie Lang. Here, they discussed in meticulous detail far into the night, how the trap was to be sprung. The details to be considered were endless; how to lure the patrol past the ambush site; preparation of the site; approaches and position of the men; procurement of weapons; outposts on approach roads; concealment and eventual withdrawal and so on. The thirty eight men picked on that night who participated in the ambush were as follows:

SEAMUS DEVINS, BRIGADIER; GRANGE
NED BOFIN, CAPT.; ROSSES PT.
PAKIE MC GOWAN, BGDE. ADJ.; CARNS
TOM SMITH, CAPT.; BARNARIBBON
EUGENE GILBRIDE, CAPT.; GRANGE
PADDY BRANLEY, CAPT.; GLENCAR
EDDIE HARKIN, LIEUT.; CLIFFONEY
EUGENE BRADY, LIEUT.; ARDNAGLASS
MICK BURNS, LIEUT.; MAUGHEROW
ALFIE LANG, GRANGE
PADDY TOM GILLEN, NEWGRANGE
PATRICK CURRID, AGHAROW
JOHN CORMAC FEENEY, GROGAGH
MICK OATES, CASHELGARRON
JOHN HARAN, CASHELGARRON

BILLY PILKINGTON, COMMDT.; SLIGO
ANDREW CONWAY, CAPT.; CLIFFONEY
WILLIE DEVINS, Q.M.; GRANGE
MICK KILFEATHER, CAPT.; MAUGHEROW
DOM JOE FEENEY, CAPT.; CASHELGAR.
TOMMY MC CANN, LIEUT.; CARNS
MICK WOODS, LIEUT.; GRANGE
JOHN GALLAGHER, LIEUT.; GRANGE
TOMMY LEONARD, GRANGE
MICK MC GARRIGLE, GRANGE
TOMMY HEALEY, DRUMFAD
PATRICK HARGADON, DRUMFAD
"BIG" DOMINICK FEENEY, CASHELGAR.
TOMMY GOREVAN, CASHELGARRON
PAT HARAN, CASHELGARRON

JOHNNY FRIEL, CASHELGARRON
JOHN MC DONAGH, CLOONELLY
JOHN JOE HIGGINS, ROSSES POINT
JIM FEENEY, CREGG

MATTIE BANKS, MAUGHEROW
JOHN FEENEY, ROSSES POINT
KENNY GILLEN, ROSSES POINT
FRANK ROONEY, ROSSES POINT
JOHN FEENEY, GRANGE

All units were on alert, members of other units north and south of the ambush site who were not actually in ambush position, served on outpost duty. A few of the above listed men were not in actual ambush position but served as lookout at points such as Langs Hill.

The night preceding that fateful 25th of October, the men worked all night with spades, picks and shovels digging trenches and preparing the site, others cleaning, loading and concealing weapons. It was almost as if a benign deity smiled on their efforts as the countryside was lit up, almost like day, with a full harvest moon illuminating the scene, as these men worked with a grim determination through the night. The following day the men moved casually in twos and threes into position beside Peter Meehans house. Four Maugherow men, among them a man named Currid and Pat McLean had baited the trap by cutting the shafts out of a cart belonging to a man known to be pro-English, knowing that he would report this immediately to the R.I.C. and this would inevitably result in the Cliffoney patrol being sent to investigate.

The youngest men in the group were Alfie Lang, seventeen and Jim Feeney eighteen years old. Along with the others, they settled down nervously to a long wait, hoping the patrol would indeed show up and anxious for the coming fight. There was time to think. Too much time! These men didn't have to be here, they had homes and farms to look after. This was a venture into the unknown! How many of them would be on the run after this, sleeping in haysheds and open fields? How many of them would have homes to go to when the inevitable Black and Tan reprisals were over? Casualties were to be expected. Will it be me? How will I perform when the shooting starts? Hated as these men are, can I point a rifle at and kill them when the time comes? Will we get away before reinforcements come? Questions. Doubts. No man wavered. They were steadfast. Determined. The dream was Ireland free! Grange, Cliffoney and Mullaghmore free! From the mountain to the sea.

Johnny Woods, on the way to the bog in his ass and cart, was moving right into the ambush. "Go back as quick as you can," someone shouted in a loud whisper. Startled, he turned the ass and cart and sped back towards Grange. It was said "He went down the street of Grange faster than anyone had ever seen. No one had ever seen the ass travelling at such speed before." Passersby shouted to him, "Whats wrong, Johnny?" "Leave it alone, leave it alone," was all he would say."

Our eyewitness was moved to outpost duty at the quarry in Cashel, his job now to observe traffic on the main road. He held this position until eleven o'clock when Patrick Gillen of Aughaged arrived with tea. Willie continues the story, "He came over with a tin can of tea and I went on with this to the rest of the lads. My oul' shotgun was leaning on a tree waiting for me while we were resting. We had barely the tea taken when nine of them came up the road on their bikes; the cry, 'Hands up' went out; they jumped off the bikes, and grabbed for their weapons and that's when the banging started. They were called on to surrender but instead reached for their weapons and started to fire."

Steady now, hindsight lined up on the vee of the foresight, centred on the target— squeeze – don't pull – aim—FIRE. Rifles kicked into shoulders. A man died, his skull shattered. The sharp crack of rifles and the screams of dying men mingled in the clear October air. The pungent smell of gunsmoke lingered, stinging the nostrils, rose lazily and disappeared into the harvest sky. The gunbattle seemed to last for hours – in reality it was only fifteen minutes. It was a bright sunny day and the shooting was heard all over North Sligo. Men lifted their heads from work and wondered. My granduncle, Pat Mc Gowan and Johnny Barry's grandfather resting on the sod ditch from their labours of digging potatoes, heard the shooting. Johnny, a small boy at the time, remembers the older men speculating that it might be the Tans on another rampage or someone target shooting on the back strand.

Our eyewitness tells us that, "when the firing stopped there was eight got out of nine, the only survivor, Spratt, emptied his gun before he threw it down and surrendered. Frank Rooney from Rosses Point who lived near Bofin, was with the ambushers. When the shooting was over Frank took off his mask. Spratt, having served with him in the British army, recognised him, – 'I didn't think I'd meet you here, Frank,' he said. Frank had been discharged and was getting fifteen bob a week of a pension for a bullet wound in his back. He used to collect his money each week in Sligo but couldn't go back after that, he went on the run with me."

Weapons and ammunition were seized and the men quickly made their escape, as Linda Kearns who had benn standing by in the event of injuries to the ambush party, tended the dead and dying R.I.C men. Some of the ambush party hastened towards the mountain and some towards the sea. "There was nine or ten of us and we went on 'till we landed at John Bruen's in Streedagh. Lucky for us the tide was out so we waded across the channel, over to where there's a moat beyond Willie Hood's in Mount Edward. We stopped here and had barely made cover when we spied through field glasses the Black and Tans at the ambush site as thick as midges. That night we went to the back of a house, Big Dominick Feeney's, he lived over at Fr. Feeney's house in Doonowney. His mother brought us out a tin can of tea while we waited for the Tans to come, to hit them again, but they went the Maugherow road; they must have been afraid of another ambush. I went from there to Martin Watters's in Cloontyprucklish and operated out of there for eleven months. From there I went to Joe Leydons beyond near hand the school where John Feeney is now over the Cloontyprucklish road."

A Rathugh woman recalls being told by her father that he was digging potatoes in Rathugh on that day when some of the ambushers passed by heavily laden with rifles and ammunition. Having nothing else at hand he gave them his belt to tie up the weapons for easier carrying. Some of the men stayed in safe houses in Drumfad and in Gleniff Horseshoe, others stayed at Kerins of Kilcar while others made their way to Ballintrillick where they set up another ambush in anticipation of the Tans coming to burn the creamery as they had done in other parts of the country. They were accompanied by some of the Ballintrillick company I.R.A. among them: Patrick Gallagher, Lecklasser; James Gallagher,Lecklasser; Thady Clancy,Lecklasser; Edward McGloin,Drinaghan; and John Gilmartin Drinaghan; John Gallagher, Gortnahowla; John Roooney, Coolagraphy; Martin B. McGowan, Mick 'the Master' McGowan and John McGowan of Glenade. The ambush was lifted when they didn't come but the creamery was burned some days later by a large force of Tans.

The Sligo Champion of Sat. Oct. 30th 1920, in addition to the news that Terence Mc Swiney, Lord Mayor of Cork, had died in Brixton prison after seventy four days on hungerstrike, carried the headline:

DEADLY AMBUSH
FOUR POLICEMEN KILLED, TWO WOUNDED
REPRISALS IN CLIFFONEY AND GRANGE

"A sensation was created in Sligo on Monday when news reached here that a police patrol had been ambushed a short distance outside Grange...... nine men under Sgt. Perry left Cliffoney about eleven o' clock...... at Derry crossroads shots rang out from behind the wall.... Sgts. Perry and Constable Laffey and McKeon were killed instantly, Constables Lynch, Clarke and O'Rourke were wounded...... Spratt, Mc Cormack and Joyce succeeded in getting away."

The account goes on to give horrific detail of the injuries,

"Sgt Perry was shot through the mouth, the bullet passing through the top of his skull and out through his cap."

116

The bullet passed through Laffey's neck and lodged in his brain; Keown was shot through the throat, portion of which was shot away. There were lorry loads of military and police at the scene.

"They found the three men lying dead on the roadway, the three wounded men lying nearby moaning in their agony...... after treatment on the roadside by Dr. Martin, and after Fr. Crehan had administered to the wounded men they were brought to Sligo Infirmary where Lynch succumbed to his injuries after a few hours."

The report went on to say that it was supposed that one of the attackers was killed or injured as blood was found at the scene. Perry (57) left a wife and eleven children, Laffey (41) an invalid wife and four children. A cavalcade drove through Sligo with the bodies of Perry and Laffey on Wednesday evening, the front lorry carrying a big inscription, "SINN FEIN VICTORY: THREE WIDOWS AND SEVENTEEN ORPHANS." The Sligo Chronicle carried an article claiming that,

" two of the constables who escaped went for the doctor and being strangers had to enquire for the doctor and priest's house. On enquiring in the village of Grange, the answer was, 'I don't know.' One party asked, "What do you want the priest for?" When the constable replied that some of his friends had been injured and were dying, the proud reply was, 'That's the stuff to give them.'

It is interesting to note here that official records and newspaper reports account for only four casualties. Yet, Willie Devins, veteran of the Moneygold ambush is adamant that "there was eight got out of nine" with only one survivor. His claim is corroborated by accounts given by other veterans. If indeed thre were five survivors they would certainly have presented a problem for the ambush party and would have to be restrained. Did they tie them up? Lock them in a byre? Did they exist? Were the four deaths admitted by the authorities a deliberate understatement, normal in a wartime situation, of the actual casualites? Certainly, the official estimate of one hundred ambushers was an exaggeration and almost three times the actual figure. The claim that at least one of the attackers was killed or injured was also false, as all of the ambush party escaped unscathed.

Some of the men who took part in the ambush later told that they regretted the deaths of some of the police, "one or two of them were good enough fella's". Almost nobody regretted the death of Sgt. Perry who was very much disliked and remembered for his sneering remarks about McSwiney when he was on hunger strike,"Did that hungry bastard die yet?"

Fear now gripped the communities as a reign of terror commenced with the inevitable reprisals of the Black and Tans. Practically every

117

house was searched as large numbers of people all over North Sligo fled their homes, fearing for their lives. The Tans went on a rampage of looting and burning; in Grange, the house of Seamus Devins was looted and burned to the ground along with all his hay and turf at the back of the house; Currid's house was burned and his son taken prisoner; Gilbride's house was visited and threatened with burning but they ransacked it instead; Lang's premises raided and looted; the fair of Grange was stopped on Thursday, people beaten and given ten minutes to get out. An absolute dread pervaded the area as Auxiliaries in their convoys of lorries spread out through the countryside, shooting at will, ransacking and burning. Grange Temperance Hall and library, along with thousands of books, was burned.

In Mullaghmore, too, many people left their homes as the rumours spread that the Tans were on their way. Thomas Boyce was one of these: "People didn't go to bed at all that night. We were without at the Big Hills, that's where we were. Ye might fall into a doze of sleep but then you'd wake up again and ye'd see a light here or there; we'd be guessing, it must be such a man's house burning." My father had been on the run for some time but the Tans came to our house again to harass and search. They accused my Uncle Patrick of hiding some rounds of ammunition they had "discovered" in a jug on the mantelpiece and threatened to take him outside and shoot him if he wouldn't reveal my fathers wherabouts. Confronted with angry denials and told that they themselves had planted the ammunition, they contented themselves with breaking the furniture and left. Our house, Gorman's, Conway's and "Big" Bernie Kelly's were the houses in Mullaghmore said to have been pointed out for Tan burning; the Tans however confined most of their destruction to the main road:-

BERNIE CONWAY, CLIFFONEY, HOUSE BURNED
WILLIE GILMARTIN, CREEVYKEEL, HOUSE BURNED (WILLIE "EDWARDS")
PETER MC CANNON, CLIFFONEY, HOUSE BURNED, FATHER AND SON ARRESTED
BALLINTRILLICK CREAMERY, BURNED
ML. HARKIN, CLIFFONEY, HOUSE BURNED
E. GILLESPIE, CLIFFONEY, CONTENTS OF SHOP BURNED
CHARLIE GILMARTIN, CARNDUF, HOUSE BURNED
FR. O' FLANAGAN HALL, CLIFFONEY, BURNED AND A PLACARD ERECTED
    WHICH READ, "VACATED HOME OF MURDER GANG".

A Sligo Champion reporter visited North Sligo shortly after these occurences on Saturday, November the 6th and reported that,
    "smokestained walls throwing gaunt shadows across the roadway in

Secret - Crime Special.

Confidential Report for month of October 1920

Part I.

I beg to state this County has been in a very disturbed state for some months past. There is no sign of improvement. On the contrary it is becoming more lawless day by day. The police are straining every possible effort to cope with the situation. Although their numbers are small and their task difficult I have no doubt but they will succeed eventually in restoring decent order. The prevailing lawlessness is all political. There is no sectarian or agrarian trouble. No one receives special police protection.

(a) There is no change as regards land-purchase. It appears to be at a stand-still. The relations between landlords and tenants and employers and workmen are good. There is no industrial development. The only topics of public interest at present are the murders and attacks on police throughout the country.

(b) There were 58 outrages reported during the month. There were probably many

The I.G.

others which have not come to the knowledge of the police. The most serious occurred on 25.x.20 when about 100 Irish Volunteers ambushed a patrol of nine policemen. Four police were murdered, and two seriously wounded. at moneygold near the village of Grange. The fight was short but terrific. The police opened fire on the attackers. When six were killed and wounded the remainder were overpowered and all disarmed. Forces of police and military from Sligo and Clogher were quickly on the scene, and have been scouring the country day and night since. For miles around the scene the male population fled in terror and have not since returned. Splendid discipline was maintained by the Forces but notwithstanding this, some reprisals followed. The houses of some leading suspects were burned. as well as the "Father O'Flanagan" Sinn Fein Hall at Cliffoney. The walls of the latter now bears the motto " The vacated home of the murder gang. arising out of the searches some arrests have been made in connection with the possession of seditious documents and ammunition.

Please see Form B. attached.

the waning light of a November evening were the objects which silently told the visitor to Grange and Cliffoney on this evening of what followed the killing of a number of police on the previous Monday...... in many instances people have been made homeless wanderers through reprisals although they have taken neither hand, act or part in the occurrence that led to these reprisals."

He reports seeing Mrs Harkin,
"an old lady of seventy years sitting in an outhouse by a turf fire. It was all that was left to her along with two chairs and a milk pail, everything else was burned. She is a wonderful old woman and tells the story of the attack which left her without a home, as if it had been an ordinary incident."

The article concludes that
"the whole thing seems one great tragedy and all because the government in power fail to understand what the aspiration of a people clamouring for their liberty means. Underlining it all is the painful thought that while no real or genuine effort is made to arrive at a settlement, England watches Irishmen killing Irishmen in guerilla warfare."

A funny sequel to the ambush and one that gave much amusement to the men that planned the affair was to hear that the police and Tans had visited their erstwhile friend in Maugherow, who had notified them of the damage to his asscart, thus causing the patrol to be sent out. Despite his protestations of innocence and loyalty they, "kicked him all 'round the yard," in frustration, suspecting that he might have helped to set up the trap by cutting the shafts out of the cart himself.

The following is taken from the secret monthly report for the month of Oct. 1920 from the Sligo County Inspector, R.I.C. to Dublin Castle:
"I beg to state this county has been in a very disturbed state for some months past. There is no sign of improvement. On the contrary it is becoming more lawless day by day. The police are straining every possible effort to cope with the situation. Although their numbers are small and their task difficult, I have no doubt but that they will succeed eventually in restoring decent order........
.... There were 58 ourtrages reported during the month. There were probably many others which have not come to the knowledge of the police. The most serious occurred on Oct X '20 when about 100 Irish Volunteers ambushed a patrol of nine policemen. Four police were murdered and two seriously wounded at Moneygold near the village of Grange. The fight was short but terrific. The police opened fire on the attackers, when six were killed and wounded, the remainder were overpowered and disarmed. Forces of police and military from Sligo and Clogher were quickly on the scene and have been scouring the country day and night since. For miles around the scene, the male

population fled in terror and have not since returned. Splendid discipline was maintained by the Forces, but notwithstanding this, some reprisals followed. The houses of some leading suspects were burned along with the Fr. O'Flanagan Sinn Fein Hall in Cliffoney. The walls of the latter now bears the motto. "The vacated Home of the Murder Gang."........

........At present there is a life and death struggle in the County between the Crown Forces and the forces of disorder and murder. The police are slowly but surely becoming masters of the situation. Their morale is improving every day and although they realize that the fight will be a bitter one for some time to come, they are absolutely confident that the battle will end in the complete rout of the revolutionary forces ...." A list of political organisations in the county of Sligo was attached:

Name of Organisation	No. of Branches	Membership
Sinn Fein	53	6,222
Irish Volunteers	10	1,727
A.O.H.	13	597
Irish T & G W Union	8	1,410
Cumainn na Bann	7	177
U I League	2	252

As a consequence of the ambush, heavy claims for damages were made against the County. In the Cliffoney area alone, the injured parties made the following claims at Sligo Quarter Sessions early in 1921:-

CONST. LAFFEY, REPS.	£10,000
SGT. PERRY, REPS.	10,000
CONST. LYNCH, REPS.	8,000
CONST. KEOWN,	2,000
D.I. BRADY	10,000
CONST. CLARKE	5,000
SGT. ML ROURKE	2,000
ML. GILMARTIN, CREEVYKEEL	3,750
B. GILMARTIN, CREEVYKEEL	1,400
BALLINTRILLICK CREAMERY	20,750
PETER MC CANNON, CLIFFONEY	2,250
BRIGID CONWAY, EDENREAGH	1,700
MARY HANNON (F. HANNON), CREEVYKEEL	650
MICHAEL HARKIN, CLIFFONEY	950
B. HIGGINS, MOUNTEMPLE	650
E. GILLESPIE, CLIFFONEY	230
P. GILMARTIN, CREEVYKEEL	100
ML. CUMMINS, MONEYGOLD	103
JAMES GARDINER, CLIFFONEY	500

SLIGO GROUP OF DARTMOOR PRISONERS

Front Row: L to R: Dominic McHugh, Seamus Devins, James Devins
Back Row, L to R: P. Brehony, Bertie Glynn, Eugene Gilbride, Andrew Conway, P. Hanrahan

Photo: Courtesy of Dr. J. Devins

JOHN GALLAGHER, CARTRONKILLERDO	70 HAY AND TURF BURNED
MARTIN GALLAGHER, BALLINTRILLICK	18 HEIFER KILLED
POSTMASTER GENERAL	80 TELEGRAPH WIRE CUT

The awards granted were somewhat less than the demands with Sgt. Perry reps. getting £9,000, Const. Keown, £2,000, Const. Laffey, £7,000, Const. Lynch, £6,000, D.I. Brady, £2,000.

Ballintrillick Creamery, £13,230, Mrs. Conway, £1,167, Brigid Gilmartin, £970, Ml. Harkin, £765, and so on.

Less than a month after this ambush and on the same day that Black and Tans killed twelve spectators at a football match in Croke Park, disaster struck the local leadership when Seamus Devins, Andrew Conway and E. Gilbride were captured near Ballisodare in a car driven by Linda Kearns. The group were moving arms and ammunition, some of which was captured in the Moneygold ambush, to set up an ambush in South Sligo. Sligo born Linda Kearns was a veteran of Easter Week, having tended the wounded in a field hospital on North Great George's Street until forced to close by the British. She then acted as despatch carrier for the men in the G.P.O. while continuing to care for the wounded; she tended to the O' Rahilly when he was fatally wounded in the retreat from the G.P.O. She now worked as a nurse but served also with the Volunteers delivering weapons to ambush sites and collecting them afterwards. She stayed to tend the wounded at the Moneygold ambush and therefore would have been easily recognised by the police when her car was stopped.

In describing the arrest later, she said: "We had with us every rifle and round of ammunition our Column possessed... I thought I could make a dash for it and put on speed, but when I got closer to the lights I saw the lorries pulled right across the road. They pulled us out of the car and when they found the load of stuff in the back, our treatment was pretty rough." The Auxiliaries were wild with drink and, "started firing all around, shouting, "Shoot them'. Orders and counter orders were issued; shoot them; line them up; put them in the lorry." Before being captured, Seamus Devins who was sitting beside the driver, drew an automatic pistol but was disarmed and along with the other occupants badly beaten. They were then questioned and beaten again at Sligo barracks before being lodged in Sligo jail. Gilbride was beaten unconscious during the arrest and Seamus Devins badly beaten at Sligo jail.

A number of the weapons found in the car were identified as belonging to the police patrol ambushed at Moneygold, the complete list comprising 10 rifles with loaded magazines, a Webley revolver, 2 police belts, a police pouch, a haversack, 2 bandoliers, a Maxim gun and belt,

124

320 rounds of ammunition and some automatic pistol ammunition.

The prisoners were transferred from Sligo jail to Raughley, from where they were taken by sea in an English gunboat to Buncrana and from there to Belfast where they were tried and sentenced to fifteen years imprisonment. Nurse Kearns was the exception, getting ten years, a sentence that at this time was the longest ever given to any woman during the War of Independence. Arrested in September 1920 and held in Mountjoy, another woman and comrade in arms, Constance Markievicz, was sentenced on Christmas Eve 1920 to two years penal servitude for,"promoting Fianna Eireann for the purpose of commiting murder of military and police, drilling men and carrying and using arms and the furnishing and training of Irish Volunteers."

Constance Markievicz may have been held in reverence, loved and respected by all those involved in the fight for independence at this time but, descendant of Sir Robert Gore-Booth, she was most certainly the black sheep in what was very much an ascendancy family. There were very many people at this time, of the older generation and particularly veterans of earlier struggles, who bemoaned the good old Fenians and disapproved very much of the methods used by the Irish Volunteers, Sinn Fein and the I.R.A.:

> *Was it for this the wild geese spread*
> *The grey wing upon every tide;*
> *For this that all that blood was shed,*
> *For this Edward Fitzgerald died,*
> *And Robert Emmet and Wolfe Tone,*
> *All that delirium of the brave?*
> *Romantic Ireland's dead and gone,*
> *It's with O'Leary in the grave."*

It seems that in every age, heroes and epic struggles live in the past. Its not surprising then, that Yeats, a scion of planter stock, bemoaned also the descent of Constance to the nationalist cause:

> *"Did she in touching that lone wing,*
> *Recall the years before her mind*
> *Became a bitter, an abstract thing,*
> *Her thought some popular emnity;*
> *Blind and leader of the blind,*
> *Drinking the foul ditch where they lie?"*

Had the Easter Rising been a failure, would Yeats then have revised his judgement and written, as he did, about this noble venture? There was surely an element of self portrait in the words as,

> "He, too, had resigned his part,
> In the casual comedy;
> He, too, has been changed in his turn,
> Transformed utterly,
> A terrible beauty is born."

Thomas Mc Shea, Battalion O/C and Patrick Johnston, Company Captain were arrested by British forces at Bundoran on 22nd April 1921. They were charged with having seditious literature in their possession and sentenced to two years in prison, serving their sentence in Finner, Peterhead Prison in Scotland, Belfast jail and Derry jail. In an attempted escape from Derry jail on 2nd December 1921 two prison warders inadvertently suffocated to death when they were gagged too tightly during the escape. Johnston, O'Shea and Mc Bride were caught, transferred to Belfast jail, tried and sentenced to hang on February 9th 1922.

In an effort to save their lives three I.R.A. units in this area, were despatched simultaneously to arrest and detain Sir Josslyn Gore Booth, Major Eccles and Parkes of Moneygold as hostages. Two of the arrested men were held at an abandoned house at Aughaged, near Mt. Edward Cross and the third at a house in Ballintrillick. The I.R.A. at this time had control of Classiebawn castle and three more hostages including Major Myles of Ballyshannon and Johnson of Kinlough were despatched here by Bundoran Co.I.R.A. and guarded by local Volunteers. A message was communicated to the British authorities that the hostages would be shot if the three condemned men were executed. The operation from an I.R.A. point of view was a complete success and the hostages released when the condemned men had their sentences commuted to fifteen and twenty years penal servitude.

Classiebawn is reported to have been mined at this time with high explosives; if the hostages had been discoverd and an attempt made to rescue them it was planned to blow up the castle. When Major Eccles was being released he is reported to have said to his captors, "Are you glad to see me go, boys?" The reply was said to be, "We are, and very glad, but we'd have been just as glad to shoot you if things were different."

Locally, there was only one more major occurrence when Constable P. Clarke was shot dead in an ambush at Creevykeel crossroads in June 1921. It is thought that he was not the intended victim but had walked into a trap which had been set for a convoy of Black and Tans.

As 1920 dragged into 1921 the war continued, the British on one side having more experienced and ruthless soldiers and superior weaponry; the I.R.A., however, had the support of the people, made even more firm by the repressive methods employed by the Black and Tans, of reprisal by looting, burning and shooting. The English, accustomed to trench warfare where opposing lines were clearly defined, became more and more frustrated with the hit and run guerilla tactics employed by the Flying Columns of the I.R.A., a foretaste of what was to come in other colonies, in Aden, Cyprus, Kenya and Northern Ireland. Tactics too which, in more recent times, have defeated the Americans in Vietnam and the Russians in Afghanistan.

An important member of what the police referred to as "the murder gang" was arrested in Maugherow in May of 1921 during a comb-out of the area. "Yank" Kilfeather received a bullet wound during the arrest and was kept in hospital for a time before being released into police custody and transferred to Dublin. Some time before this, members of this battalion area had a narrow escape at Drumcliff when re-opening trenches in the road which had been filled in by the Tans. Bridges at Bunduff and Drumcliff had been destroyed and the roads trenched some time previously so as to make travel as difficult as possible for British forces. The trenches at Drumcliff had been filled in by the Black and Tans using I.R.A. prisoners and men were immediately dispatched to re-open these. Willie Devins and some others who were standing guard, noticed a blue light coming from the trench and suspecting a bomb, shouted to Tom Watters and John "Cormack" Feeney, who were clearing the trench, to jump clear. Just as they dived clear there was a massive explosion, which afterwards, people said could be heard as far away as Bundoran. The Tans were now planting booby trap bombs in the trenches they filled in, so from that time on, trenches which were filled in by British forces were not touched.

The pressure was kept on the British. On the 1st of July 1921 in an almost exact replica of the Moneygold incident, a party of seven R.I.C. suffered casualties in an ambush at Culleens near Dromore West. While the British were coming to the realisation that they couldn't win, Sinn Fein/I.R.A. knew that while they could not lose, it was not in any way certain that they were going to win either. Peace feelers had been sent out by both sides which resulted eventually in a truce being agreed on July 11 1921,thus bringing a cessation to hostilities while de Valera met with Lloyd George to agree plenipotentiaries for peace talks.

While the Truce was a welcome respite for all concerned, local units, realising that hostilities could be commenced at any time, continued drilling, making dugouts, running Sinn Fein courts, doing sentry duty at and manning Bofin's North Sligo H.Q. at the Glebe house in Moneygold, present home of the O'Connor family. The Divisional Commisioner demanded action as he regarded the occupation of this house, "as a provocative display of force and a menace to my R.I.C. force at Cliffoney." A local veteran, recalling the events of the time remembers a prisoner being brought to the Glebe House H.Q. from the Sinn Fein court in Grange having refused to pay a fine. In an attempt to bring the man to a more co-operative frame of mind, he was given a spade and shovel with instructions to start digging his own grave. The men guarding him, not being unfriendly, would occasionally give him a hand to dig while advising him that his best interests lay in paying up his fine. This he eventually did and was released.

During the period of the Truce, the R.I.C. kept a watchful eye on events, reporting a breach of the truce by the I.R.A on the 29th August:

> "I beg to report that on the 29th inst. some person or persons called on the residence of Sir Josslyn Gore-Booth and asked for the keys to Rahelly House. On being refused, they later in the same day broke in the door and a large party of I.R.A. men took possession, moving in bedding and possessions and carrying out target practise. Some men called at Sligo Assylum and carried away twenty bed ticks and twenty blankets – it is believed in connection with this house."

The report went on to say that the I.R.A. were enforcing a form of conscription by which all the young men of the area had to go through a period of training. It was deduced that the I.R.A. were preparing for war and demanded an appropriate investigation by the I.R.A. Liason Officer. Commandant Fintan Murphy, District Liason Officer stationed in the Prince of Wales Hotel in Athlone replied that he, "does not consider training to be a breach of the truce any more than training by the British Army."

On 25/9/'21 the R.I.C. reported that, "the rebels who were encamped at Rahelly House have now moved to a vacant house belonging to Charles Rogers near the village of Carney." Rogers, they reported, gave the key "without demur" when asked for it. The move to Carney, they felt, was to give I.R.A. units in Sligo a better opportunity of drilling. In October, Constables Manus Loughry, 67469 and Frederick Gonnigale, 78564 reported a large body of men drilling and marching at Mullaghmore. A shot was fired at them which they believed was meant to intimidate them and prevent them from coming any closer.

On 16/10/'21, the police report a public Sinn Fein meeting at Grange where Fr. Greene C.C., James Devins, M.P. Grange, Thomas

O'Donnell M.P. Gurteen, and others adressed an audience of more than 500 young men. "No police were present but it is stated that Devins used strong language and advised all Volunteers to be ready for action at any moment." The report concluded that, "the meeting can have no effect in Grange as the locality cannot be any more revolutionary than it is."

These Treaty negotiations have engendered much bitter debate, controversy and recriminations over the years but in retrospect it would seem that the result of these discussions were a foregone conclusion when it is considered that the Government of Ireland Act passed in 1920 had already divided Ireland into six and twenty six county entities, George V having already visited Belfast to open the Northern Parliament. On the 6th of December the Articles of Agreement for the Treaty were signed in London by Michael Collins and the other delegates under Lloyd George's threat of "immediate and terrible war within three days." Opinions are sharply divided to this day as to whether the conditions of the Treaty should have been accepted or not; it is certain that its signing was a death warrant for many thousands in the civil war which followed and in the struggle which continues in the six north eastern counties of Ireland at the time of writing. After much bitter and acrimonious debate the Treaty was ratified in the Dail on the 7th of January 1922 by a margin of 64 to 57.

Republican forces under de Valera were bitterly disappointed that the delegates didn't hold out for a thirty two county nation. Michael Collins went with the pro-treaty side considering the agreement to be a "stepping stone to the Republic." Two days after the vote, de Valera resigned as President and Arthur Griffith, one of the signatories to the Treaty, was elected as President of Dail Eireann in his place. Gradually the two sides moved towards conflict and faced each other in a bloody civil war. Britain, anxious to maintain her newly established foothold in Ireland, resorted to the old colonial policy of divide and conquer, a strategy as old as war itself; she armed the pro-Treaty National army, which was bound by oath and interest to England, urging them to take action against the anti-Treaty side. The Republican or anti-Treaty forces had none of these advantages or support and were further disadvantaged in that the men they now faced were former comrades in arms, who knew every trick and hiding place they had employed together to defeat the Black and Tans.

The first shots of the Civil War were fired at 4.07 A.M. on the 28th of June 1922, when eighteen pounder artillery pieces, loaned to Collins by the British, opened fire from across the Liffey at the Republican garrison stationed in the Four Courts.

County of Sligo.

District Inspector's Office,

Sligo. 3/10/21.

C.I.

I beg to submit statements from two Constables from Cliff oney as to drilling by I.R.A.at Mullaghmore on 1st Inst. and the firing of a shot,evidently to intimidate the police,who were unarmed, from coming closer.

An I.R.A. training camp was established at Moneygold,near Cliffoney on the 27th Ult, already reported,but it seems this body of men were not from there. As about 8 o'c same evening this party came from the direction of Mullaghmore (which is on the seashore two Miles N.W. of Cliffoney) and on to the main road at Creevykeel,a mile north of Cliffoney. They then march- ed towards Bundoran,and are believed to be from Tullaghan, Co. Leitrim, where I understand a camp was established about a fort. night ago,

The police did not know any of the party,and did not see who fired the shot.

This seems a flagrant breach of the Truce,and looks as if the I.R.A. want to force trouble. If much of this thing occurs it will be hard to answer for the police,who resent this dril- ling,and carrying of arms by rebels in an open display of sed- ition and antagonism.

Illegible signature 1st D.I.

County Inspector's Office, .
Sligo, 4 : 10 : 21

130

CHAPTER 7

The Civil War and After

The first shots of the Civil War were fired in Dublin but the first serious confrontation took place in Sligo town some months before that, in April. North Sligo, by and large, took an anti-Treaty stance when the split came and conflict loomed once more for war weary men, this time with a very different foe, as local units were ordered to mobilise once again.

Their orders were to assemble in Sligo under the command of General Billy Pilkington of the Third Western Division to enforce a ban on President Griffith, who was due to hold a monster rally in Sligo to speak on behalf of the Freestate. The day before Griffith's arrival, Freestate forces captured and held large areas of Sligo, including Sligo jail. Determined to defy the Republican ban, Griffith arrived in Sligo, but was forced to deliver his speech at the corner of Grattan and O'Connell Streets, as the Town Hall was in the possession of the Republicans. Massive forces were assembled on either side on that Easter Sunday 16 April 1922. The time was not yet ripe for war though, and Pilkington, a man who later on was to become a Redemptorist monk, was given much of the credit for restraining his forces and defusing a dangerous situation, thus avoiding the loss of many lives.

The first major battle of the Civil War came to an end in Dublin, when Rory O' Connor and the Republicans were forced to surrender on the 30th of June with the loss of 29 dead and 59 wounded. Regrettably, many historical documents were lost forever in the shelling of the Four Courts during this battle. The conflict now spread throughout the country, reaching Sligo during the Summer of 1922; Sligo town became a battleground as Republicans and Freestaters fought for control of the town; The Sligo Champion which had taken an anti-Republican stance was raided by the Republicans and had type broken up; Bank of Ireland raided, £14,000 taken to finance anti-Treatyites; Teeling St. and Wine St. barracks taken and burned by National forces; Custom house destroyed; Rosses Point and Raughley coastguard stations burned.

In North Sligo, Republican units were active and participated in the dismantling of Cliffoney and Mullaghmore Post Offices, destruction of roads and bridges to impede movement of National forces and in a raid for arms at Tawley, shots were exchanged and one of the raiders injured. During the War of Independence, Mullaghmore was a much used departure point for Volunteers and arms enroute for Donegal; this has always been an attractive alternative, even in more recent times, as it was considered to be much safer than transport by road. Landings were made then at St. John's Point and at Teelin but this route was not completely without danger either as it was patrolled by British gunboats during the Tan war and later by the armoured cruiser, the "Tartar", captained by J.J.Clancy for the Freestaters during the Civil War.

A major ambush mounted by the Republican forces at Rockwood on the shores of Lough Gill in July 1922 resulted in three Freestate casualties and the capture of the legendary armoured car known as the 'Ballinalee'.

This armoured car had been the strong arm of the Frestate armoury in the area, being used to especially good effect during Arthur Griffiths visit to the town. Later, mounted with a deadly Vickers machine gun, she had devastated the I.R.A. position at the Wine St. barracks. She was now to pose a major worry for the Freestate forces as the Republicans now used it to deadly effect when on the day after its capture, July 15, under the command of Brigadier Seamus Devins the town was attacked. All the main buildings which were occupied and heavily fortified by the National army were taken. The National forces were forced to retreat to the Courthouse and on being issued an order to surrender by Devins were saved only by the action of Bishop Coyne when he entered the Courthouse and refused to leave. The Republicans now found themselves in an invidious position and not wanting to harm the Bishop, thereby handing a propaganda coup to the enemy, evacuated their position and withdrew.

In the hands of the Republicans, the 'Ballinalee' continued to wreak havoc going through the town firing bursts of machine gun fire on the night that a massive explosion partially wrecked the Ulster Bank. Ballina was taken and later Collooney:

> *You may talk of Patrick Sarsfield*
> *And the siege of Limerick town*
> *But their deeds they were downrated*
> *When you mention Ballina town*

Like a thunderbolt from heaven
They rushed up Ard-na-Righ
A handful of Republicans
In the famous Ballinalee

After an attack on Tubbercurry the Ballinalee was closely followed by National troops. In the running battle that followed, Commandant General Ring ran into an ambush and was killed. Clearly, the Freestate forces could not allow this state of affairs to continue and now laid plans that would lead to events in North Sligo that would add another bloody chapter to an already tragic history.

For some time, Rahelly House in the Maugherow area had been H.Q. for Republican forces in the Northern half of Sligo so it was not unexpected that this would now become the objective of a massive military assault by Freestate forces. On the 1st of September, National troops, heavily armed with motor lorries, armoured cars and field guns advanced on Rahelly. In an encircling movement and under the direction of Generals Sean Mc Eoin, Duffy and Lalor, they advanced northwards from Sligo and Southwards from Finner Camp and Manorhamilton moving through Cliffoney and Grange towards their objective.

"They came in their fast Crossley tenders
And many a strong armoured car
With Lewis guns, Maxwells and rifles
All England's equipment of war.

The 'Ballinalee' and Republican forces were engaged near Drumcliffe and after fierce fighting the National forces gained the upper hand, forcing the I.R.A. to withdraw and taking nine prisoners, three of whom were wounded. Advancing to Rahelly the Freestaters found the house deserted, the occupants having withdrawn to the wooded and mountainous areas for cover. Contact was once again made later with the Ballinalee but according to reports in the Sligo Champion, " that elusive Vickers gun car was well handled and avoided the dangers of artillery fire; long distance sniping then ensued."

The ring of steel continued to close though, as troops from Dromahair and Finner Camp continued to close in on the area capturing the I.R.A. held villages of Tullaghan and Kinlough as they came. The 'Ballinalee', along with the main body of Republicans under Gen. Pilkington and Brig. Seamus Devins, T.D. were now surrounded, every avenue of escape being cut off by National troops to prevent any attempt at a successful dash through the cordon with the armoured car. On the 19th of September, at Carmamadow near Ballintrillick, heavy fighting which continued all day resulted in the hard pressed Republicans having to blow up the Ballinalee when capture seemed inevitable and then taking to the hills for cover.

On the following day, six Republicans were shot dead on the mountain, four of the bodies being discovered immediately. They were Brigadier Seamus Devins, T.D. of Grange, Brian Mc Neill, son of Prof. Eoin MacNeill, the man who had given the countermanding order for the Easter Rising, Joseph Banks, Abbey St. Sligo and Patrick Carroll, John St. Sligo. These four were discovered shortly after the engagement but it was not known for weeks afterwards that two others, Harry Benson and Tommy Langan had also been killed. It was bad enough that six men were dead, but now a wave of revulsion swept the countryside when it was discovered that the National forces had left the area without burying the dead or informing anyone that there had been casualties. They were found by a man tending sheep on the mountain.

> *"They took to the hillside for cover*
> *While the State poured its merciless rain*
> *They shot them like partridge in clover*
> *And six of the bravest were slain"*

One of the men who participated in the events of the time, Willie Devins of Aughaged near Grange, tells us: "We got word that there was men shot on the mountain and went up at night searching for the bodies. We got four of them shot into the river. We were fourteen days looking for two other men, Harry Benson and Tommy Langan, but we didn't know if they were shot or on the run. Langan lost an eye in France in the 1st World War and his Daddy was killed in the same war. Anyway, there was a man on the mountain, Michael Watters, looking after sheep... the dogs wouldn't come when he called them and he found them barking at this hole. When Watters looked down, he saw four shoes up — they had been shot and dumped into the hole. Dr. Moran from Cashelgarron was the local doctor, he was out in the 1st World War. When he examined the bodies, he said, 'I've been on the battlefields of France and Flanders but never have I seen anything like this; never was it known for a bayonet to go through a dead man.' They cut them up with bayonets and them dead."

The Freestaters overran Rahelly Camp and took over the Glebe House in Moneygold which now belongs to Frank O'Connor and family; Frank can still point out the positions where the machine guns were

134

mounted in the gable of the house at that time. Martin Bernard Mc Gowan of Glenade, veteran of the War of Independence now took over Seamus Devin's position as O/C No.1 Brigade, Third Western Division I.R.A.

It was a sad fact of the Civil War that Irishman inflicted as much atrocity on brother Irishman as was ever done by the Black and Tans. The carnage continued as the new State endured its birth pains until in May 1923 de Valera gave the Republicans the order to lay down their arms. Millions of pounds worth of property had been destroyed, hundreds of lives lost and thousands imprisoned but the saddest loss was the deaths of so many brave men who, side by side, had beaten England and the Black and Tans and made a break with Britain possible.

Tommy Mc Cann, Northern Divisional Adjutant and veteran of the War of Independence in a letter to his sister dated 21/12/'22 gives us a glimpse of the feelings of these veterans at the time:

"…. Things are quiet here, the imperial troops have not been around for some time so for the moment we have peace; but of course they'll come again and then probably some other veteran of the Black and Tan war will have to make the supreme sacrifice for the Republic. Oh, when will it end, when will the Irish people see the crimes commited in their name by a gang of renegades? I see they have murdered seven more poor fellows — all for the Free State, we are told; no, these things are done in order that Ireland will be bound more firmly to the Empire than it has ever been before. If people would only think! Lord Gleneavy, better known as Sir James Campbell, Orangeman and Freemason, chairman of the Senate, eighteen Freemasons nominated for the Senate by Cosgrave. Liam Mellows and Rory O'Connor in prison graves and the lion-hearted de Valera hunted like a wild beast and all this done in the name of the Irish people. Oh, God that we should live to see the day!….."

The number of military prisoners in the Freestate was soon to be estimated at over 11,000, with several men from this area including my father among them. The author of the above letter, Tommy Mc Cann, Eddie Harkin, Petie Mc Gowan, Patrick Mc Gowan, Thady Conway, all of Mullaghmore, Willie Devins, Grange, Dan Jones, Streedagh, Mick Mc Gowan, Carns, (later to win a Silver Star for distinguished service in the U.S. Army), Paddy Blaney, Lisadell, Petie "Red" Gilmartin, Charlie Gilmartin, Carnduff and hundreds of others were arrested in a countrywide swoop by Freestate soldiers in January 1923.

Tommy McCann's next letter was written from Hut 19 in Finner Camp near Bundoran, where he was taken with most of the internees from this area, before being transferred to Tintown, Co. Kildare. The

Mullaghmore men were held prisoner in Classiebawn Castle, which was then garrisoned by the Freestate army,before being transferred to Finner. Some were released here, but most were held for some time here before being transferred to internment camps in Newbridge, Tintown and other parts of the country.

My father was a taciturn man who spoke very little about his experiences during these troubled times but he would occasionally tell about some of the funnier little incidents which happened in these camps. Like the one about the warders who were guarding the prisoners, who would sometimes use the tin can which served as a urinal for the prisoners. This was somewhat of a routine, so in anticipation of his next visit the men procured a length of wire which they stuck into an electrical socket, attaching the other end to the tin can. The warder nearly jumped through the roof when the stream of urine came in contact with the electrical current, causing a severe shock to the mans waterworks and mental state, not to mention the threat to potential descendents.

One of the prisoners, Dan Jones, a tailor from Streedagh, spent his time making blankets and mending clothes for his fellow inmates. He was "stone deaf" and as he couldn't hear his name being called at roll-call, his brother used to pluck his sleeve to indicate that he should answer. When the other prisoners caught on to this they would pull his coat at the wrong time and he would shout 'Annseo' out of turn, much to the annoyance of the prison guards and to the great amusement of his fellow cellmates.

Another amusing incident which had rather more serious consequences at the time was brought about by the sending of a note by a Mullaghmore internee to Lizzie Love, a local Cumainn na mBan member, asking her to take good care of the 'pet hen'. When the prison guards discovered the note they became immediately suspicious that the object of the note's attentions was a code and something much more sinister than a pet hen. They took the sender of the note outside, forcing him on his knees, advising him to say his last prayers and threatening to shoot him on the spot if he wouldn't reveal the secret identity of the pet hen. A party of soldiers were despatched to Lizzie's house and her home, byres and gardens were torn asunder and searched. The note-writer's home was "turned up-side down" too but nothing was found; we are assured that there really was a "pet hen" which escaped detection – hidden in the cow's byre in the hay manger!

On the 24th of May 1923, de Valera, declaring that, "military victory must be allowed to rest for the moment with those who have destroyed the Republic", called for a dumping of arms and so the Civil

War came to an end. Time hung heavy now for my father and the other prisoners, detained at this time in Tintown internment camp. With the state of war now over, the men expected to be released momentarily but this was not to be; in August the Freestate government passed the Emergency Powers Act allowing them to detain the internees indefinitely. Later in August Cumann na nGaedheal was returned to power and hope of an early release faded. On the 14th of October several hundred Republican prisoners went on hunger strike, these included my father, Willie Devins, Tommy Mc Cann and many more of the local men.

In a letter written on 17 December from Hut 15, No. 3 Camp, Tintown, Mc Cann echoed the feelings of his fellow prisoners when he wrote,

"I wonder what pleasure it can give our jailers, the keeping of us away from our homes and all that we hold dear during this holy season......... however I suppose we must suffer on, God in His own good time will give us our freedom......."

His next letter, postmarked Dublin and written on the 21st December brought the good news,

"I was released yesterday together with the four other boys from my own place, so you see our Christmas will be happy after all...."

Johnny Barry of Mullaghmore, twelve years old at the time remembers that the imprisoned men, "were missed badly when it came time to make the ricks", and remembers Pat Kelly putting him up to, "tramp the rick"; Pat had taken over the running of the farm in my father's absence and even the twelve year olds had work to do. He remembered too the neighbours coming to the house to welcome my father home when he was released with many of the other prisoners at the end of 1923 following the pressure exerted by the hungerstrikes, which lasted from the 14th of October to the 23rd of November and resulted in the deaths of two men, Andy Sullivan and Joseph Lacey.

Cairns,
2/12/02

My dear Sister,
I'm sure you wont think me for this letter now seeing that its so long overdue however I hope youll forgive me for the long delay.
I thought I'd have seen you last summer as I intrnda going there for a few days but the terrible war prevented that. if peace comes & that I'm alright I'll surely go.
Things are quiet here now

the imperial troops have not been round for some time. so that for the moment we have peace. but of course thayll come again & then probably some either return of the Black & Tan You was will have to make the supreme sacrifice for the Republic. Oh! when will it end. when will the Irish people see the crimes commited in their name by a gang of renegades. I see they have murdered seven more poor fellows. all for the Free State. we are told. no, these things are done in order that Ireland shall be bound more firmly

to the Empire than it hasever
been. Before. Of people would
only think. Lord Glenavy,
better known as Sir James Campbell,
Brangeman & Freemason, chairman of
the senate, eighteen Freemasons
nominated for the senate by bygone.
Liam Mellows & Rory O'Connor
prison graves and the blackest
DeValera hunted like a wild
beast & all this done in the
name of the Irish people
Oh? God that we should
live to see the day.

But enough of this. I won't
bother you any more with such
thoughts, of a mind made
bitter by the events taking

place all around. We are
expecting M.B. home some of
these days I haint seen her
since she went to town. I con't go
there you see, we are all
fairly well, John & Mary are
getting very big. the Abint had
any letter from America as yet
I hope they'll write so I'll it will
know how they are. I hope
this letter will find you very
well & that it will reach you
before xmas which I doubt, as
the mails are delayed a good deal
lately. I don't think there is
any more I have to say now.
Wishing you a happy Xmas &
bright New Year, from your

Your
loving Brother
Conor

Plan of Bay
in Drawing room.

Classiebawn Castle as it might have been had this artists impression dated 1867, by the architect Rawson Carroll, been accepted.

Sketch: Courtesy of Broadlands Archives

AFTER THE CIVIL WAR

The aftermath of the civil war is an area that has largely been ignored by historians. Maybe it was not exciting enough when compared with events which ended in 1923. I have spoken to many men who lived through this period and feel that they too deserve their place in history as they too suffered for their beliefs but still were willing and prepared to carry on the struggle for freedom when and where needed. I will attempt to redress in some small way this neglect in the following pages.

The Republican side may have been physically beaten but most still stood to their ideals and beliefs and were true to Sinn Fein and de Valera. Discontent was not confined to the defeated I.R.A. and was to be found too in other places; in March 1924 Free State army officers mutinied, demanding an end to demobilisation and a declaration of the Free State government's intention to achieve an Irish Republic. The fact that there were large numbers of young men in every country house in the area with no prospects of employment encouraged in many a more pragmatic acceptance of the new order and large numbers joined the new Army and "Civic Guards". In this area, the men of the "Old I.R.A.", having "done their bit", now moved into the background and took only an advisory part when drilling and weapons training continued as a new generation of young men emerged to rekindle the dream of a "bold Republic". These veterans continued to be involved in social issues and one of the strangest of these was the struggle involving the tarring of "Denis's Hill". It's difficult for us today to understand what all the fuss was about but this fight which happened in the early '30's was taken very seriously by the residents of Mullaghmore, Cliffoney, Bunduff, Creevykeel,etc.

To put the incident in perspective we must bring our minds back to this time and visualise the rough stone paved country roads dotted with ass and horse drawn carts driven by men bringing milk to the creamery or turf home from the bog, some drawing supplies from Sligo to the local shops; hardly a motor car to be seen anywhere! When word went out that the Council were about to tar "Denis's Hill", there was uproar. This madness had to be stopped! How were the asses and horses going to negotiate the hill in their iron shod feet on this new smooth surface? How indeed? In frosty weather one could reasonably suppose that the commerce of the whole countryside would grind to a complete halt. Committees were formed; Eddie Harkin, Charlie Gilmartin, Petie

McGowan, Thady Conway and nine or ten more formed the nucleus of resistance in this immediate area.

The authorities were determined to go ahead and men signing on the dole were re-directed to Eddie Mc Gloin to report for work. This really put the cat among the pigeons as if the order was accepted and the men went to work they would be going against their principles, not to mention putting themselves in opposition to their neighbours. On the other hand, if they didn't go to work,they would lose the few bob of dole as they were refusing to work. Never mind! A united front was presented and no workmen could be found to participate in the hated project.

The Council, being just as determined to go ahead with the job, hired men from Grange and commenced to draw materials from Hoey's quarry. On the morning the work was to commence, the local men converged on the site and scuffles broke out, some of the men, "gave the ganger a bit of a 'crunging' and threatened him". The work was stopped; Eddie Harkin gave a speech and he and Bernie Barry (later to become interned in 1939 and later still, a Sinn Fein councillor for the area) were arrested and released. The row tapered off and everyone went home, satisfied with a good morning's work, which resulted in the postponement of the road-tarring for many years. When it was eventually tarred, a band of only eight feet wide in the centre of the road was covered; a four feet wide strip was left at either side of the road for horse and ass drawn traffic. Cars were so scarce then, that not a lot of consideraton was given to them; on the odd occasion when two cars would meet, one or the other would have to get off the tarred strip in the middle to allow the other to pass. A wider band of tarred surface was laid on the main Sligo Bundoran road with rough strips on either side, similar to the side roads for non motorized trafic. The "water tables" beside these strips were maintained in those days by local men who were paid on contract by the mile to keep them clear.

These disputes about the tarring of the roads were going on all over the country. In some areas, when the tarring went ahead despite local opposition, locals went out at night with picks and shovels and lifted the paving which had been laid by the workmen on the previous day. Work was scarce in the twenties and thirties and to complicate matters, a mans political persuasion could make the difference in whether he worked or not. Veterans of that era will still talk about losing jobs because they didn't support one political candidate or another, belong to one political party or another or if they didn't buy their groceries in certain shops.

Veterans of the War of Independence and Civil War became involved in the running of the Mullaghmore Races for a time and many

Republican names can be recognised in a report in the Sligo Champion on the races to be held on Wednesday, July 7th 1926:

"Officials; President, Mr. P. Burke; Secs. Bernie Conway and Petie Mc Gowan; Treasurer. Mr. Willie Mc Cormack; Judge Mr. R. Kerins; Starter, Mr. J. Gilmartin; Clerk of Scales, Mr. Eugene Gilbride; Handicapper, E. Condell, 37 Drumcondra Rd. Dublin; Committee: Martin Bernard Mc Gowan, T.D., R. Wymbs, Charlie Mc Garrigle, D. Devins, T. Gilmartin, P. Farrell, Tommy Hannon, Bernie Kelly, James Gorman, Mac Barry, T. Meehan, J. Gilmartin, J. Curneen, Charlie Gilmartin, Johnny Barry and Thady Conway."

The good weather must have had a pleasing effect on the "Champion" reporter as he opened the report on the meeting in flowery language:

"The weather was perfect. The mountains of Sligo and Mayo from Slieve League around by Benbulben and to Neifean More, formed a circle of beauty unsurpassed throughout the length and breadth of Ireland. About three thousand people were present, some of whom came from places as far apart as Galway, Dublin and Derry. Each of the six races were kenly contested."

THE FIRST RACE, THE CLIFFONEY PLATE of £25 was won by Mr. E. Browne's Curfew with Mr. J. Gray's Butterfly coming in second.

SECOND RACE; THE MULLAGHMORE PLATE OF £15, 2nd, £2. Mr. J. Harans, Holy City, 1st and Mr. T. Gillespie's, Little Peter, 2nd. Also ran; Mr. J. Dolan's, Beauty and Mr. J. Harans, Red Apple.

THIRD RACE; BENBULBIN PLATE OF £25. Mr. E. Browne's, Cappy Ricks came 1st and Mr. J. Deane's, Ambush 2nd.

FOURTH RACE; THE CREEVYKEEL PLATE OF £10. Confined to Ahamlish parish for ponies 14 hands and under. 1st, Mr. J. Mc Gowan's, Black Prince, 2nd, Mr. Michael Clancy's, Rebel Lad and 3rd Mr. L. McGowans, Angelina.

ALSO RAN; Mr. E. O'Connor's Blackberry, Mr. P. Mc Sharry's, Paddy and Mr. H. Mc Cormack's, True Light. "A very exciting race, Black Prince winning by half a length from Rebel Lad."

OTHER WINNERS IN THE OTHER RACES WERE; Mr. B. Doherty's, The Visitor; Mr. E. O'Connor's, Blackberry.

I.R.A., VOLUNTEERS AND BLUESHIRTS

In the eyes of many, young and old, Ireland was only partly free and there was still work to be done. From the mid '20s on, Johnny Barry with his friends, Pa Dowdican, Jimmy Barry and dozens of young men from Cliffoney and surrounding areas would meet near the home of that old veteran of Carnduff, Charlie Gilmartin, for weapons practice or at the racecourse flats, or the Treilya for arms and foot drill under Martin Bernard McGowan of Glenade. Johnny recalled my father showing him how to make a "dump" for three rifles belonging to their unit. It was made of galvanised iron and wood and concealed by Johnny and Pa Dowdican in a stone ditch at a field known as the "Big Garden".

Dev remained as de facto head of the I.R.A. and as leader of the abstentionist Sinn Fein party with 44 seats. In a gradual derogation of principle he resigned as President of Sinn Fein and formed the Fianna Fail party in 1926; after the elections of 1927 he still refused to take the oath of allegiance to a "foreign power"; in August he subscribed to the necessary form of the oath declaring it "merely an empty political formula" and walked into Dáil Eireann with 42 of his followers.

Even though Dev. had now moved to a more constitutional position he straddled the fence quite successfully and held on to I.R.A. support. Johnny and his comrades continued to drill and train in the belief that there was work still to be done in achieving the dream of a thirty two county Republic. Looking back in later years, Johnny was to come to the belief that they were used by de Valera for publicity and as a threat on the road to gaining power. Johnny may be considered to be right in this cynical manipulation theory in light of Lemass's declaration of Fianna Fail in 1928 as a "slightly constitutional party", further declaring their objective of establishing a republican government in Ireland and going on to state "if that can be done by the present methods we have, we will be very pleased, but, if not, we would not confine ourselves to them".

Sinn Fein and the I.R.A supported Dev in his bid for power at the general election of 1932 and Johnny remembers canvassing in this area with Shaw Carty of Bundoran advising people how to vote and arranging lifts to the polling booths for older people. Dev swept into power, winning 72 seats to Cumainn na nGaedheal's 57 and formed the first Fianna Fail government shortly afterwards.

It was a time now for far reaching change as Dev gradually distanced himself from old comrades and political alliances. From this point on constitutional politics was going to be the only vehicle for change in the Free State! Initially, with Dev's rise to power, pressure on the I.R.A.

eased; drilling and training became more open as the Civic Guards turned a blind eye to their activities. As time went on though it became obvious that the I.R.A. no longer suited Dev's purposes, his association with the organisation was now becoming an embarrassment. As a preliminary to the eventual banning of the organisation, the Volunteers were formed with the intention of giving young men an option for legal military service and to cause an erosion of support for the I.R.A. Further, as Dev didn't trust the allegiance of what was essentially a Freestate army, the recruitment of an army that would be loyal to him would be a two-headed spear. With an eventual membership of 40,000 men, this represented a very formidable spear indeed.

Andrew Conway of Cliffoney, recently returned from America, was given a commission in the army and became local organiser of the Volunteers. An activist of the time recalled the night when Conway, "took two big cases of rifles into an assembly of I.R.A. in Cliffoney Hall offering them to anyone who would join" (the Volunteers). Pressure was now also exerted by the authorities on young men in the I.R.A. to join the new force. Johnny Barry of Mullaghmore and Thomas Barry of Bunduff were the first of many to join the Volunteers from this area.

On the other hand the Army Comrades Association, commonly known as the Blueshirts, staunchly loyal to Cumainn na nGaedheal and a Free State, rose to prominence at this time. Clashes between members of this organisation and the Volunteers and I.R.A. contributed to an escalation of tensions for some time. Again, when we take a look at events of this time we must visualize a countryside very much different from that of today in that the indigenous population of families and young men was much more dense than today. The heavy outward flow of emigrants which ended in the late '50s had yet to take its toll. Political tensions were high, confrontations between opposing political factions were common, fist fights were frequent and served as an outlet of energy among the masses of unemployed young men.

Michael Leonard of Bunduff, a member of the Volunteers, told me that, "we were getting fourteen shillings a week but ye'd want to have yer boxing gloves on"; he tells us about an incident that happened at Cliffoney hall c.1933, which gives a vivid illustration of these turbulent times:

"We had our training in Cliffoney Hall and this time Andrew Conway sent word to all members to be at last Mass on Sunday in uniform. We all headed away for Cliffoney any way, meself and Pa Mc Cannon, Jose Harrison, Michael "Patsy" Harrison, Jack "Patsy", Michael McGowan, Tim Gonigle, Dan Herrity, Andy "Jack" Harrison, Danny Foley, John Leydon. Anyway, Conway informed us that the Blueshirts were going to take over the Hall that night but that we weren't going to let them. "We have the key", says he, "so be up here tonight and we'll show them".

We assembled at the Crossroads that night and marched to Cliffoney where we were joined by other units. In we went to the hall and started drilling. We weren't long at it 'till Pakie Mc Cannon came to the door and demanded the key; Big Thomas Barry and Pa McCannon were first to the door and refused to give over the key. That was alright, we continued drilling and the next thing we knew the windows were put in with stones – Dan, Jose Harrison's brother was hurt with glass. Next to arrive was Fr. Kane, he had a funny way of speaking; 'Oh, tut, tut, tut', he said, 'will ye not give over the hall to them'. Andrew Conway refused".

"About twelve o'clock we formed outside and marched towards Bunduff; the Blueshirts were massed outside Charlie Mc Cannons armed with sticks and stones. They fired at us but it went over our heads and no-one was hit". There was another confrontation on the following Wednesday and it's interesting to note that I.R.A. units led by Terry Joe McSharry of Ballintrilick and 'Big' Bernie Barry of Bunduff were stationed in the fields behind the hall to give assistance to the Volunteers if it was needed.

The wounds inflicted by the Civil War were unhealed and very fresh at this time. Blueshirts battled with the I.R.A and both factions were now alienated from the de Valera government. An already tense situation was aggravated as the "Economic War" with England intensified and prices for cattle fell through the floor. A local man who marched with General Eoin O'Duffy's Blueshirts at different venues in North Sligo told me how he felt at the time:

"Sure it was a grand country before the Troubles – before there was anyone shot or killed in the country. I joined the Blueshirts to back up Cumainn na Gaedhel, they were the best and dacentest party. Fine Gael followers was more of a kind of people to try and have something, Dev's crowd was a kind of riff-raff, the smallest in the place – have it anyway no matter how you got it!" The feeling of many of these men was that Dev was a foreigner and a manipulator, "he didn't fight or need to fight, he was at the devilment with the pen."

The Blueshirts in this area marched under the leadership of Terry Connolly, an ex-army man; quite often they carried sticks and other weapons and, "we weren't a bit afraid to use them if it came to the point. There was a few of our crowd beaten up y'know and that's what rose the right trouble." The feeling was that concessions such as dole was given to the poorer classes, men with two cows now got farmers dole, the men with four cows or so, "got nothing". "When Dev got in, he wouldn't let the cattle over to England with the result that there was no price for cattle— the best of calves were sold for three pounds ten shillings in the fair of Kinlough, before that you'd get sixteen pounds for a year old calf. It left a lot of poor people in the country and mind you, anyone that lost money that time – he never forgot it."

People, as neighbours must, eventually worked out their differences; hostilities that were inevitable as a result of the Civil War cooled as the years went on and the ballot box became the only weapon used between the Soldiers of Destiny and the Blueshirts. The names of Collins and Beal na mBlath and what they mean can now be scrutinized with a more dispassionate gaze as old animosities and divisions melt away.

The Volunteers evolved into the L.D.F. and eventually became the F.C.A., an organisation which is still in existence and with which I served for some years in the late fifties, until my departure for the U.S.A. in 1961. Blueshirt influence flourished in the area for awhile and eventually faded in the late thirties. It is only recently that the bitter divisions of these years have quite faded into insignificance and must now be remembered, even by the older survivors of the period, as the inevitable birth pains of a new state.

In 1939, a bombing campaign carried out by the I.R.A. in England resulted in many deaths, injuries and damage to property. Two Irishmen were executed as a result of this and many imprisoned; two of those imprisoned were local men Terry Joe Mc Sharry and Pakie Connolly of Castlegal who spent many years in prison in Maidstone and the Isle of Wight. Pakie was caught with bomb making equipment. Mc Sharry operated a supply route from Scotland and was given a sentence of fifteen years when he too was discovered with a cache of explosives. In 1920 Pakie, a small boy at the time, was asleep in the same room as his grandfather on the night the old man was shot dead by Captain Small, during a raid on the family home during the War of Independence. His uncle was shot dead while defending Finner Camp for the Republican forces during the Civil War.

Pressure for internment in Ireland increased as the bombing campaign in England continued and as tensions in Ireland were heightened with the death by hungerstrike of Darcy and Mc Neela in April 1940. The discovery of a transmitter used for communicating with the German Abwehr and the capture of Hermann Goertz when he landed by parachute in Co. Meath led to fears that the I.R.A. might help to facilitate a landing in Ireland of German forces wishing to establish a back door to England. The radio announcer, Lord Haw Haw, in one of his famous broadcasts, declared, to the Irish people, however, that the Germans had no interest in Ireland, assuring them that German interests lay in "oil wells not holy wells".

Empowered by the Emergency Powers Bill, the authorities swooped on the early morning of the 4th of June, interning many young men countrywide; these included two Bunduff men, "Big" Bernie Barry and Hubert Barry. They served many years of internment before being released. Bernie came to know the aforementioned Goertz while in prison and became quite friendly with him.

Despite persecution, the I.R.A. and Sinn Fein have survived as a potent force to this day, but the arrests and internment throughout the country of the leaders, during this period, marked their end as a force of influence or change in politics in the south of Ireland.

THE COAST WATCH SERVICE

On the outbreak of World War II the Dept. of Defence set up the Marine and Coastwatching service under the aegis of the Volunteer force with a view to protecting Ireland's neutrality. This was known as the "Emergency" and they were the eyes of the Irish nation, their brief being to monitor sea and air traffic and report all movements to their Army superiors. Lookout posts were erected along the coast at "all strategic locations where combatant troops could conceivably be landed". L.O.P.s were erected at Raughley, Aughris, Lenadoon and Mullaghmore.

The words EIRE in letters ten yards high were cut into the field at the back of Mullaghmore on Johnny Barry's hill. The cutaway letters were then filled in with whitewashed flagstones to warn approaching aircraft and shipping that they were approaching a neutral Ireland. Pilots who had crash landed confirmed that these signs, which were positioned all around the coast, were very useful aids to navigation.

Recruitment practice was to give first preference to old I.R.A. men, the age limit being widened for them to allow their entry as a recognition of their service during the War of Independence. Second preference went to members of de Valera's Volunteer force and third preference to members of Fianna Fail. On the 3rd of September 1939, Andrew Conway, area commander of the Volunteers, and Gus Mulligan, Captain in the Regular Army arrived at our house to recruit my father for service. He and a neighbour, Thady Conway, went immediately to the stone tower at the top of the Quay Road where local men had stood watch in the previous world war. A bell tent was erected as temporary accomodation and this was used until the coastwatchers hut was erected the following year on James Rourke's land, where it's ruin can still be seen.

The Tower was used during the First World War as a look-out post and as an extension of the Coastguard service. Alfie Pearson, gatehouse keeper to Classiebawn, along with local men, James Rourke, James

Leonard and William "Stoker" Leydon patrolled the coast from Streedagh to Ballyshannon and reported to the Coastguards. Local people recalled that it had a good fireplace and fire then and was a good place to "ramble".

During the Second World War, the men served on two man teams on twelve hour shifts, keeping a lookout for and noting all shipping and aircraft traffic in their area. Most of the air traffic in this area would have been from Allied bases in Northern Ireland. To enable the men to make accurate identifications they were required to recognise the silhouettes of ships and aircraft of all nations. They were also required to recognise all flags and to receive and send Morse code. Each L.O.P. was provided with a logbook, telephone, telescope and binoculars, fixed compass card, Admiralty charts, silhouettes of ships and aircraft, morse lamps, semaphore flags and a bicycle. The bicycle was used in the early stages before the telephone lines were completed to convey a coastwatcher to the nearest telephone in case of urgency.

Josie Harrison, was made corporal in charge of the unit. Other members serving in this period were Dan Heraughty, Mick Gilmartin, Owenie Conway, Jimmy Dowdican, Pa Mc Cannon, Jim Moffit, Petie Mc Gowan and Thady Conway. Each watcher received Army pay of two shillings a day (10p) and an extra half a crown (12$\frac{1}{2}$ p) as a basic subsistence allowance. Josie Harrison recalls that the most tragic happening of the time was the crash landing of an American flying Fortress in the Atlantic off Mullaghmore Head. He remembered seeing the crew walking on the wings before the great bomber slid beneath the waves taking all on board with her. (See Chapter 1) A mine which came ashore on the Long Flag at the back of Mullaghmore caused a major furore until it was detonated by the bomb squad. Everyone living on the Hill Road was evacuated to houses in the front of the village as a precaution against flying glass or debris.

It is much more difficult to elicit information on a visitation from the ghostly otherworld which happened on a wild and wintery January night. On being relieved of their watch in the morning, Pa Mc Cannon and Jim Moffit, the two men on duty on this January night, claimed that they had witnessed a headless man parading back and forth all night along Rourkes ditch, while from the sloping hillside below came a wailing and crying they had never heard before or ever experienced again after that night. The strange occurences became much more understandable when the men on being relieved of their watch in the morning, were told that John Hannon, proprietor of Hannon's Hotel and owner of the fence where the ghostly apparition had been seen, had died earlier in the night in a Dublin hospital.

Neighbours claim that his death was as a result of his cutting down a lone whitethorn tree in a lane near this field some days earlier, despite being warned of the possible consequences. The coastwatching hut is built near an old court tomb and some may say that this offers an explanation of why there were so many unusual occurences here. On different other occasions, other men on watch claimed to have heard noises and seen figures which presaged sudden deaths in the village. Unbelievers may scoff, but who knows what shadowy spirits keep watch in the faerie night, even today, as the ruin of the coastwatchers hut stares out to sea with vacant ghostly eyes as it awaits the arrival of another "Emergency"?

MOUNTBATTEN ASSASSINATION

Southern Ireland has been remarkably stable since its formation, the only threat to that stability now being the ongoing violence in Northern Ireland where a civil resistance campaign which started there in 1969 has evolved into an armed struggle by the Sinn Fein/I.R.A. of today, who demand unification of the island and a British withdrawal from the North of Ireland. The violence is mostly confined to the six northeastern counties but occasionally spills across the border. Such was the case with the assasination of Mountbatten off Mullaghmore Head on Aug. 27 1979 — the explosion that was heard around the world.

Occupiers of Classiebawn were for the most part, absentee landlords and the subjects of much anger from time to time, most notably during Land League times and also in the period leading up to and during the War of Independence. During my lifetime though there were no disturbances, which was probably due in large part to the good relations which existed between the Brackens, gamekeepers and caretakers of the estate, and the local population. Mountbatten and his family, absent for many years had started to come on a regular basis on annual holidays to visit Classiebawn and the Mullaghmore estates. Apart from the flying of the house flag from a turret on the castle and the employment of some local people as house staff, their arrival created no great stir. Living in such an isolated location it was not unusual that Mountbatten and his guests had little contact with the affairs or social life of the village. He and his family did, however, visit the harbour frequently, spending a considerable amount of time fishing and pleasure cruising in his timber built pleasure boat, the Shadow V, built by local boatbuilders, the Mc Canns' of Milk Harbour and maintained by Rodney Lomax of Lomax Boats, Mullaghmore.

150

Given the campaign in Northern Ireland it was almost inevitable that this grandson of Queen Victoria, uncle of Prince Philip, retired Admiral of the Fleet, one time Commander of Allied forces in Southeast Asia, last Viceroy of India, First Sea Lord, and Chief of Defence Staff would have been a prime target for some kind of political demonstration. Shadow V had narrowly escaped sinking when she had been bored under the waterline with an auger some years previously; this might have served as a warning, but it was generally dismissed as merely an act of vandalism and of no significance.

Mountbatten scorned a major security presence and even though the authorities insisted on some protection, he wanted his Special Branch minders out of sight, saying that he was "used to giving orders, not taking them". Government papers released recently under the thirty year rule, revealed that in 1960, questions were raised with the Gardai by Mountbattens agent, Patrick O'Grady, about the Earl's safety. The conclusion reached in the reply was that, "While everything points to the fact that no attack of any kind on the Earl, by subversive elements was at any time contemplated, it would, in my opinion, be asking too much to say in effect that we can guarantee his safety while in this country." It is not clear which subversives he was under threat from, as in this article it indicates that he (Mountbatten) was not favoured by such bodies as the League of Empire Loyalists, who felt that his views on partition were too liberal and that he was "very friendly disposed towards the Catholic clergy, particularly the Jesuits." This, of course was a misconception and may have arisen because the castle was rented to Jesuits in the 1950's, as it was to many other groups, for hard cash.

Local whisperings that Mountbatten was homosexual are given credibility by claims in Gordon Winter's book, 'Secrets of the Royals' that it was "no secret that Mountbatten was a bisexual". It is also claimed in this book that British Intelligence leaked rumours to authors and journalists that the Earl was a Soviet sympathiser who secretly helped the Russians during the Cold War. Just as incredible is the claim that he was killed on the order of the K.G.B. who feared that he was on the point of disclosing his role as a Russian agent. These are matters for speculation but certainly all could not have been what it seemed in that fateful Summer of 1979. Behind the serene, peaceful appearance of the tranquil, picturesque village of Mullaghmore, it seems that other passions simmered and his movements were surely monitored by secret watchful eyes.

The weather had been wet and windy for most of the month of August, unpleasant for pleasure craft but ideal for drift netting for salmon. The salmon, apparently weren't aware of this and the pickin's were slim for Paul Maxwell and myself crewing on Freddy Conaghan's half decker, the "Kilkilloge". Paul was a pleasant lad who loved Mullaghmore and the sea and held a summer job as boatman on the Shadow V. Rough weather and Paul did not agree and he suffered with seasickness on our last night at the salmon. When he bade the salmon fishing and the "Kilkilloge" goodbye, we were not to know then that it was for the last time.

Monday came in bright and clear and it looked like there might at last be some good weather ahead. Mountbatten and his family were among the many holidaymakers putting to sea and everyone on board was in a good humour as Paul steered the Shadow V around Mullaghmore Head and past Thumb Rock to the fishing ground. Martin Dowdican worked the hay and watched from his field on the heights overlooking the bay as the green boat moved towards the lobster pot markers outside of Oillean Roudh. Suddenly there was a massive bang and a fountain of water and debris blasted into the air. Windows shook as far away as Cliffoney and Bunduff; no-one in this area had experienced anything like it since the time when the Army exploded the mine which had been washed ashore on the Long Flag at the back of Mullaghmore during the closing months of World War II. Windows vibrated and people for miles around looked up from their work, wondering what it was that had made such a great noise. Finbarr Hegarty looked up from his work on the pier in shocked amazement at the sound, in time to see fragments of the Shadow V falling back to earth.

Four died on that day; Mountbatten, his grandson Nicholas, Lady Brabourne and Paul Maxwell. Lady Patricia, her husband and Timothy were badly injured, but survived. Fortunately for them, the day was good and rescue boats were on the spot immediately. If the incident had happened any time in the bad weather of the preceding days and weeks it is more than likely that no-one would have survived as there would not have been so many small craft about. Splintered planks and fragmented, shattered wood, no bigger than matchsticks and barely recognisable as part of a boat were picked up by fishing boats for days after the explosion and pieced together by Gardai in an effort to find out more about what had happened. On the same day as the Mountbatten killing, the British army suffered the biggest number of casualties in a single incident in the North of Ireland, when eighteen British soldiers were killed in an explosion in Warrenpoint Co. Down. The I.R.A. claimed responsibility for both incidents.

The upheavels caused by the hunger strikes in Long Kesh sent shock waves southward again in 1981 as tens of thousands took to the streets in sympathy with Bobby Sands and his comrades, on hunger strike in Long Kesh; Classiebawn castle was taken over in a demonstration designed to bring attention to the hunger strikes; committees were formed, masses said and black flag vigils held in Sligo town, in north Sligo and in towns and villages all over Ireland as once again history repeated itself. The spectre of Irishmen on hunger strike in English jails in the ultimate form of protest, was nothing new, and was seen by many as being reminiscent of an earlier period in our history when Thomas Ashe, Terence McSwiney and local men took on a similar form of protest.

Bobby Sands elected as M.P. for Fermanagh-South Tyrone in April, while still on hunger-strike, compared with Terence McSwiney, T.D. also an elected representative of the people who died on Oct. 20th 1920 following seventy four days on a similar fast. One month after his election, on the 5th May, Bobby Sands died after sixty six days without food. Another striker, Joe McDonnell, ran for election in the Sligo-Leitrim constituency in the general election held in June, almost gaining a seat when he polled over 5,000 votes. Ten of the hunger strikers died before the protest came to an end in October. The events of 1981 had widespread repercussions in political terms; in the associated disturbances sixty one people were killed including thirty members of the armed forces in the north of Ireland.

In 1983, on the second anniversary of the hunger-strikes, Mullaghmore reluctantly became once again the focus of world attention, when a commemmoration planned on the anniversary of the hungerstrikes was condemned as an anti-Mountbatten affair by Loyalist politicians Paisley and Molyneaux. Despite dire warnings of violence and public disorder the event went off quietly with dozens of marching bands and brightly coloured banners marching into Mullaghmore The gathering was addressed by members of the families of the hunger-strikers and by local Councillors, Tommy Higgins, Harry Blaney, Larry McGowan and Declan Bree (now a T.D).

The most recent spillover of the Northern troubles into this area was a much more sordid and macabre affair which came to light when the body of Margaret Perry of Portadown was discovered buried in the Mullaghmore woods in June 1992. The story which then came to light involved the I.R.A., R.U.C., Special Branch, British Intelligence and M.I.5 in a sordid chain of events which revealed brutality, murder, intrigue and subversion of justice at the highest levels of government.

The gruesome discovery, in the woods underneath Classiebawn Castle, was made when the I.R.A. informed a local priest of the whereabouts of the body and he in turn informed the authorities. The I.R.A.'s involvement in the affair came about when they discovered that one of their members, the boyfriend of the dead woman, Gregory Burns, was a police informer. Burns admitted recruiting two accomplices to assist in the murder when she threatened to expose his deception to the I.R.A. The I.R.A. allege that in June 1991, at the woods near Mullaghmore, Starrs "overpowered her, bound her hands and gagged her mouth with tape, proceeding to strangle her with the cord from a set of venetian blinds. Believing her to be dead he left to retrieve a shovel from the car and on returning found Margaret Perry alive and struggling. He then beat her around the head with the shovel and buried her in a shallow grave." The next day Starrs and Dignam returned to the scene of the murder as Starrs had remembered he had left the tape which he had used to gag the woman and feared his fingerprints might be found on it.

Shortly after this Dignam was routinely arrested on another matter by the R.U.C., broke under questioning, admitted the murder and implicated Starrs and Burns. Starrs and Dignam were then passed on to MI5 and recruited as informers on the promise of immunity from prosecution over the killing of Miss Perry. From that point on the three worked as informers, handled by the R.U.C. Special Branch and passing on to them information on I.R.A. personnel and arms dumps. Some months later a Sunday newspaper covering the story of the mystery of the disappearance of Miss Perry, reported that North Armagh Republicans were responsible for her death. On reading this, Burns panicked, contacted his R.I.C. handlers and was instructed by them to "frustrate any possible identification of the womans body".

The three men then returned to the grave in Mullaghmore with the intention of cutting the womans fingers off and smashing her teeth so as to avoid identification by means of fingerprints or dental records, in the event of her being found. "When they got to the grave the head was above ground as a result of the heavy rains so they decided to smash the skull and proceeded to do so with lump hammers". I.R.A. personnel, suspicious for some time of the three men, arrested and interrogated them. They admitted to being informers and to the murder of Miss Perry and pinpointed the location of the grave. The I.R.A. executed the three men and set in train the sequence of events which led to the recovery of the body and the disclosure of the sordid details surounding the whole affair. The Sunday Press of 5th July '92 in reporting the incident, concluded that:

"the British Army is prepared to go to almost any lengths to protect an informer. A top informer will be allowed to involve himself in illegal acts, up to and including murder....... the moment an informer becomes a liability, or of limited use, those who have been handling him are unable to protect him or unwilling to do so." It goes on to say that if "the I.R.A. statement of last week is correct, the R.U.C. knew a year ago, When John Dignam cracked up under interrogation, that Margaret Perry was murdered. They did not inform the Perry family, indeed they carried on insisting that she may have committed suicide. They were prepared to allow her murderer to go free in return for information on the I.R.A. Aidan Starrs whom the I.R.A. allege was also responsible for the brutal murder, was allowed to run around Portadown, a free man". The article concludes that,"the epithet often attached to the North of "the dirty war", has never seemed truer than at the end of this week."

Dirty, indeed! After 800 years of suppression, manipulation and exploitation by a colonial power, as traced in these chapters, and over 3,000 deaths in the last twenty three years, we are still engaged in a downward spiral of violence, murder, intrigue and dirty tricks. Will the realisation of the aspiration for the union of the geographical entity that is the island of Ireland, bring an end at last to these centuries of tragedies which have affected and are affecting our country, the last act of which is now being played out primarily in the six northeastern counties? As yet there is no end in sight as today, as in ages past, the failures of history bear the fruit of the crude violence of rage. The "bell tolls" for us all, as down through the centuries to the present day, outside events over which we have no control, touch each and everyone of us, to some extent, in some way, in every town and village in Ireland. North Sligo, and particularly in recent years, Mullaghmore, has had more than it's share of such tragedy. A study of the local history of an area can be a reflection in miniature of acts played on stages further afield, sending out ripples which affect all our lives. For too many, Yeats' words have as much or more relevance now than when they were written:

"What need you, being come to sense,
But fumble in a greasy till
And add the halfpence to the pence
And prayer to shivering prayer, until
You have dried the marrow from the bone?
For men were born to pray and save:
Romantic Ireland's dead and gone,
It's with O'Leary in the grave."

155

APPENDIX No. II.

(See Vol. I., pp. 178-9.)

The following Census (printed now for the first time), giving the number of inhabitants, English and Irish, in the townlands, parishes, and baronies of the county, together with the names of the Tituladoes, shows the desperate state to which the population of Sligo, town and county, was reduced in 1659, near the close of the Cromwellian regime.

COUNTY OF SLIGOE.

BARONY OF CARBURY.

Parishes.	Townlands.	No. of People.	Tituladoes' Names.	English	Irish
Aghamlish	SligoeTowne	488	Humphrey Booth, gent. Rowland Thomas, gent. Henry Crafford, gent.	130	358
	Ballyconnell	8		2	6
	Lislarry	3			3
	Shrehidagh	13			13
	Grange	27	Thomas Soden, gent.	2	25
	Monidualt	2			2
	Carne	7		2	5
	Cliffney	9			9
	Cryickeele	16			16
	Creenimore	9			9
	Mullaghmore	6			6
	Bunduff	24			24
	Mardneglasse	7			7
	Killsard	21			21
	Derilchan	16			16
	Cloonergo	4			4
	Inismores	3	Philip Sulevane, gent.		3
Drumcliffe	Dunawna	17			17
	Ballyconnell	8			8
	Ballyknocke	10			10
	Dunfuard	10		4	6
	Ballynagallagh	9			9
	The Rosses	28		2	26

CHAPTER 8

Landownership
and
Development

O'Connor Sligo, being the chief landholders in the barony of Carbury, were lords of Mullaghmore and the surrounding areas of the parish of Ahamlish, with the exception of Grange, where the gallowglass O'Harts held land within the O'Connor lordship. The O'Connors and O'Harts were the last of the great old Irish families in this area before the arrival of the usurpers. The rentals of the estates of 1633-6 list the O'Connor lands in Cliffoney as being mortgaged to Lady Blondon, who had an income of £24 from the re-letting. It was described as good arable land with grazing for 88 cows also having "good turffe and six days mowinge". The headland of Killcoroge (Kilkilloge) that is now popularly called Mullaghmore was listed as being part of, "my Lady Cressey's joynter from O'Connor, having an area of 1 qr. and along with the qr. of Drombalre being worth 27 pounds per annum."

Later in 1665 the Book of Survey and Distribution, supported by the 1654 Down Survey maps, list a Lady Dunboyne as being the proprieter of Mullaghmore, Kilculloge and a strip of adjoining land which included Roskeeragh and was known then as Rosculeth. Some of these maps support the oral tradition that Mullaghmore was at one time a tidal island similar to Dernish, with the turf being loaded on boats at Denis's Hill and off-loaded at Port na h-Eoarna near Barry's lane at the woods near the beach in Mullaghmore. Lady Dunboyne is also listed in 1665 as the proprieter of Moneygold, Derry and Drumfad, while O'Connor still held Cliffoney, Bunduff, Clunerko and so on.

The Confiscation of Connaught was at this time put into effect by the Earl of Wentworth, Lord Strafford, who took possesion of most of Donegal and large tracts of Connaught for the crown. In the scramble for land by Cromwellian adventurers and soldiers that followed, Thomas

Soden, Philip Sulevane, Roger Parke and Sir Francis Gore are shown as "Titulados" in the census of 1659, claiming the parish of Ahamlish and large areas of the parish of Drumcliff. According to O'Rourke's History of Sligo, the exception to this was the town and castle of Grange and about 300 acres in the neighbourhood which was passed to Thomas Soden.

One of the big winners in this lottery was Sir Francis Gore, son of Sir Paul Gore whose mother was the niece of the Earl of Strafford. Sir Paul had served under Essex and Mountjoy and had escorted Sir Donough O' Connor, the last of the Irish Chieftains to submit, to Athlone on his way to see Elizabeth. The lands acquired at this time went eventually by succession to the Gore-Booths of Lisadell. Grange and much of the surrounding area went to Roger Parke and Thomas Soden while the winner in this area was Sir John Temple, Master of the Rolls in Ireland at the time of Charles 1. Under William of Orange he was promoted to attorney general for Ireland and Speaker of the Irish House of Commons. He was granted 10,000 acres in Sligo which included 123 acres in and near the town of Sligo, also the parish of Ahamlish to include Inishmurray, Mullaghmore, Cliffoney, Bunduff, Grogagh and other various townlands as far away as Cloughboley in the Maugherow area.

His claim is stated in a case and legal opinion in 1828 by Sir Henry Meredith regarding claims to the Tithes of Ahamlish. The claim is traced from an original grant by the crown in 1666 to,

"William, Earl of Strafford and Thomas Radcliffe, of the Manor, Castle, Town and Lands of Sligoe and several thousand acres throughout the county, several Rectories and among others the Rectory of Ahamlish in said County (the subject matter of this case) were conveyed to these patentees and their heirs and assigns forever."

The claim is traced by stages to a Margaret Trapps in 1694 and on that date,

" Margaret Trapps by deed of this date conveyed all these estates and Rectory of Ahamlish, so conveyed to her by said Dr. John Leslie unto Sir John Temple of East Sheen, to hold to him and his heirs forever......

The legal pretext for the dispossession of the O'Connor Sligo and the grant to the Earl of Strafford is described in a case stated for John Irwin in 1737:

"Donough O'Connor Sligo being feized in fee (inter alia) of the lands of Fannagh one quarter, and one Cartron or Moiety of the lands of Caftlegarron, did, in 1526 for valuable confiderations, mortgage the fame (inter alia) to Lord Vifcount Powerfcourt and others for the term of 99 years, with a claufe of Redemption, That the faid mortgage ..... to be in truft for Dame Joyce Blundell and her affigns; that the faid Joyce Blundell marrying afterwards Francis Little, they in the year 1662, affigned their intereft to

158

Thomas Griffith of Ballinacar ......
    The faid O'Connor, the Mortgagor, being attainted of High Treafon in 1641, the Equity of Redemption was vefted in the Crown, and the fame was (inter alia) granted to William the Earl of Strafford and Thomas Ratcliffe; Radcliffe by will or otherwife, devifed his Moiety to Jofhua Wilfon and Margaret Trapps ....

Sir John died in 1704 and left a son, Henry Temple, who continued to expand the family fortunes. As a child of seven he received an honorary position in the Court of Exchequer worth £2,000 per year; in 1723 he was created the first Viscount Palmerston of Palmerston in County Dublin. It was he who bought Broadlands in Hampshire as a second country estate. He outlived his son and was succeeded by his grandson, the second Viscount Palmerston. The second Viscount who lived from 1739 to 1802 was a typical 18th century aristocrat who inherited from his parents an income of £11,000 a year of which £6,000 came from rentals from his properties in Sligo and Ahamlish. He spent £23,000 on the aforementioned Broadlands, making it into a magnificent residence. In Co. Sligo his properties were managed by agents and middlemen. Even though a high proportion of their incomes came from the Sligo estates, "neither he nor the first Viscount had any feelings towards their Irish tenants and never invested any money in their lands in Sligo," according to the biographer, Joseph Ridley. In fact hardly anyone in England or anywhere else cared, when in 1739 one fifth of the population of Ireland died of hunger. The death of three and a half percent of the population shocked the world in 1847, but the deaths of twenty percent in 1739, went unnoticed, and historians hardly even bothered to mention the incident.

At the age of twenty two the second Viscount became an M.P., sitting also on the Board of Admiralty and on the Treasury Board during the American War of Independence. When his first wife died he married in 1783 the daughter of a wealthy English merchant who had a residence in Dublin; he had been nursed back to health by her when he was injured by a fall from his horse when riding through the city. Henry John Temple, the third Viscount Palmerston was born to them in 1784. England was at the height of the industrial revolution when at the age of twenty four, this man made his first visit to his Sligo estates in September 1808, bringing the dawn of a new era, which was to change completely the face of the land in this area. Any study of the development of Mullaghmore or Ahamlish from this time into the early twentieth century, is intertwined with Palmerston as he proceeded to develop his properties, leaving the main topographical features, particularly in Mullaghmore, essentially as we see it today.

DEVELOPMENT OF MULLAGHMORE
AND ENVIRONS

The preceding information is necessary to establish the origins of land ownership in this area and to trace the succession from the original land grantee to the third Viscount Palmerston. This is the man who after centuries of neglect, now proceeded to change the face of Ahamlish and particularly Mullaghmore into, essentially, what we see today. On this first trip, he probably travelled by private coach on the mail coach roads, undertaking a long tedious journey over what in those times amounted to little more than cart tracks. A private coach would have been somewhat faster than the mail coach, which was drawn by from two to four horses and managed all of four miles an hour. It would be 1830 before speeds of seven m.p.h could be achieved with improvements in the roads.

We are told that he found on his arrival a destitute tenantry who held their small plots, most of which comprised about five acres, from four or five middlemen. These middlemen or petty landlords held the land from the landlord on long term leases, and let it to tenants in rundale, a system of joint occupation, in which one man could hold half a dozen detached pieces of land in different places. These middlemen held their leases for periods of time which was sometimes set and determined by the lives of prominent people in the locality or elsewhere. The middlemen in this instance held the leases for the life of William IV, expiring therefore in 1837. The rent rolls of 1788 show William O'Beirne as holding Kilkilloge and Gortnaleck; James Johnson holding Mullaghmore & Warrens[1]; Owen Cassidy, Ballinabrock; William Coane, Bunduff and Castlegal, Ballinfull and Cartronplank; The Right Honorable Owen Wynne holding the island of Inishmurray and so on. The land itself was described at the time as being boggy and poor on one side of the property and consumed by blowing sand on the other. From 1806 to '35 thousands of acres of arable land were overwhelmed by sand, "the unfortunate citizens retreating before the deluge, clinging to their wretched hovels as long as the roofs were able to sustain the weight of sand".

---

1. Rabbits were unknown in Ireland until they were introduced by the Normans in the 12th century. For centuries these 'rabbit warrens' were a valued possession providing hunting for sport, food for the table, and skins for clothing. Many old estate maps and even deeds carried details of warrens. It is only in recent years that the rabbit has been considered a pest.

BUNDUFF SOUTERRAIN

Seamus Moore In Smaller inner chamber of Bunduff souterrain. Note quern stone built into wall near passage to outer larger chamber

Photo: J. McG

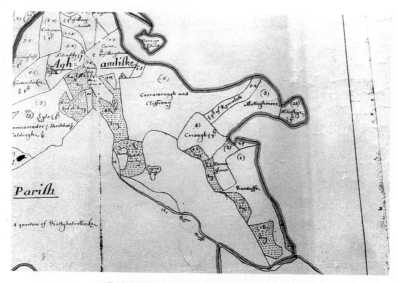

DOWN SURVEY MAP 1654
Showing Parish of Ahamlish
Photo: Courtesy of Sligo County Library

BRONZE AGE BURIAL CIST
*Discovered at Carrigans Maugherow 1992. Cist, dating from 1800 to 1500
B.C. is only third of its kind ever found in Sligo. Urn contains cremated
remains of several bodies.*

Photo: J. McG

'TIC TAC MAN'
at Mullaghmore Horseraces c1930
Photo: Courtesy of Lillian Mitchell

PETIE WATTERS, CASTLEGAL 1992
Note built-in kitchen bed, a common and practical feature in country homes up to the middle of this century

Photo: J. Mc G

INISHMURRAY ISLAND C.1900
Mary Donlon grinding corn on stone quern

Photo: Courtesy of Ulster Museum

GRANGE N. S. 1949 *(Teachers: Master Burke and Mrs. Kelly)*

Back Row, L to R: Eileen Cunningham, Noreen Watters, Brid Watters, Maureen Meehan, Brid Gillen, Margaret McHugh, Pauline McHugh, Margaret Feeney, Margaret Haran, Katie Feeney.
Middle Row: Sally Stephens, Martin Currid, Ann Stephens, Michael Gillen, Pat Kilgannon, Eily Kilgannon, May Devins, Kathleen Meehan, Anna Quinn, Mary Feeney, Veronica Gilbride, Una Stephens, Cassie Gilroy, Lizzie Kilfeather, Sheila Gillen, Eileen Waters, Bernie Feeney, Michael Gilbride, Sean Nicholson, John Currid, Annie Meehan.
Front Row: Paddy Feeney, Joe Feeney, Jim Campbell, Patsy Barry, Petie Haran, John Joe Kilfeather, Tommy Meehan, Noel Campbell, John Gilbride, Michael Leydon, Jimmy Killoran, Jim Joe Bruen, John Gillen.

GRANGE N. S. 1949

Back Row, L to R: Ann Gillen, Kathleen Lenehan, Ursula Gilbride, May Feeney, Chrissie Bruen, Nonie Devins, Theresa Mitchell.
Third Row: Kathleen Leydon, Nell Jackson, Angela Gilbride, Mary Gilmartin, Nora Ann Gilmartin, Gertie Jackson, Theresa Feeney, Rita Devins, Mary Jackson.
Second Row: Andy Sexton, Paddy Kilfeather, Joe Taheny, Paddy Gilmartin, John Mitchell, Michael Feeney, Leo McSharry, James Gilmartin, John Keegan, Tom Keegan,
Front Row: John Oates, Jim Joe Keegan, Jim Currid, Rory Kelly, Liam Kelly, Eugene Feeney, Enda Jackson. Photos Courtesy of Eileen Feeney.

MULLAGHMORE N.S. 1924 *Teacher: Miss Nanny Hannon*
Back Row: *Tommy Rourke, Patrick Kelly, Violet McCafferty, Celia McCannon, Patrick Duffy, NoraMcCannon Tom McGowan.*
Middle: *Dan Kelly, Jim McGowan, Maggie Duffy, Isa Duffy, Delia McGowan, Mary McGowan, Delia Kelly*
Front: *Bernie Kelly, Mary Rourke, Delia Rourke, Margaret McGloin, John McCannon, Mary Kate Kelly, Ellie McCannon Maggie Kelly, Bee McCannon*
Photo: Courtesy of Nelly McGowan

MULLAGHMORE N.S 1967
Back Row, L to R: *Mary Ellen Kennedy, Kathleen McCannon, Kathleen McHugh, Mary McGowan, Kate Leonard, Annie Nicholson, Margaret Leonard, Eithne Davison, Noreen Duffy, Martin Boyce, Mary McHugh*
Front Row, L. to R: *Evelyn McCannon, Noelle McHugh, Marion Meehan, John Callery, Jean McHugh, John Meehan, Peter McHugh, Pat Barry, Liam Carey*
Photo: Courtesy off Mrs. T. Kennedy

I will go with my father a ploughing
To the green field by the sea
And the rooks and the crows and the seagulls
Will come flocking after me.

Photo: J. McG

MOWING AT MULLAGHMORE 1933

James Gallagher (on machine) and Pat Kelly pausing for the camera
at Lena Boyce's, Mullaghmore

Photo: Courtesy of Anne O'Dare

Picture taken by Robert Welch c. 1900, at Cliffoney

Photo: Courtesy of Ulster Museum

In a poignant description of the plight of the natives at this time Woodmartin[2] describes the discovery of one such house in Raughley which had been buried in the blowing sand;

> "we almost waded through this wilderness, saw no house, and were wondering how much farther we had to go when suddenly the constable stopped opposite to what appeared to be a thatched potato pit, nearly covered with sand. We went round, saw an opening in the thatch, and the end of a ladder protruding; by this means we descended and dimly descried the poor man and his family, by means of the light given by the hole in the roof and by the chimney. His recovery was slow, and when able to be moved, he was at once carried off to his neighbours in the adjoining townland, as by that time the sand had completely covered the roof of his former dwelling."

The mass movement of sand extended from Rosses Point almost to Bundoran and was attributed to the over-cultivation of areas close to the coastline.

During his visits to this area Palmerston stayed in what was formerly known as the "Cliffoney Inn", recently owned by John and Vincent Cummins and now owned by David Carmody and known as Ena's Pub. Nimmo, the designer of Mullaghmore Harbour supervised extensive renovations to the Inn in 1826 at a cost of £385.15s.0d. The refurbishment included provision of a stone staircase, yard, stables and gateway.

In a letter sent from here to his sister on this first visit, he expressed the hope that both the boggy land and the blowing sands could be brought into cultivation, with a resultant trebling in value of the property, and set about immediately to achieve this. Looking at the peninsula of Mullaghmore he saw a potential for development and planned to, "establish a little manufacturing village in a central part of the estate and to build a pier and make a little port near a village that stands on a point of land projecting into Donegal Bay, called Mullaghmore." He planned to build roads and schools and noted that, "the thirst for education is so great that there are now three or four schools upon the estate." The schools that existed then were primitive, the schoolmaster living next door in a mud hut and supported by the

2. W.G. Woodmartin, author of history of Sligo, was born in Woodville, Co. Sligo on July 16, 1847. He was ecudated at private schools in Ireland and later in Switzerland, in Belgium, and at the Royal Military College, Sandhurst. He was a Justice of the Peace, High Sheriff and Deputy Lieutenant of Sligo and Colonel commanding the Duke of Connaughts Own Sligo Artillery from 1883 to 1902. His history of Sligo was published in1882-92.

parents of the pupils in his school. Palmerston spoke about the thirst of the people for education and we are told that even though the conditions were bad, there was nothing inferior about the education being given there, as in addition to reading writing and arithmetic, Latin and Greek were also taught.

Palmerston set out at this time on a programme of development that continued until his death:

Land Management and Housing

The people's cry was, "Give us roads and no petty landlords." On the expiration of the leases he abolished the middlemen and the rundale system; setting about "squaring the land" he proceeded to lay out roads through the townlands. Roads were made through the Ahamlish estates, crossing the main road evey mile at right angles. It is interesting to note today, the uniformity with which the side roads are laid out off the main road from Bunduff to Grange through the former estates. The old established villages were then razed to the ground, some of the inhabitants persuaded to emigrate, the remainder made to build new houses along these new roads on sites pointed out to them and chosen by the landlords agents. Two roomed fishermens cottages with adjoining plots of one rood were built by the landlord along the length of the eastern side of the Hill Road in Mullaghmore, many of which are still in existence at the time of writing. The slates for these came from a slate quarry owned by Palmerston in Caernarvonshire and for which quarry he sometimes recruited labour locally, providing labour for his quarries and an outlet for a surplus of displaced and evicted tenants. According to old sketches, one of the sites considered for the fishermens cottages was the strip of land opposite the avenue leading up to the White House.

Farmers with average holdings of eighteen to twenty acres were settled on the western side of the Hill Road but had to build their houses out of their own resources. This explains why the houses on the east side of the road were two-roomed slate structures and those on the west, three roomed thatched houses. The Hill Road did not exist before this time and remnants of the old road which this new road replaced can still be seen running parallel, several hundred yards to the west. According to local lore this new road and houses were built on an exposed hill in the hope that the tenants would be driven out by the Atlantic gales and harsh Winters.

The ordinance survey map of 1836 and some of the early estate maps clearly point out one of the old villages or "clachans" near the stone "tower" at the top of the Quay Road. This village was very old indeed and oral history tells us that it was known as Bally tSeampaill; the area still being known by that name until recently. The existence of this village is also recorded on an estate map of 1812, although anglicised and marked as Ballintemple. There was an early school and Church here, the Church giving Kilkilloge (Cill Caolog, Cill Coroge) the name it retains to this day. Underground chambers or souterrains which are commonly associated with early settlements, honeycomb this area; the evidence would indicate a continuum of settlement from medieval and even iron age times. Workmen uncovered an old cemetery here some years ago while resurfacing the Quay Road; some of the inscribed slabs from here may be viewed in the National Museum (see photo).

There was no evidence at this time of anyone living at, or near the ringfort near the old Post Office, or at the much older settlement of Dun Balra, remains of which, along with an associated megalithic tomb can still be seen near the big hill at the back of Mullaghmore. Dun Balra, where Balor probably lived for a time, belongs to a classification of settlement known as a promontory fort, dating from the late stone age to early bronze age. Ringforts are by far the most numerous Irish field monument. The Mullaghmore ringfort provides the only remaining evidence over ground, of settlement here from Iron age to medieval times; examples of similar early settlements abound on the Bunduff hillside facing west on the sea side of the main road, with one of the finest examples in Ireland of a court cairn to be seen at Creevykeel.

On Palmerston's arrival, houses in existence above Claddagh Dubh and on what is now the village green, were also levelled by his planners to provide open space around the holiday village which he planned and to allow for development of the harbour. It is said that an old pub was run by a Gonigle family near Claddagh Dubh at the Iron Gate. This family name no longer exists in Mullaghmore but the remains of the house, to which they were moved at the time, can still be seen near the place where sea rods are stacked at the southern end of the Hill Road. The houses which existed at Claddagh Dubh were built along what was formerly the main access road to the lower village and ran directly from the end of the Burra road past Port na hEorna, branching at the end of the Green road. This Green Road is one of the oldest thoroughfares in Mullaghmore and ran directly to the old village of Bally tSeampaill. Lewis's Topographical dictionary describes "Ballintemple" (BallytSeampaill) as containing 20 houses and 110 inhabitants in 1837.

Outlines of houses and old walls can still be seen of another village, known as Mullagh Gearr, which existed in the area between where

Classiebawn now stands and the gatehouse cottage and fields, to the north-east. The removal of the inhabitants of this village, to provide more open space around the recently completed Classiebawn castle, was completed in 1888. Some of the family names and heads of households removed at that time were Pat Gunnigle, Pat Bruen, Pat Gilmartin, McHugh and Owen Fowley. Thomas Boyce recalls the old people telling about a boat which was built here by Johnny "Neddy" Gilmartin and was pushed on rollers to a launching at the harbour. Johnny's people were moved to a house at the bottom of the Quay Road and another tenant, Bruen, moved to a house halfway along the little lane that leads from the Green Road to the Hill Road.

Another one of the old villages razed at this time existed in Cliffoney near Bernie Kennedy's, south of the existing village on the borders of East and West Cartronplank. Locals still point out another of these "old towns" which existed near Brian Narry's in Bunduff, at the top of the steep hill, on the road leading from Lower Bunduff to the main "coach" road.

A report to a commision of enquiry reported that in the years 1838 to '41 there were 94 new houses built on the Sligo estates with 56 in progress; 1660 Irish perches of new roads were made with 523 in progress and 19,000 Irish perches of ditches and fences built. The labour for these roads was provided by the tenants with the landlord bearing half of the cost. The names of some of the workmen or "contractors", as they were called, working on the road from Grange to Lyle in 1826 are as follows; perhaps some of your ancestors are here:

Fencing, Forming, Gravelling and Building Gullets: Gortnaleck; John Laydon, Patrick Mc Gowan, Michael Mc Sharry, John Branley, Bryan Mc Gowan, Dan Kilmartin, Patrick Kerin, Patrick Kilmartin, Cormac Kerin. Kilcat: Matthew Walsh, Mc Sharry & Co.

Kiltykere: John Leydon, Barth. Currit, Patrick Kilfeather, Denis Feeney. Grogagh: Michael Mc Gowan, Barth. Currit, John Feeney, John Gilmartin, James Gilmartin, Michael Feeney, John Laydon, Michael Mc Sharry, Patrick Mc Gowan.

Newtownward: Thomas Haran, Luke Gilmartin, James Kelly, Richard Costello, Patrick Kilfeather, Thady Moffit, William Gallaher, William Kelly, Charles Waters.

Ardnaglass: Patrick Gilmartin

It was at this time too, that the bent grass was introduced from Denmark; it naturalised very quickly and had a remarkable effect in stabilising the shifting sands; so successful indeed that Robt. Gore-

Booth, Gethins and other landlords procured some of the bent from Mullaghmore, planting it with an equal amount of success in their own area. In 1826, Palmerston had planted 140 acres of bent at a cost of only £50, almost completing his objective of planting 600 acres. Gethin, whose properties lay near Ardtermon, when advised to plant bent grass and the Maritime pine, replied that he couldn't afford to import it from Denmark on which he was allowed to send carts down to Mullaghmore to load up with bent and young trees. This may have given Palmerston the idea of providing a nursery, which he proceeded to establish in Cliffoney and which continued in existence to the early part of this century. A front page advertisement in the Sligo Journal of November 23rd 1832 carried the following information:

"Forest trees to be sold on Lord Palmerston's Nursery, Rundle Cottage:-

10,000 ASH	30,000 SCOTCH FIR
10,000 ELM	24,000 LARCH
22,000 CANADA POPLAR	30,000 ALDER
5,000 HUNTINGTON AND REDFORD WILLOWS	10,000 OAK
10,000 BIRCH	10,000 NORWAY SPRUCE
11,000 LAURELS	10,000 WHITE AMERICAN SPRUCE

Above trees have been twice transplanted and are growing in an exposed place close to the Atlantic.
Orders to John Lynch, Rundle Cottage."

In 1825, Palmerston's civil engineer and adviser had recommended building an iron railroad six miles long to, "bring up a shelly sea sand from the beach to reclaim the bogs, and to carry down in return to my new harbour, turf from the bogs prepared as fuel", considering that an export trade could be carried on to the town of Sligo and beyond. He considered raising a portion of the £6,000 required by Government loan but must have considered the project too daunting, as it never got beyond the planning stages.

This did not hinder his plans to develop the bogs though as by 1826 he had got thirty acres producing potatoes, turnip and rape, which previously had been unworkable bogland. His method was to first drain the bog in April; "then to dig up the surface and pile it in heaps and burn it; then to level the ground, and form it into ridges and plant it with potatoes or sow it with turnips and rape, throwing the ashes on as manure and adding a top dressing of sea-sand and clay". His plan was to rotate the crops, planting potatoes, turnip or rape the first year, oats the second and third, and hay on the fourth. It's not hard to imagine

THE CENSUS OF IRELAND

FOR THE YEAR

1851.

COUNTY OF SLIGO.

BARONIES, PARISHES, AND TOWNLANDS.

BARONY OF CARBURY.

PARISHES, TOWNLANDS, AND TOWNS.	AREA.	POPULATION IN 1841.			POPULATION IN 1851.			NUMBER OF HOUSES IN 1841.				NUMBER OF HOUSES IN 1851.				POOR LAW VALUATION IN 1851.
		Males.	Females.	Total.	Males.	Females.	Total.	Inhabited.	Uninhabited.	Building.	Total.	Inhabited.	Uninhabited.	Building.	Total.	
AHAMLISH P.:	A. R. P.															£ s. d.
Agharrow, . .	206 2 14	56	57	113	49	61	110	20	.	.	20	17	.	.	17	108 10 0
Ardnaglass, Lower, .	109 0 37	41	44	85	32	30	62	15	.	.	15	11	.	.	11	63 15 0
Ardnaglass, Upper, .	87 3 1	11	12	23	12	12	24	3	.	.	3	5	.	.	5	19 0 0
Ballincastle, .	141 0 31	67	75	142	16	10	25	24	.	.	24	5	.	.	5	38 0 0
Ballinphull, .	77 1 25	90	88	178	56	55	111	39	3	.	33	16	3	.	19	78 15 0
Ballynabrock, .	64 0 21	46	56	102	40	39	79	22	1	.	23	14	.	.	14	31 15 0
Ballycannel, .	423 3 11	161	159	320	111	124	235	50	1	.	51	38	.	.	38	224 10 0
Breaghwy, .	371 1 9	136	139	275	93	86	179	40	.	1	41	30	.	.	30	185 5 0
Busduff, .	893 2 0	288	289	577	231	211	442	109	1	.	110	79	1	.	480	300 5 0
Carrownamaddoo, .	479 2 21	48	51	99	44	49	93	17	.	.	17	13	.	.	13	93 10 0
Cartronkillerdoo, .	29 2 19	62	80	142	46	55	101	31	.	.	31	17	.	.	17	68 5 0
Cartronplank, .	188 0 27	20	13	33	93	98	191	5	.	.	5	32	.	.	32	59 10 0
Castlegal, .	461 3 34	118	127	245	87	93	180	41	.	.	41	29	.	2	31	184 0 0
Castlegowan, .	256 2 25	11	7	18	5	7	12	4	.	.	4	3	.	.	3	20 0 0
Cloonerco, .	333 1 1	10	7	17	7	5	12	3	.	.	3	3	.	.	3	24 10 0
Cloontyprocklis, .	123 1 35	55	70	125	44	55	99	24	6	.	30	19	.	.	19	64 10 0
Cloyragh, .	314 1 12	1	.	2	.	.	.	1	.	.	1	.	.	.	.	28 15 0
Cloysparra, .	202 3 33	75	57	132	37	37	74	19	.	.	19	13	.	.	13	69 10 0
Creevykeel, .	623 1 34	204	218	422	151	165	316	67	4	.	71	56	1	.	57	174 0 0
Creevymore, .	598 3 33	291	298	589	174	166	340	95	1	.	96	54	.	3	57	220 15 0
Derry, .	176 2 28	36	37	73	31	28	59	13	.	1	14	8	.	.	8	74 15 0
Derrylehan, .	583 1 29	145	137	282	94	90	184	48	.	.	48	33	.	.	33	174 10 0
Dooaghnakin, .	190 3 20	73	83	156	64	55	119	22	.	.	22	18	.	.	18	98 15 0
Dragna or Mountelward, .	307 0 26	130	145	275	97	103	200	43	1	.	44	34	.	.	34	140 15 0
Drumfad, .	640 3 25	170	176	346	115	103	218	55	.	.	55	31	.	i	32	151 10 0
Edenreagh, .	246 2 27	44	42	86	39	52	91	15	.	.	15	16	.	.	16	61 5 0
Gortaderry, .	170 0 21	25	19	44	27	21	48	7	.	.	7	8	.	.	8	52 0 0
Gortnaleck, .	1,182 2 11	82	93	175	54	47	101	26	.	.	26	15	.	.	15	130 5 0
Grange, .	350 1 36	230	201	431	185	168	353	75	.	i	75	67	1	.	68	363 5 0
Grellagh, .	418 0 13	87	118	205	68	91	159	35	.	i	36	27	1	.	28	125 10 0
Gregagh, .	192 1 10	71	55	126	35	34	69	19	.	.	19	13	.	.	13	92 0 0
Kilsas, .	249 1 29	11	18	29	13	12	25	4	.	.	4	3	.	i	4	109 10 0
Kilkilloga, .	486 3 8	.	.	.	269	269	538	.	.	.	.	86	.	1	91	215 10 0
Kiltykare, .	176 0 2	42	40	82	41	41	82	12	.	.	12	14	.	4	15	81 15 0
Lislary, .	347 3 26	125	140	265	109	95	204	45	.	.	45	33	.	.	33	176 15 0
Lyle, .	651 3 0	38	30	68	20	21	41	10	.	.	10	7	.	.	7	51 0 0
Moneygold, .	471 2 2	155	156	311	81	85	166	53	4	i	58	31	2	.	33	214 10 0
Mount Temple, .	410 1 27	200	258	458	167	172	339	77	1	2	80	56	1	.	56	212 0 0
Mullaghmore, .	886 1 17	13	12	25	40	36	76	3	.	.	3	11	.	.	11	216 0 0
Mullaghmore, West, .	133 3 1	172	176	348	3	2	5	57	2	.	59	1	.	.	1	12 5 0
Newtown, .	154 3 8	68	64	132	37	36	73	21	.	.	21	13	1	.	14	80 15 0
Newtowncliffony, .	105 0 30	38	51	89	26	32	58	13	.	.	13	11	.	.	11	38 5 0
Rathfrank, .	201 2 30	20	12	32	13	12	25	8	.	.	5	3	.	.	3	22 10 0
Rathbogh, .	247 2 33	25	20	45	19	20	39	8	.	.	8	7	.	.	7	57 0 0
Silverhill, .	149 3 35	31	45	76	23	25	48	13	.	.	13	11	.	.	11	23 10 0
Sraravagh, .	74 1 21	26	24	52	28	30	58	10	.	.	10	8	.	.	8	17 0 0
Streedagh, .	490 1 37	105	107	212	78	78	156	38	.	.	38	26	.	.	26	232 5 0
Cosors Island, .	111 0 30	8	7	15	3	1	4	1	.	.	1	1	.	.	1	26 10 0
AHAMLISH P.—con.	A. R. P.															£ s. d.
Dernish Island, .	103 1 16	20	22	42	26	23	49	5	1	.	6	6	1	.	6	65 10 0
Inishmurruy, .	209 0 5	45	50	95	27	26	53	16	.	.	16	8	.	.	8	40 0 0
Inishnugor, .	5 0 16	.	.	.	.	.	.	.	.	.	.	.	.	.	.	.
	16,413 2 2	4,025	4,186	8,214	3,160	3,166	6,326	1,389	27	5	1,421	1,025	19	7	1,084	5,464 0 0
Ballintemple T., (*)	.	92	86	178	.	.	.	32	.	.	32	.	.	.	.	.
Grange T., (*)	.	70	70	140	85	86	173	27	5	.	32	32	3	.	35	.
Kilkilloge T., (*)	.	95	93	188	.	.	.	49	3	.	32	.	.	.	.	.
Total, .	16,413 2 2	4,285	4,435	8,720	3,245	3,254	6,499	1,457	35	5	1,497	1,090	22	7	1,113	5,464 0 0

Census showing population changes during famine years

166

what the comments of the local farmers must have been when these schemes were first mooted and this mad stranger from England started putting them into effect. However, this mad stranger considered that after the fourth year the land could be let at 30 shillings an acre and assuming a net cost of £8 per acre for development that he would make 12% on his money while at the same time giving employment and enlarging the holding's of his tenants. He planned to develop at a rate of 60 acres a year; looking at these boggy areas today it might be reasonable to surmise that his estimates of his abilities and the capacity of bogland were somewhat exaggerated and highly optimistic.

Palmerston himself listed the:
"Crops and Stock on my Estate in Ahamlish" in Oct. 1858 to be:

Crop	Acres		
Wheat	85		
Oats	397.3		
Barley	8	Total arable	1345.2
Potatoes	805.2	Meadow	470.2
Turnips	27.3		
Clover	17.2		
Flax	4		

Cows, 1650; Heifers, 680; Horses, 223; Asses, 226; Sheep, 720; Pigs, 1272

A report written by John Hannon of Rundale Cottage for Palmerston earlier that year on May 20th 1858 (11 years after the famine) gives us a good idea of the condition of some of the affairs of the estate and surrounding areas at this time, particularly as regards plantations. He reported planting for the season to be completed and went on:

"The nursery is planted and cleaned and will require only two men to keep it clean as well as attend to the Hotel Garden and assist and direct the tenants in keping their flower gardens in order from Cliffoney to Edenreagh."

He reports the tenant's crops as coming on well despite very stormy weather early in the month. There is an abundance of seaweed providing a plentiful supply of manure for the crops. He reports having carried out Mr. Kincaid's orders to visit all the tenants urging them to grow good crops of turnips, mangolds, clover and other green crops.

"Bunduff, Grellagh and Castlegal plantations: The planting along the Bunduff river from the Cloontabawn wood to the waterfall near the sea has a good appearance and requires thinning." It consists of oak, ash, Scotch fir, American Spruce and common sea willow. "This plantation with the Cloontabawn Woods has a very pleasing effect, particularly when seen from the other side of the river....... This planting is continued from the Bunduff Bridge through Grellagh and

167

Castlegal and on to the road leading to the sea at Second Bunduff.......
plantation along Mr. Dixons mearing from Cloontabawn to Carnduff
and planted in the Spring of '57 and '58 has a promising appearance
and so far is doing well....... The plantations on the Rev. Brennans
land on the Rundale Cottage ground and in the nursery are all doing
well, also a plantation on mountain side of mail coach road from
Rundale Cottage gate to to the Cartron river. This planting is 26 feet
wide and well planted with oak. ash, Pinus Maritima, Pinus Sylvestus
and Spanish chestnut. Several trees are from 16 to 20 feet in height
and in a most thriving condition....... The plantations on the
Cloonkeen and Cliffoney bogs are not doing well; the trees have a
stunted and sickly appearance except in parts where the late Mr.
Lynch had seeds of the Pinus Maritima put in."

He believed that more of the maritime pine should be introduced, believing
also that the bog was in a better condition then than twenty years before
when it was not so well drained.

The plantations at Milkharbour, Moneygold, along the Coach road
and on the road leading to Ahamlish Church were all doing well with
the average heights of trees on, "the older parts of the plantation of from
15 to 20 feet and some are 30 feet each." About 9 acres of Dernish Island
had been planted, four of these required replanting, having failed but
now with some of the trees well established he believed that they would
give good shelter to re-planted areas. One acre of Pinus Maritima was
doing remarkably well and was an average 20 feet in height, requiring
thinning. The cost of putting the fences on the island in order was
estimated at five pounds. Aughaged was planted on cutaway bog along
Mr. Wymes mearing and on each side of the Coach road, about ten acres
in all. This area was planted with Pinus Maritima, Pinus Sylvestus, oak,
ash, Spanish chestnut and willow; pine were taking the lead in growth at
from 8 to 12 feet in height. Nothing had been done to the fences since
the woods were planted eight years before and they would now require
repair at a cost of from 8s to 10s per perch. Glengaragh was reported as
doing equally well except where the tenants were cutting turf.

The pine plantations on the Mullaghmore sand hills near the
Cliffoney passage to the sea were doing well, many of them exceeding 20
feet in height with the Pinus Sylvestus almost as high as the Pinus
Maritima. Although thinned the previous Spring they now required
further thinning as the bent grass had disappeared from under the trees
where they were too close to each other.

"The width of the plantation which is doing so well is from 100 to 200
yards and extends from the Cliffoney passage to the sea to about the
centre of the great sand hill, but from here to the road leading to
Mullaghmore is not in such a thriving condition. The trees are fewer

in number and not in such a thriving condition, this portion of the sands having a North Eastern aspect and exposed to the winds from that quarter which prevail here in the Spring months when the pine is making its growth."

He reports that the flat inside the Cliffoney- Mullaghmore road has been drained and planted with pine seeds and believes that so long as the drains are kept clean that the trees should do well and provide shelter for further planting to the West.

"The fence along the road between the two Iron gates is not finished, 58 perches remain to be done; if the wall was built on this portion there would be no danger of the grazing cattle breaking in on the plantations at nights. It would cost between 5 to 6 shillings a perch, the stones not being convenient and must be carted from the Cliffoney fields."

BENT "There will be a considerable portion of bent planting required to be done next Winter. That portion of the sands East of the road leading from Creevykeel to Mullaghmore and containing upwards of 40 acres, now in the hands of Hugh Gilmartin, has broken up in many places; the sand blowing along on the track of the old road leading to Claddaghduff, covering the land up to the new road and leaving several heaps of sand on the new road near the "Well" or what is called "Tobergall". I understand that your Lordship's agents have given Hugh Gilmartin notice to quit in order that they may plant this portion next Winter. There are several acres of sand required to be planted with bent under the Bunduffs, which is also in a bad state. The rabbits are becoming so numerous that they have the sands very much broken up in many places and if your Lordship would allow them to be sold to some party for a few pounds they would soon be rduced in number. The hares are also rather numerous and do much injury to the young larch, oak, chestnut and Scotch fir.

I am, My Lord, Your Lordships most

Obedient and very humble servant

John Hannon

Palmerston's schemes were financed partly out of his own pocket and partly by annual grants of £5,000 from the Government. However mad they may have seemed, his plans seemed by and large to bear fruit, as despite the considerable amount of money expended, the net rental income from Dublin and London had risen from £6,100 in 1805 to over £8,300 in 1811 and by 1840 to £11,000.

Looking at official scources and figures this seemed to be an era of landlord-tenant harmony and bliss. Certainly the figures look good! The views of the tenants are not so well recorded, except orally and some of this through the Folklore Commision collection. Here the picture changes as we hear and read of "crowbar brigades", evictions and ruthless bailiffs; if we are to believe these accounts there was a cost of human misery behind the statistics; the replacement of the petty landlords of the pre-Palmerston era with harsh overseers like Kincaid, Tom William Higgins and Barker, merely meant the replacement of one tyranny with another. No perusal of estate records gives any indication of the condition of the people at any time. Even during the famine era!

Some may argue that harsh measures were necessary to achieve change. The communist experiment of this century, gives proof, if proof was needed that real progress and advancement for the ordinary man comes about only through outright ownership of property; the Land League and the formation of the Land Commision was decades down the road. It was to be a full century yet before Fr. O'Flanagans slogan of, "The land for the people and the people for the land", was to be heard.

In 1860, two years after Hannon's report was written, the Attorney general passed an Act which restated, as if any restatement was necessary, that the land of Ireland belonged to the landlords and that tenants had no rights of their own! In the third Viscounts favour, it must be said though, that he was a man for his time and a vast improvement on his forebears, who stopped the clock of progress in this area for centuries.

CHAPTER 9

Schools, Churches and Commerce

Fr. Roger Burns was Parish priest on Palmerstons arrival in 1808, but of him or his successors, Fr. Stephen Fallon and and Fr. John Hanly, we know little nor are their opinions of this new arrival on record. We do know that Palmerston was ambivalent in his attitudes towards Catholics, making it clear many times that Roman Catholics had no right to hold political, or any other position in a Protestant country, regarding, "any approximation to Popery, Popish doctrine and Popish practises with special dislike and even fear", according to his associate, Shaftesbury. In a letter to Minto in 1847, the year of the famine, he wrote of his conviction that the best way of solving the unrest in Ireland would be to "hang a half dozen Catholic priests". The archetypical politician, though, his anti-Catholic prejudices were frequently tempered by pragmatic considerations which were influenced by political, financial and managerial realities concerning the very substantial incomes from his Irish estates.

He gave a measure of support to the Catholic Emancipation Bill, believing that it was the only way to prevent civil war and defuse the tensions which Daniel O' Connell had brought to exploding point. Speaking in favour of the Bill in 1813 he made it clear that he could not support Catholic rights on its merits, but viewed the question, "entirely on the grounds of expediency". Of the Catholic movement he said that it was for them to consider, "whether we will force it to spend its strength in secret and hidden causes, undermining our fences and corrupting our soil, or whether we shall, at once, turn the current into the open and spacious channel of honourable and constitutional ambition".

Prior to the opening of the new schools c.1826 the following interesting letter was sent to, "The Right Honourable Henry John Temple Lord Viscount Palmerston":

171

"The humble petition of Andrew Harrison of Cartron Killerdoo who in the most humble and supplicating manner makes to your Lordship this melancholy appeal imploring of your Lordship to grant him that request which he now presumes to express which is one of those free schools which we are told will be opened immediately by your Lordship, as I have been teaching in the townland of Cartron Killerdo those three years past. Moreover your Lordship was in my school the last time you were in Ireland and further expects your Lordship will be kind enough to assist me with the improvements I have in hands at the present as I am void of money to finish my house.

N.B. Your Lordship will give me a trifle of money to buy windows and lime, I expect. Petitioner, duty bound will pray for your Lordships felicity here and hereafter."

In 1826, with Catholic Emancipation still very much an isssue, the Parish Priest in Cliffoney, Fr. John Mc Hugh, had locked horns with Palmerston, forbidding the people to send their children to the two schools he had built, until Catholic teachers were appointed. Palmerston on the other hand seems to have expected that in a short time his tenantry would have turned Protestant. The following letter is dated at Cliffoney, 29th October 1827:

Mr. John Newburn,

I hereby authorize and desire you to read the Scriptures to all my Tenants on the undermentioned Townland (Cliffoney) and also request my Tenants to give you a patient and attentive hearing, and I particularly desire that you will let me know if any person on my estate, whether man woman or child should ill-treat you in any manner whatever."

The words "man woman or child" are marked with an X and footnoted:

"These words were put in at Newburn's particular request as he said the women and children annoyed him the most."

One of the stories of this era still told in Cliffoney is of a Barry woman, (her descendants still live in Cartronplank) who threw a pot of hot gruel over the landlord's agent when he came to her house demanding that she send her children to the school.

The following letter was sent from Cliffoney on January 25th 1827:

"My Lord, I fear you will think it impertinent in so humble an individual as I am to trespass on your time by sending you so many letters. But I hope your Lordship wil do me the justice to believe that it was far from my intention to dispute the propriety of your orders or to think myself in any instance at liberty to deviate from them. Yet as I thought your Lordship wished to engage the priest to give his assistance, I took the liberty of communicating to you the proposals he had made as I have seen no gentleman more anxious to have things brought to an accomodation than he appears to be. The Revenue Police have been removed from this place and consequently six of my pupils have been withdrawn. There are remaining four Roman Catholic boys who are tolerably advanced in Grammar and Arithmetic. Three of them do not belong to this parish.

I trust your Lordship does not think my attendance here unworthy of some compensation and as I depend solely on your Lordship's bounty for my support, certain pecuniary difficulties oblige me to your Lordship for relief. Mr. Walker will not give any money without particular orders from you Lordship and if you will be graciously pleased to direct him to grant me a supply, it will be of essential service to me, your Lordships most obedient

        Servant,

        Felix Connolly

Later in that year, Palmerston had reached agreement with the bishop by agreeing to his demands, which on reflection, he found to be, "not unreasonable". Writing on Oct. 1827 from England three weeks after his return from a visit to Cliffoney, he mentions his satisfaction at having heard, "that my girls school has increased from five scholars to one hundred". and of his hopes that on finding a suitable master for the boy's school, it would do well also.

The boy's school, built at a cost then of £385.15s.8d, was a two storey building housing the bigger boys underneath and the infants overhead; it fell into disuse when the new school was built in 1914 and was taken over by Sinn Fein/I.R.A. during the War of Independence and used as a meeting place and drill hall. It was burned to the ground by the Black and Tans as a reprisal for the Moneygold ambush, rebuilt shortly afterwards by the parish, and is used at this time as a parish hall for community and parish functions. Very few people today in this area, even among those who use the hall, realise the rich history and important events in which this modest building played a central role.

The girl's school was also a two storey building, the senior girls being taught on the top floor and the younger ones underneath. There was provision here too for living accomodation for the teachers, on the ground floor. This house may have been just a renovation of an earlier structure. Known as Market House in the early 1800's it is believed that it was used originally to store grain, which was collected by the landlords as rent payment from the people, and stored here, prior to transportation by horse and cart to the port of Sligo for export.

According to Miss Kathleen Clancy, retired postmistress of Cliffoney Post Office, one of the most famous visitors to the girl's school in the 1870's, was the old Fenian John Devoy. Miss Clancy's mother, Delia Quinn, who taught in this school recalled that Devoy's sister, who taught in the school, was visited by him prior to his departure for America. This building too fell into disuse when the new school, which was a mixed school housing boys and girls, was opened. Charlie Mc Cannon operated a grocery shop from the old school for many years; it is now owned as a private residence by the Macarthur family.

There were separate boy's and girl's schools in Castlegal also, these being replaced by the present school which was built on the site of the old boy's school in 1951 at a cost of £2,200. The boy's school which it replaced was built in 1901 for £235. The girls school now owned by the Mc Gee's since 1951 was built in 1891 at a cost of £200.

Mullaghmore N.S. was built in 1895, replacing an earlier thatched building which stood on the same site, and shown on an 1865 map as being the holding of James Mc Gloin. These schools had replaced an earlier rough structure near the old village of Bally tSeampaill at the top of the Quay Road. On the arrival of the Sisters of Mercy in Mullaghmore, Miss "Nanny" Hannon, sister of John Hannon, proprieter of Hannon's Hotel, was replaced by Sr. Peter Doran as principal, in 1930. Miss Bridie Moffit continued as assistant for many years afterwards.The fact that there were 51 children on the roll then, is a sober reflection on the changing times and fortunes of Mullaghmore..

Mass was said in the school for many years prior to the opening of the present chapel and convent in 1929. This was done at the request of the local people who pleaded with Fr. Crofton that the long walk to Cliffoney for Sunday Mass and the various devotions was an unecessary hardship. Some of the older residents of the village recall Fr. Shannon giving fiery sermons here, in opposition to dances in the country houses, maintaining that the "devil is in the house there's a dance in". Priests in those days took their obligations as moral guardians of their flock, quite seriously!

It is said that a sort of class distinction existed when the Mullaghmore people attended Mass in Cliffoney chapel. Back in those days, going to Mass was as much of a social occasion as the fulfilling of a moral obligation. After Mass, all would gather around the church gates, exchanging pleasantries and catching up on events of the week. The fact that the landed farmers of Mullaghmore would congregate with their landed counterparts of the Cliffoney district, gave rise to a sort of amused resentment by the fishermen and labourers of Mullaghmore, who would reprove their neighbours for what they perceived as snobbery.

What is now known as Pier Head House served, into the middle of the 19th century, as a store house, watch house and accomodation for the Coastguards while the station buildings were under construction. Usage then gradually changed until by 1862, "Harbour House" could boast of "hot baths" as an inducement to visitors. It was probably prior to its takeover as a Coastguard station that one of the first public houses in Mullaghmore, owned by a family of Gilmartins, stood in a little thatched house on this site. Gilmartin also owned the buildings in the block starting from Mc Hughs grocery shop over to the Beach Hotel. It is said that these Gilmartins were moved by the landlord to a house which stood until recently at Creevykeel crossroads known as Felix "Edwards" Gilmartin's.

It is ironic then, that a century later, the descendants of these Gilmartins, during the War of Independence, played a leading role in the demise of landlordism in this area. Part of Pier Head House served as a Protestant church and schoolhouse until it was struck off as such in 1913 for lack of pupils, Miss Maria Glenny being the last recorded teacher there. The older people remember the Church of Ireland minister from Kinlough arriving for service at 3.00 P.M. on Sundays. Matthew Mc Hugh of Mullagh Gearr was employed to drive the children of families who lived outside of Mullaghmore, such as the Eccles and Lowes, to this school. It was also attended by the families of the coastguards stationed at Mullaghmore. A Miss Currid ran the store there at the turn of the century and is listed as caretaker and shop assistant, free of rent, at this time. The Protestant schoolhouse at Mullaghmore was eventually acquired by a Mc Dermott woman from Cliffoney when she retired as caretaker at Classiebawn; she eventually married Johnny Mc Hugh and is listed as Mrs. Mary Mc Hugh in the rentals of 1907, paying £7.3s.6d for the rent of the Pier Head House; the old watch house, schoolhouse and Church were eventually taken over and incorporated into the building now known as Pier Head House which is still owned by the Mc Hugh family.

The old Carns school was built in 1864, the money coming from the Education Co. and partly financed by Palmerston. It is now a private residence, being replaced in 1951 by the existing school. Grange school which was opened on Oct. 1st 1870 was replaced by a three roomed building in 1968, this in turn being replaced by a new National School in

175

1985. Derrylehan N.S., built in 1935 replaced an earlier school which was built by the Healy's on land owned by them, close to the existing school. The first teacher there was Brigid Healey, who served from 1885 to 1915. Benbulben school, which had 80 pupils on its rolls in 1900, has long fallen into disuse, finally closing its doors c.1950, it has been used since as a private residence.

CHURCHES

Palmerston is credited with the building of two Catholic churches, one at Cliffoney and one at Grange; he assisted also with the Church of Ireland building, now in ruins, in Ahamlish cemetery. According to Church of Ireland records, the wording of the Deed of Consecration, "rebuilt, erected and constructed a church", indicate that a Catholic church or abbey already existed on this Ahamlish site, and indeed an inspection of the walls where plaster has fallen off recently, also seems to bear this out. Some historians have deduced from the writings of de Cuellar, survivor of the Armada wrecks, that it is here and not at Staad Abbey, that he found, "twelve Spaniards hanging within the Church by the act of the English Lutherans." This old church, now deserted, was completed in its present form in 1813 with a loan of £700 from the Board of First Fruits and a contribution of £100 from Palmerston. The church was consecrated by the Bishop of the Diocese of Elphin, the Hon. Power Le Poer Trench in 1813 assisted by the Vicar of Ahamlish of that time, Rev. Charles West. Rev. Charles West was preceded by Rev Matthew Browne and succeeded by Rev. Michael Obins. The Glebe house, now occupied by the O'Connor family, was also built at this time.

Cliffoney

When the pressure of the Penal Laws abated somewhat, towards the end of the eighteenth century, Catholics became bold enough to start building houses of worship which consisted of mud cabins or rough stone buildings with thatched roofs. One of these crude buildings existed at a site behind Cliffoney hall, on the sea side, some few hundred yards down the Mullaghmore road; this is clearly marked on estate maps drawn about 1811. According to some maps, Pat Watters and Pat Cannon lived in close proximity to this site; in 1810 widow Hoy is listed as tenant on 1 rood 36 perches on which there stood a "house and chapel".

Lewis's Topographical Dictionary printed in 1837 credits Palmerston with having built the present St. Molaise's Church in Cliffoney. According to diocesan archives, it was built either in 1827 or 1830 and according to local scources seems to have been a rectangular thatched building. The O.S. map of 1837 marks the site of another "Church" west of the "nursery" at Rindaly Cottage; this is now known as tSeampaill Buí and was used for burying unbaptised children into the early years of this century. The present St. Molaise's church in Cliffoney village was reconstructed c.1865, being re-roofed with the present slates and changed in shape from rectangular to the present cruciform.

Seamus Conway of Cliffoney claims that the massive ceiling beams were brought into Sligo harbour on a sailing ship captained by one of his ancestors, a Captain Conway. This Captain Conway was taught navigation by Celier, one of the early teachers in Cliffoney who bridged the gap from hedge schools to the early established schools; this was the same Conway who smuggled Hayes out of the country to America. The timber beams were transported by horse and cart to Cliffoney, each timber requiring two horse carts, one at either end. The iron fixings, visible today on the ceiling joists, were forged at Mc Garrigle's blacksmith shop which stood just south of Cliffoney village on the main road. It was here too that the ironwork for Classiebawn castle was prepared.

Around this time, the parochial house, still being used as a residence by the Parish priest, was granted by Palmerston to Fr. John Mc Hugh, P.P. of Ahamlish from 1826 to 1836. It consisted of a house and lawn only, the grounds being enlarged to their present size in Fr. Malachai Brennan's time. It is told that when on Fr. Mc Hugh's departure, Fr. Malachai Brennan applied to have the house, a reply did not come from Palmerston for twelve months; when eventually it did come, with apologies, Fr. Brennan was not alone granted the house for his use but also an extra acre of ground around it, for every months delay. John Harrison of Cliffoney recalls his father telling him that it was at this time that the Wymbs's of Cloonkeen were moved to their present location. James Gallagher recalls ploughing in a field adjacent to Peggy's Lane and noticing the blacker earth in the area where Peggy had her garden. It is said that even though this woman had her Spring planting done she was forced to move to make room for Fr. Malachai's new fields.

Palmerston and Fr. Malachai Brennan became firm friends and O' Rourke tells us that,

"he and Lady Palmerston could hardly digest their dinner if they had not Fr. Malachai with them to help them to eat it; few things in later life supplying them with such pleasant reminiscences as the racy anecdotes and the sparkling wit of the genial P.P. of Palmerston Glebe".

The parish house is currently held on a 999 year lease which was issued by Wilfrid W. Ashley to Bishop Coyne in 1927. It cannot be sold and if it is not used for the purpose for which it was intended, reverts to the Classiebawn estate.

Grange

Church records tell us that St. Molaise's church in Grange was built in 1845 or 1875; other scources tell us that it was built at Palmerstons expense c.1837 around the same time as Cliffoney even though the church records say the Lessor in this case was Mr. Johnson of Kinlough. This church is said to replace an earlier church which existed approximately one mile north of Grange village, off the existing main road, and marked R.C. Chapel on the O.S. map of 1837. Grange presbytery which stands next to the church was built by Dr. Healy in 1875. Dr. Healy, later to become Archbishop of Tuam, was C.C. in Grange from 1871-75 and according to his biography built the presbytery in two months. Sligo County Council acquired some of the church lands and developed an amenity area in 1985-'86, this includes a shrine in honour of St. Molaise.

Mullaghmore

A block of four of Col. Ashley's holiday "lodges", Numbers 8,9,10 and 11, originally built in 1866, which had previously been let to wealthy tenants for the Summer season, were burned out in 1920 and purchased by the Sisters of Mercy in 1927 for £1,400. This burning, which was not thought to be politically motivated, cost the ratepayers four thousand pounds, as this was the amount of the award given by Judge Roche as a result of Col.Ashley's claim which was levied on the county. At a meeting of Sligo County Council, reported in the Sligo Champion of May 28 1927, it was decided to devote the amount of the award to the Sisters of Mercy. Items of furniture from the lodges, some of which may have come from the Coastguard station, can be seen in homes in the area to this day, as prior to the burning the furniture was transferred to the lodges.   Work commenced immediately following the acquisition in 1927 and a new convent and chapel emerged from the ruins of Ashley's lodges. Stones were taken from Claddagh Dubh and sand from Moffit's

Burra for the reconstruction which was supervised by stonemasons, Jerry Cummins of Mullaghmore and Peter Cummins of Cliffoney. The new convent and chapel was opened and consecrated on 19th August 1929. The main contractor was Donnelly of Enniskillen.

The numbers of nuns using the convent has dwindled dramatically from then to the present time but the convent and chapel serve the community as well now as it did in 1929. Number 2 lodge was bought from Lady Mountbatten in 1948 for £450, reconstructed and used as a presbytery by C.C.'s assigned to Mullaghmore. In 1988 a new presbytery was acquired on Castle Road, the old one being sold off and converted to commercial use and is now known as Eithne's Restaurant.

As noted elsewhere, an early church existed in Bally tSeampaill near the old stone tower in Mullaghmore. It is likely that another place of worship existed, in some form, under where Classiebawn now stands. This spot is known as Cill na Muckaun (Mboctan?) and as with tSeampaill Bui in Cliffoney, unbaptised children were buried here into the early years of this century.

INDUSTRY AND COMMERCE

There is no evidence that Ahamlish had any business or industrial infrastructure in the early 1800's. The old village of Mullaghmore, Bally tSeampaill, anglicised to Ballintemple, along with Grange were considered to be the main villages; Grange[1] being the biggest having a population of 221 with 40 houses, four of these described as "decent houses, the rest being thatched cabins". Ballintemple, as noted earlier, had twenty houses and 110 inhabitants. Farming and fishing were the main occupations of the people; small industries such as salt pans and malt houses produced enough to supply local needs. Illegal distillation might well qualify as the worlds second oldest profession, if somewhat more illegal, as malt houses then seemed to be as much outside the law as poteen making is now. One such malt house existed in Bunduff and was owned and operated by John Harrison. It was dug into the face of the sandbanks and could be reached only by being lowered by rope down the face of the bank. This business came to an unfortunate end

1. O'Donovan reported in 1836 that the oldest names in the area were: Kilmartin– T. Mac Giolla Martain; Mac Sharrys – S. Mac Searraigh; Gillan – T. Ua Giollain; Ronan – T Ua Ronann; Crolly P.A. Craolaigh,; O'Harts – S. Ua Harit

when the sand collapsed, wiping out the malt house and smothering the unlucky owner.

Farm produce was marketed at fairs in Grange on June 2nd and 28th, July 25th, August 25th, Sept. 29th, October 28th and December 10th. By 1826 a linen market had been established in Cliffoney and was run on a monthly basis. A market house existed also at the turn of the 19th century beside what is now Ena's Pub; a fair and market known as the Cliffoney Pattern, its origins lost in the mists of history, was held here on St. Brigid's feast day, the 1st of February each year. When the rounds were done and the prayers said at St. Brigid's well (neglected, but still in evidence in Cliffoney) the people then crowded into the village to barter and sell all kinds of farm produce — livestock, vegetables, poultry, and drink too! More often than not these fairs ended in faction fighting and bloodletting because of rivalry between different townlands and families. The priests eventually denounced the practice from the altar, causing the fairs to die out, and with them eventually, the devotion and visits to St. Brigid's well in Cliffoney. It was quite common in Britain and Ireland to have fairs on calendar feastdays, until 1750, when the Gregorian calendar was introduced and an Act of Parliament passed, which decreed that fairs be held eleven days after whichever feastday they had formerly been held on. The purpose of this Act may have been to diminish the importance of the fair thereby reducing the attendance and as a consequence, providing less opportunities for disturbances on a large scale.

In 1781, Henry Viscount Palmerston was given a grant by George III of England to hold fairs in Cliffoney. A levy was to be charged and the fairs were to be held on the 18th day of May, 18th of June, 5th day of October, 6th day of November and the 15th day of December. In addition to this, a weekly market was to be held, "in or near the town" on every Thursday. Shortly after this, the rent rolls show cash being allowed to a Lawrence Sweeney, being Mr. Johnson's tenant for Mullaghmore, to establish this fair and market at Cliffoney.

Nos.	Denominations	Tenants	Arrears due			

Proof of Years Rent

Years rent to March and May 1887 per last Rental furnished £ 5819 5 10

Deduct Decrease

for Nos. See Rental Decrease being the difference between the old and the
Judicial Rents fixed for several holdings, as shewn
in last column of the foregoing present Rental of
the Ahamlish part of the Estate _____ 367 11 11

65 Kilkilloque. Widow Mary McAnnon : Conacre Rent entered
in last Rental as £2.10.0 instead of £1.5.0 _____ 1 5

71 Mulloghmore, Owen Fowley, holding taken up and added
to Demesne _____ 1

81ᴮ Do. Salmon Fishery, James McGlone, surrendered, now
let to Christopher Donleavy at £5. per ann. Decrease 2 10

82 Do. Grazing proceeds. — Decrease this Rental _____ 2 19 6

103 Cloontybawn: Pat McMorrow. portion of his holding taken
up for planting, rent reduced proportionately _____ 2

287 Creevymore, Grazing proceeds. Decrease this Rental _____ 7 14

362 Cliffoney Dr. Tate. holding surrendered and sold to S. Commons 8

365½ Do. Policemens Cottages, Decrease in Receipts this Rental 1

367³ Do. Mary Gilmartin, house taken up. proportion of rent to time
of leaving entered & paid in this Rental only. Decrease _____ 1 7 6

482 & 617 Middle Mount Temple, Widow Kath. McSharry, holding sold
to her under the Ashbourne Act _____ 13

494 + 495 Do. + Moneygold. Edward Parke. Do. Do. _____ 79

640ᵃ + 641ᵃ Kiltykere : Roger Connolly. new letting to him as one
holding at £1. per ann. Decrease _____ 10

709 William Street. William Gilmour, holding included in
No. 708. in lease made to Mrs. Gilmour. Dec. 1885 _____ 2 2

Forward £ 489 19 11 5819 5 10

181

Nos.	Denominations	Tenants	1 Year's Rent due May 1890		
			143	3	13
58	Kilkilloque contd	Widow Nabby Barry	7	1	
59		Peter McGowan	7	8	
60		John Gilvarry Senr.	3	10	
61		Michael Martin	5	17	
62		Bridget Kelly	7	3	
63		Martin Boys	2	4	
64		Widow Mary McCannon	3	9	
65	aa31	Do.	1	5	
67		Martin Doodican	1	14	
68	Mulloghmore	Paddy Gunnigle	2	2	
69		Pat Bruin	4	3	
70		Pat Gilmartin (Ned)	2	2	
72		Thomas McHugh	J.K. 1	10	
72		Do. 3rd Install of Loan £6_	1	8	
73	White House	Christopher Bracken	free.		
76	Watch House Boat Ho. & Flag Staff	H. M. Board of Customs	68	10	
77	Six Coast Guard Houses	Do.			
78	Old Watch Ho. Boat Ho. Store				
" A	No 1. Lodge	R. I. Constabulary Barracks	20		
" B	No 2. Lodge	Kenneth Kerr	14		
" C	Metrological Society	Robert H. Scott. Secy.		1	
79	Harbour Pier, Keep Shed	Martin Gilmartin	5		
" A	Do. 2 Barytes Sheds	Colonel Tottenham	10		
81	House Plot	James McGlone Senr.	2	8	
" A	New House Plot	James McGlone Junr.	8		
" B	Salmon Fishery	Christopher Donleavy	5		
82	Fields Near Lodges	Grazing, Season 1890	62	8	
83	Classiebawn Bent Hills & Small Burrow	Do. Do.	172	9	10
		Forward	562	5	10

182

'THE LODGES'

Palmerston, realising the potential of the area as a holiday resort, is said to have set about building a terrace of lodges for "the better classes" by the sea in Mullaghmore. Early maps and records indicate that buildings already existed on the site of these lodges on his arrival in Mullaghmore, so a sizeable portion of the work would have been reconstruction. Part of this block of buildings, probably what is now used as a disco area by the Beach Hotel seems to have been converted to a corn store and drying kiln in 1829, at an estimated cost of £340. Shortly after this the Sligo Journal carried advertisements advising of the letting of the Corn store and kiln, with a 300 ton capacity, at Mullaghmore harbour. The northern portion of this block of houses belonged to a Hugh Gilmartin, who, it seems, may have been the first man in Mullaghmore in the business of renting lodges. The following advertisement was inserted in the Sligo Journal in 1836:

BATHING LODGE

TO BE LET FOR THE SEASON, OR MONTHLY, THAT SUPERIOR BATHING LODGE AT MULLAGHMORE, WITH SUFFICENT APARTMENTS TO ACCOMODATE ONE OR TWO FAMILIES, ALSO BUTTER, MILK, POTATOES, HAY OR GRASS, AND ALL WITHIN ONE MILE OF THE PUBLIC ROAD, WHERE DAILY COACHES AND CARS PASS BETWEEN SLIGO AND BALLYSHANNON. THERE WILL ALSO BE IN A FEW DAYS, ATTACHED TO THE PREMISES, COMFORTABLE WARM BATHS.
FOR FURTHER PARTICULARS, APPLY TO HUGH GILMARTIN, MULLAGHMORE.

Gilmartin was still listed as owner of the lodges in 1858. Some of the buildings were unoccupied at this time and it is likely that Palmerston acquired Gilmartins property shortly after this, having previously acquired Pier Head House. These lodges were built as self contained units – the self catering cottages of their day and the forerunner of a style of accomodation which is still popular in Mullaghmore and all over Ireland even today.

The lodges started at No. 1 where the Mc Hughs now have a grocery shop, Eithne's restaurant stands where No. 2 lodge was, and so on up to No.'s 8,9,10, and 11 where the convent and chapel now stand. A water supply to all the lodges was piped from water storage tanks near Tobair Geall well, both tanks and well are still in existence near the entrance to the beach. Mullaney's house, on the approach road to Mullaghmore, was originally a wash house, where the washing was done for the lodges and Classiebawn. Leydons were the last family to live here while it was being used for this purpose.

Coach houses and stables were built behind the lodges to house the carriages and horses of the tenants, a list of which tenants could fill a Who's Who of landed gentry and officers of the county of Sligo and further afield — O'Hara's, Wynne's, Perceval, Hosie, Eccles, Cooke, Le Strange, Earl of Granard, Gore-Booths and so on. The ruins of the stables and coach houses which were built c.1843 at a cost of £86.8s.10d by Martin Connor, contractor, and approved by John Lynch of Rundale Cottage, are still to be seen behind the Beach Hotel at the old iron water pump that once provided all the water for the yards and horses. The lodges were let for ten to twenty pounds a month; rentals of stables, if required, was extra.

The noted attorney, Bob Lyons, was one of the most famous residents of the lodges in the early years of the last century. He is given the credit for starting that famous barrister and orator, John Philpot Curran, on his career. Curran, a frequent visitor to Mullaghmore, had his most famous case in the defence of William Orr, who was tried and hanged at Carickfergus in Co. Antrim in 1797 for administering the oath to the United Irishmen.

Palmerston's agent, Kincaid, of the Dublin firm of Stewart & Kincaid spent his summers in the lodges and kept a yacht under the green at the "Lugger Quay"; this quay was scavenged by Sligo County Council in the middle of this century to build roads in the area, but its foundations can still be seen at this time. Kincaids apartment in the lodges was burned down in mysterious circumstances in the early 1900's; some old postcards of this time show No. 4 lodge as a ruin. According to Miss Kathleen Clancy the caretaker, a retired coastguard, Attridge, and his wife, had a narrow escape from burning at this time.

No. 1 lodge was used as an R.I.C. barracks for some years after White House was discontinued for use as a barracks. The estate rentals at the end of the 19th century list the occupation of No. 1 lodge by the R.I.C., at a rental of £20. Older residents recall Tommy Fowley's mother, who lived where Maxwells now have a holiday home, paying a fine to the police when they were garrisoned at White House. The fine was levied for allowing domestic fowl to wander on the "green" in front of the lodges. This green was the preserve of the visitors who came to the lodges; the area in front of the present convent was reserved for lawn tennis and from there over to Pier Head for other games and leisure activities. The local fishermen were allowed the use of the green from the Iron Gate to the lawn tennis area for spreading and mending their nets. Pat Leonard of Bunduff was one of the last greens-keepers on the golf course, which was located behind the sand banks, in an area where visitors and locals still practise the odd round of golf from time to time.

The development of the lodges, complemented by the harbour was a very successful undertaking, which continued under Ashley's patronage into the early years of this century. Surviving the test of time in a changing world, it has continued to this day, although now privately owned, to cater to holidaymakers wishing to enjoy the many hobbies and sports Mullaghmore has to offer. During the early years of its development though, it was not without its critics; O'Rourke writing at the close of the last century reprimanded that it was accomodation of too exclusive a kind which catered only to the rich, "who have already so many of the good things of Ireland", making no provision, he said, "for the lodging of persons belonging to the humbler classes."

An English author, Stanley Lane-Poole who visited here in 1903 commented that the village was in danger of being over developed along the lines of Brighton in England, making this "delightful but little known spot accessible to thousands who never heard of it. It would all mean Progress and everything that is profitable and detestable. Mullaghmore would make an ideal seaside resort but it would no longer be Mulaghmore."

The lodges were sold to various private interests following the formation of the Freestate. John Hannon, who worked for the estate and whose family had long connections with the Classiebawn estates, was listed as leaseholder of the old corn store at an annual fee of £15, in 1901. Hannon eventually acquired the portion of the lodges now known as the Beach Hotel, completely renovated the old store and the burned out lodge, giving it the basic form we see today and naming it, "Hannons Hotel". It retained this name into the 1960's until the death of Mrs Hannon who survived John by many years. Ownership then passed to Hannon's nephew, Tom Cartin and it has changed ownership every few years from then to the present day. The view from these lodges out across the harbour towards the mountains, is unrivalled anywhere in Ireland or the world, and will always ensure the popularity of these historic old seafront buildings as a centre of the tourist industry in this area.

LIME AND LIME KILNS

Cement did not come into use until the beginning of the 20th century so lime kilns were essential to any building project at this time, as lime mortar was the binder used to bond the stones, used in the building, together. The earliest lime built construction dates from the beginning of the 11th century; prior to this no bonding was used and all building was of dry stone. The ruins of old lime kilns can still be seen in many places throughout the country but lime mortar is not in use today, except in specialist reconstruction work. The use of lime kilns for any purpose was finally discontinued in this area in the middle of this century.

In 1826, Palmerston had proposed three lime kilns for Derrylehan with a railroad running to Mullaghmore. He projected that each kiln would burn 100 barrels of lime every three days at a cost of 5d per barrel. The cost of erecting the three lime kilns was £100 and the lime was to be sold at 10d per per barrel.

An old lime kiln, built in the early years of the 19th century, existed at Mullaghmore until recently, when it was torn away and replaced by the existing toilets at the harbour. Locals can still remember hearing the older people saying that the limestone was brought in lots of three tons by boat from St. John's Point, as the limestone for the kilns had to be brought into areas from outside if the rock was not indigenous to an area. Two Mullaghmore men, John Clinton and Jamesy "Visit" Mc Court, ferried limestone in this manner during the building of Classiebawn castle. (Jamesy was nicknamed "Visit" as he was possessed of many cures and "visited" sick people; he eventually went blind on one of these healing visits.) The preparation of the kiln and manufacture of the lime was an interesting process.

Two men worked full time at the kiln; this looked like a big chimney, three to five feet inside diameter, standing 15 to 16 feet high and tapering slightly inwards towards the top. When setting up a burning, the first layer on the bottom consisted of a layer of kindlings, turf and coal topped with slack, over which was laid a layer of limestone which had been broken into three to four inch lumps. This was followed with layers of coal, turf and limestone, these being laid alternately until the kiln was full.

It was then set alight and left to burn from four days to a week, at which time the lime was separated from the ashes and removed through a trap door at the bottom of the kiln. The rough lumps of lime were then covered with sand and slacked with water; care had to be taken at this stage, as when water is added to lime, it can blow up violently. The heaps of lime were then covered, to keep the air and water out, and left to cure for about two weeks at which time the lumps were broken, the lime turned and sand added. It could then be left for a longer period; the longer it is left, the stronger it gets.

When required for building the lime was mixed and mixed again until it formed into a very sticky substance which rivalled any modern building material for strength and adhesion. Buttermilk was sometimes added to improve adhesion and hardening and also when the lime was used for the glazing of windows. Cowhair was sometimes mixed with the lime when used for plastering and building to strengthen the mix and prevent cracking, and bullocks blood was added for fine stone work. This lime had other uses too as it was also spread on the land to counter acid soil and in its raw state, uncured, for decorating and whitewashing the plastered stone walls of country houses. Palmerston had several of these kilns in operation in this area by 1826, producing lime at a cost of fivepence to sixpence a barrel, and selling it at tenpence, relating that he was quite pleased with himself that he could undersell the competition by twopence a barrel.

DIAMOND

Boot Polish

Nov. 30, 1893

M

Bought of

JOHN LANG,

Draper, Grocer, Wine and Spirit Merchant,

GRANGE, Co. Sligo.

7 st. bag flour	8	9
6 lb. bacon	2	0
1 qt. oil		2
herrings & snuff		7
? lb. tea	3	0
1 st. sugar	2	9
Coffin boards & nails	4	2
2 gra paper	6	0
1 qt. malt	4	0
Bottle rum	2	11
3 lbs. tobacco	10	6
Bag meal	13	0
2 bottles claret	2	6
	3 0	4

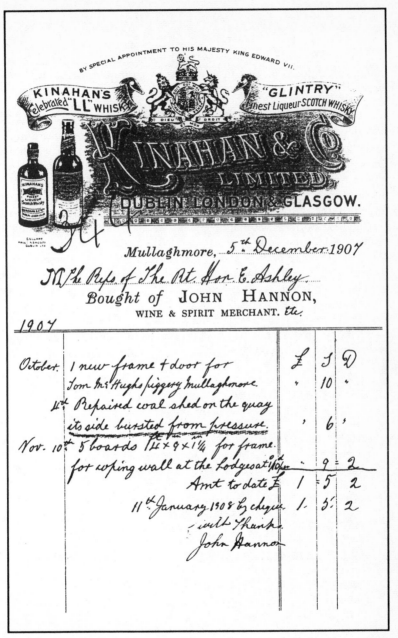

BY SPECIAL APPOINTMENT TO HIS MAJESTY KING EDWARD VII.

KINAHAN'S Celebrated "LL" WHISKY

"GLINTRY" Finest Liqueur SCOTCH WHISKY

KINAHAN & Co LIMITED.

DUBLIN LONDON & GLASGOW.

KINAHAN'S FINEST LIQUEUR Scotch Whisky

Mullaghmore, 5th December 1907

M/The Reps of The Rt Hon E. Ashley

Bought of JOHN HANNON,

WINE & SPIRIT MERCHANT. etc.

1907

		£	S	D
October	1 new frame & door for Tom McHughs piggery Mullaghmore.	"	10	"
4th	Repaired coal shed on the quay its side bursted from pressure.	"	6	"
Nov. 10th	5 boards 14 × 9 × 1¼ for frame for coping wall at the Lodge at 10½	"	9	2
	Amt to date £	1	5	2
	11th January 1908 by cheque	1.	5.	2
	with Thanks			
	John Hannon			

189

A DIRECTORY

John Gilmartin of Grange P.O, 70 years old in 1937, related to the Folklore Commission that in Penal Times Grange consisted of a single row of houses on the south side, where the village now stands. A double row of small drab huts stood on either side of the road, known as the old road, southward of the present village. This, the village proper was known as "Sraid Tra". The huts of "Sraid Ard" were occupied by tradesmen; shoemakers, weavers, patchers, wheelwrights, smiths, basketmakers, millers and coopers. A large granary or storehouse, from which Grange gets its name stood where the Catholic Church now stands and was at that time the property of the monks of Boyle Abbey, some of the monks actually living in Grange. They supervised the granary and the storage of food there, by the people of the surrounding districts, pending transferral to Boyle.

The O.S. map of 1837 shows a Tuck Mill and mill race south of the village. Correspondence of the Palmerston estate indicates a flax scutching mill being built, "at the river above Grange", in 1864. Six sets of scutching machines were being made at Belfast and the builders, finding a new wheel too expensive, were on the lookout of a second hand water wheel.

Kilgannon's Almanack and Directory published in 1907 gives the following information on Grange:

CHURCHES

Roman Catholic ...	Rev. M. Kelly
C. of Ireland ...	Rev. J. McCormack

SCHOOLS

Grange ...	Wm. Devins & Miss K. Conway
Benbulben ...	John Kilfeather & Miss Hannon

POLICE STATION ... Sergeant McSteer, Constables Clarke, Mackey, Magee and Roche.

POST OFFICE ...   Miss McSharry

MERCHANTS AND TRADESMEN   * Indicates a spirit license
Costello, John
*Harte, Bernard (also Draper and Bakery)
Finnegan P.
*Lang, John (also Draper)
Lang T.

190

*Leonard, Owen
Lindley Miss
Lang, John (Draper & General)
McSharry, Miss, Stationer, Newsagent etc.
*Moffat, M.
Moore, Mrs. Restaurant
*Watters, C.
Pugh, M. Tweed Manufacturer
Tivnan, Mrs. Restaurant

INDUSTRIES
Creamery & Co-Operative Society, Ballinfull
Flanagan, P. Tweed Manufacturer

A directory of 1912 adds the following:
Barry, P. Wines and Spirits;
Gilmartin, J. Grocer;
Kilfeather's Wine & Spirit Merchants;
Kilgannon, W. Restaurant;
Leonard, Eugene, Chemist;
Sweeney, Francis, Hardware & Cycle accessories, Cars for hire.

BREAGHWY (1907)

CHURCHES
Roman Catholic ...	Rev. M. Kelly C.C.
C. of Ireland ...	Rev. Mr. Mc Cormack

SCHOOLS
Breaghwy ...	Bernard McGovern, Joseph McGovern and Miss Agnes McIntyre.
Derelehan and Mount Temple ...	Miss B. Healey and Miss Moffit

R.I.C.   Sergeant Higgins, Constables Alexander, Finiane, Fitzpatrick and Gillooly

POST OFFICE   John McGovern

MERCHANTS AND TRADESMEN
*James Harte, Lislary, Ballinfull
Peter Cunningham, Mount Edward, Breaghwy
Thomas Hargadon, Ballyconnel, Breaghwy
John Foran, Lislaryy, Ballinfull

AUCTION

OF
A VALUABLE
LICENSED PREMISES

In the Town of
GRANGE,

On WEDNESDAY, 29th SEPT, 1897.

SUBSCRIBERS has been favoured with instruction from Mr Martin Brearty, to sell by PUBLIC AUCTION, on above date, that Valuable Licensed Premises in the town of Grange, which he holds under Lease from James Johnston, Esq, J P, for a term of 31 years (unexpired), at the very low rent of £3 10d per annum.

For further particulars see posters or apply to
T H M^cLOUGHRY, Auctioneer.
The Mall, Sligo, 24th Sept, 1897.

1897 Auction of what is now Barry's Pub & Lounge in Grange

Rental No. *198* *Bundcliff*   **£ 3 : 0 : 0**

RECEIVED from *Anthony McNutty*
James McCormick

sterling, for   *One*——Year's Rent

Due to THE RIGHT HONble. EVELYN ASHLEY,

the *1st* day of *November* 189*1 (One),*

out of the above Holding—Received this *14th* day of *November* 1894

Rent   ....   .   £ 3 : 0 : 0

Poor Rate £   : 6 : 0
@ 2/£ — : 6 : 0

ONE PENNY

£ a : 6 : 0   *John McKinnen*

Nett £ *2 : 14 : 0*

PAGE

192

PUTTING UP WRACK

Pollyarry, 1933; John Leonard on left with unidentified boy sitting on ass. Fr. Browne who took this picture stayed with the Jesuits during the years they rented Classiebawn for Summer holidays

Photo: Courtesy of the Father Browne S.J. Collection

WINCHING HAY
Coen Brothers 'winching' haycock on to hayfloat

Photo J. Mc G

THE BASKETMAKERS
Michael McGroarty and Connie McHugh, 1977

Photo: Courtesy of Colman Doyle

'MULLAGHMORE BARYTES RUSH' 1927

Members of the group positively identified starting at the back, L to R: Danny McCannon, Nicholas Joe McGovern, Jack McHugh, Mary McDermott, Jack Hargadon, May McHugh, Petie McHugh, Francis McGowan, Martin Mullaney, Pa Barry (Jimmy's brother), Bartley Gillen, Mac Barry, Johnny Gallagher, Paddy ('beag') Barry, Pa Duffy

MIdle, L to R: John Hannon, Dinny Rourke, Martin Mullaney, Paddy Gallagher, Michael Duffy, Hughie Cawley, Alf Hill, James Rourke, Francis Duffy('Meman'), Petie McGowan, 'Youth' Harrison, John Rogers, Jamesie Duffy, Dan McGowan,

Sitting on ground, L to R: Jack McHugh, Danny McHugh, ? , Tom Currid, Thomas Boyce.

Sitting on Chairs: L to R: Sutherland, Mrs Sutherland, ? , Mrs. John Hannon, Fr. Keane.

Not all members of the group can be identified   Photo Reproduction: Courtesy of Hugh Barry

GRANGE PIPE BAND

T. Burke, N.T. (Leader), Bernie Friel, Jack Friel, Jim McLean, Mick Gilbride, Paddy Kelly, Jim Moore, Paddy Joe Keagans, Jimmy Gilmartin, Johnny McGarrigle, Jim Feeney, Paddy Currid

Photo: Courtesy of Mrs T. Burke

BUNDUFF BAND 1940

Michael Leonard, Hughie Cawley, John Leydon, William Barry, John Leonard, Tommy McGowan, Paddy Curran, Pat Judge, Patrick O Connor, John Clancy, John Gardiner, Johnny McGee, Tommy McGee, William Mc Gee
Lower Bunduff: *Matie Leydon, Jim Leydon, Jimmy Harrison, Hubert Barry, Tommy Barry, Stephen Barry, Michael, Martin and Andrew Harrison, Owen Leonard.*
Frolic: *Thomas Wymbs, John Wymbs, Bernie, Thomas and Jim Barry.*

Photo: Courtesy of Lilian Mitchell

GRANGE FAIR C. 1945

Jim Leonard and Patrick Branley among those pictured

Photo: Courtesy of Mrs T. Burke

COSTELLO'S, GRANGE: PETROL DELIVERY C. 1925

Photo: Courtesy of Joe Barr

WALTER DIXON, STONEMASON
with Mullaghmore 'Tower' in the background, 1992

Photo:J. McG

CUTTING THE TURF
An essential part of country life in times past, 1977
Michael Dunleavey, Joe McGowan, Michael Mc Groarty
Photo: Courtesy of Colman Doyle

QUENCHING A 'RICK-MAKING' THIRST AT DERRY 1943

Jimmy McSharry (on Ladder) Back Row: Paddy Kelly, Tom Currid, Peter Meehan,
Middle Row: Jamesy Moohan, ? McSharry, Kay McSharry
Front Row: Mick McSharry, John Joe Leydon, Mick Brennan

Photo: Courtesy of John J. Leydon

A 'CONVOY' 1928

Back Row, L to R. Mattie Burns, Pakie Currid, John Moore, Peter Meehan,
George Costello, Tommy Moore, John Barry with John Joe Leydon in arms
Front: Kathleen Currid, Tommy Moore, John Burns, Eddie Towey, Mary
Currid (gong to U.S.A.) Jack Hoey, James Moore, Phil Costello.

Photo: Courtesy of John Joe Leydon

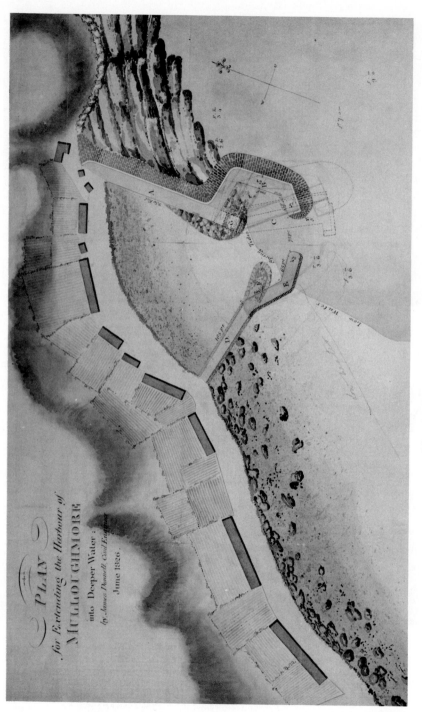

PLAN
for Extending the Harbour of
MULLOGHMORE
into Deeper Water :
by James Donnell Civil Engineer
June 1826.

CLASSIEBAWN HARBOUR

Pat Waters, Lislary, Ballinful
Carney
Merchants and Tradesmen
McKim, George, Ballinfull
*McLaughlin, James, Ballyconnell
*Barber, I.L. Carney
Mrs. P. Currid, Ballyconnell
*Martin, I., Carrigans
Mrs. M. Doherty, Ballyconnell
*Michael Harte, Carney
Mrs. J. Currid, Ballyconnell
*McMorrow, I.M. Carney
John Chrystal, Castletown
*J.P. Jordan Carrigan

LACEMAKING, DOONFORE ...   Miss Breslin, Teacher

An earlier directory for Carney printed in 1889 gives the following:
William McVilly, Publican and Grocer;
Michael Hart, Publican;
John Wallace, General Merchant;
Owen Leydon, Blacksmith;
Thomas Meehan, Blacksmith;
James Ewen, Carpenter.

NATIONAL SCHOOL
Headmaster ...   James Mulligan
Headmistress ...   Miss McGowan
Medical Officer at dispensary ...Dr. Roe
Postmistress ..   Miss Jones

GLIFFONEY/MULLAGHMORE

Alexander Nimmo, architect and designer, was busy in 1826 drawing up plans for the "Cliffoney Inn" (now Ena's Pub). Every detail was attended to:

"A door is to be opened on the yard side at the gable, between the kitchens a flight of stone steps 4 feet broad to the level of the yard. A small hole within the door with single doors opening into new kitchen and old one which is to be converted into a bar room ... the stables are to be fitted each with a plain rack and manger on one side and on the other two stalls as shown in the drawing ..."

Some details concerning Canavaun Pub are given in a separate chapter where the incident concerning Hayes is covered. In addition to this, Bernie Barry told me that his fathers grandmother, a Miss McNelis, came from here before Foley's time. The McNelis's were woolbuyers and kept a large shed at the back of what is now Canavaun, for the purpose of storing the wool. The proud boast of McNelis's grandfather, O'Donoghue, who came from Creevykeel, was that when he looked towards Donegal on a clear day he could see the smoke rising from the chimney's of all of his three daughters who were married there.

A directory for Cliffoney written in 1889 gives the following information:

CHURCHES
Irish Church ...	Rev. Mr. McDermott
Roman Catholic ...	Rev. M. Crofton, P.P.

SCHOOLS
National School (male) ...	Mr. Kearns
National School (female) ...	Miss Quinn
National School (infant)...	Miss Heron

DISPENSARY
Medical Officer ...	Dr. John Tate
Police Station	

Sgt. Carty in charge

HOTELS
Mr. Commons (late Palmerston's Hotel)

POST OFFICE...   Miss Davy

MERCHANTS AND TRADESMEN

Patrick Cummin, Grocer & Publican
Henry Brennan, Baker and Publican
Hugh Clancy, General Merchant and Publican
Owen Dunleavy, Publican
Edward Hannon, Bunduff, Blacksmith
Patrick Hannon, Creevykeel, Blacksmith
McGarrigle, Blacksmith
Thomas Hannon, Carpenter (not included)
Oates, Carpenter
John Commons, Wheelwright
John Commons, sen., painter and glazier

Kilgannon's directory of 1907 give the following:
Local agent for Mr. Ashley ...   William Lowe

CHURCHES
R.C. ...   Rev. W. Crofton P.P., Rev. P. Clive C.C.
C.of Ireland ..Rev. Mr. McCormack

SCHOOLS
Cliffoney ... Mrs. McGloin and Mrs. Clancy
Castlegal ... Mr. O'Connor and Mrs. McGloin
Mullaghmore ... Mr. P. Conway
Church of Ireland ... Miss Noble
Derelehan ... Miss Healy
Mount Temple ... Miss Moffit
Inishmurray ... Miss Heraughty

DISPENSARY
Medical Officer ...   Dr. Gibbons

POLICE STATION
Sergeant Gaughan, Constables Butler, Fahey, Feely and Perry

POST OFFICE
Cliffoney ... Mr. Clancy
Castlegal ... J. O'Connor
Mullaghmore ... Miss Barry
Ballintrillick ... Hugh Gallagher

MERCHANTS AND TRADESMEN *Those marked with * hold licenses*

*H. Brennan, Cliffoney
*I. Cummins, Cliffoney
*H. Clancy, Cliffoney
*D. Dunleavey, Cliffoney
P. Clancy, Cliffoney
J. Timoney, Cliffoney
AndrewHiggins, Castlegal
Henry McGovern, Castlegal
John Wymbs, Bunduff
*Mary Hannon, Creevykeel
*Mrs. McGowan, Creevykeel

*John Hannon, Mullaghmore
P. Duffy, Mullaghmore
Thos. Hannon, Carpenter, M'more
John Oates, Carpenter
John Commons, Wheelwright
John Commons, Painter & Glazier
*Bonnar, Mrs. A. Tullaghan
*Bonnar, John E., Tullaghan
Maguire, T., Egg Exporter, Tullagh
Thos. McGuire, Grellagh

Did you know that:

According to John Harrison, Conor Commins, possibly related to the Commons mentioned above was a carpenter and wheelwright who also made firkins for butter and churns etc. He lived where Miss Jennings now lives.

The license to sell spirits for James Patrick McGloins pub in

Mullaghmore was, according to Seamus McGloin, originally held next door at what is now Quinn's shop, owned at that time by the McGloin family. The location of the present licensed premises is shown as an empty lot on a map drawn in 1865, and was probably built c.1880.

Mullaghmore Sea Farms is one of the more unique and interesting businesses in Ireland, buying lobsters and crawfish all along the north west coast of Ireland and storing them live in ponds until ready for export to points all over the globe, but mainly continental Europe. The business was founded by Michael Watters of Streedagh in 1947 and the storage ponds built in 1959. Michael was born on Innishmurray island of which he was titular king, this title having been handed down for many generations.

Correspondence between Palmerston and his agents Walker of Rathcormack and Lynch of Cliffoney in 1830 discuss the details of removing the roof and raising the walls of Pier Head House. The cost was estimated at £16,10.0 for labour, materials extra, depending on how many of the old slates could be reused. Further information on Pier Head House is given in a separate chapter.

Rodney Lomax, originally from Rosses Point, fulfilled the ambition of a lifetime when he established his boatbuilding business in Mullaghmore in the winter of '61/'62. Lomax Boats are still going strong and since that time have built over 200 boats here, varying from sailing dinghies to 30' fishing and cruising boats.

No reference to boats would be complete without a mention of that fine builder of model boats, P.K. Malone, whose precise scale models of square riggers, galleons and schooners can be seen throughout Ireland and in many countries abroad.

BATHING LODGE.

TO be let for the Season, or monthly, that superior BATHING LODGE at MULLAGHMORE, with sufficient apartments to accommodate one or two families, also, butter milk potatoes, hay or grass, and all within one mile of the public road, where daily coaches and cars pass between Sligo and Ballyshannon. There will be also in a few days, attached to the premises, comfortable WARM BATHS.

For further particulars, apply to Hugh Gilmartin, Mullaghmore.

Sligo Journal 1836

CHAPTER 10

'Clashybaan' Harbour
to
The Barytes Rush

The jewel in the crown of Palmerstons achievements on his Irish properties must surely be the harbour at Mullaghmore; an enduring tribute in stone to the abilities of the stone masons and a monument to the genius of its architects and engineers.

There is no evidence to indicate that anything more than the most rudimentary facility existed to shelter boats here previous to the building of this harbour. Ships and cargo boats were unloaded by being driven aground on the beach, propped in an upright position by timbers and unloaded by horse or ass and cart. A local historian, Bernie Barry, once recalled being told by his grandmother that one of these merchants receiving goods in this manner, was a man named Lynch, a part time smuggler, he was also an agent for the Palmerstons. Smuggling was rife in the 1700's both in England and Ireland and went on pretty much unchecked until the Customs Service and communication along the coast was improved in the early 1800's. Two of Lynch's associates were Bunduff men Harrison and Mc Quaid, who helped him to land tea, rum, silks, whiskey and tobacco, bringing the goods ashore at the "channel" and storing them in sheds at Bunduff, prior to being sold to merchants in Sligo. Bernie claimed that one of these ships of 50 to 100 tons carrying flour, meal and timber was wrecked near the little bridge on "Fanny's" road at the time when Mullaghmore was an island, and that the top of the mast could still be seen protruding from the sand in his fathers time.

Lynch lived where Mark Hannon lives now in what was formerly known as Rundale House, his property extending to the Burra road to an area still known as Lynch's Ditch. Lynch fell into disfavour with the landlords and was replaced by Hannon who had served with distinction during the Crimean War (1853-'56). Lynch's sister, still resident in the house, was moved to the cottage now owned by Rattigans while Hannon took over Rundale House and Lynch's duties. Hannons eventually acquired this house also, renting it out to various people including a Dr. Tate and at one time to Dr. Gibbons, who lived here while practising medicine at the dispensary, which at that time was located where Kilfeathers now run a grocery shop. John Harrison, Cliffoney,relates that Captain O'Beirne, a captain of the local yeomen, (a volunteer cavalry unit) lived in Rundale House some time before Lynch. The existence of a Captain O'Beirne is confirmed by a reference to this name in correspondence from Rundale House in the early 1800's, held in the Palmerston archives in Southampton.

Work on the harbour commenced in 1822 on what we now call the Old Quay; so called because it is the oldest of the two piers, being the first one to be built. Alexander Nimmo, the engineer who designed the harbour, in a report dated 29 April 1822, stated that the bay of Mullaghmore was the best place on the south side of the Donegal bay to site a harbour, having good anchorage and being sheltered from the prevailing winds by the peninsula. In addition,

> "There is a productive Turbot bank from Mullaghmore to Bunduff and clean trawling ground from there to the Donegall side. The herrings when in this neighbourhood frequently set into Mullaghmore and were last year so abundant as to be sold for five shillings per thousand .... even in its present state it is the chief place for supplying the counties of Fermanagh and Leitrim and the neighbouring parts of Sligo and Donegal with white fish .....
>
> At the rock called Elanna Clashybaan a little to the right of the village is a landing place for boats at low water ...... This landing place is covered by a ledge of sandstone rock running obliquely from the shore and presenting a sloping side to the swell. It is very confined and in heavy gales of wind affords so little shelter that the boats have to be hauled upon a steep bank .... In the high tides of last Winter eleven out of the fourteen boats belonging to the village were washed off this bank and totally wrecked.
>
> I should propose to build up this ledge to 3 feet over high water Springs with a stout parapet and sloping pavement on the sea side ..... This beach affords abundance of loose stones for building and filling the pier and especially what will be obtained from the low ledges that must be quarried out of the centre of the harbour are in their natural state the finest building ashlers I have ever seen, requiring no dressing of any kind. The quay wall may be built dry with these stones ...."

He expected the harbour to be an English acre in extent and when finished, to be capable of handling any of the coasting vessels of the day. He estimated the cost at £1,182.

Originally there was no intention to build anything other than the short pier and jetty at the northern end of the harbour, but when this was finished, in 1827, Palmerston decided to continue building, and extended the harbour to its present configuration. Construction was still in progress on the New Quay when he wrote in Nov. 1841,

"My harbour, which I have been obliged to enlarge lately, is nearly finished, and though it has cost me more than I reckoned upon, it will now fully answer all purposes. It will be about 800 feet long by 300 wide and will have thirteen or fourteen feet of water at Spring tides...... enough depth to admit vessels of 300 tons, as much as any harbour on the West coast of Ireland."

At one point during the building he had discussed with Nimmo, the engineer in charge of the project, the possibility of getting the authorities, "to lay down a railroad to it from the end of Loch Erne; it would become the exporting and importing harbour for a large tract of very fertile country lying on the banks of that lake."

Nimmo seemed to be quite enchanted with railways, as these were just gaining ground in England as a mode of transport at this time; the use of crude railways with wagons pulled by horses along wooden rails had spread to England during the 17th century the first scheduled passenger service was put into effect there in 1825. He didn't get his railroad to the bogs but he did plan and put into operation the first rails in these parts and possibly in Ireland when track was laid from Gubaun, a promontory north of Mullagh head, to the works at the harbour. The bogeys or cars were horse or ass drawn and conveyed the rocks, which were quarried at the base of the cliff and raised by two derricks to rail level. The remains of the base of one of the derricks which raised the stones, could be seen at Gubaun until recently; lengths of the rails are still used to barricade gaps into pasture fields, to this day.

Some of the stones used to build the harbour were quarried in place, while others were taken from the Blackrocks at Bunduff. These latter stones were loaded on to lighters or boats with platforms installed on the decks; these craft were beached near the quarry at low water, loaded, and when the tide came in, towed or sailed across the bay to the harbour.

Shortly after the harbour was completed it became severely silted up, with large accumulations of sand threatening to make it unusable. This problem was completely alleviated by the simple expedient of building an opening and bridge at the southern end of the harbour thus setting up a scouring action which has kept the harbour relatively free of any major build-up of sand since then.

The harbour was completed in 1842 at a cost somewhat in excess of

£11,000, part of which was financed out of his own rental income and partly from Government grants, the first grant of £5,000 being received in 1826. The harbour when completed was a great boost to fishing and shipping and has been of incalculable worth to North Sligo generally from its completion to the present day. Ships of up to 300 tons used the port regularly up to the latter part of the first half of this century, bringing in commodities such as coal and timber and taking away kelp, barytes, logs and grain, etc. Without this harbour it would have been impractical to develop the barytes mine at Gleniff, the development of which we will look at later.

SHIPWRECKS

Very few harbours are without their stories of seafaring tragedies and shipwrecks and Mullaghmore is no exception. In the 17th century, vast tracts of Ireland's woodlands were cut down to provide fuel for the smelting of iron ore and for export to England. The ruins of one of these smelters, established by Sir Charles Coote prior to 1640 and burned down in the rising of 1641, can still be seen at Creevylea near Dromahaire. The manufacture of staves, used in the making of barrels, pails, casks, etc., became a prime industry in the 17th century also, causing the exploitation of the woods of Sligo on a massive scale, as these and other timber products as well as rough sawn logs were exported from the port of Sligo.

The "Idwal" was one of the ships involved in this export of timber and in January 1868 she arrived at Mullaghmore, where she had to dock at the Old Quay because of her great size. She then proceded to take on a load of rough timber which was drawn from the woods at Tawley, on the Dickson estate in Co. Leitrim. Some of the older people remember being told of the great shipments of oak going out of the harbour, remarking on a peculiar kind of oak, which was unique for the fact that it would not float and sank when it fell in the water. The trees were cut down by employees of the Dickson estate, the bark taken off by local women, and the logs roughly squared by hatchet and adze before being drawn by horse and ass carts to the waiting ships at Mullaghmore. The 'Idwal' had completed loading her cargo on Saturday January 25th and was made ready by her captain and crew to sail on the first tide on Sunday morning. Local fishermen who came down to the quay to secure their boats spoke to the captain, warning him that the signs were that a major storm was on the way and advising him to move his ship to a safer place and make it secure. A measure of the impression made by the response, and the tragedy that followed, must be that the scornful reply which was given well over 125 years ago is still remembered in the locality to this day. His response to the warnings of the locals was the retort that he, "always took as much of another man's advice as would do him good."

The storm that came on that long black winter's night was a howling westerly gale accompanied by a mountainous groundswell which lashed the ship with wind and wave in her exposed position.

> *"Hour by hour with sleepy light*
> *Glimmering. All without this lair*
> *Was darkness and the noise of night,*
> *Where the wide waste of ocean roll'd*
> *Thundering with savage crash, and air*
> *In one tremendous torrent stream'd*
> *Across the rocks, across the wold,*
> *Across the murky world. It seem'd*
> *There never could be daylight more*
> *From earth to sky, on sea or shore."*

In the middle of the night the Idwal could no longer withstand the severe battering she was receiving at the quayside, and eventually breaking her moorings, was driven before the gale out between the two quays and all the way to Tullaghan where she was driven ashore and completely wrecked near the townland of Redbrae. According to local lore, the cook, who was the only survivor, was saved when he made a desperate leap on to the jetty of the Old Quay as the ship struck this projection when she was being swept out of the harbour. The bodies of the rest of the crew were washed up on the shore on the following day and following an inquest, buried in the old cemetery in Kinlough. On Feb. 1st 1868 the Sligo Champion carried the following story:

DREADFUL SHIPWRECK AND LOSS OF LIFE

"On Saturday the 21st inst. about three o'clock in the morning "The Idwal", a Welsh schooner, laden with timber for Mr. Jackson of Manchester, was forced from her mooring at Mullaghmore, by the violence of the gales and a furious sea which rolled with terrific force from the north side of the breakwater into the harbour, so completely overwhelming the captain and crew – a mate and two sailors, as to deprive them of any assistance. One of the sailors, giving up all hope, jumped in the breakwater as the vessel passed out of the harbour and would have consequently perished, being washed onto the docks by the waves, had not the chief boatsman rushed to his assistance. The

MULLAGHMORE CROSS INSCRIBED SLAB

Kept at National Museum in Dublin, found in 1936 built into the gable of 'Pateens' old house near the stone tower (in Bally tSeampaill)... The seastone cross inscribed on two concentric circles, was also found at 'Pateen'. The stone hammer head was found at Bunduff

SLIGO JOURNAL 1832

Yearly Subscription, £1 3⁵.

Tower

FRIDAY, NOVEMBER 30, 1832.

Mercantile Sale,

TO BE SOLD BY

A U C T I O N,

On MONDAY, December 3rd, 1832.

At the Stores of

ABRAHAM DOBBS,

Wine-street, at One o'Clock:

Jamaica Sugar, of superior quality, in Hhds. and Tierces.

Refined do. in Hhds. and Tierces the Lump.

10 Hhds. Molasses (of a moderate size.)

300 Dozen of Russian-Bass Mats.

30 Casks of Cod, Seal, and Lamp Oil.

30 Ton of British Oak Bark.

Terms at Sale.

S. DOYLE,
Auctioneer.

Wine-street, 26th November, 1832.

CAUTION.

I CAUTION the Public not to give my Wife A.ne Kerriolds, otherwise Reagan, any Credit, as I am determined not to pay any debts she may contract from this date—November 29, 1832.

PATT REAGAN.

Cloteara, Co. Sligo.

NOTICE

To Persons desirous of Emigrating to Van Diemen's Land, or New South Wales.

FOREST TREES,

TO BE SOLD

At LORD PALMERSTON'S

Nursery, Rundle Cottage,

Midway between

Ballyshannon and Sligo,

On the Main Coach road, near Cliffony, as follows:—

30,000 Scotch Fir.

24,000 Larch.

30,000 Alder.

10,000 Oak.

10,000 Norway Spruce.

10,000 White American Spruce.

10,000 Ash.

10,000 Elm.

20,000 Canda Poplar.

5,000 Huntington & Bedford Willows,

10,000 Birch,

11,000 Laurels,

THE above Trees have been twice transplanted, and are growing in an exposed situation, within about 150 perches of the Atlantic Ocean. Any Nobleman, or Gentleman, that has final planting to get done, should visit this Nursery, and see the trees, where they can be purchased on the most reasonable terms. Any orders directed to John Lynch, Nursery-man, Rundle Cottage, Cliffony, Sligo, will be punctually attended to.

AUCTION.

202

schooner did not go far after she was driven from the harbour. The chief boatsman (Coastguard) found her two miles east of Mullaghmore, without mast or bulwark, not even a shred of sail. All was a total wreck."

The inquest which was held by Robt. Corscadden Esq., Coroner, returned a verdict to the effect that, "the four men came to their death by their bodies coming into contact with the rocks, after they were washed off the deck of the vessel. Mr. John Dickson J.P., Tullaghan, was present. Much credit is due to Mr. Sling for his noble exertions in saving the remaining seaman's life."

These four seamen lie buried now in a quiet graveyard in Kinlough, their gravestone of Welsh slate which was brought over from their native hills, their only connection with their own land. The slate bears the Welsh emblem, the leek; underneath an inscription bears their names and the story of their awful fate on that January night so long ago:

"Sacred to the memory of Thomas Jones, aged 61 years, Master of the schooner Idwal of Bangor, who, with his nephew Thomas Jones, aged 22 years, son of John Jones of Tynrhos Farm, Parish of LLanwinllwyfo (Anglesey), lost their lives in the wreck of the above named vessel at Red Brae on the night of the 25th January 1868."

In 1843, the Tolagazone, carrying corn for the port of Sligo, went aground on Bomore Island and was completely wrecked. The captain and crew were rescued by coastguards from the Mullaghmore station.

A Greencastle yawl with her crew of six Mullaghmore fishermen was wrecked on the rocky shore, known as the Long Flag, behind the big hills at the back of Mullaghmore c.1860. The men were engaged in lobster fishing when a wave broke over the boat; both boat and crew were lost.

CLASSIEBAWN

Palmerston was never to see the results of his labours on his last major project in this area. The building of Classiebawn Castle was left to his stepson, the First Lord Mount Temple, to complete when Palmerston died in 1865, at the age of eighty one. The English author now living at Strandhill, Gordon Winter, in his book 'Secrets of the Royals' tells us that the Third Viscount was an amorous old lecher who was well known for his many adulterous shenanigans. Even Queen Victoria was aware that his accomplishments ran to somewhat more than politics and engineering when she described him as "an old sinner" after some of his escapades as a guest at Windsor Castle. It seems that he died somewhat as he had lived, as his death is supposed to have come about as the result of his exertions, in an amorous struggle with one of his parlour

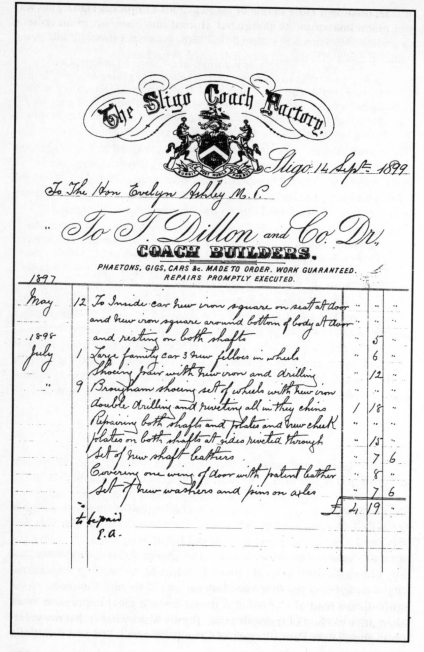

The Sligo Coach Factory,

Sligo 14 Sept 1899

To The Hon Evelyn Ashley M.P.

To T. Dillon and Co. Dr,
COACH BUILDERS.

PHAETONS, GIGS, CARS &c. MADE TO ORDER. WORK GUARANTEED.
REPAIRS PROMPTLY EXECUTED.

1897				£		
May	12	To Inside car new iron square on seat at door	"	"	"	
		and new iron square around bottom of body at door	"	"	"	
1898		and resting on both shafts		"	5	"
July	1	Large family car 3 new felloes in wheels		"	6	"
"		Shoeing pair with new iron and drilling		"	12	"
"	9	Brougham shoeing set of wheels with new iron		"	"	"
		double drilling and riveting all in they chins		1	18	"
		Repairing both shafts and plates and new cheek		"	"	"
		plates on both shafts at sides riveted through		"	15	"
		Set of new shaft leathers		"	7	6
		Covering one wing of door with patent leather		"	8	"
		Set of new washers and pins on axles		"	7	6
				£	4 19	"

to be paid
E.A.

maids, on a pool table in one of his mansions at Brocket Hall. This was not made known to the public but at least one historian in an oblique reference to the incident claimed that some correspondence found in the house proved that the old man had "died in harness."

The first site chosen for Classiebawn Castle was on Dernish Island but this plan had to be abandoned when the architect, J. Rawson Carroll, found it impossible to construct an access causeway because of the very strong tides running into Milk Harbour. The site near Dostann na Breena or the Fairy Rock as it is more commonly known was the one finally chosen. This was not the first building in this area as the Admiralty chart of 1860 marks a "gazebo" here. An earlier estate map drawn in 1813 clearly shows an area marked Mount Temple Lodge encompassing a collection of houses and gardens, some of which at least more than likely belonged to tenants. The list accompanying the estate map of 1810 lists Messrs. Park and Sweeney as tenants of "Mount Temple Lodge, House, Garden & front Field", along with 564 acres of land in the same area. The reduced circumstances of the Sweeneys can be deduced from the following letter written many years later in a very shaky hand, begging alms:

"To the Rt. Honorable E. Ashley,

The petition of Rose Sweeney of Mount Temple, (part of Carns named after the Temples) widow of the late Arthur Sweeney most humbly showeth that herself and her husband has from time immemorable been on the most cordial terms of amity and friendship with the rulers and heads of this estate. *That father to your petitioners husband lived on the site where your castle now stands ......* that from the facts mentioned above that you would be graciously pleased to allow a poor old woman 83 years of age an annual pittance that would enable her to get a box of matches to light her pipe in the night when sleep would fail her and a little grain of tea. Petitioner states that she would not or cannot trouble your honour long and she will

sincerely pray

18th Sept 1886

Most of the stones used in the building of the castle were brought over by sea from Donegal, the stonemasons working on the project being paid 1d. per hour (threequarters of a penny by today's currency). The flagstones used on the steps to the castle were quarried at Leac Ina on the rocky shore nearby. It is said that the steam engine bringing the slates to Classiebawn was the first horseless carriage seen in these parts. As it sunk on the road at Carns hill it didn't make a great impression as an alternative method of transportation. Family history has it that my great-great-grandfather Pat Gallagher of Creevykeel was killed as a result of a fall while erecting the steeple on the castle. As a result of this and in lieu of compensation, his family and their descendants were offered employment on the estates in perpetuity. John Wymbs of the Frolic in Bunduff, forebear of the late Thomas Wymbs also worked on the steeple.

Lord Mount Temple completed the venture in 1874 passing on the castle and estates on his death to the Honourable Evelyn Ashley who was succeeded by his son Col. Wilfrid Ashley, M.P., father of Edwina Ashley who was later to marry Mountbatten — a scion of the German house of Battenberg. A Mr. Hugh Tunney is now in residence in Classiebawn, completing the return to Irish control of this part of North Sligo, which was broken during the confiscations by Strafford and the crown in the 17th century. Slowly but surely, grazing farms have been divided, cut up and taken over, castles and lodges, coastguard stations and towers returned to native ownership.

Classiebawn castle was fortunate to survive destruction during the War of Independence, having been occupied by I.R.A. units during that time and later during the Civil War by Freestate troops. It was slated for burning at one time but saved by the intervention of the local I.R.A.; it had another narrow escape in 1920 when Major Myles of Ballyshannon and some other hostages were held there to force the release of the Bundoran prisoners, Johnston, O'Shea and Mc Bride. It was mined with explosive charges at this time and made ready for detonation, should a rescue be attempted.

Lighting in the castle was provided by candles and oil lamps until 1948, when a generator was installed to provide light and power. Prior to the installation of a petrol pump and pump house at this time, water to the castle was supplied by rainwater from the roof and by donkey and cart from a spring well some distance away. In the late fifties when mains power came to the village, it also came to the castle and in 1965 piped water made the donkey and cart, at least where Classiebawn was concerned, redundant.

1895: THE WAY WE WERE

We will pause here, on our stroll through history's pages, as we are given a unique opportunity to see how the people of this area lived just prior to the turn of the 19th century. This opportunity is given to us by F.G. Townsend Gahan, an inspector with the Congested Districts Board, who visited this area in 1895 to survey the living conditions of the people and suggest improvements. Similar organisations today would be B.I.M., Teagasc, I.D.A., B.I.M. and so on. Gahan was given this brief by the C.D.B., which was set up in 1891 to evaluate and improve the conditions of people living in these "congested" districts along the west coast. This district came under the heading of Grange, which comprised the four electoral divisions of that time; Cliffoney North, Cliffoney South, Lisadell North and Lisadell West, effectively covering most of the area of interest relevant to the writing of this book. The confidential report which he filed with his superiors is a valuable reference for information on living conditions of the time:

Methods of Cultivation

The district is described as having 496 farms of from £10 to £4 valuation; 768 families at and under £4 valuation; 343 families at and under £2 valuation and 95 families in very poor circumstances. The area covered under the survey was 18,133 statute acres, having a population of 6,673 persons. The fact that the area of a farm of £4 valuation ranged from 4 to 6 acres, depending on the quality of the land, gives us an idea of the size of the holdings.

On a six acre farm, three roods would be given over to the cultivation of oats and potatoes; cabbage, half a rood; turnips, half a rood; an acre to an acre and a half given over to meadow and the rest to grazing. A little wheat, barley and rye were grown by a few farmers, but only in small quantities. Cabbage was frequently planted in the "brows" or sides of the potato ridges.

Potatoes were planted at the end of March in lazy beds or ridges; the use of drills was not common but was becoming more popular. Horses and ploughs were more common than in Donegal but even so, most of the labour was done with the spade or loy. The potatoes were "moulded" about six weeks after setting, when the stalks were nine inches above the ground, and not interfered with from then to the time of digging. Some farmers continued to keep the crop clear of weeds but in general he reported that the "weed crops exceeded the potato crops". (this man, obviously, hadn't seen the potato crops in Mullaghmore!).

The crops were manured with farmyard manure, seaweed, guano and shells which were scraped off the rocks. This district, he reported was more dependent on seaweed than Donegal, because the farms, being of a smaller size, didn't produce as much farmyard manure. Grassland was top-dressed with farm manure and seaweed, lime being seldom applied as the soil is on limestone formation. Guano was used at a rate of one bag to a rood and a half of potatoes. Two crops of potatoes were taken off lea land, oats being sown the third year, mixed with grass seed or clover, for letting out to meadow the following year. The report continues:

"General Information On Stock

The stock in this area is, on the whole, superior to that in the Donegal districts. The cattle are a very fair class, and some very fine beasts are to be found. The landlords, Sir Henry Gore-Booth and the Hon. E.

Ashley, both keep bulls for the benefit of their tenantry, the service of which they get at a low price although the bulls kept now by Mr. Ashley are not so good as formerly, with a resultant deterioration in stock got from them. The breed preferred in the district is the Shorthorn and although opinions differ as to their suitability, they are much more in favour than the Polled Angus breed. The location of bulls at different points in the district would be of great benefit, as all cannot take advantage of the bulls kept by the landlords, some on acount of the distance and some for other reasons.

There are not many sheep in the district; probably about ten per cent of the tenantry keep sheep. The breed is good, being a cross on the Roscommon breed; they produce from five to six pounds of wool, which is very fine in quality and much softer than that obtained from the black-face sheep.

The horses in the district are small, but strong and fairly well formed. About 25% of the farmers have horses and 70% of the remainder, donkeys; these latter are very small but are used for every conceivable purpose — carting turf, seaweed, manure, provisions, etc., etc. The Board have a stud horse in the care of Major Eccles at Moneygold, but it would be wiser to place the horse in Grange village, as country farmers do not care, as a rule, to take their mares to a private house, and many who would apply for and get the service in Grange, would not go to Moneygold. Three or four good jackasses placed at, say, Grange, Lisadell, Cliffoney and Bunduff, could not fail to be of the greatest benefit in improving the local breed.

The pigs in the district are, on the whole, good, and are really the staple stock of the smaller farmers; on their good or bad sale depends their balance to profit or loss each year. Each farmer has two and very often, three pigs and unlike the farmers in the pig districts of Donegal, they sell two lots of pigs, as a rule, in the year. Two or three good boars in the district, at suitable centres would be of great service. At present, sows have to be taken some miles for service.

As regards the poultry, the hens are of the ordinary barndoor breed, there is room here for improvement. Owing to the proximity of Sligo and Bundoran the poultry trade should be a very valuable one but very little use is made of it. Geese are kept by a few but not largely. The establishing of poultry farms in the district as distributing centres and the distribution of some good geese and ganders, and some bronze turkeys would be of immense benefit. The neighbourhoods of Carney, Grange, Cliffoney, Mullaghmore and Bunduff would be good centres. The number of poultry generally kept on the smaller farms is from twelve to sixteen and on the larger from twenty to thirty; twice this number could be kept easily if more care were exercised and the fowl properly looked after, for the same cost. Here, as elsewhere, no attention is paid to the housing and feeding of the poultry; as a general rule they are left to look after themselves. The usual quota of ducks is kept attached to each house, but as these are maintained for pleasure rather than for profit, they call for no remark.

208

Markets and Fairs

The principal fairs in the district are Grange with thirteen fairs yearly, and Sligo, Ballyshannon and Kinlough, outside. Grange is the principal fair and Sligo the principal market, twice weekly. Sugar, tea, tobacco and other groceries are generally obtained in small quantities from local shops. Baker's bread is bought from carts which make daily rounds; these come from Ballyshannon, Bundoran and Sligo.

Eggs are sold to the local dealers, being paid for in tea or sugar, never in cash. Butter is often made into firkins of 70 lbs. and sold in Sligo and locally. There was a poultry market in Sligo but it was given up by the people of the district. The dealers who come around in "tea carts" often buy poultry in exchange for tea. There is a good market in Mullaghmore and Bundoran in the bathing season. Eggs vary in age from five days to three weeks before they reach the English market; how old they are when they reach the consumer is difficult to ascertain. Local dealers, if they think there is a prospect of a rise in the price of eggs will often hold them over for a fortnight in order to take advantage of it.

Rail, Posts and Telegraphs

Properly speaking, the area has no railway facilities, Sligo being the nearest railway station on one side and Bundoran on the other, each one being thirteen miles distant from the centre of the district. The construction of a railway (1) from Bundoran to Sligo, connecting Sligo with the Great Northern Railway or (2) from Sligo to Ballyshannon, connecting with the Donegal Railway Company (proposed line). This latter would be the best for the district as it would connect the whole district at once with Derry, Glasgow, Liverpool etc.

Steamer:	A steamer plies between Sligo and Liverpool.
Sailing boat:	nil.
Roads:	very good.
Postal facilities:	sufficent for the district.
Telegraph:	good. There are two telegraph offices, one in Cliffoney

and one in Grange. As Grange office is not that busy, one is suggested for Ballinful.

Employment and Migratory Labour

There is no constant employment of labour in the district other than that given by the landlords (who employ some thirty to forty men) and the road contractors. There is a fair share of irregular labour, and an ordinary family, with a man and a strong boy, may count on making about £4 per annum in wages. The general rate of wage is 1s per day with food, and 1s.6d without. There is no migratory labour; all the young men who go to Scotland generally remain away for some time before they come home. A number emigrate yearly to America.

Weaving, Spinning, Knitting and Sewing

There is comparatively little weaving and spinning carried on in the

209

disrict. Some years ago there used to be a good deal of work done, but since the mills in Convoy, Lisbellaw, Galashiels, and other places, have been established, the farmers send their wool there to be made into cloth, and sell any surplus wool they may have either in Sligo or to the factory.

The district itself is not a wool producing one, though immediately adjoining one. There are at present some three or four working weavers in the district. These weave linen almost more than frieze; petticoats for the women, towels, coarse sheets and such like, but the demand, as well as the supply, is local and small.

There should be a good opening in the district for a profitable woolen industry, as the quality of the wool is good, but there does not appear to be any local interest in the matter. In this lies a demonstration of the great difference in position, financially, of the farmers on this side of Donegal Bay and those on the west side. There they must work in order to live at all, as their stock and their farms cannot support them, while here, the industry would only be taken up as a means to better their position, and as on the whole, they are without ambition, there is no real anxiety shown in the development of any industry.

Knitting, there is practically none, except for home use, and that only sometimes.

Sewing in the shape of "sprigging", has gone out, but quite recently a local industry of limited extent has been started, with Sligo as its headquarters, giving out work of different sorts to girls in the district. This is not likely to be constant, although at present, the number earning at it is quite considerable.

Mrs. Eccles of Moneygold, still employs girls at sprigging work and turns out some very beautiful work, which she disposes of privately to friends and others, but the supply and demand is limited.

Turf and Bogs

The sale of turf on the estates is prohibited, but nevertheless, all the tenants who have the opportunity, sell it. The money they make is a very large increase on their yearly receipts — getting 1s.6d to 2s for a small cart and 3s to 5s.6d for a large one. Selling about fifty cartloads in a year produces earnings which would range from £3. 15s to £10. This practice, combined with those who rightfully draw their fuel is rapidly reducing the extent of the bogs so that in another sixty to eighty years time, all the bogs will be cut out and the community will have to face the very serious problem of how to provide fuel. It is in the interests of the people themselves and their descendants that this indiscriminate sale of turf should be put a stop to.

Each tenant pays 2s.6d a year for 200 barrels, or about 33 cart-loads of turf, which is all they are supposed to cut. Tenants not on the estate, pay from 10s to 15s for the same. The total extent of bogland in the district is about 1,000 acres, and a good deal of that is partially cut. The turf is generally of an inferior quality. The lowest strata of the bog is generally worked with the hands. The turf are formed into round balls and squeezed very firmly together, these when dry turn somewhat like coals, with an intense heat.

Banks and Loan Funds

There are no banks in the district, the nearest being at Ballyshannon, on one side and Sligo on the other. A branch from Sligo is open at Grange on fair days. There is a loan fund at Drumcliff and another one at Bundoran. The general opinion is that the loan funds do a great deal of harm in the districts in which they are placed, and so far as I could gather, about 50% of the farmers in the district have borrowed from them. The borrowing is a very costly process, for not only has the borrower to repay the interest on the loan, but he must also bring in and pay two securities; if his loan is not paid to date he is fined. The interest charged is very high, and it is difficult to see where the profits, and they must be very great, go to.

Cash Credit or Barter

This district is placed similarly to congested districts in Co. Donegal, as regards its credit dealings with the local shopkeepers. A great deal of credit is given; indeed the greater number of families exist mainly on credit, all debts being cleared up as far as possible, half-yearly. The only goods for which a present equivelant is given are tea and sugar, and they are generally paid for with eggs or butter. Meal and flour are always obtained on credit but the same quantity on these commodities is not consumed here as in Donegal. In this district the people live very largely on bakers bread and do not make much home-made bread, and do not eat much "stirabout".

Barter in the way of getting an equivelant in kind for eggs, butter and poultry is common; indeed the two first named articles are never paid for in cash, with the one exception, when butter is sold in the firkin, it is then generally paid for in cash, but in all cases of retail, it is paid for in kind.

Receipts and Expenditure of an Ordinary Family

The income varies in different localities. Kelp is made in some areas, in others fishing is carried on, some where turf is largely sold and some that have none of these advantages. They are all noted in the following table, those items which are not common to all are noted as such:-

CASH RECEIPTS		EXPENDITURE	
*Sale of cows	£9.0.0	Rent and Taxes	£4.0.0
Sale of three pigs	8.0.0	*Tea	4.10.0
+Sale of sheep	2.0.0	Sugar	1.10.0
Sale of ?	5.0.0	Bakers bread	4.0.0
Sale of poultry	1.0.0	Meal and flour	8.0.0
<Sale of oats	13.4	Clothes	7.10.0
<Sale of hay	2.0.0	Tobacco,drink, etc.	3.15.0
<Sale of butter	6.2.6	Fishermen, £2 extra	2.0.0
>Sale of turf	5.0.0	Church dues	16.0
#Sale of kelp	12.0.0	Farm implements	15.0
#Sale of fish	20.0.0	Artificial manure	1.10.0
+Sale of wool	1.0.0	Oil, candles, salt, etc.	1.10.0
Earnings in a year	5.0.0	Carting & saving turf	2.0.0

Buying 3 pigs   2.5.0

* Fisherman, only one, £3.0.0	Replenishing stock	2.0.0
+ Only inland	If keep horse	8.0.0
< Only inland	Interest on loans	10.0
> Inland, certain districts	TOTAL	£55.1.0
# On coast	Without horse	£47.1.0

* The tea purchased in this district seldom under 3s.6d per pound

The estimated value of home grown food:-

Potatoes, 10 barrels at 12s	£6.0.0
Poultry	5.0
Milk and butter	5.0.0
Turnips (house consumed)	10.0
TOTAL	£11.15.0

Potatoes generally last until the middle of April, or beginning of May, in a very good year, until June; in a bad year, only until the new year. Turnips, hay, manure, etc., can hardly be looked on as assets by themselves, as they are consumed in the produce of stock, cultivation of land etc.

Diet and Variety of Food

Here, as in Donegal, the people are almost completely vegetarian. Again, the most marked difference in the diet here is the large amount of baker's bread consumed; the amount at home being very small by comparison. Bacon is the only animal food eaten, and that seldom, fish occasionaly, and perhaps once or twice a year, a fowl or two. Eggs are more eaten here than in Donegal; not so much in the winter as in the summer months, as in winter, they are a more marketable commodity than in the summer. Oatmeal is sometimes eaten but not largely. For dinner, cabbage and dripping is a favourite dish. Breakfast is generally taken at eight o'clock and consists of tea and bread, sometimes porridge. Dinner at one p.m. consists of potatoes mainly, which is eaten with buttermilk, and cabbage and dripping sometimes. When the potatoes are finished, bread and tea and sometimes porridge are taken.

There is generally some sort of meal about four o'clock, consisting of dry bread or tea and bread. The regular "tea" is taken sometime between seven and eight and consists generally of stirabout, or if potatoes are plentiful, of potatoes and milk. When potatoes are scarce, between April and August, stirabout and bakers bread is the principal food. Tea is taken twice a day and very often three times; it is made strong and very unwholesome, through the habit of stewing it. Stirabout is almost always made with Indian meal, seldom with oatmeal.

Clothing

Clothing, including underclothing, is almost entirely bought. Blankets and undershirts were made locally when weaving was common in the district but now the farmers prefer to send their wool to Convoy and Lisbellaw. In return, they get a quantity of cloth; those who have no wool generally buy as much as will make all the clothes they will need, sending it to the factory and geting a return in cloth or blankets and paying extra for the weaving. The women generally have their linen petticoats woven locally as they wear better than those they buy; the men's socks and the women's everyday stockings are also home made. A quantity of second hand clothes is purchased at the fairs in Grange from itinerant vendors. These are generally shawls, childrens garments and men's overcoats.

On Sundays and holidays the young women dress up in remarkably fine clothes; some in the district remark that the female portion of the community spent a great deal too much on dress.

Dwellings

On entering the district from the north-east side, one is struck with the cleanliness and comfort of almost all the cottages. They are well built and have large good windows, a marked contrast to the tiny light holes one is accustomed to see in County Donegal. The reason for this is that the former landlord, Palmerston, used to give prizes for the best built and best kept gardens, etc.; he also supplied windows to all his tenants. Beyond this and the building of the harbour at Mullaghmore, there does not seem to have been any organised effort made to improve the condition of the people in any way, or to develop the industrial resources of the district. On the south side of the district the houses are not so good, especially in the townlands of Ballyconnell and Cloonagh, where some very poor houses are to be found. There are other very poor townlands where the houses are in keeping with the poverty of the people. On the whole, though, the houses of the district betoken a much greater degree of prosperity and comfort than exists in the districts on the northern side of the bay. It is said, however, that the poverty of the people should not be judged by the appearance of the houses. The home life is simple and quite similar to that of other districts.

In summer, they get up about six and in winter, seven or later. The stock is attended to, the cows milked somewhat later — as the cows are let out on the grass for an hour or so before milking. Breakfast is eaten about eight o'clock after which they all go about their various duties; the men to the farms or the bog, the children to school and the women to churn and herd cattle, etc. On account of the better fencing here, herding is not as much required here as in Donegal. Dinner comes on about one o'clock, and after dinner, the same routine until tea-time. At night the cattle are housed (generally both winter and summer for the sake of the manure) and milked, the pigs put in and fed and about ten o'clock, they all retire. There is practically no such thing as a cottage with only one room in it in this district; they have all a sleeping room for the women and often one for the men — if not, the men sleep in the kitchen or living room."

On his tour of Donegal some two years earlier, Gahan described the homes there as consisting of two rooms,

"the outer room being the public room of the house, for fowl and farm stock as well as human inmates; the inner for a sleeping room for the women of the family".

213

The fact that he doesn't mention something similar here is surprising, but must mean that this practise was not as prevalent here. The older people of this area can remember Dan Mc Gowan keeping cattle in the dwelling house shortly after the turn of this century, and also remember Anthony Rogers having an ass tied to the kitchen bed. It was quite common, as recently as the 1950's, for newly born calves to be kept in the kitchen for some weeks after being calved.) The report continues to observe that:

"there are no distinctive customs, wakes are held, but not to the same extent as formerly. In former days. a good deal of smuggling was done on the coast but is now entirely done away with.

Conclusions

There are many internal indications that this district is in many respects better off than the majority of congested districts on the north side of the bay. The chief reasons for this are (1) the large price obtained for fish; (2) the fact that nearly all the population wear boots and shoes, and all the women on Sundays, hats and bonnets; (3) the fact that there is no home industry; (4) the character of their dwelling houses; (5) the quantity of bakers bread bought.

Recommendations

There are many means which might be adopted to improve the condition of the people of the district. The first among these would be an improvement in fishing methods with new and bigger boats and more modern equipment.

Secondly, an improvement in the railway development of the district as mentioned earlier.

Thirdly, industrial development; the people as a rule, have enough to live on, and are not, for the most part, ambitious to improve. It seems too, that the younger women of the district seem to think it rather beneath them to spin in the woolen industry. The Board have made a small grant to Mrs. Eccles of Moneygold for the development of the industry but the conditions appear to be vague. The weaver and loom are there but no one seems to want to learn unless Mrs. Eccles pays them for it. There follows a list of suggestions for the development of this industry for a trial period of two years.

Fourthly, the improvement of various stock as suggested earlier.

In addition, improvement in agricultural methods is much needed; drainage is badly attended to; the land insufficiently laboured; the crops not properly attended to.

Bee-keeping could be introduced with satisfactory results, as there would be a good market for honey in Sligo and Bundoran.

Osier growing and basket-making could be introduced as an industry as the soil seems suitable, although it might be difficult to establish a market as local demand would be small.

214

Migration of Inishmurray

There is one scheme of migration which should be effected for the benefit of the district and that is the Inishmurray islanders. The island is a flat barren unsheltered rock of very limited extent; under the present conditions the people must always live on it in wretchedness.

If they could be migrated to land that might be obtained for that purpose, that is the portion of Ballyconnell and Kilmacannon townlands which lie east of Knocklane Castle, it would be of immense benefit to them. There is a great waste tract here of some 1,000 acres or more, which was once inhabited and cultivated, but a great many years ago the sand drove the people out. There is a certain depth of sand over the soil, but not very deep. The surface is now covered with short sweet grass and portions of it with bent grass. The greater portion belongs now to Captain Gethin, the remainder to Sir Henry Gore-Booth. Under the circumstances it might not be advisable, at this time, to enquire into the probable cost of the land but it would, at present, not be worth very much. There would probably be a great difficulty in inducing the Inishmurray people to leave the island, and there is always the danger of the migrated families saying 'You have brought us here and must now look after us.' The matter though is one which is worthy of consideration."

Kelp and fishing are covered in detail in the report and are included in other parts of this book under those headings. The report is signed F. G. Townsend Gahan and dated 12th December, 1895.

CLIFFONEY LACE

We know that the C.D.B involved itself with the promotion of Irish lace throughout the country, but apart from the Eccles experiment there is no mention in the report of a lace industry in this area at the time. Clones Crochet Lace — the variety made in the Cliffoney area — was widely known and practised in Europe from the 16th century onwards. It was brought to Ireland in the 1840's and to Clones, Co. Monaghan by Mrs. Cassandra Hand in 1847; 1500 workers were eventually employed in the industry in this area within a few years. Around the turn of the century, girls specially skilled in the art of crochet, were selected from Clones Centre and taken to Dublin for further training in design and management and then sent to such areas as were deemed most suitable.

In 1901, Miss Catherine Cosgrove was sent from Lisnaskea to Cliffoney, opening a Crochet School in a building near the bridge north of the village. Eventually becoming Mrs. John Rhatigan, she taught and supervised the production and sale of this handcraft to markets in Dublin, London, Paris and the U.S.A. After the foundation of the state,

Gaeltarra Eireann took over responsibility for this type of industry. On Mrs Rhatigan's death in 1944 her work was carried on by her niece, Teresa Cosgrove, to whom I am indebted for this information on Cliffoney lacemaking. She retired from the Cliffoney Gaeltarra Lace Centre on her marriage to Sean Daly in 1950 and was succeeded by Miss Anna Mc Cluskey until she retired, at the closure of the centre in the 1960's. Mrs Daly continued the lacecraft in connection with her Craft Shop in Cliffoney village.

The economic necessity which led to the introduction of this craft at the turn of the century faded away gradually and no longer existed in any great measure in the 1960's. The era of prosperity which Ireland enjoyed for two brief decades has declined; now, as a response to rising unemployment, there is an effort being made at the present time to revive this craft in Cliffoney. Time will tell whether the revival of this age old skill is economically viable. Even if its not, some enthusiastic craft lovers wish that the making of such exquisite lace should be revived, if only for personal fulfillment.

CLIFFONEY'S BOY'S SCHOOL, 1925 *Teacher, Master McHugh*
Back Row, L to R: *V. Cummins, Mick Burns, Luke Leydon, Michael Higgins, Joe Barry, P. Watters, Thady Whyte, Danny McHugh, T. Hargadon, F. Cummins*
Middle Row: *Michael Wymbs, Frank Mullaney, James Barry, Dr. Heraughty, Jim Cummins, Jack McHugh, Tom Leonard, C. Watters, ?.*
Front Row: *Mick Gilmartin, John Mc Cannon, John Harrison, Pakie Barry, Cornelius Rooney, John Rhatigan, Peter McHugh.*

KELP

The building of the Mullaghmore harbour was a great boon to the kelp industry; on its completion it became the main port of export in the northwest for this commodity. Kelp was an important scource of income for families all along the west coast, contributing substantialy to survival in difficult times for families and indeed, whole communities. When the schooners came into the the harbour, horse and ass drawn carts came heavily laden with the product from points all along the coastline, from Bundoran and Tullaghan and all along the shore they came, from Raughley, Cloonagh and Streedagh. From the sea, too, they came,as the Inishmurray men brought their kelp in boats from the island.

The manufacture of kelp was first commenced about the middle of the 18th century for the purpose of extracting sodium carbonate from it; it was also used by the Irish bleachers. Demand was high and prices of £2.5.0 per ton was the going rate in the 1750's, rising to £11 and £14, and in the English markets, £20 a ton by the beginning of the 19th century. Kelp making at this time became so remunerative that fishermen all along the shore, gave up their fishing and turned almost exclusively to the gathering and processing of the seaweed.

After the Napoleonic Wars (1812-14), when the high duties were taken off foreign imports of barilla and salt, kelp declined drastically in value and became hardly worth the effort, at prices in 1831 of £2 to £3 pounds per ton, even though it continued to be used until 1845 in soap and glass manufacture. About 1845, according to Woodmartin, iodine began to be extracted from it, "producing about 8 ounces of iodine to a ton of good kelp and a by-product of large amounts of potash salts. Halogen iodine contained bromine and chlorine, essential at that time in medicine and commerce; paraffin oil and naptha could be obtained by distillation." Prices now rose rapidly and the best kelp sold for 10 pounds per ton. In 1875, nitrate of soda, from which iodine could also be extracted, began to be imported from Chile and Peru and the price of kelp plummeted again to between £2 and £3 pounds per ton. People were desperately poor at this time and as £2 or £3 pound per ton was better than no pound, the manufacture of kelp continued.

Townsend-Gahan, in his report for the C.D.B. in 1895, reported that 1,000 tons of kelp was shipped out of Mullaghmore in schooners in that year, 600 tons of this coming from the Maugherow shore and 400 tons from the Carns and Mullaghmore areas. Three hundred and fifty families worked to supply the buyer and were paid an average of £3 pounds ten shillings per ton, the dealer sometimes offering the seller 10 or 15 shillings less than he was entitled to. Those travelling ten or fifteen miles were especially victimised in this regard and would sell at the lower price rather than bring the product back. The report concludes that:

"On the Hon. E. Ashleigh's estate a small amount is added to the rent of each tenant, and all have the right of gathering the weed. On Mr. Jones' estate, the seaweed is on the landlord's land and is divided among the tenants, they paying so much; on Captain Gethin's estate a somewhat similar practise prevails, and on Sir Henry Gore-Booth's estate, the tenants along the shore have the seaweed rights, and if those inland want it, they must pay at from 5 to 7 shillings per cart."

Despite the fluctuations in price, the production of kelp continued well into the first half of this century and was a vital income supplement to farmer and fisherman along the coast until the practice died out in the late '40's. It took 20 to 40 tons of sea-rods and wrack, which was gathered at the waterline, to make one ton of kelp. The tides, as they still do, carried the sea-rods to certain spots on the sea shore, with certain places, such as Pollyarry, Pollachurry, Powarleide and a few others being well known to be prime locations for a plentiful supply. Pollyarry and Pollachurry were worked by the Mullaghmore men on a first come, first served basis while Powarleide and the far shore were worked by the "ones from the country,"— men from Cliffoney and the surrounding areas who worked the shore on a share basis. Each man here had a short stretch of shoreline marked out for him, leaving fate and the vagaries of wind and tide to decide what his portion of wrack and sea-rods would be.

Wrack and famluc were needed, too, for use as a fertiliser for the crops and meadows. Fishermen and farmers worked their plots well into the 1900's with loys and spades to plant potatoes, rye, oats, barley, cabbage, carrots and turnips; cabbage, turnips and mangels were grown too as animal feed. The horse drawn plough made inroads, but only very slowly, as, far from being seen as a labour saving benefaction, it was viewed with great suspicion by these conservative tillers of the soil. Men shook their heads dubiously when an adventuresome neighbour took a chance and allowed a horse team into his field; it could do no good! The experts wagged their heads as they predicted the evils that would befall if this new foolishness was encouraged; some opined that the fields would be filled with scutchgrass as the ploughs propagated the weed by dragging the roots about the fields; others listed more reasons why this could not be a good thing; and who was to know at that point that there might not be some good sense to what the doubters were saying? Best to wait and see!

Whether it be plough, loy or spade, the fields had to be manured and kelp had to be made; men lined the claddaghs along the shore after a storm or ground swell, each one anxious to get his quota. The sea unfailingly delivered it's bounty every year when it was needed and just as surely as Spring came, so did the periodic deliveries of seaweed arrive with the "cuckoo storm" or again with the "May wrack." Men sometimes fought over the "tor" of wrack when it came in. One of the older men who worked the kelp and fields recalled: "Pollyarry corner, over on the Carraig na Calwa side was a great place for wrack. When it came in, ye'd have two or three men in the corner holding the tor of wrack; sometimes holding on to it and staying all night with the intention of working it in the morning. After all that, sometimes the morning tide would come and sweep it away out again."

Some men went out in boats at a Spring tide to Garwoge, at the top of Ros Caoireach to cut the seaweed, stacking it in huge bales. When these rafts of seaweed floated with the incoming tide they were towed to the old quay and taken bit by bit up the steps to waiting carts where they were then taken to where they were needed, in the fields or kilns.

Famluc was cut too at Murlyin in the Eastland, the boats going in at high water, the men cutting the famluc when the tide went out and then waiting for the tide to rise so that their prize could be towed home.

A spade or new shovel with the metal tip squared off and sharpened was used to cut and scrape the famluc off the rocks; only the young tender shoots would do as the old mature stalks were too tough and would not provide the nourishment necessary when needed for crops.

For kelp making, the sea-rods were gathered at points along the shore, carried to a dry place, or purpose built stone ditch, stacked and dried and then thatched with bent grass. In Spring, "when the May wrack came in, ye'd be a week or a fortnight at that until ye had enough wrack to put with the sea-rods." Sea-rods and wrack were taken from the shore or up the cliff face by ass and creels and carried to the kilns.

At the start of the kelp burning, in the late Spring, the kilns were made. Pits were dug to a depth of about 9 inches or a foot and in the bottom of this, layers of sticks and turf were placed; layers of the dried sea-rods and wrack were placed on top of the sticks and turf and the whole thing was then set alight. In the kelp burning season dense clouds of smoke could be seen billowing all along the coasts of Sligo as well as Mayo and Donegal. Free from worries about greenhouse effects, global warming or holes in the ozone layer, the men tended the blazing piles all day. Scores of years later, Mattie Joe Barry, then an exile in America, recalled the scenes and the verse:

"With the wind from the west
And the smoke blowing o'er,
We'll have a day's burning
In sweet Mullaghmore."

With plenty of fuel and "a good air of wind," rods and wrack were eventually reduced to a molten mass which then had to be "lumped." Special sticks were used for "lumping" which involved the shaping and mixing together of the residual gruel in the pit and the unburned bits of searod into lumps of about 1 cwt. each. At this point, men were known to add "weight enhancers"; a certain kind of stone, found at "Cruc na Gabhair", when added to the burning kelp had the same texture and colouration as the kelp, but was much heavier. When the "lumps" of kelp hardened they were brought to the harbour where they were stored in sheds in readiness for shipping. Estate rentals for 1889 show a sum of £5 being paid by Martin Gilmartin for one years rental of the "Harbour Pier Kelp Shed". One of the men who worked the kelp told me, "A man might have 5 or 6 tons for a season, but it was heavy work, night and day for only £3 pounds to £3 pounds ten shillings per cwt., the most you could get at the finish up of the kelp was £7 pounds a ton." Readers will bear in mind that this price was much lower than that given one hundred years before. Tom Cummins supervised the weighing and testing of the kelp for the Scottish firm which bought the product. Tommy Fowley, who worked here too, was fond of a drop of poitin and when the time came for the buying of the kelp, he was assured of a plentiful supply of the liquid from the Inishmurray and Maugherow men who came to sell their kelp; "Tommy never was sober from the time the kelp would start until it would finish."

On one occasion a raid for poitin coincided with the Inishmurray mens preparations for bringing the kelp for sale to Mullaghmore. The authorities on this occasion carried off a large quantity of the illegal brew from Inishmurray, and on arrival in the harbour stored it temporarily in a shed belonging to McHughs guest house pending transportation to the barracks in Cliffoney. The island men, having made some judicious and discreet enquiries during the course of their business transactions with Tommy Fowley and Tom Cummins, on discovering the location of their treasure, repaired to McHughs where they joined the management in an evenings joviality over a few drinks. As the evening wore on and after some lengthy persuasion, McHugh's co-operation was secured and access to the precious liquid gained.

When morning came, no trace of Inishmurray men or poitin could be found about Mullaghmore, leaving Mc Hugh with some awkward questions to answer when the authorities came looking for their seizure of poitin, finding only an empty shed with no sign of a forced entry.

As work was hard to get, there was keen competition among the boatmen for the piloting of the ships into the harbour and later for the loading of the kelp from the sheds into the boats. Tommy Fowley was overseer on the loading and there was a keen rivalry here too among the local men for appointment to the temporary job of stevedore. The following story is written down exactly as it was told to me, it needs no retouching and recalls in vivid detail the colour and atmosphere of the time:

"This boat was supposed to be coming and Cawley says to me, 'If you see any sign of her coming, cut for here.' I got out of the bed and went out to the gap at two or three in the morning and could see a dim light coming at Rathlin O' Beirne. It looked like it might be a schooner alright so I went and told the bucks, Jimmy Cawley and Big Dan Mc Govern; they were sorta half ready too!

Out we went in Cawley's boat. We weren't long out 'till Willie Duffy's boat, the "Shamrock" was out after us. There was no wind for a sail but we were all good rowers and we were a bit ahead of them anyway. The rowing took place anyway but they couldn't pass us and had to turn back after a while, no one would have it to say they were fighting over the piloting in any case. Like most of the kelp boats, she was about 3 or 4 hundred tons and we had to wait for high water to bring her in to her berth at the New Quay where most of the ships took on cargo. Most of the big boats could only come in at high tide then so when the tide went out they would be completely aground. There was five or six pounds out of it for bringing her in. When we came into the quay, Tommy Fowley asked me would I help to put in the cargo. "I will," says I — I was mad for work that time! Along with me there was John, God be good to him and Pa Barry in Bunduff, Hughie Cawley and Jimmy Cawley — the whole kit of them is dead now. We went up home for a bite to eat and came down again at ten o'clock but couldn't do a thing as the tide was high and the chute for loading was away up in the air. We started at half past eleven when the tide and the ship went down a bit.

It was Tom Cummins that was buying at the time. He told us that there was 150 tons in the shed and a few new wheelbarrows. It was all tack shoes that time; two pounds of anchorhead nails — a pound in each shoe and sure there was every head on them yon size. We all started wheeling into the hould; if you weren't careful, the barrow, if it hit you there, (pointing at his hip) would knock ye into the hould, d'ye see! Ye be to have a bit of action about ye as well, ye know (laughing). This time any way, Tom Barry, Lord have mercy on him, came along, and Pa tipped the barra' and he nearly went in himself along with it. When he heard the commotion, Tommy Fowley came out of the shed and him half asleep and he gave out hell. Jimmy Cawley, Lord have mercy on him, and me, we were only young, I'd be twenty two or twenty three; well for laughing part of it the whole night, they couldn't shut us up!

The shed, anyway, was cleared in the morning and there was supposed to be only 50 tons in the other shed. All hands agreed to go home and get some sleep, but to get to sleep wasn't easy as for the kelp part of it, ye'd be sweating and with the heat of your hands and the burning of them, from the kelp going into the pores, it was wild. We came down again in the morning anyway to put in the other 50 ton — no man could sleep! We went to bed alright but no man could sleep, what with being overtired and the burning of the hands and the burning of the feet and "druith" (thirst).

Well, we got down two dozen of stout from James Patricks — started to drink the stout anyways but still we were fit to make no headway with the rest of the cargo, what with the heat of the sun and dog tired from the work of the night before and then, no sleep. Well, anyway, there was an old sailor on the ship; — "Say, me boys," he says, "ye're making no headway and ye're only killing yerselves. Drinking that porther is only killing ye and knocking more sweat out of ye!"

"Well, what'll we drink?'

'Is there a good spring well about.'

'There is," says we, "Tobair Watcha in the farm is as good as ye'll get'

"Get a pound of oatmeal,' he says, 'and put it into a bucket of spring water. Let it dissolve and then drink it and ye might be fit to do something.' There was plenty of oatmeal about that time for making stirabout and we did what he said and there was some improvement after that. Max, Lord have mercy on him, came down to see had we the stuff cleared in; Pa's brother Tom Duffy came down too and the two of them took off their coats anyways and gave us a "shive" until we got the job done. That was 200 ton going by Tommy's talk but I'm afraid it was a lot more than that!

Tommy Fowley says, 'Will ye go over to James Patricks for a drink?' Tommy, of course had the poitín in – ye wouldn't know when he'd be drunk or sober. We said we'd go anyway and Tommy got a drink for all hands in the shop. The first bottle of porter didn't last long anyway and when the second bottle was near drank, every man was talking a bit funny, y'know, and out of the funny talk, all hands was drunk. I suppose it didn't take much, with no man having a right bit to eat and tired from lack of sleep.

The next thing, Tommy says, 'The two best men that ever put in kelp for me was Jack Harrson and Martin, the son.' (They lived on the lower Bunduff road.) Pa Barry jumped on him right away, 'I worked along with Jack Harrison and I worked along with the son and they could do no more than any other man!' The next man that spoke up was John, God be good to him, 'Arra God may blast ye,' he says, "ye son of a bitch ye, ye're talking about good men! Did you ever get in as much stuff as you got in today? There was 160 ton in the first shed and 60 or 70 more ton in the second and did you ever know men to put it in as good?" Tommy had no answer for that.

222

There were no blows struck that day, but if there was, Tommy wouldn't be the last man to get one. There was another round of drinks called for but James Patrick (Mc Gloin) wouldn't give it. Home, then, and into bed and couldn't sleep with the burning of the hands from the handling of the kelp and the sweat "mulching" it into the palms. John Fowley was a good while in the bed after that and the doctor had to come to him; he was stooped after that, it happened him right away. It nearly finished us all and that was for one skithery thirty bob, and that was ould money at that time!"

Famluc (ascophyllum nodosum or bladder wrack) and sea-rods (Laminaria Hypornoea) are still gathered along the coast but only in relatively minute quantities by very few people. Arramara Teo., based in Dungloe, is now one of the main buyers of the seaweeds for processing into Alginate, a substance which is used in foodstuffs, pharmaceuticals, dental impressions, printing and even the froth on your beer.

Ships no longer come into the harbour and the sites of the kilns where kelp was burned are now overgrown; by careful observation, though, these sites can still be identified at Pollyarry and other places along the shore, by the traces of the depressions left when the pits were dug. The shores where hordes of men watched and waited for the tors of wrack are deserted now. Times have changed and like so many other things, the day is long gone when men depended on, and were prepared to fight and strive over this great natural resource. The "tors" of May wrack still come into Pollyarry, but no one notices, or cares, as the weed rots on the stony beach or is carried out on the stormy tide.

MULLAGHMORE BARYTES RUSH

There was keen competition between boatmen Willie Duffy, Jamesy "Charlie" Gallagher, and Hughie Cawley for the piloting of the S.S. Crosshands when she was spotted on her approach to Mullaghmore. Willie Duffy secured the honour and the fee, took charge of his prize and brought her carefully around Mullagh Head, well clear of the shallows at Thumb Rock, towards a place in history at Mullaghmore harbour.

The older people of the village can still recall the excitement created in the village on the arrival of the 800 ton Belfast built vessel at the harbour during Christmas 1927 with 400 tons of railway material. Because of her size and a ground swell running, she couldn't enter the harbour and had to tie alongside the breakwater to unload the railway equipment, bogies, rails, etc. Dozens of men from the surrounding areas were recruited immediately and worked around the clock under the supervision of Jack Hargadon, paymaster and Petie Mc Gowan, ganger, in a race against time; it was vitally important to unload as fast as possible, as even in good conditions the breakwater was a dangerous place to berth; any deterioration in the weather would mean a serious setback.

A small boy at the time, Bernie Kelly remembers the clear frosty weather and the ringing sound of the iron rails that carried on the frosty air as far as their house on the Hill Road, as the men dropped the rails on to the stone paved quay. Johnny Barry worked with the men unloading the ship and recalled that it took two men to carry each heavy iron rail. He relived the agony of bruised and blistered shoulders as he told me how they worked long into the night carrying the rails down the gangplank of the ship, along the breakwater, through the "eye", and along the quay. It seemed inevitable that the Crosshands was going to receive some damage and she was holed, but not badly, as after some repairs in Killybegs she made the return journey safely.

It was barytes, or sulphate of barium, used in glassware, paints, chinaware, wallpaper, pre X-ray barium meals, linoleum and various other products that was responsible for this gold, or rather, barytes rush. Gold was to be had alright, for the exploration and recovery of the rich veins of this substance which ran through the nearby mountains; this was not a recent discovery though, as these veins had been worked long before Barium Consolidated Ltd came here in 1927. Barytes was first mined by a Mr. Williams in 1858, on top of the Glencar mountain, and transported by donkey and creels around the top of the mountain to

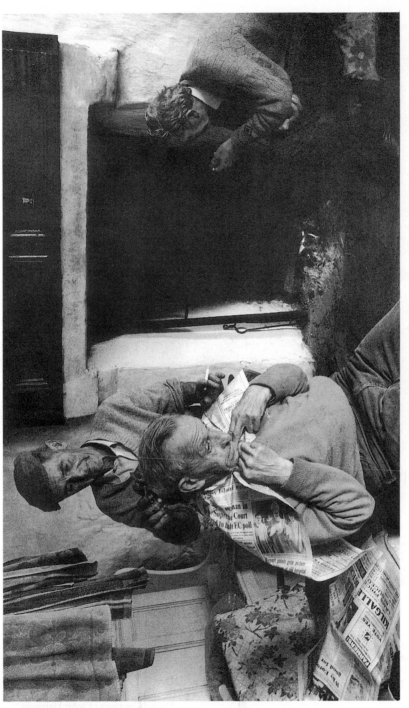

GETTING A HAIRCUT

The Way it Was. Bernie Kelly, Paddy McGrath and Mick Mc Grath

Photo: J. McG

MULLAGHMORE BARYTES RAILWAY 1928 -31
Bridge near Barytes 'Pilot Factory' at Ballintrillick
Photo: Courtesy of William McGrath

CLIFFONEY BOYS SCHOOL 1940
Back Row, *L to R. Seamus Burns, Willie Gilmartin, John McGovern, Patrick Chrystal, Gerard Lalor, Bernie Oates, Frank Cosgrove, Mark Hannon.*
Third Row: *Phelim Burns, Frank Burns, Pakie McSharry, Hubert McGovern, John Connolly, Roddy Burns, Eddie Gallagher, Harry Gallagher.*
Second Row: *Vivian Conway, Michael McCannon, John Harrison, Danny Clancy, Joe McGowan, Paddy Gallagher, Eddie Gilmartin, Patrick Connolly*
Front: *Paddy Joe Tehan, Michael McSharry, Denis Lalor, Tommy Haran, Michael Harrison, Hugh Gallagher, Sean Grimes.*
Photo: Courtesy of John Harrison

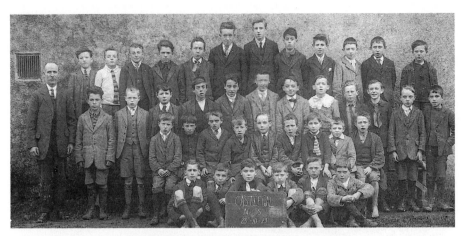

CASTLEGAL BOYS SCHOOL 23/10/1923

Teacher *Master John O'Connor* . **Back Row:** *L to R: Bernie Higgins, James McGovern, Josie Harrison, Paddy McIntyre, Patrick Costello, Eugene McGloin, Martin O'Connor, ? , Steven O'Connor, Tommy Barry, John Costello, Paddy McIntyre.*
3rd Row: Eddie Higgins, Kenneth Dickson, Robert Pye, Ned Gallagher, ? *Dickson, Steven Barry, William Barry, Thomas Barry, Hubert McGloin, John 'Judge' Gallagher, Pakie Mc Gloin, ?,*
2nd. Row: *Eugene Higgins, Willie Leonard, Patrick Joseph Watters, ? Higgins, Jimmy McGloin, James Eddie Costello, Paddy Harrison, Johnny O'Connor, ? Tehan.*
Front Row: *? , Dan Harrison, Jack Harrison, ? , John Leonard. ?*

Photo: Courtesy of Ellie B. Barry

CASTLEGAL GIRLS SCHOOL 1927

Teacher: Mrs Gilmartin on left. Back Row, *L to R. Mary Kate Clancy, Annie Curneen, Katie Harrison, Mary Margaret Harrison, Molly Leonard, Minna O'Connor, Eithne McIntyre, Katie Killerlane.*
Middle Row *Brigid Langan, Kathleen Watters, Rose Ann McGowan, Katie Warnock, Mary K. McGowan, (Tawly), Ellen Tehan, Ellie Bee Barry, Mary Kate Cleary, Dotie Gonigle, Delia Watters.*
Front: *Katie Harrison, Bee Cleary, May Watters, Kathleen Leonard, Brigid Killeralne, Teresa McGowan, May McGloin, Rose Laden, Nellie Killerlane, Ismay McIntyre.* Photo: Courtesy of Ellie B. Barry

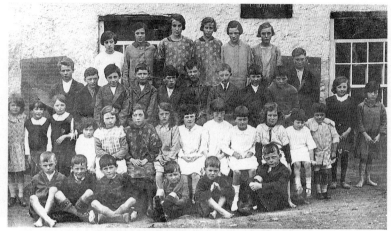

CLOONTY NATIONAL SCHOOL 1930

Teacher *Michael Steven McGowan and Mrs Sarah Conolly* **Back Row:** *L to R: Kathleen Gallagher, May Connolly, Maggie Connolly, Rose Ellie Connolly, Molly McDermott, Una Rooney..*

3rd Row: *Macklie Gillespie, Jery Clancy, Joe McGowan, Jim McSharry, Jimmy McGarrigle, Eugene Crean, Andy McGowan, Liam Gallagher, Hugh Gilmartin, Johnny Clancy.*

2nd. Row: *May Likely, Bridie McSharry, Katie McSharry, Delia McDermot, Mary McSharry, Kathleen Connolly, Emily Likely, Brigid Connolly, Nora McDermot, Maisie Gallagher, Margaret Mc Sharry, Dympna Gallagher, Tessie Connolly, Bernadette Connolly, Teresa McGarrigle* **Front Row:** *Brian Crean, ?Connolly, ? Kelly, ? Connolly, John Crean, Patrick Connolly*   Photo: Courtesy of Mrs Kate Heraughty

PARENTS PROTEST CLOSURE OF CARNS SCHOOL, 1972

Included in group are parents: *Christy Heraughty, Tommy and Annie Gilroy, Eileen Coyne, John C. & Liz O'Connor, Mary Langan, Sophie Keegan, Michael James Healy, Katie Heraughty, Mary Keaney, Michael J. & Mary A. Burns, Mary Rooney.*

Children *Aidan Gilroy, Fiona Gilroy, Michael Healy, Michael John, Christine, & Jimmy, Langan, John & Cathy Rooney, Mary, Agnes, & Margaret Burns, Teresa, Christina, Josephine, Patricia, Jacqueline and Bernadette Keaney, Paula, Katherine and Adrian O'Connor, Martin Heraughty, Philomena Keegan, Neasa Coyne.*   Photo: Courtesy Mrs Heraughty

ON THE WAY TO MASS, BALLINTRILLICK 1948
On the way to Mass by car, Bike and Pony and trap
Photo: Courtesy of The Father Browne S.J. Collection

HEYDAY OF THE NUNS C. 1956
Sisters of Mercy at Bishops Pool
Photo: Courtesy of Sister of Mercy, Mullaghmore

This card was commsioned by Hannon's Hotel' and shows Mullaghmore Quay shortly after the turn of the century

Courtesy Aidan Mannion Collection

Posted at Cliffoney on July 8, 1904; showing cargo ships and sheds used for storing Kelp, Coal and later Barytes.

Courtesy Aidan Mannion Collection

MULLAGHMORE COAST GUARD STATION
Posted on August 20th 1918

Courtesy Aidan MannionCollection

MULLAGHMORE QUAYSIDE
Posted at Cliffoney on April 3rd. 1911

Courtesy Aidan Mannion Collection

UNLOADING SHIPS BY HORSE AND CART

Portrayal of days when, "ships were driven aground and unloaded by horse or ass and cart"

MILK HARBOUR C 1905

L to R ; Johnny Mc Cann, Johnny 'Ruadh' McCann, Thomas Mc Cann, James Gillen

Photo: Courtesy of Tom & John Mc Cann

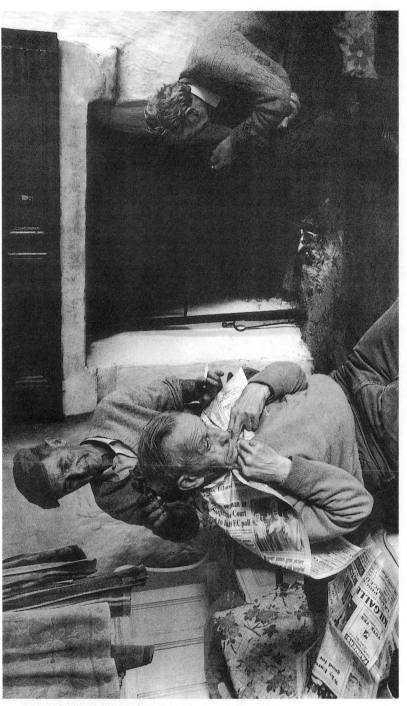

GETTING A HAIRCUT

The Way it Was. Bernie Kelly, Paddy McGrath and Mick Mc Grath

Photo: J. McG

MULLAGHMORE BARYTES RAILWAY 1928 -31
Bridge near Barytes 'Pilot Factory' at Ballintrillick
Photo: Courtesy of William McGrath

CLIFFONEY BOYS SCHOOL 1940
Back Row, L to R. *Seamus Burns, Willie Gilmartin, John McGovern, Patrick Chrystal, Gerard Lalor, Bernie Oates, Frank Cosgrove, Mark Hannon.*
Third Row: *Phelim Burns, Frank Burns, Pakie McSharry, Hubert McGovern, John Connolly, Roddy Burns, Eddie Gallagher, Harry Gallagher.*
Second Row: *Vivian Conway, Michael McCannon, John Harrison, Danny Clancy, Joe McGowan, Paddy Gallagher, Eddie Gilmartin, Patrick Connolly*
Front: *Paddy Joe Tehan, Michael McSharry, Denis Lalor, Tommy Haran, Michael Harrison, Hugh Gallagher, Sean Grimes.*
Photo: Courtesy of John Harrison

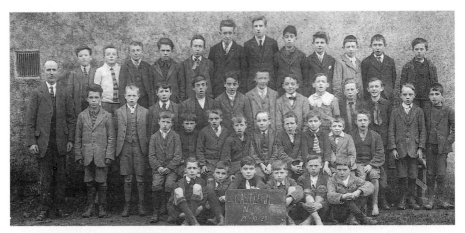

CASTLEGAL BOYS SCHOOL 23/10/1923

Teacher *Master John O'Connor* . **Back Row:** *L to R: Bernie Higgins, James McGovern, Josie Harrison, Paddy McIntyre, Patrick Costello, Eugene McGloin, Martin O'Connor, ? , Steven O'Connor, Tommy Barry, John Costello, Paddy McIntyre.*
3rd Row: Eddie Higgins, Kenneth Dickson, Robert Pye, Ned Gallagher, ? *Dickson, Steven Barry, William Barry, Thomas Barry, Hubert McGloin, John 'Judge' Gallagher, Pakie Mc Gloin, ?,*
2nd. Row: *Eugene Higgins, Willie Leonard, Patrick Joseph Watters, ? Higgins, Jimmy McGloin, James Eddie Costello, Paddy Harrison, Johnny O'Connor, ? Tehan.*
Front Row: *? , Dan Harrison, Jack Harrison, ? , John Leonard. ?*

Photo: Courtesy of Ellie B. Barry

CASTLEGAL GIRLS SCHOOL 1927

Teacher: Mrs Gilmartin on left. Back Row, L to R. *Mary Kate Clancy, Annie Curneen, Katie Harrison, Mary Margaret Harrison, Molly Leonard, Minna O'Connor, Eithne McIntyre, Katie Killerlane.*
Middle Row *Brigid Langan, Kathleen Watters, Rose Ann McGowan, Katie Warnock, Mary K. McGowan, (Tawly), Ellen Tehan, Ellie Bee Barry, Mary Kate Cleary, Dotie Gonigle, Delia Watters.*
Front: *Katie Harrison, Bee Cleary, May Watters, Kathleen Leonard, Brigid Killeralne, Teresa McGowan, May McGloin, Rose Laden, Nellie Killerlane, Ismay McIntyre.*

Photo: Courtesy of Ellie B. Barry

CLOONTY NATIONAL SCHOOL 1930

Teacher *Michael Steven McGowan and Mrs Sarah Conolly* **Back Row:** *L to R: Kathleen Gallagher, May Connolly, Maggie Connolly, Rose Ellie Connolly, Molly McDermott, Una Rooney..*
3rd Row: *Macklie Gillespie, Jery Clancy, Joe McGowan, Jim McSharry, Jimmy McGarrigle, Eugene Crean, Andy McGowan, Liam Gallagher, Hugh Gilmartin, Johnny Clancy.*
2nd. Row: *May Likely, Bridie McSharry, Katie McSharry, Delia McDermot, Mary McSharry, Kathleen Connolly, Emily Likely, Brigid Connolly, Nora McDermot, Maisie Gallagher, Margaret Mc Sharry, Dympna Gallagher, Tessie Connolly, Bernadette Connolly, Teresa McGarrigle* **Front Row:** *Brian Crean, ?Connolly, ? Kelly, ? Connolly, John Crean, Patrick Connolly* Photo: Courtesy of Mrs Kate Heraughty

PARENTS PROTEST CLOSURE OF CARNS SCHOOL, 1972

Included in group are parents: *Christy Heraughty, Tommy and Annie Gilroy, Eileen Coyne, John C. & Liz O'Connor, Mary Langan, Sophie Keegan, Michael James Healy, Katie Heraughty, Mary Keaney, Michael J. & Mary A. Burns, Mary Rooney.*
Children *Aidan Gilroy, Fiona Gilroy, Michael Healy, Michael John, Christine, & Jimmy, Langan, John & Cathy Rooney, Mary, Agnes, & Margaret Burns, Teresa, Christina, Josephine, Patricia, Jacqueline and Bernadette Keaney, Paula, Katherine and Adrian O'Connor, Martin Heraughty, Philomena Keegan, Neasa Coyne.* Photo: Courtesy Mrs Heraughty

ON THE WAY TO MASS, BALLINTRILLICK 1948
On the way to Mass by car, Bike and Pony and trap
Photo: Courtesy of The Father Browne S.J. Collection

HEYDAY OF THE NUNS C. 1956
Sisters of Mercy at Bishops Pool
Photo: Courtesy of Sister of Mercy, Mullaghmore

This card was commsioned by Hannon's Hotel' and shows
Mullaghmore Quay shortly after the turn of the century
Courtesy Aidan Mannion Collection

Posted at Cliffoney on July 8, 1904; showing cargo ships and
sheds used for storing Kelp, Coal and later Barytes.
Courtesy Aidan Mannion Collection

MULLAGHMORE COAST GUARD STATION
Posted on August 20th 1918

Courtesy Aidan MannionCollection

MULLAGHMORE QUAYSIDE
Posted at Cliffoney on April 3rd. 1911

Courtesy Aidan Mannion Collection

UNLOADING SHIPS BY HORSE AND CART

*Portrayal of days when, "ships were driven aground and unloaded
by horse or ass and cart"*

MILK HARBOUR C 1905

L to R ; Johnny Mc Cann, Johnny 'Ruadh' McCann, Thomas Mc Cann, James Gillen

Photo: Courtesy of Tom & John Mc Cann

Gleniff, where it was taken by horse and cart to Mullaghmore and shipped, unprocessed, to Liverpool. This venture came to an end following a disagreement with the owners of the mineral rights.

Mining was undertaken again in 1870, this time in Gleniff on Sir Robert Gore-Booth's property by a Mr. Folliot Barton. The great difficulty was always getting the material down the mountainside, and Barton at first attempted this in a novel way, by using a long tube. This proved unworkable, but not to be beaten, he then introduced a system of cables, quite innovative for it's day, which brought the ore down to the valley,"by small buckets carrying two stone weight each; the buckets were then hooked on to an endless wire rope, and moved by the weight of the full buckets round the inclined drum at either end." It was a thousand foot drop from the workings where the buckets were hooked on, to the terminal on the valley floor below where the buckets were emptied and raised again to the rim above. It was carted from the end of the cable system along the valley to a small water mill on the Bunduff river, where it was processed and packed in bags and barrels in preparation for shipment from Mullaghmore.

Barton ceased operations in 1875 and the workings lay fallow until 1888, when Sir Henry Gore-Booth and Mr. George Tottenham of Largydonnell, Co. Leitrim put the mines into production again. Classiebawn estate records for 1890 and some years following, show a sum of £10 per annum being paid by Col. Tottenham for two Barytes Sheds on the Harbour Pier in Mullaghmore. Timber ladder-roads were installed on the face of the cliff to give access to the mine face from above and from below. One of these ladders started on the valley floor and went 140 feet straight up the sheer cliff face to where the borings were blasted into the face of the rock. Cables were again used, this time on a bigger scale, with a span of 3,000 feet between supports, carrying the spar in steel buckets, with a capacity of 5 cwt., to the washing sheds below, from where it was carted to the stone mill near Ballintrillick bridge. It was further ground here and processed into a powder, packaged and brought to Mullaghmore for shipment.

This enterprise continued for many years and was continued by Sir Josslyn Gore-Booth who worked the mines into this century, shipping huge amounts of the product through Mullaghmore and Sligo port, before production again ground to a halt and the mines and mills once more fell silent. A trip to the rim overlooking the Gleniff Horseshoe is well worthwhile, where remnants of this and other operations can still be viewed from the dizzy heights. Parts of the cableway, starting near the old Gleniff school, could still be seen until recently, along with some other rusty and forlorn remnants of rusting machinery, strewn on the mountainside.

It was Barium Consolidated Ltd., an English concern financed by a Swede, Mr. Wallenburg, who now spearheaded this latest assault on the barytes resources locked up in the mountain. The venture had a most auspicious beginning when the company signed a contract with Sligo County Council, owners of the harbour, "guaranteeing 300 pounds a year to the council for the shipment of 30,000 tons of barytes from the Mullaghmore pier." Quite understandably there was great excitement and enthusiasm for the venture, as vistas of a new era of employment for the young men, and prosperity for the harbour and area as a whole, opened up.

The entire village turned out for the laying of the first rail on Jan. 2nd 1928. This surely, was no will o' the wisp; the fact that this company was actually laying a railroad, inspired confidence, and gave hard evidence to the community of their commitment, practically ensuring the establishment of Mullaghmore as a railhead and centre of commerce. Things would never be the same again! If there's a life hereafter we can be sure that Nimmo and Palmerston smiled down on the project as their much sought after railway came to the little harbour at last.

The Sligo Champion sent a reporter to the village along with Mr. J. Hennigan T.D. and duly reported in the issue of Feb. 18 1928 that:-

"The babel of voices and the clanging of hammers told that the silence had been broken and that the opening stages of a new era had begun. Approaching the village one found a line of narrow gauge railway already in course of construction. Hordes of men worked like bees in a hive, each at his own particular section, hurrying through the laying of the rails across the main road at Creevykeel before darkness set in..... The rails are prepared in sections of about 18 feet each, this work being done by a number of men in a large shed erected by the harbour. The sections having been assembled, they are placed in a small lorry or bogey and carried along the line already laid, to where they are required for the further extension of the work."

The engineer in charge of the work was a Capt. Mc Namara; John Mitchell the overseer, was Scottish; he settled down in this area after the railroad was built. Other men who came to build a railroad and settled in the area, building a home too, were Jack Deery of Pettigo, lorry driver; Jack Hargadon of South Sligo, mechanic, and Alf Hill, from England, no one knows exactly where, but he was the ganger and expert on intricate rail sections and exchanges. The two foot gauge tracks starting their journey at the harbour, were laid along the "Old Quay", out along the "burra" behind Mullaneys and running parallel to the road went through the stone pillars (which still stand) at Fanny's Road. It ran alongside the road between the lakes, up "Denis's Hill" crossing the mail coach or main Sligo-Bundoran road at Creevykeel heading towards Ballintrillick. The rails could be seen embedded in the road here as recently as the fifties. The little railroad went on through Carnduff, passing through Leitrim at Cloonty, and on to the corrugated iron building housing the steam operated mills at Ballintrillick, where the spar was purified and broken down into a white powder.

The spar started its journey to this refinery from the top of the Gleniff mountain, where the cars were pushed manually by the workmen along another mile long 18 inch rail track, which was laid from the mine itself to a cable worked track. The cars were hitched on to a cable here and lowered down these vertical tracks, the full ones going down hoisting the empty ones from below. At the bottom of this track is where the Mullaghmore railway proper started, running down the western side of the valley and crossing a trestle bridge over a gorge on the left of the Ballintrillick river, but at a higher level. On reaching the mills at Ballintrillick (where my father worked as a timekeeper) the rails ran onto a raised platform where the rough material was dumped from the wagons down a chute to the mills. A bypass line was built here which allowed the trains to travel directly from the cable track at the foot of the mountain, with unprocessed material, for direct shipment from Mullaghmore.

The line took nine months to complete, the last rail being laid at Gleniff on Sept. 22nd 1928 with operations being commenced some short time thereafter. The locomotive used to pull the cars was a petrol powered Simplex, supplied by Motor Rail Ltd. of Bedford England. It weighed two and a half tons, measured nine feet long by five feet wide and was chain driven from gear box to axles. The engine was a water cooled Dorman and the whole affair could be driven in either direction without the driver changing seats, as he sat in the centre facing to the side. Considerable quantities of barytes were processed at the pilot shed and moved by road for shipment out of Sligo. For some unknown reason it seems that Mullaghmore was little used as a port for export of the material, as not more than three shipments were made out of here altogether. The length of track from Mullaghmore to Ballintrillick was used mostly for bringing coal up to the mill.

The Gleniff barytes was a very high quality product, samples of which were shown at an international exhibition in Buenos Aires in 1929. Despite this the whole project flopped and mills and rail engines ceased operation and fell silent once more in 1930-31. The tin concerns which controlled and were the main scource of income for Barium Consolidated fell into decline; when these markets collapsed, the capital to finance the operation and expansion of the Gleniff project disappeared. The Irish Governments newly formulated policy of exercising 51 percent control over foreign companies in Ireland acted as a further disincentive. Within a few short years the commercial success of the mines, railroad and harbour, the bright hope of employment for the young people was blighted, faded away and died. Bernie Kelly remembers the rusting cars and rails and recalls playing with the other young boys of the neighbourhood, as the bogeys lay idle in the Burra under Port na hEorna until they were uprooted and sold for scrap to a Mr. Lynch of Ballisodare in1935.

In 1942 another Irish company, Benbulben Barytes Ltd., reactivated the mines, installing yet another cable car system, this time on the Sligo side of the mountain. This operation has ceased too, possibly for the last time as it seems that there are no commercially viable deposits of the ore left in the mountain. Nothing much is left now to show that there ever was a thriving industry here; the rails are gone and only the scavenged ruins are left of the pilot shed and mills; the mines are desolate and silent. Looking at the peaceful village of Mullaghmore today it is difficult to believe that such great hopes for it's harbour were ever envisaged, that a "babel of voices and a clanging of hammers" ever disturbed the tranquility of the area or, indeed, that a railroad ever ran here.

Mullaghmore Harbour.

THIS well sheltered Harbour, which is now fit for the reception of Trading Vessels, contains an area equal to an Irish acre, and has alongside the Quay 13 feet water at high spring tides, and 11 feet water at high neap tides.

It is so situated on the Southern side of Donegal Bay, that Vessels of suitable draught can get in and out at every tide, and with almost every wind; and there is good anchorage on a clear sand off the mouth of the Harbour.

Mullaghmore is connected by good roads with Sligo, 13 miles distant—with Ballyshannon, 10 miles distant—and with Belleek, 13 miles distant. Its local and natural advantages adapt it to serve as the Port of communication for the County of Fermanagh for all articles of export and import, and especially for the Timber Trade.

Several Lots of Ground well calculated for scites of Warehouses and other Buildings, have been marked out contiguous to the Harbour, and any applications respecting them will be duly attended to, if addressed to JAMES WALKER, Esq. Rathcarrick, Sligo.

May 1st, 1828.

228

CHAPTER 11

The Last of the Windjammers

Herring of Sligo
And salmon of Bann,
Have made in Bristol
Many a rich man

It is indisputable that man, from time immemorial, has found the harvest of the sea as crucial to his survival as any land based wealth. Detailed information from earlier times is difficult to come by, but we do know that in the early part of the 15th century the exploitation of the fisheries resources of Sligo town, and coastal villages of the county, contributed immensely to the growth of Sligo itself and the development of its commercial life. The boom times of the 1450's were attributed in large measure to the shoals of herring that appeared off our coasts then; shoals which in addition to native boats, also attracted English and continental fishermen. Boats that came to fish brought luxury items and other goods, which included wine, and of course, salt, which provided the ingredient at that time for a new way of preserving fish, by salting them in barrels. This provided the key for making the herring industry into a very profitable industry.

The Creans, a Gaelic family from Donegal, came to prominence in the commercial life of Sligo town at this time, sharing the boom times with the O'Connors, O'Donnells, McDonaghs and Burkes. Much of this wealth was generated from custom's revenues of hides, meat and wool, as well as fish exports through Sligo harbour. Indicative of the importance of this valuable natural resource and the revenues from the fishing industry, was the decline in trade and general prosperity recorded when the shoals of herring disappeared from these coasts in the late 15th century.

Salmon and eels were a valuable natural resource too, and in the middle and late 17th century were again listed as two of the most important exports from Sligo town. The River "Sliceach" of course had the advantage of being blessed by St. Patrick which according to the 11th century "Life of St. Patrick" made it the "milch cow of the waters of Ireland." The River Duff, we are told was not nearly so lucky though, as St.

229

Patrick, not being a man to trifle with, cursed this river, "because of the refusal which the fishermen gave him." The River Drowes fared somewhat better and we are told that he raised his hand in kindness here: "Howbeit he blessed the River Drowes owing to the kindness which the little boys who were fishing in it did unto him. A salmon of Drowes is the finest of Irelands salmon."

'S nach breá i mo bhaidín ag snamh ar an gcuan,
    O-ro mo churraichín o
'S na ceaslai dtarraingt go laidir 's go buan,
    O-o-ro mo bhaidin!

As recently as the beginning of the 18th century the boats used by the inshore fishermen on the Sligo coast were primitive craft indeed, consisting merely of a wooden frame covered with horse or bullocks hide. "For a boat or currach, two cowhides were sufficent, the hairy side being turned inwards, and they were sewed together with worsted thread, which swells when it becomes wet; the outside was sometimes tarred." These boats were usually about fifteen feet in length with a beam of five feet and had a two foot draft, with no keel. Both bow and stern had the same shape, so they could go equally well in either direction; cost of building was estimated at a guinea and a half. These boats were common in the province of Connaught and were described by Beranger on his visit to Inishmurray Island in 1779 as a "frail craft" differing in construction from other areas only in that the inner structure was of basketwork. It looked to him like a vessel made of glass as when the sun shone, the water could be clearly seen through the almost transparent hide.

In 1775, bigger boats of three to five ton, worked the herring fisheries offshore, with five to seven of a crew. There were seven lengths of net to a boat, each sixty yards long, which was made by the fishermen; each net was 24 feet (160 meshes) deep, made of flax or hemp and soaked in a preservative. The boats operated then as they do now, on a share system: the owner then had a fifth, the nets two fifths and the crew two fiths. The share for the crew was divided up into sixths, one for each of the crew and two shares for the skipper. Location of the fish shoals in these days was by visual observation of the seabirds, the presence of gannets being a sure indicator, as these birds fed off the herring shoals. Despite todays electronic marvels for locating fish shoals, the smaller inshore boats until very recently, still depended on observation of the movements of seabirds to determine where nets should be shot, using

230

the depth sounder for verification. The average catch for a boat then was listed as a maximum of 10,000 fish with an average catch from 3,000 to 5,000 which were sold at an average price of one shilling and eight pence per hundred, sometimes going as high as two shillings and sixpence.

The herring fishery, which started in October, continued to be of great importance to the economy of the region at this time, but as in earlier times, it was unpredictable, and in some seasons could fail completely. This failure happened again in 1783, around which time it collapsed almost altogether. Even in the 1820's the Sligo boats were forced to fish in Donegal Bay and further north in search of the herring shoals. In 1840 the silver shoals returned to Sligo Bay once again, where an extensive herring fishery was carried on for the next thirty five years until 1875, at which time they moved North to Donegal Bay once more. From this experience it would seem likely that herring have a pattern of cyclic movement from one area to another.

These failures have happened in more modern times too and, interestingly, fishing lore has it that these disappearances have been attributed to quarrels among the fishermen, over the catch. Herring were caught in abundance in Sligo Bay less than two decades ago; their abrupt departure from here shortly after disputes arose among the boats, giving credence to the old superstitions.

The herring fisheries in the North-west at this time are carried on almost exclusively from Killybegs in Co. Donegal, Sligo having long ceased to be a fishery port of any significance. Driftnetting for herring has almost ceased for the inshore "half-deckers" too, as the catching abilities of the huge tank boats and supertrawlers threaten the very survival of the herring shoals. The decline of the driftnetters is regrettable as this method of fishing was kinder to stocks, taking only mature fish and allowing the smaller fry to escape through the meshes. It also distributed the wealth more evenly among the smaller villages and communities on the coast giving everyone a share in the silver bounty. The move to these bigger boats and factory ships, and the promotion of this aspect of the fishing industry by national bodies, has resulted in a decline in demand for the smaller boats by inshore fishermen and has had the follow-on effect of a virtual elimination of the small, local boatyards which catered to this market.

A report issued by the Commisioner of Irish fisheries in 1824, gives us a glimpse of the condition of the fisheries of 170 years ago. Mullaghmore is stated to be the principal fishing village in Donegal Bay supplying, "the markets of Leitrim and Fermanagh; it also sends much fish to Sligo." It goes on to give an evaluation of the fishing grounds of the area, saying that it has,

"betwen Mullaghmore and Ballyshannon Bar.....good ground for haddock with spilliards, also for flatfish, viz. plaice, turbot and sole. On
the Bullocks rocks, between Mullaghmore and Milkhaven, there is
good lobster fishing, also at Ennismurray. The cod fishing is chiefly
from hence to Ennismurray, with foul ground called Bankrea, but
inside is an excellent turbot bank at Stridagh in two or three fathoms
water; the best is on the East side of Stridagh." [1]

It records Milkhaven as being an excellent scource for slugs, mus-
sels and flatfish for bait and indeed, as will be noted later, Milkhaven
was used extensively for this purpose, until the demise of the last generation of fishermen in the middle of this century. The report gives only a
passing mention of Raughley but tells us that the village of Cloonagh
has, "twenty to thirty yawls, which are employed in fishing in good
weather, but in bad weather must be hauled up."

A question that has always puzzled historians is how the famine
could have had such devastating effect along the West coast of Ireland
when it seems that shoals of fish were to be found in abundance off the
coast. The explanations that have been put forward, that in extended
periods of bad weather, when the fishermen could not put to sea, they
were forced to sell their gear, seemed rather thin and unlikely. Looking
at it from the protected, relatively affluent 1990's, this seems like a fool-
hardy, unwise course of action. Whatever the reason, this situation
seems to have prevailed here too, as evidenced by a letter of an Inspector
of the Board of Guardians to the Commisioners in Dublin written in 1848
at the height of the famine. He outlined Mullaghmore's favourable position on the coast as a fishing port but also describes it as being in the
neighbourhood, "of the most destitute part of the Union." Describing the
plight of the fishing community he goes on to say that,

"the men are all brought up to support themselves and their families
by fishing; but since the failure of the potato crop have been so
reduced and become so poor, that they cannot obtain the necessary
fishing gear to continue their former ocupations."

He then makes a case for a loan of £500 to help the fishermen to re-
establish the fisheries and start a curing station.

We can well imagine that the potato crop was an important element
at that time for survival as even in more recent times, people depending
completely on fishing for a living, could not survive as well as those
with farms to work also. As late as the middle of this century many of

1 According to Palmerston's agent, Walker, a trade in poteen and potatoes existed at
this time too; fishermen from the Donegal shore bringing poteen and returning with
seed potatoes and other goods.

the boats were not "shoved" or prepared for sea until the farms were in order and the crops were in; when the potato and other crops were secure, then and only then did the summer fishing begin. At a Board of Guardians meeting in Sligo in April 1886 the fishermen of Inishmurray were reported to be in dire straits having lost their nets in a storm. Here, poteen was an important income supplement, but a constabulary barracks, which had been established on the island some years previously, effectively prevented poteen making. A petition signed by the Brady's, Heraughty's, Thomas Hoey, Michael McGovern, John Boyle and Michael Dunleavey requested the Board for financial assistance to procure new fishing gear and seed for the crops of 1886.

In the early 1880's, according to Woodmartin, Raughley seems to have overtaken Mullaghmore as the premium fishing port in this area. Even though the boats here were larger and had better equipment than those at Raughley, he maintained that the harbour was a failure, the only good achieved by it being, "to prevent the fishery, of which it was the centre, from completely dying out." In Raughley, there had apparently been some opposition to trawling previously, but in 1884, trawling was constantly carried on from this port, "one of the greatest opponents of trawling now having the most successful boat". In a twelve month period, the boats there had taken 40,000 cod, 20,000 pollock, 2,000 sole, 100 turbot, 25,000 mackerel, 20,000 herrings, 40,000 flatfish, 6,000 lobsters and 2,000 crabs. We are not told who was counting but they certainly came up with some nice round figures! Mullaghmore may have fared badly in this report but Rosses Point fared even worse, the boatmen there being described as being mostly farmers and pilots, "who did not fish much unless the herrings or mackerel came close to the shore."

A fisherman's life was a hard one then, but time was made long ago for sport too, and so the annual Mullaghmore Regatta was duly held in Aug. 1886. A reporter from The Sligo Independent attended the affair and tells us in that paper on Aug 25th, that the "conduct of the people who assembled to witness the sailing and rowing matches was very good." A Mr. Mc Gloin was Secretary and three sailing boats started in the first class. The winners in this race were:

JOHN GILMARTIN	HELENA	1ST
B OR S HARKIN	MARIA	2ND

In the second class race four yachts started and the winners were:

MARTIN BOYCE	JANE	1ST
CHRISTOPHER DONLEVY'S	ANNE	2ND

Six boats started in the third class race for Greencastle yawls carrying sails and the winners here were:

Pat Gallagher	Rose	1st
Brian Callery	Lily	2nd
John Mc Cann	Linnet	3rd

In the mixed class, all boats started at the same time, on a course from the pier to Bundoran, a dead run before the wind. The light Greencastle yawls ran clear away from the bigger boats on the first leg, but on rounding the marker boat at Bundoran, and heading close hauled for Mullaghmore, the situation was reversed, and the bigger boats forged ahead. One of the second class yachts, Martin Boyce's "Jane" made fine work and beat John Gilmartin's "Helena" which was in the first class. A few rowing races followed and these were pulled over a four mile course. Martin Heraughty's "Belle of the Isle" manned by a picked crew from Inishmurray Island won the yawl race in this class, John Roger's "Linnet" came second and Brian Callery's "Lily" a boat length behind. Being "King" of Inishmurray at the time, I suppose it was only fitting that Martin Heraughty should have had the honour of winning the race and the opportunity to lead his loyal subjects to the victory!

PRE 1900 FISHING RETURNS

In 1890 ten Mullaghmore boats along with a large number of Donegal boats participated in a mackerel fishery at St. Johns Pt. from August to the end of September. Some of the fish were sold at Mullaghmore and the balance at Ballysaggart and Ballyederlan, where they were bought for curing. Ten men, twenty women and nine boys were employed at the curing and packed 556 barrels of mackerel during the period. Men were paid 15 shillings per week, women, 9 shillings and boys, 9 shillings.

Coastguard stations kept an eye on the local fishing communities and filed yearly returns on catches. The following information is gleaned from the reports of the Sligo Division some years before the turn of the century:

"1889: In addition to nets and lines, trawling is carried on in Sligo and Drumcliff bays. About 30,000 cod, 25,000 pollock, 1,500 soles, 150 turbot, 15,000 mackerel, 300,000 herrings, 50,000 flatfish, 7,000 lobsters and 1,800 crabs were taken.Large shoals of herring and mackerel appeared off Cloonagh in January and February and again in Oct. November and December, from one to four miles off the coast.

In Mullaghmore division there is good trawling ground availed of by local boats of a small class for about 3 or 4 months of the year. About £10 per year can be made at the trawling. Large shoals of

234

mackerel appeared in August, September and October, and herrings at Inishmurray island the whole year. About 11,900 lobsters were taken by the Mullaghmore men.
The salmon fishing of the Sligo district is improving. The highest price for salmon was 3s.3d. per pound and the lowest was 7 $1/_2$d."

In 1890, twenty three to thirty, third class boats (an increase of seven) took part in the Spring and Autumn fishing out of Mullaghmore, fishing for herring and mackerel. The highest number of boats fishing in any one day was fifteen. Fish were landed at Mullaghmore and Streedagh.

At Raughley during the same period, twelve boats landed fish at Ballyconnell and Cloonagh. The total catch of lobsters here for 1890 was 7,000 and 2,500 crabs. Mullaghmore had a catch of 13,900 lobsters for the same year. According to the coastguard reports, the catch of lobsters in Mullaghmore was down to 5,000 in 1892; these were shipped "by passing steamers from Sligo to Liverpool".

By 1894, lobsters in the Sligo district continue to show a decline, from a gross of 18,900 lobsters in 1890, to 13,955 in 1893 and 13,205 in 1894. These were sent to the Dublin market and sold for a price of 30 shillings a dozen. This price was considered to be exceptionally high for the time, but it was stated that at 18 inches long, the size was also exceptional.

In 1893, 25 tons of periwinkles were picked at Raughley by about twenty people, from April to December. They were exported to Scotland where they fetched a price of £2. 10s per ton.

These reports are accompanied by remarks on the difficulties and obstacles faced by fishermen, regarding the condition of their gear and disposal of catches: "The Raughley and Mullaghmore men would, no doubt do better, if better transport than carts were available. The men at these ports send principally to Sligo and the roads are very bad. None of these ports are very far from markets; provided enough fish was landed to make it worth while to provide better transport." A suggestion is made that small tugs towing proper lighters should be experimented with as a more efficient way of getting the fish to market in time.. Further difficulties are reported in that:

"The Raughley and Mullaghmore men fish fairly regularly, but their boats are not able, on account of their size to work the outlying grounds to advantage....... the boats and nets of the fishermen are becoming worn out and they have not sufficent means to produce new ones....... The lack of means of communication renders it extremely difficult for the men to get rid of their fish before it becomes unfit for sale, and consequently they show a lack of energy for their calling."
It seems that a fisherman's life has, indeed, always been a hard one!

GREENCASTLE YAWLS

Greencastle yawls were common in Donegal Bay at this time and were the workhorses of the inshore fishing fleet on the West coast of Ireland. These boats had their design origins in Norway; originally known as "Druntheim" boats or "Norway yawls" they were imported along with timber, tar and general cargoes into Ireland in the late eighteenth and early nineteenth centuries from the Norwegian ports of Trondheim and Christiansand. These boats were part of a north-west European building tradition, centered on Scandanavia, where these double-ended clinker built boats had been built for over a thousand years. They rowed and sailed well, were generally about 24 feet on the keel with 6 feet beam, carrying two spritsails, and sometimes a jib. It is not clear why they were called "Greencastles" as when the building of these boats was begun in Donegal they were built in Moville, where in addition to supplying local demand they were exported from here to Scotland, where they became known as "Greencastle skiffs."

Large numbers of these went to Kintyre and the Islands of Islay and Colonsay where they were delivered on the Derry-Clyde steamer; they were delivered to this area at the railhead in Bundoran by the narrow gauge railway which ran at that time through Donegal. The Mullaghmore men would then go to Bundoran to take delivery of their new boat, push it on rollers through the streets of Bundoran to the slip and row it across the bay to its new home.

These boats were the back bone of the fishing fleets of the north and west coasts until the introduction of the internal combustion engine in the early part of the twentieth century. This brought about inevitable design and structural changes, but nevertheless elements of the old craftsmanship design and style can still be detected in localities that, even today, still carry on the old traditions of boatbuilding.

These Greencastle yawls were so highly regarded that about 1900 the Congested Districts Board had large numbers of these boats built for poor fishermen all along the west coast. The C.D.B. was instituted in 1891 with the intention of improving the living conditions of the people of the west coast through farming, fishing and small industry and the provision of financial aid and practical help and advice. The development of fisheries was seen almost immediately as a priority as this great natural resource lay at the door of most of the "districts". As outlined earlier in the section on farm life, their first work was an evaluation of the areas under their control so that they could estimate the extent of the problem and establish a baseline for progress in the ensuing years. This area along with Cliffoney and also Maugherow including north and west Lisadell, is listed in the report as being part of the district of Grange; the survey was carried out in 1895 by one of the Board's Inspectors, F.G. Townsend Gahan. The report comprises a comprehensive evaluation of the way the inhabitants of this area lived at the time and makes very interesting reading as a whole but as this section deals primarily with fishing and related matters we will confine ourselves as much as possible to that.

The report states that there is no steady employment of labour in the district other than that given by the landlords who employ about thirty or forty men altogether. A certain amount of casual employment is available and an ordinary family, "with a man and a strong boy", could count on making about four pounds a year with the daily wages being at a rate of one shilling per day with food, and one shilling and sixpence without (one shilling = fivepence in todays money).

The two principal fishing centres in the area were Raughley and Mullaghmore with a certain amount of fishing being carried on also at Milkhaven, Streedagh and Ballyconnell; Mullaghmore is stated to be the more important of the three, as the greatest quantity of fish is landed there. Inishmurray is considered to have good potential being situated close to the cod banks, "but at present the men seem rather apathetic about it." The possibility of opening a curing station was considered to be of immense benefit to the islanders but some doubt was expressed as to whether they would sell their fish to the Board at three shillings when they could get five to six shillings on the mainland.

At Mullaghmore, at least eight shillings could be got for cod and ling and twenty shillings per thousand for herring; the average local prices were seven to twelve shillings per dozen for cod and ling; three shillings per dozen for haddock; between ten and thirty shillings per thousand for herring and ten pence per dozen for whiting. There were some twenty boats fishing for lobster at times during the season, carrying three of a crew per boat who could make eight to ten shillings per man each week. There was a good local market for lobsters in Bundoran and Sligo with a number being shipped to Liverpool by steamer. Ballyshannon, Bundoran and Sligo gave consistently good markets for fish and large numbers of cadgers or fish hawkers supplied these markets as well as the more local demand.

There were very few boats in the district engaged solely in fishing, the fisher families in Mullaghmore, numbering forty or fifty, coming closest to this; even these had "little patches of land and keep one or two pigs and sometimes a cow." Twenty five boats are listed as fishing out of

Mullaghmore and Moneygold, of which seven were trawlers; crews averaged six to a boat making a total of 150 men and boys employed. The number of boats on the Raughley/Ballyconnell and Inishmurray side were thirty five of which four were trawlers, a large number of the boats here were considered to be "old and indifferent" and not very active at the fishing. Most of the boats, both on the Raughley and on the Mullaghmore side were used extensively in the Springtime for carrying seaweed (probably famluc) as this was at the time an essential ingredient for the cultivation of crops. One or two boats at Milkhaven were employed occasionally in the transport of turf to Dernish Island.

Consideration was given to the setting up of fish curing stations in the district similar to that which was set up in Raughley in 1894 but some doubt was expressed about the success of such a move as there was such a ready market for fish in Mullaghmore. The fishermen of Raughley were more likely to be satisfied with the prices given by the Board, the village being "more out of the way and not so frequented by hawkers."

In any event a curing station was set up at Mullaghmore shortly after this to take the excess of fish left over when the normal markets were supplied. Another one was started on Inishmurray where curing of cod, ling and glassin started when prices fell to three shillings for thirteen full size cod and five shillings for thirteen full size ling. (In 1896 the Inspector of Constabulary led a hue and cry for the discovery of the villain who had stolen salt and curing utensils from the Mullaghmore curing station.)

Conclusions drawn at the end of the survey were that the people of this district were much better off than the majority of the congested districts on the Donegal side of the bay. Reasons given for this were the better prices for fish which could be got here, a better standard of dwelling house and as noted in another chapter,

"the fact that nearly all the population wear boots and shoes, and all the women on Sundays, hats or bonnets.......also the quantity of bakers bread bought",

Among a list of recommendations for the improvement of the area was that new boats should be procured to replace the existing ones which were very old and in poor shape; also recommended was the introduction of more modern fishing methods to replace the outdated ones being used. Mullaghmore, having an enclosed harbour was considered suitable, from a safety point of view, for the introduction of larger boats. The fishermen there, too, were willing to club together to purchase one or two on a trial basis. Even though the harbour was privately

238

owned, the board, in recognition of the importance of the fishing industry to the economy of the area as a whole, granted three hundred pounds for the repair of the quay walls and breakwater and the re-making of the roadway. Raughley pier, constructed by the Board of Works a few years before, was considered to have several drawbacks, one of these being the shallow water in the approaches; a major drawback was the lack of a road, as the land around the harbour was privately owned by the landlord, Mr. Jones, who charged a royalty on all carts going through his property.

The C.D.B. did, in 1903, introduce one of the large Zulu luggers to Raughley. The St. Derible, along with an instructor, was sent to Raughley to participate in the herring fishery of that year, but had to be withdrawn when no one could be found to go as crew. It was felt, at the time, that in any case, the boat was too large and the harbour too shallow for such a venture.

A landing stage was suggested for Knocklane to prevent the fishermen getting wet on landing and launching their boats, a sum of fifty pounds was recommended for this. Streedagh was considered to have the same drawback as Raughley in that the land approach was through the private property of another Mr. Jones (no relation to the Raughley landlord) although he closed and locked his gates only once a year to maintain his property rights. Streedagh was considered to be relatively important though, as it served as a landing place for the Inishmurray fishermen and as a place to pick up doctors, police, clergy etc., going to the island. It served too as a port for many of the boats of the area who landed here, particularly during the herring season. A landing stage similar to one the board had installed at Magheroarty in Donegal, was recommended.

The Board concerned itself too with the setting up of and instruction in industries immediately associated with fishing, such as fish curing stations mentioned before and also net making, barrel making and boat building. By 1902, twenty three decked fishing boats had been built at shipyards on the coast of Conemara and at Killybegs, where building was first started under instruction provided by the Board. Including these twenty three, the total number of boats built by the Board up to that time was ninety one, some of these being built to the Boards order in Scotland, at a total cost of £15,000.

Some of these boats were built by local boatbuilders, Mc Canns of Milk Harbour, Moneygold, who in addition to boats, also supplied the community with ass and horse carts, wooden wheelbarrows etc. In the late 19th century, double ender yawls of 21ft. keel, 6ft.2inch beam, with

239

four oars and rudder were built at this yard at a cost of £12 each. One or two of these yawls were built each year, one at least of which came to Mullaghmore, at the order of James Rourke. Boats were also built then at "Oldtown", Carns, by travelling boatbuilders who came and built to supply local demand, moving on to the next town along the coast, when their job was finished.

The sea faring tradition of the McCann family can be traced back to the middle of the 19th century, when Johnny "Ruadh" Mc Cann, grandfather of the present Mc Canns, ferried cargo in his 28' yawl from Killybegs to points along the coast as far as Sligo town. After the turn of the century, his son, John, delivered post to Inishmurray "once or twice a month". Twelve pounds won't get you much anymore, but the Mc Canns still turn out fine boats in this location to this day. The demand for the skills of "shoeing" wheels and building of carts has practically disappeared but nevertheless, these skills are still alive and well at this location, should they ever be needed.

Mr. Townsend Gahan finished his report with some interesting commentary on the Irish psyche, observing that one of the greatest impediments to the success of many of the villagers was, "a feeling of false shame and fear of being laughed at by their less enlightened and unambitious neighbours, keeping those who would gladly rise, tied to the same position." He believed that the feeling was deeply ingrained through long years and it was this fear of being laughed at for trying to better his condition and so raise himself above his neighbours that kept many a young man, "who would otherwise rise, down in the old grooves." He predicted that with increasing education, each individual would determine what was best for themselves and was in their own best interests, and act accordingly, disregarding the mocking of "those who would live themselves at a lower level and keep others there if they could." One hundred years later, things have changed, and these observations could no longer be valid — could they?

FISHING LIFE AND LORE

Decca and satellite navigation hadn't even been thought of in those days, let alone invented. About the turn of the century, when the compass was first introduced, it was treated with a healthy dose of scepticism; one local fisherman, after an unsuccesful attempt at unlocking the secrets of this new gadget remarked that "you might as well have a cow's shite in a boat." The fishing grounds then, and until well into this century were pinpointed solely by a very accurate system of alignment of landmarks, many of which are disused and forgotten, but some of which are still used, albeit to a lesser extent, today.

One of these old fishing grounds was found by steering a course with the "hatchet" (a vertical cliff face on one of the Leitrim mountains) in line with an old quarry on Mullaghmore head until the Rotten Island lighthouse was "opened" clear of St. Johns Point. Lines or nets were then "shot" until the lighthouse was "closed" on the other side. Skate, cod, haddock, whiting, etc. were caught on this mark, other marks yielded herring, mackerel, pollack and so on. Six or seven man crews were common when fishing lines, each man being responsible for the baiting and shooting of his own line, as if the lines weren't prepared properly they would go over the side of the boat in a tangled mess. The lines as well as nets were made of cotton and "catacued" before being used. The "catacue" came in dark brown lumps which were boiled to produce a heavy brown liquid which was then applied to the lines or nets and acted as a preservative. Sometimes the job of digging "slugs" (lugworm) for bait was given as a permanent chore to one of the crew members but more often it was common practice for each individual crew member to be responsible for getting his own bait. In this case the fisherman's work, when fishing lines, was not done when he came ashore after a strenuous days work at sea.

Some of the old fishermen still tell stories of long trudges on foot, wearing heavy tack boots, over by Classiebawn and past the "Hungry Bank" to Poll Brane, near Milk Harbour, and further afield, with tin cans and spades in hand to dig slugs, enough to bait about 400 hooks per man, for the next days fishing. On arriving there, they quite often met with a hostile reception from landowners in the area, who claimed the shore as their own. They objected to the Mullaghmore men turning the sand over on to the "famluc" and thereby, in their opinion, retarding the growth of the weed. Neither could they dig along the shoreline under the property of Parkes and Eccles — at least not when they were looking!

Competition for places on the shore was fierce among the dozens of men involved in the fishing, necessitating travel further along the coast and on to Dernish Island to find bait. Until recent times some of the boatmen in that area were employed, at sixpence a trip, to row the Mullaghmore men across to the island; the Classiebawn estate rentals as far back as 1886 record a sum of one pound being paid to a Bartley Gillen for "services of his boat to the Mullaghmore fishermen getting bait on Dernish Island." In later years sixpence ($2^1/_2$ pence today) per man was paid by the fisherman for passage to the island.

After strenuos hours of digging these men walked home by the shore to spend further laborious hours meticulously baiting hundreds of hooks by hand with the slugs, sometimes mixed with "borneocs", for the next days fishing. Quite often, when bad weather intervened and the lines had to be left for a time, the hooks would have to be stripped of the rotten bait, fresh slugs procured and the whole time consuming process repeated. It was not unusual, in extended periods of bad weather, for the whole tedious process to be repeated three or four times before the weather cleared and the boats could put to sea.

Just as our boats fished and sometimes landed their catch on the Donegal side so the Donegal fishermen did likewise on this side sometimes bringing back grain and potatoes as the market demanded; many Mullaghmore surnames have their origins on the northern side of the bay viz. Duffy, Gallagher, Keaney, McDaid, as men who came to fish made a permanent home here, or in other cases where Mullaghmore fishermen met women on the Donegal side and brought them home as wives. A by product of this commerce between the two shores was the introduction of stories told on the Donegal side to the folklore of this area as the Donegal and Sligo fishermen swapped yarns on many a long and stormy Winter night. This is how one of these stories was told in rambling houses here:

" A 'witch' and her pretty daughter lived by the shore on St. John's Pt. When a local fisherman who was responsible for the young girl finding herself in the family way, refused to marry her, the mother became distraught, as in those times it was a great disgrace and a blot on the good name of the family to have an illegitimate child. Despite the young girls tears and the mother's pleading the young man would have nothing to do with the girl even when after some time a child was born.

Time passed but the old woman never forgot or forgave; she would have her revenge; biding her time she watched one bright calm morning as the young man and his crew boarded their boat and hoisted their sails for a days fishing in the bay. When the witch saw that they were well out at sea she went to her kitchen and filling a milk pan with water she placed a "coppin" (churn lid) to float on the surface of the water. Placing the milk pan and it's contents near a window overlooking the bay she called her daughter and told her to look out and scan the bay and tell her what she saw.

The old woman then commenced to splash and dash and cause a commotion on the surface of the water in the container causing the coppin to dance wildly about. Simultaneously, a storm sprang up at sea where the men were fishing and their boat tossed and rolled and struggled to stay afloat in the rough seas. The witch continued to cast her spell on the water while questioning the daughter, who was still looking out to sea, "Are they still afloat?" She continued to dash the water about in the pan until after some time, the girl told the old woman that she could no longer see the boat. The witch ceased to stir the water, the storm abated, but neither boat nor fishermen were ever seen again.

This story is still told in Donegal but has a slightly different introduction. One of these old story-tellers, Mickey Mc Groarty, in his version, tells that the disaster had its origins when the old woman, who lived in Inver and was very poor, went down to the herring boats to ask for some fish. The fisherman on the pier refused to give her the fish for nothing, as many people then believed that if you gave goods away for nothing you were, "giving away your luck". On being refused, the woman angrily replied, "This time next week, you'll have fish neither to sell or give away."

Some say that the gulls along the quayside are the reincarnation of old fishermen who have passed away. Perhaps they come back in other forms too, to revisit the dockside where they spent so much of their lives. In the old days, fishermen in their frail sailboats were much more subject to the vagaries of nature than today; any thing was possible and natural or supernatural things were not understood and were not to be interfered with:

"Hughie Cawley and Jimmy the brother, Dan Mc Govern and meself were, one day, going down to fish mackerel early on a Summer morning. At the eye of the new quay, there was always a rat seen running; he used to come to the edge of the quay and run down in between two stones. This morning, I decided to have a go at him, lifted a stone at the Iron Gate, and fired it. I tumbled the bugger anyway and he disappeared in between two stones; thinking no more about it we hopped into the boat and away."

When the fishermen came in and tied up the boat in the evening they normally stowed their handlines along the side of the boat in different places, taking care to take the "drove" of mackerel bait off the hook so as not to attract rats into the boat. Next morning, on arriving at the boat, our storyteller noticed that his handline was cut. "Had you the drove off the handline?" says Cawley. "I did," says I. "We used to take the droves off the handline the night before, as the rats would eat the drove of mackerel and cut the line along with it, if you didn't. That was alright; we arrived the next morning and it was the same thing, two cuts in the line and no gear but mine was touched! The third morning, the same thing happened! The Cawleys and Dan McGovern told me that I'd have to go altogether, that whatever it was that I fired at, it was no rat! Well, this went on for awhile, but to make a long story short, it quit eventually anyway, but I can tell you that I fired at no more rats after that."

THE LUGGERS

The greatest era of sail was introduced to Mullaghmore about 1913 when John Hannon and Pat Duffy, with the help of the Congested Districts Board, introduced the lugger to Mullaghmore. What matter if it was the twilight of sail, no discussion of fishing here could ever be complete without a reference to these great sailing boats. Designed originally and built in Scotland they became known as "Zulus", as England at the time of the development of these boats, c.1880, was involved in a colonial war against the Zulus in Africa.

Ranging in size from 40 to 75 feet long, one of their more unusual features was that they they caried a huge mainmast unsupported by any rigging. One of the fishermen who worked one of these great boats here told me that the mainmast "couldn't be spanned about with a mans arms." These masts, which were often shaped from a two feet square by sixty feet long baulk of timber, could be lowered into a crutch alongside the mizzen mast when fishing. They were "awful rollers" when they were not under sail; hoisting the sail took at least three men who would sometimes swing out over the side on the halyards as they hoisted and she rolled. The rudder was controlled by heavy chain attached to a great wheel and once under control of helm and sail, they were "as steady as the road." Four eighteen foot oars were carried, but these were used only as a last resort as these boats were considered to be nigh impossible to row, being fully decked. The deck to gunwale measurement was only 12 inches, so there was an ever present and real danger of being tossed overboard especially in heavy weather. When stranded at low water a man could almost walk upright along the keel as they had a draft of 6 to 7 feet. They were not without some comfort though, as below decks they boasted a coal burning stove for heating and cooking; bunks were also provided here and in a separate area, storage compartments for fish.

John Hannon owned four of the luggers; they were the 'St. Ita,' skippered by James Rourke; the 'St. Mary', skippered by Jamesy "Charlie" Gallagher; the 'Rosebud', skippered by Petie McGowan and the 'Veronica' by Pakie Mc Cannon. Pat Duffy brought in two of the luggers; the 'St. Drostane', skippered by Bernie Rourke and the 'St. Colmcille' by John Callery. Prior to 1900 the Board brought the luggers into Ireland from Scotland and after this time, as a general rule, it was more usual to have them built in Ireland. According to local information, the 'Rosebud' was built in Killybegs and according to records in the National Library the 'St. Drostane' and 'St. Ita' were built in Scotland in 1906. Both the Drostane and Ita had a registered length of 50 feet and cost £192 and £187 respectively, at the time they were built.

The 'Rosebud'was brought down from Downings about 1913 by Petie Mc Gowan, Hughie Cawley, Tom Cartin and "Big" Dan Gallagher. James Cawley recalls his father telling him of the clear frosty morning when the Rosebud with her crew, left Downings. By the time they had made Rathlin O'Beirne on the last leg for home, the weather had changed and the crew and boat were struggling in the teeth of a full gale. In danger of being driven on the rocks and wrecked, they turned about and made for shelter in Aranmore, which they reached in a few hours. The approaches to Aranmore being treacherous, two island men in a small boat came out to meet the Mullagh men and pilot them in, one staying in the little boat and one boarding the lugger.

The man in the smaller boat had a narrow escape from drowning when the bigger boat, being hit by a strong squall of wind surged forward, dragging the small boat with its helpless passenger, under the water. The other men watched helplessly from the lugger as the storm drove their boat on and the Aranmore man clung desperately to the submerged boat until somehow, both boats and crew made it safely ashore. The story had a funny but almost tragic sequel when the man who almost drowned, after celebrating his good fortune on surviving in the local pub that night, had a narrow escape from drowning again when he fell into a drain on his way home. The Mullagh men spent a few days on the island and when the weather cleared, made their way safely home.

With eight or nine of a crew, the luggers were used mostly for trawling and driftnetting; they were not considered suitable for longlining because of their great weight and size. For herring fishing, drift nets of fifty to sixty feet in length per "sheet" were used; floats made of cork were used on the headrope for buoyancy with stones on the footropes to sink the nets to the bottom. A "fleet" of twenty or so of these nets were fished by each boat with buoys of expanded pigs bladders or canvas used to mark the ends of the nets. When fishing at night the boats would sometimes tie on to the end of the fleet of nets so as not to become separated from them in the darkness and to provide a respite for eating and rest.

The boats followed the shoals of herring along the Donegal shore from Rosnowlagh as far as Teelin and Rathlin O'Beirne and from Mullagh Head westwards beyond Inishmurray and Bomore. Catches were sometimes landed at Teelin and Killybegs, but more frequently at the home harbour where they were auctioned to a waiting assemblage of rival cadgers or fish 'hawkers' who would bid keenly for the fish. Looking at the harbour now it is difficult to visualize what a busy place this must have been then, as a dozen or more cadgers waited for the boats to land; when they did land, competition was fierce and tempers often flared as the rival cadgers bid for the fish. These men would then fan out through the countryside transporting their wares by horse drawn springcart or ordinary horse and ass drawn carts, travelling to Sligo, Ballyshannon and beyond until the catch was sold. Sometimes the herring were packed fresh in barrels and brought to the railhead at Bundoran, the carters geting paid seven shillings and sixpence for an ass cart and nine shillings for a horse cart for the fourteen mile round trip.

With so much sail and manpower about it was inevitable that there would be great competition between boats, not only in the amount of fish caught in a trip, but in a hard wind and a close haul to home, in speed. One of these stories was told to me like this:

"The 'Rosebud' got thirteen cran of herring at "Inismorra"; there not being great sale for them here at the time we set sail for Killybegs, to see if we could do any better there. Killybegs was worse, and only we met a man who had been treated well here at John Kelly's wedding some time before that, the whole thing was a dead loss. This fella took us away and got sale for us anyway and we were glad to get rid of the lot for a pound a cran. We stayed in Killybegs for a while anyway and got well steamed before we left there in a stiff westerly wind, along with six or seven other boats from different parts to try the herring off Teelin. The Rosebud was a very fast boat; whatever it was about her, she had a crooked mast, but she could sail like the divil, and we passed them all.

Next thing, what did we see up in front of us but the Pimpernel, a Teelin boat and well known to be the fastest anywhere in the bay. We kept gaining on them and you could see the Donegal men sticking their heads up like "cutees" (cormorants) and looking back, one now and one again. There was a full gale blowing from the west by this time and our gunwale was buried in the water. "You'll sink her," Mc Govern shouted. "God damn yer sowl, give it to 'er," someone else roared. 'Twas full sail ahead anyway and she flew past the Pimpernel; that was the day that finished the arguments about which was the fastest boat in the bay."

The introduction of the internal combustion engine shortly before the First World War spelled the end of these magnificent luggers and brought an end eventually to the picturesque and romantic era of sail, not alone for the luggers but for all commercial craft powered by sail. Motorboats came to stay in Spring 1933 when Willie Duffy helped Jamesy Charlie Gallagher bring his new 32 foot "Pride of Mullaghmore" down from Beatty's boatyard in Moville, Co. Donegal. She was driven by a 9 H.P. Bolander diesel engine, the noisy thump of which served often as a timely warning to the islanders of Inishmurray, when Jamesy was obliged to take the Gardai on poteen raids to the island. Other motor boats followed and for a time continued the traditional fishing methods, with a new freedom though, as they were no longer tied to wind power and long tacks home, or worse still, a long row. Longlining, as a method of catching fish has long vanished from these shores and the lugworm of Poll Brane are safe, no longer threatened by the hordes of Mullaghmore men with their spades and tincans. The great majority of the boats in the harbour now are pleasure craft, reflecting the great changes that have taken place here in the last few decades, changes that have transformed the harbour from a facility for a thriving fishing community to a convenience for a holiday village peopled by a transient colony of Summer visitors.

Only a handful of fishermen are now to be found and these operate their boats single handedly for the most part. Lobster fishing is still carried on with very little of anything else except for some angling boats which cater to sport fishing continentals and a scattering of Irish anglers.

John Rogers sailed his Greencastle, the St. Patrick, well into the noisy, smelly, diesel engine populated 20th century; "the last of the windjammers," my father said as we watched John one balmy Summer's day in the late 1950's from a hill overlooking the harbour, as he tacked back and forth, making his way tediously in a light Summer breeze towards the harbour. The last of the windjammers indeed; the luggers were long gone at this time; my father had long ago given up fishing to tend the family farm full time; the skeleton of his beloved Rosebud lay rotting near the bridge at the harbour. In other ports some of the luggers were changed to gaff rig, a few became coasters carrying cargo while most became derelict and mouldered quietly away at quaysides.

Some had engines fitted, but as with the Pimpernel of Teelin, these efforts to modernise the luggers proved a failure as they never handled right afterwards and were fraught with problems. Late in 1911, the C.D.B. accepted a tender of £425 by Killybegs boat yard to build a motor Zulu boat. It seemed, though, that these great boats were reluctant to change, their spirit at one with the untameable, wild wind. A death at the quayside was fitting, and preferable to prostitution by the ugly, noisy but efficient monster created by Rudolph Diesel in 1892. Redmond John Bruen of Rosses Pt. bought the St. Mary and the Rosebud; the St. Mary was brought to the Point but the Rosebud while on her way there, broke the hoist for the lugsail off Mullagh Head and had to turn back to the harbour, never to leave again. So we are told — I believe, though, that this was no accident — I believe that she wanted to spend the last of her days at peace, with the Mullaghmore fishermen who sailed in her. Most of the other luggers were broken up for firewood, and so it was with these great boats, bringing an end to the greatest era of sail that Mullaghmore and the waters around it had ever known.

247

MENDING THE NETS
Hugh Barry 1985

Photo: J. Mc G

'THE LAST OF THE WINDJAMMERS
John Rogers in his Greencastle Yawl, the 'St. Patrick'
Photo; Courtesy of Padraig Callery

CHAPTER 12

Of Signal Stations
Sea Fencibles and Coast Guards

This section was intended to deal exclusively with the Coastguard Stations which existed at one time in Mullaghmore, just north of Mullaghmore Sea Farms, on the opposite side of the road, where private houses now stand. On trying to determine exactly where to begin, I shortly discovered that, however reluctantly, I had to go back to the 17th century to follow the metamorphosis that resulted in the formation of the Coastguard service, as they existed in Ireland and Mullaghmore. In fact this research led to the discovery of a related service in this area, of which there is now very little trace and of which, until now, very little was known.

In the early 17th century, long before the establishment of H.M. Coastguard, it was the responsibility of the Board of Customs to collect revenues payable on imported goods and to prevent evasion of payment by smugglers. These Preventive Officers, as they were called, in times of war, were expected, in addition to their normal duties to prevent the coming and going of passengers, intelligence and correspondence, with England's old enemy, France. Later in the century, with the evolvement of the Riding Officer Force, increased efforts were made to prevent the movement of smuggled goods which had eluded the Revenue cruisers at sea and the customs officials in the ports. Even this force, whose job it was to patrol the coast on horseback, were largely ineffective in making any great contribution to the prevention of smuggling. Until the beginning of the 18th century, no organisation existed which was capable of preventing the smuggling of tea, silk, laces, brandy and so on.

In 1743, there was an excise duty of 4 shillings on a pound of tea, which sold from bond at 5 shillings and 9 pence to 6 shillings and 10 pence per pound. While the English Exchequer derived a handsome £160,000 pounds a year from 650,000 lbs. weight of tea sold, it was reckoned that one smuggler alone brought no less than half a million pounds weight yearly into England, from Zeeland in Holland. Some idea of the vast profits to be made from smuggling can be gathered from an item in a pamphlet published at this time called, "A Proposal for the Preventing of Running Goods," where an instance was given of a man who some years before, "had been an ordinary sailor, was now married to a woman who had a china shop, and had so well managed affairs that he had four sloops of his own constantly employed in smuggling and that he had more guineas and English specie in his house than any banker in England." More than enough temptation indeed for our friend, Lynch, mentioned elsewhere in this book, whose ships landed cargoes of contraband on Mullaghmore strand for the markets in Sligo and elsewhere.

This state of affairs continued until the early 1800's when concerns about national defence caused the government to reorganise and upgrade the Customs Service and its Riding Officer Force. In England this resulted in 1809 in the establishment of a Preventive Water Guard to operate in coastal waters and in 1816 the formation of the Coast Blockade to complement the existing forces.

Ever since the start of the war with the French Republic in 1793 the British were constantly in fear of a foreign invasion force being landed on the West coast of Ireland. Their worst fears were realised when General Humbert landed in Killala in August 1798 with a French expeditionary force of over 1,000 troops, in support of the Irish uprising of that year. These feelings of insecurity were aggravated still further when Admiral Bonaparte arrived off the Donegal coast in October of the same year, in charge of a fleet of ships with 3,000 soldiers on board. These were defeated by a superior British force; two weeks later, three French frigates and a corvette which arrived off Killala with 1,100 troops on board returned to France on learning of Humberts defeat. Not withstanding this, little was done to fortify the Irish coastline up to the end of hostilities with the French in 1801. It wasn't until war with the French broke out again in 1803 and Robert Emmet's uprising in Ireland in July of the same year, that the British started to draw up plans for a chain of Martello towers, batteries and signal towers along the Irish coast. In the following years, signal stations were constructed starting at Dublin on the East coast, around by the South coast and northwards along the West coast, to Malin Head in Co. Donegal. These stations were built with the intention of giving an early warning of any hostile intent by enemy shipping to British forces in Ireland.

Along the Sligo coastline, these stations were built starting at Carrowmably in Dromore West, the next one at Knocklane Hill and another one on the next prominent headland northwards at Streedagh.

The next station was built at Mullaghmore (Kilcologue) near a point of rock known as Cromadach where the remains of the foundation can still be clearly seen. Claims that this was the site of an old lighthouse had always been rather puzzling to me, as a more logical location for any kind of warning beacon, if one were needed at all, would have been a mile and a half north on Mullagh Head. However, when looked at as a link in a chain of signal stations, everything falls into place, as this site at Cromadach is clearly visible from Streedagh Point to the south and from the next Station to the north, which was sited at St. John's Point. The 14' X 14' inside dimension of the ruin also conforms to a size which is known to be standard in the construction of these stations. This station is clearly marked as a "telegraph" on an estate map drawn c.1810, but must have ceased to exist, even as a ruin of any significance, by 1837 as the Ordnance Survey map of that year gives no indication of the existence of the station or its ruin at that time. The next station in the chain was across the bay in Donegal at St. John's Pt. and so on around to Malin Head, completing a line which had started at the Pigeon House in Dublin.

Some written accounts which are available tell us that these towers were built to a standard plan of thirteen to fourteen feet square on the inside, by 43 feet in height. They incorporated the round tower method of defence in that they had a small door in the upper storey, which was reached by a ladder that was drawn up when not in use. They were generally not sited on high ground because of the danger of signals being obscured by mist and fog. These towers were built of stone, had slated roofs and cost from £600 to £900 pounds to build. A signal mast was set up close to the station consisting of a 50 feet high ship's topmast with a cap and crosstrees, to secure the thirty feet high flagstaff above. Below the crosstrees was a thirty-foot long gaff or inclined spar. Signals were made by showing the Union flag, a blue pendant or long triangular flag, and four black balls (hoops covered with canvas) in various combinations on the flagstaff and gaff; it seems that a system of signalling by lights at night was also used. The stations were generally manned by one or two naval officers and two signalmen with sometimes a detachment of the local yeomanry to act as a guard. Communications were made between adjacent signal stations along the coast and with ships of the British Navy offshore.

About the time of the erection of these Martello towers and signal stations, a naval reserve force was created consisting of fishermen and merchant seamen commanded by naval officers and called the Sea Fencibles. These Sea Fencibles were part of the coastal defence system too, having a number of gunboats at their disposal; men and gunboats being used in conjunction with the newly built signal stations along the shore. In Ireland, the British government were again faced with a dilemma when considering the arming of these men, many of which were recruited locally. The English were under no illusions about Irish loyalty and thought it likely that large numbers might join an invading force to overthrow British rule, rather than resist the incursion. Keeping the recent Rising of 1798 and Emmett's Insurrection of 1803 in mind, it was decided to limit numbers of recruits bearing arms and to restrict them to numbers required to man the gunboats as crew.

The Sea Fencible District in this area was No. 4, covering the coastline from Ballyshannon to Killala, having a fleet of three gunboats along with a smaller number of fishing craft and boats under the overall command of Capt. Lecky. Altogether, there were 74 men serving on 43 boats in our No. 4 Sea Fencible District. The gunboats in this area were sloops, each one armed with an 18 pounder gun and four 18 or 32 pound carronades.

In September 1809, Admiral Whitshed, who had been responsible for selecting the sites of the signal stations some five years earlier, was informed that the Government intended to close down most of the stations. There was a renewal of interest in the stations for a short time during the War of 1812-14 with the U.S., when American naval vessels and privateers were active around the Irish coast, but this interest faded when war with America ended in 1814; most of the stations were abandoned then and shortly thereafter torn down and scavenged for other purposes. It is quite open to speculation that the stones from the signal tower at Cromadach may have helped build the Coastguard station near the harbour a few years later.

In the early years of the 19th century there were several preventive services operating on the coasts of Britain and Ireland, resulting in much overlapping of function and duplication of effort. A committee set up in 1821 to enquire into the operation of the Customs service recommended an amalgamation of the different groups; this took place in 1822, with the Coast Blockade being the last unit to be absorbed into the Coastguard in 1831. After 1831 the Coastguard became effectively a reserve of the Royal Navy, all appointments in the Coastguard, of any rank, being held equal to a similar rank in the navy. Ireland was divided into 28 Districts or Divisions, each District being placed under an Inspecting Officer holding the naval rank of Commander. There were two Divisions in Sligo, one having Headquarters at Pullendiva while the District covering this area had Headquarters at Rosses Point. Each Division had several stations; there were four stations in this area;

Rosses Point having a Divisional Officer and seven men; Raughley with a Chief Boatman and five men; Streedagh, a Chief Boatman and four others and Mullaghmore having a Chief Officer and eight men with three of these being detached to Ballyshannon.

The duties of this newly constituted Coastguard included the manning of the Royal Navy in the event of war or emergency and military drill and training for coastal defense in connection with this, (three thousand Coastguards served with the Royal Navy during the Crimean War in the years 1853 -56). Their duties also included the prevention of smuggling, assisting vessels in distress, taking charge of wrecks, operating life-saving apparatus, participating in the lifeboat service, searching for mines and torpedoes lost at sea and various other duties in connection with signals, telegraphs, buoys, lighthouses etc. In Ireland their duties included, in adition to this, assisting the police and army in detecting and suppressing revolt and, worse still, helping the police to search out stills and prevent the distillation of poteen in the country areas. These additional duties guaranteed their unpopularity in many areas in Ireland as they were seen as just another uniformed branch of a foreign police force.

Distribution of seizure awards was according to the rank of those belonging to the station or vessel at the time of the seizure:

CHIEF OFFICER	25 SHARES	COMMISIONED BOATMAN	8 SHARES
CHIEF BOATMAN	10 SHARES	BOATMAN & EXTRA MAN	6 SHARES
RIDING OFFICER	10 SHARES		

In 1831 a Chief Boatman's salary was £9-4s-8d per annum or 2s-9´d (14p) per day; a Commisioned Boatman or Boatman was paid £4-12s-4d or 7p per day in today's money. Here are the names of some of the men serving at Mullaghmore in 1827 according to records in the Public Record Office in Kew in London:

NAME	PERIOD	PAY
HENRY RAYE C.O	6 JAN. – 5 JULY	£6-18s-6D
JAMES PEMBEDRLEY C.B	"	£4-12s-4D
JAMES JOHNSTON E.B.	"	£2- 6s-2D
THOMAS DAVIS, BOATMAN	6 JAN. TO 5 APRIL	£1- 3s-1D

Following are the names of some more of the men who served at Mullaghmore and Raughly in the early 1800's:

Mullaghmore

DATE OF APPT.		NAME
Chief Officers		
SEPTEMBER	1822	LT. MC GLADDERY
OCTOBER	1824	MR SAMUEL PARSONS
JULY	1825	MR. J WEISS
NOVEMBER	1832	LT. KEITRIGHT
MARCH	1833	LT. LAWR. CARVEY
AUGUST	1839	MR. G. CULMER
AUGUST	1833	LT. CLAYTON MCLEAN
NOVERMBER	1840	MR THOMAS WEBB
NOVEMBER	1843	MR THOMAS HAMILTON
Chief Boatmen		
SEPTEMBER	1822	JAMES PEMBERLY
MAY	1829	HENRY HEAISON
OCTOBER	1830	JOHN BRIGGS
JULY	1834	GEORGE LINDSAY
JULY	1939	GEORGE THOMAS
MARCH	1943	GEORGE SINNETT
Comm. Boatman		
NOVEMBER	1822	WM. WEST
NOVEMBER	1822	FRANCIS KENDALL
NOVEMBER	1823	JAMES JOHNSON
AUGUST	1825	THOMAS LEMARE
JULY	1827	JOHN BRIGGS
JULY	1828	GEORGE KEEBLE
JULY	1829	DANIEL DIGNAM
JULY	1830	JOHN LOUGHNEY
JULY	1832	ROBT. CAMPBELL
APRIL	1833	MICHAEL PARSONS
SEPTEMBER	1833	CHARLES GREER
DECEMBER	1836	ZACHARIAH DAVIE

Some Boatmen who served during the same period: Daniel Bernard, Daniel Sullivan, Timothy Donoghue, Michael McGinley, Michael Perry, Peter Rogers, Thomas Blowsher, James Mc Carthy, Duncan Graham, Michael Kenney, Thomas Browster, Francis Rogers, Michael Kennelly, John Naughton, Thomas Davie, Arthur Breen, David Woolner, Alec McDonnell, John Harvey, Wm. Manning, Geo. Mc Creevy, John Mc Niece, Thos. Curran, John McNeely, John Brown, Matthew Smith, Samuel Mitchell, John Campbell, Henry Crump.

Raghly

DATE OF APPT.		NAME
Chief Boatmen		
MAY	1828	JOHN BRIGGS
MAY	1828	MICHAEL O'DRISCOLL
MAY	1828	CHARLES KINGSMAN
MARCH	1844	THOMAS ROBINSON
OCTOBER	1830	ALEX GREIG
DECEMBER	1844	THOMAS CRIMLEY
Comm. Boatman		
FEBRUARY	1823	ANDREW GILLESPIE
JANUARY	1823	JOHN BRIGGS
JULY	1829	EDWARD LAMB
OCTOBER	1830	THOMAS MCCARTAN
APRIL	1833	WM. GRILLS
OCTOBER	1843	MATTHEW MORRISON

Some Boatmen who served during the same period: George Stephens, Wm. Chesnut, Andrew Chesnut, Robt. Fagan, Richard Davies, James Crowley, William Moody, James Conaghan, John Freeny, James Keown, Hamilton Blakeney.

Pier Head House and some of the lodges were rented from Palmerston and used by the Coastguards as temporary accomodation and watch house while the Coastguard Station complex of Watch house and six houses for use as family quarters for the men were being built. Records in the P.R.O. at Kew show a sum of £1-3s-1d being paid as rent for this accomodation on 5th April 1827. The construction of new stations which included six houses, a watch house, Mullaghmore tower and a flagstaff, (see Ordnance Survey map) wasn't finished until c.1870 when the last two of the six Coast guard houses were completed. Records of the Classiebawn estate show the old coastguard quarters, now Pier Head House, being used as baths and a store, during and after this time; later again it was used as a Protestant Church and as a schoolhouse for the children of the Coastguards and other Protestant families of the area. Estate Rentals of 1858 give the following information:

DENOMINATION	TENANTS	YEARS RENT RECEIVED
Watch house	H.M. Board of Customs	£ 4-12s-4d
Boat house	do.	£ 4- 0s-0d
Flag staff	do.	10s-0d
4 Coastguard houses	do.	£18- 9s-4d
2 do. addl.	do.	£ 9- 4s-8d

The following information is from a report now held at P.R.O., Kew, and published in the year 1868 'Returns Relating to Costguard Stations':

RETURN of the Names and Situations of all Goast Guard Stations, with the Total Cost of each, for the Year ending

NAME OF STATION.	Name of nearest Seaport.	Number and Rank of Officers.	Number and Rating of Men.	Number engaged on Day Duty.	Number engaged on Night Duty.	Pay.	Allowances
SLIGO DIVISION:							
Rosses Point - - -	Sligo - -	1 inspecting officer - (Captain, R.M., half-pay).	6; 1 chief boatman, 1 divisional carpenter, 2 commissioned boatmen, 2 boatmen.	1	5	422 12 7	276 1 4
Rachley - - - -	Sligo - -	1 chief boatman -	5; 2 commissioned boatmen, 3 boatmen.	1	5	243 17 9	151 3 9
Streedagh - - -	Sligo - -	1 chief boatman in charge.	4; 2 commissioned boatmen, 2 boatmen.	1	5	229 9 7	119 15 11
Mullaghmore - - - Detachment, Ballyshannon.	Sligo - -	1 chief boatman in charge,	7; 3 commissioned boatmen, 4 boatmen.	2	6	323 8 2	213 19 2

Very few Irishmen ever joined the Coastguards and this resulted in the posts being filled mostly by Englishmen, which meant that these men had to be posted away from their home towns to what most considered a foreign land. Although, as mentioned earlier, they were mostly regarded as another arm of an unpopular English lawkeeping force, there is nothing to indicate any hostility towards them in this area; if they weren't taken into the bosom of the populace, they were at least, tolerated. As with most human relationships it is probable that the level of their acceptance could be measured by their own attitude to the local people. Ransome, the last Chief Boatman, who lived with his family in the two storey Watch house at the end of the station complex, is remembered as being a "bitter man", hostile to the local people and disliked by them. In any event, his daughter married a Catholic man against his wishes and much to his displeasure and disappointment. On the other hand, some of the older local people still remember a coastguard called Purchase and recall being invited to children's parties which were given in his own quarters.

The building directly behind No. 1 Lodge is still known as Attridge's, as a Coastguard of this name and his family, lived there for some time after his retirement from the service.

During the 1914-18 World War, most of the men were removed and posted to the Navy and their duties taken up almost entirely by local men. They were: Alfie Pearson, who was not a native of this area but served as gatehouse keeper at the end of the avenue leading to Classiebawn; others serving were local men, James Leonard, "Stoker" Leydon, James Rourke. Their tours of duty were served at the Mullaghmore tower on coast watch and on night patrols along the coast from Tullaghan to Streedagh. Some of the older people, recalling these years, remember the cheery fire in the stone fireplace at the "Tower" as a great place to "ramble".

The latent hostility of large elements of the local populations towards the Coastguards inevitably resulted in a series of attacks countrywide on these stations in the closing years of the War of Independence. It is interesting to note that despite these attacks, Admiral Tupper, Commander-in-Chief, Western Approaches, in a Colonel Blimp-like appraisal of the situation, assessed in 1920 that when the present rebellion subsided, "it would be a sound policy to increase the Coastguard force in Ireland, establishing in this country men and their families who have had more experience of civilised life than obtains in these localities normally. This would have the effect of civilising the neighbourhood."

Admiral Tupper's pompous and naive expectations of civilising the Irish were not to be fulfilled as attacks on these stations all over Ireland increased. Mullaghmore Coastguard station was attacked and burned on Saturday 26th June 1920, the details of which are covered elsewhere in this book. The Irish Times of 28th June carried the following item:

COASTGUARD STATION BURNED

"Mullaghmore Coastguard Station, two miles from Sligo, was burned to the ground on Saturday night. It was occupied by the coastguard's families only. They were ordered to clear out before the place was fired. Marines have landed from a destroyer, and are now guarding Rosses Point Coastguard Station."

A year later, on 12th June 1921, Teelin station across the bay on the Donegal coast was burned, one casualty being sustained in this incident when Coastguard William Kennington was killed during the attack.

Kilgannon's History of Sligo tells us of the demise of Raughley and Rosses Point:

"8/7/'22 A week of thrills and terror to the residents of Sligo and neighbourhood! Scarcely a night passed that the rest of the inhabitants was not disturbed by rifle and revolver fire, punctuated by explosions of bombs. The Coast Guard stations at Rosses Point and Raughley were burned to the ground, and Colloney was the scene of considerable activity during the week."

It was five days after this that National troops were ambushed at Rockwood in Sligo, suffering three fatalities and the loss of the armoured car, the Ballinalee. Kennington was the only casualty in the Donegal Bay/Sligo area as in these attacks the families of the Coastguards were generally treated well, and furniture where possible removed before the building was set alight. The attacks on these stations continued all over the country up to the signing of the Truce and the setting up of the Irish Free State, when 109 of these stations were abandoned, and passed into the hands of the Irish Provisional Government.

It seems like poetic justice that stones from the ruins of the Mullaghmore stations were used to rebuild the house of Bernie Conway in Cliffoney; his house had been burned down by Black and Tans in 1920 following the Moneygold ambush. Some years later, Petie Mc Hugh, on acquiring the property and ruins, sold the remains, c. 1959, to Sligo County Council, who crushed the stones into gravel to pave the Carnduff roads.

'THE ROADWORKERS' BUNDUFF C. 1937
L to R: Jerry Markey, Martin Murtagh, Peter Harte, Maugherow(Ganger)
Patrick Waters, Bernie Barry, Lower Bunduff. (Family Photo)

THE ENVIRONMENTAL SETTING

by Dr. Don Cotton
Lecturer in Environmental Science

The people, events and lore described in this book were set on the stage of north Sligo, sandwiched as it is between the cliffed walls of the Dartry Mountains and the vastness of the Atlantic Ocean. This is a romantic and most attractive landscape setting when the weather is good or as viewed from a car window or when imagined as one reads this book from a comfortable armchair with electric light and central heating. In these circumstances it is so easy to forget how the natural environment with its inheritance of rocks, soils, vegetation and climate has generally shaped the course of human history rather than being just a passive backdrop. One only has to go back 50 to 100 years to appreciate how people worked with and around the constraints of the environment whereas today we have grown away from nature to an alarming degree and often expect to dominate and work against it. To fully appreciate the wealth of information in this book one has to get into a frame of mind where nature is more in control of human destiny and the people are living a more harsh life than we can easily imagine from our own modern experiences. In this short Appendix I am going to try and build the landscape from its very foundations to help you understand what we see and experience today. I will start by going back in time to the very beginning of this geographical region, as far as we know it from its rock history.

Geologically this region neatly falls in a basin between the ancient rocks of Donegal and the equally ancient rocks of the Ox Mountains which are between 500 and 700 million years old. All rock in this basin dates from the Lower Carboniferous age and is between 350 and 330 million years old. Even in geological terms these rocks are quite old, but they don't have a patch on the Ox Mountains! These Carboniferous rocks were laid down under water as a warm tropical sea advanced from the south over an ancient land that lay to the north. Like all sedimentary rocks, they were laid down in layers or beds. The first to be laid down,

259

and therefore the oldest, are found underneath the younger more recent beds. Because of the way that they now slope, the oldest beds poke out from under the younger ones to the north-west at around Ballyshannon, and as one moves south to Bundoran and Mullaghmore they become higher in the sequence and younger. So far so good, but due to a number of cracks or faults in the rocks, this simple sequence is upset midway between Cliffony and Grange and the rock story south of here has to be read going from west to east. That is, starting from the main road and going towards the mountains, one sees the same sequence as between Ballyshannon and Mullaghmore, but at the base of Ben Bulben and Ben Whisken an additional part of the sequence is encountered forming the cliffs and the mountain tops (see map 1).

Now to tell the story revealed by the rocks in more detail. Parts of the ancient land mass over which the sea was advancing from the south in Carboniferous times are still to be seen to the north of Ballyshannon, and in a small wedge of rock near Rosses Point, and best of all as the Ox Mountains. Indeed the Ox Mountains were probably off-shore islands at this time with the main land mass stretching far to the north from Ballyshannon.

The first layer of Carboniferous rocks can be seen at Ballyshannon where they lie directly in contact and on top of the ancient rocks. They are a thin bed of a conglomerate made up of pebbles, just like some beaches in north Sligo today. They are followed by a thick layer of limestones formed as the sea became a little deeper and in which a diverse community of animals formed coral reefs. These rocks stretch from Ballyshannon to Bundoran and also occupy a triangular wedge making the lowlands of Grange-Drumcliff-Lissadell of the west-east sequence. (See Arrow on Map 1) The farm land over these limestones is generally well drained and quite fertile and is used for good quality permanent pasture. There is an abundance of ground water for wells but it is also easily polluted by septic tank and farmyard effluents.

As the Carboniferous sea advanced northwards and the water deepened the sediments became finer and more muddy and beds of shales are the evidence of this period. In the north-south sequence there is a band of this shale at Bundoran and the softer nature of this rock has resulted in it being eroded by the sea to form Bundoran Bay. In the west-east sequence of rocks, the band of Bundoran shale has formed a low lying boggy area with poor, wet soils, midway between the main Sligo-Donegal road and the mountains behind Drumcliff, Grange and Cliffony. The peat bogs here are nearly all cut-away and some are planted with conifers but good examples of the sort of environment formed over these shales can be seen between Cloonty and Uragh. In years gone by this area must have been difficult to cross and useless for agriculture.

A temporary retreat in the Carboniferous sea resulted in a return to shallow water conditions and the rocks from Tullaghan along the cliffs of Castlegal, Mermaid's Cove, Mullaghmore Head and even out to Inishmurray all belong to this period. There are therefore plenty of places to see this rock type which is named the Mullaghmore Sandstone after its most obvious outcrop, and it is worth taking a closer look at it. First of all, it is clearly laid down in great sheets or beds which would have been horizontal as they were formed but are now sloping or dipping at an angle of about 5-10o usually to the south-east as a result of earth movements. What is really interesting are the details of ripple marks, cross bedding and animal tracks and burrows that can be found upon close examination. All of these features are clues that indicate the sands were deposited in shallow water and it is generally believed that they were a part of a delta of a huge river flowing from the north into the warm tropical sea. Very occasional fossil tree ferns help confirm this view. The Mullaghmore sandstone also appears in the west-east sequence and here forms a band of rising land running all around the foot of the mountains but not making any notable feature in its own right. In fact the road running n-e to s-w through Ballanatrillick is on the sandstone and avoids the wet boggy ground over the shale. The soils formed from the Mullaghmore sandstone are acid, nutrient poor making them only good for rough pasture land. One benefit is that coastal exposures tend to form cliffs which are very scenic and offer nesting ledges for sea birds.

One has now reached the foot of the Dartry mountains where there is a thin band of shale upon which the whole of the mountain range is sitting. Like the previous beds of shale this is a very impermeable rock and along the top beds there are many springs where it comes into contact with the limestone above, and in some instances the limestone beds have slipped away from their main block to form free-standing pinnacles of rock. The Eagle's Rock in Glenade is a prime example of one of these 'rotational slips'.

The very hard Glencar limestone has resisted erosion and now rises vertically for over 250 meters from the lowland plain to form spectacular cliffs that are capped by a limestone reef called the Dartry limestone. The mountains Ben Whisken, Ben Bulben (526 meters) and Castlegal are the well known landmarks formed from these ancient deposits that are full of fossils of marine animals right to the reef at the very top. An outlier of this same rock succession is the very distinctive hill of

Knocknarea (327 meters) that lies between Sligo town and the seaside resort of Strandhill. Due to the effects of geological faults a block of the Dartry limestone can also be seen at sea level where it forms the coast all the way from Milkhaven to Streedagh, Ballyconnell, Raughly and Lissadell. From the fossils we know that the environment was very similar to the coral reefs of tropical waters today and we can assume that similar warm, clear and shallow marine conditions must have existed when these limestones were formed. Serpent Rock near Cloonagh is named after the distinctive 'cabbage stalk' fossils which are in fact large solitary corals. Other fossils in these rocks include shellfish called brachiopods, some snail shells, relatives of the starfish called crinoids, and distinctive 'knolls' of colonial corals. Streedagh Point and Serpent Rock are listed as of great scientific interest and are given nominal protection from fossil collectors and are well worth a visit. Apart from the great scenic value of these limestones in forming cliffs and mountains, there is also an economic aspect to them because they contain veins of barites (barium sulphate) that has been mined. The barites was not a part of the original deposit but has accumulated in cracks in the rock mass over hundreds of millions of years. The exact process is not fully understood but the miners knew how to find and follow the veins and their activities have left various landscape features, some of industrial-archaeological interest and others that mar the landscape as has happened at other mine sites world-wide.

The final rock types in the sequence are found in the highest places like Truskmore (647m). These are named the Glenade shale and Glenade sandstone but they are not very extensive in distribution and have little effect on human activity in this region. The sequence of Carboniferous rocks in north Sligo is thus fully described and passes through a succession of limestone-shale-sandstone-shale-limestone-limestone with reefs-shale-sandstone; all are of a marine or deltaic origin and all were laid down in a 30 million year period during the Lower Carboniferous.

The rocks that I have described are all that can be seen in this geographical region and are the skeleton of our landscape. However, the last of them were laid down 330 million years ago, so what happened since then? I think we can assume that more rocks must have been formed on top and that there were periods of erosion, more deposition and more erosion. These chapters in Sligo's history have all been lost, almost without trace. A clue to a period of intense erosion comes from the presence of Dermott and Graine's cave high up in the limestone cliffs of the Horseshoe Glen. It is generally believed that this cave was at ground level, or just below ground level when the Tertiary era started about 65 million years ago. The cave was most likely a part of an underground system of streams eroding down through the landscape and attacking the soluble limestone. Why the cave is now more than 250m above the valley floor can be explained by the last chapter in Sligo's geological history which started 1.83 million (1,830,000) years ago and is the story of a period of erosion called the Pleistocene ice ages.

The ice ages are a prolonged period of ice cap advance and retreat with sub-tropical conditions in Sligo during some of the warm inter-glacials. Each glacial effectively destroyed the evidence of the preceding one so that what we see today in Sligo can only be assigned to the last glaciation known in Ireland as the Midlandian. Imagine a thick layer of ice and snow lying over the Irish Midlands, in places 1500m thick, and spreading out sideways to produce glaciers that were 'rivers of ice' radiating out and pushing between the hills to carve deep valleys out of the rock skeleton. In North Sligo major glaciers gouged out the Lough Melvin basin, Glenade, Glencar and even the basin of Lough Gill. (See Map 2) Small pockets of ice formed in our mountains and spilled over the tops of ridges to carve the Horseshoe Glen and Ardnaglass. The ice also over ran the coastal area of Sligo and shaped the sandstone of Mullaghmore Head into a series of 'crag and tail' features with a long smoothed slope from the south-east followed by an ice-plucked crag as the ice moved north-west. Classie Bawn Castle is built on the highest of these and in this respect is similar to Edinburgh Castle which is also on a crag and tail.

Whenever ice moves over a landscape in glaciers it erodes, transports and deposits rock and rock debris, and when it melts the melt-water transports and dumps sediment or some of the larger debris may be dropped in situ. The ice that crossed the Dartry Mountains left features of erosion as just described, but more significantly it led to the deposition of large amounts of sands and gravels along the sides of the mountains and across most of the lowlands. The glacial deposits of north Sligo are not well understood or studied but there are some interesting features, especially around Grange. Inland from Grange at Ardnaglass Bridge there is a complex landscape of undulating hummocky ground and a clue to its origin can be seen in the disused sand and gravel quarry next to the bridge. The way in which the sands and gravels are bedded shows that they were deposited by melt-water rushing off the melting ice in the mountains, and in other places the lack of any sorted structure suggests that the heaps of material were just dumped as the ice melted away all around them. Another similar area can be seen at Mount Edward townland where there are also hills and hummocks. The presence of large amounts of glacial debris over the solid rock usually has major effects on the sort of soil that develops and on the native and agricultural floras.

It is now over 10,000 years since the last glacial finished and we are probably in an interglacial at the moment. In that span of time the landscape has continued to change, one of the more obvious features in this region being the growth of accumulations of fallen rock forming a talus or scree slope all around the base of the mountains making the cliffs less sheer in appearance. Most of the scree would have fallen in the first thousand years after the ice melted when processes of freeze and thaw would have been a feature of the sub-arctic climate that Ireland was experiencing 9-10,000 years ago. Another thing that happened as the ice melted was that the land upon which the ice had been sitting began to rise as a reponse to the great weight being lifted, but also the sea level around the world rose due to the increased amount of water released by the melted ice. The rise in sea level would have been very rapid compared with that of the land and consequently all around the Sligo coast there are indications that the sea covered places that we now know as dry land. These raised beaches are sometimes deposits of shingle and other beach materials, but more typically they are erosion features such as cliffs and ledges running along hillsides a few hundred metres inland from the current coastline. There can be no doubt that Mullaghmore Head, Conor's Island at Streedagh, Raghly and probably Knocklane were all rocky islands separated from the mainland by the sea at some time in the last 10,000 years. It is also probably the case that the first three of these locations were islands in historical time. The area between Cliffony and Mullaghmore called Bunduff is very low lying and is entirely composed of sandy deposits. It is not hard to imagine that the hillside below Cliffony was once the sea coast. A small cliff of sandstone in the field to the north of Bunduff Bridge was also once a piece of the coastline.

The fluctuating relationship between sea level and land is a complex phenomenon which is not fully worked out, but evidence from peat deposits under the sandy beaches at the Bunduff River mouth, Cloonagh beach and Loughaun (Ballyconnell) indicate that at other times in the last few thousand years places that are now under the sea were once land. So from our land-based perspective it could be said that the sea has encroached on the land and retreated further back than it is now since people set foot in Ireland, and it will probably continue to encroach and retreat in the future.

Stories of tropical coral reefs, the advance and retreat of glaciers and the rise and fall of sea levels seem fanciful when one looks at the landscape of north Sligo today. However, these have given us the land on which we tread and have provided generations of people, stretching back thousands of years, with their living. During the course of making that living the vegetation has been greatly modified and the wild animals have also altered so we have become one of the great forces of change of our environment. The natural vegetation would have been various kinds of broadleaved woodland with oak, ash and elm on the better drained soils and alder, willow and birch on wetter or more exposed areas. The mountains would have had some bushes and trees but the exposed and windy places may only have supported grasses and heathers and some low growing juniper. Wild animals like red deer, wild boar, bears and wolves were still around just a few hundred years ago and are remembered in the oral tradition of songs and stories.

Today things are very different and continue to change. It is only on the most inaccessible cliffs of the mountains that some now rare plants hold on to their precarious existence, and in poor agricultural situations like the dune grassland at Bunduff or on the bog remnants at Cloonty that other special kinds of plants survive. These places should be treasured and to give a taste to the flora of the dune grassland or 'machair' at Bunduff let me name a few special plants : adder's tongue, lady's tresses orchid, marsh heleborine, field and autumn felwort, butterfly orchid, frog orchid, bee orchid, fragrant orchid, twayblade, pyramidal orchid, water dock, and many more. Places like this have been called 'Areas of scientific Interest' but they are more than this, they are the biological remnants of our heritage and are better called 'National Heritage Areas' for they belong to everyone, born and yet to be born.

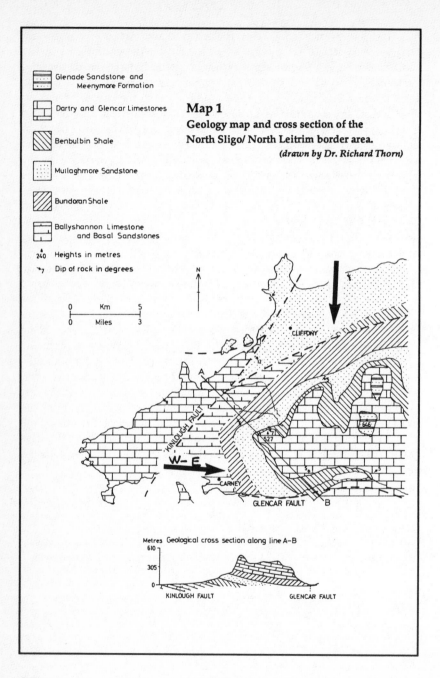

Map 1
**Geology map and cross section of the
North Sligo/ North Leitrim border area.**
(drawn by Dr. Richard Thorn)

Glenade Sandstone and Meenymore Formation

Dartry and Glencar Limestones

Benbulbin Shale

Mullaghmore Sandstone

Bundoran Shale

Ballyshannon Limestone and Basal Sandstones

240 Heights in metres

7 Dip of rock in degrees

0 Km 5
0 Miles 3

N

CLIFFONY

KINLOUGH FAULT

W—E

CARNEY

GLENCAR FAULT B

A

527

646

Metres Geological cross section along line A-B
610
305
0
KINLOUGH FAULT   GLENCAR FAULT

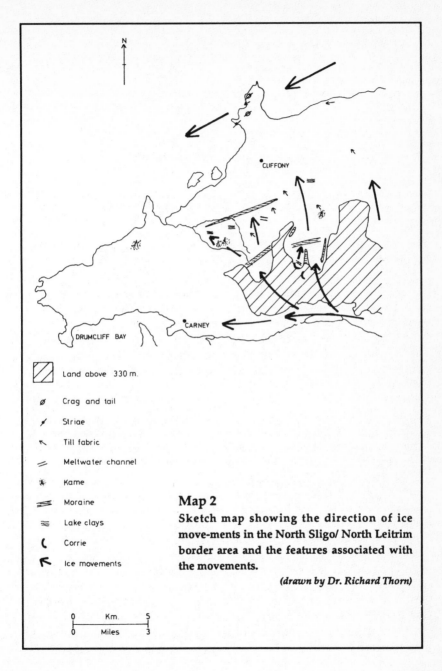

CLIFFONY

CARNEY

DRUMCLIFF BAY

Land above 330 m.

ø Crag and tail

↗ Striae

↖ Till fabric

= Meltwater channel

☀ Kame

≋ Moraine

≈ Lake clays

(Corrie

↖ Ice movements

Map 2
Sketch map showing the direction of ice move-ments in the North Sligo/ North Leitrim border area and the features associated with the movements.

(drawn by Dr. Richard Thorn)

	Km.	
0		5
0	Miles	3

MINERAL WATER WEALTH

and the

SCENERY OF SLIGO

His Royal Highness the Duke of Connaught

To save and to soothe life is a higher function than to enjoy it. The Right Honourable W. Cowper Temple, M.P. , contributed much towards that philanthropic object by directing the mineral water at Mullaghmore to be analyzed for the information of the visitors in search of health.

To extinguish maladies in the light of sanitary science is the noblest work of the physician, for prevention is better than cure.

Disease is not to be cured by drugs alone ("traditional empirieism" – Stokes) but by whatever influences the varied electro-chemical changes of the material tissues of the animal body – the matter changes while the man remains, once another and the same, no longer the same matter but still the same man. I believe that the Mullaghmore Spa belongs to that class of mineral waters which are essential to recruit the normal constitution of the blood, and thus promote those electro-chemical changes so necessary for the renewal of animal life. As invalids are recommended to respire an ozoniferous ocean atmosphere at the sea coast, Hufeland, a German authority, states, that they should drink mineral waters, at the subterranean laboratories, from the hand of living nature. These two conditions are happily combined at Mullaghmore, where electro-muscular exercise – on the high, dry, sandy soil – can be enjoyed, to develop animal electricity, to promote all the electro-chemical functions, and thus prolong life in good health.

The confidence of Mr. Cowper Temple in this healthful sea-coast at Mullaghmore, warmed by the gulf-stream, is fully proved by the splendid mansion he has erected on the high, dry, sandy soil, overlooking the sea, in which, as heretofore, we may expect his annual visits to his tenantry, whose health, comforts, welfare, and education, he consults for, believing that education is to the mind what food is to the body, for it not only enables man to become a good and loyal member of society, but also to know himself, through his Almighty Creator, and to prepare for eternal happiness.

I know of no places more worthy of public notice than Mullaghmore and Donegal, in consequence of their mineral waters. I believe the sulphur spa at Donegal to be one of the strongest in Ireland. Its proximity to Mullaghmore, about five miles across the sea, renders them essential to each other.

Mind, matter and electricity are the three conditions that constitute the whole man, which should be considered together. Mind is the immortal spirit that directs, through which alone he is man, and a "hymn in honour of the Deity," created to the image and likeness of the three Divine Persons in one. Matter is the passive principle that is acted upon, while electricity is the vital active agent of all works that I have briefly referred to. All the mineral matters that form, as it were, the bricks and mortar of our living tenements, as lime, soda, magnesia, potass, iron, carbonic acid, phosphoric acid, muriatic, and sulphuric acid, &c., are found in mineral waters. We can, therefore, quickly perceive the vital importance of having our constitutions physically refreshed, at such electro-chemical fountains of health. Since all science is now popularised, it is the duty of the physician, if he be a philosopher of nature, and a merchant of sanitary light, for the prevention and cure of disease, to render man familiar with these subjects, which form the alphabet of his own life and constitution. The mineral alkaline, chalybeate spas of Mullaghmore, which the Right Honourable W. Cowper Temple, M.P., directed to be analysed last October, was found fully equal to the waters of Vichy, Ems, Fachingen, Carlsbad, Wiesbaden, or Aix-la-Chapelle in Germany, while the locality affords one great advantage over any German spa, that invalids can enjoy the bracing billows of the Great Western Atlantic, and inhale its singularly salubrious ozoniferous ocean atmosphere, for these two spas are on the sea shore, though in no way contaminated by the sea water, while the locality is a high, dry, sandy soil. The bold marine and mountain scenery of the place exhibits the majesty of nature in full perfection.

I give as follows the analysis of Mullaghmore alkaline chlorinated chalybeate water: – One Imperial Gallon contains, carbonic acid, free and combined, 15-421 grs.; chlorine, 23-919 grs.; sulphuric acid, 5-714 grs.; phosphoric acid, 0-001 gr.; iron, 0-545 gr.; calcium base of lime, 5-246 grs.; magnesium, 2-067 grs.; potassium, 0-301 gr.; sodium, 12-420 grs.; slight traces of silica, manganese and volatile organic nitrogen.

To drink the Mullaghmore alkaline chalybeate spa, which can be safely taken at or before meals, in draughts of half-a-pint, for it does not contain too much iron or other minerals to cause it to disagree – to frequent hot or cold marine baths – to respire the ozoniferous ocean atmosphere – and to take daily electro-muscular exercise, which supports the magnetic intensity of the iron of the blood, so necessary to attract magnetic oxygen from the atmosphere through the lungs into the circulation, therein to promote the oxydizing electro-chemical influences for the removal of the refuse matters of the animal body, and for the renewal of animal life in healthful existence – are sanitary conditions well calculated to promote personal and public health, and to refresh vital constitutions physically and mentally, which are so happily attainable at Mullaghmore, and worthy of the notice of the crowned monarchs of Europe, and of the nobility and gentry of the United Kingdom of Great Britain and Ireland.

Dr. Lee says that there are only two sulphur spas of any reputation in Germany, that far famed mineral water country. Periera, a learned author, seemed to recognise only one sulphur spa there, that of Aix-la-Chapelle, which is of great antiquity, was frequented by the Romans of old, at which place Charlemagne the Great, lived and died and held levees while in the baths. In the county of Sligo I know of three sulphur spas. They are specially recommended for gout, rheumatism, congested livers, skin diseases, haemorrhoids, or piles; they act as aperients, as diuretics, and diaphoretics. Baron Liebeg said they are mildly aperient and alterative, in small quantities. They are recommended for hypochondriacs, for chronic bronchical expectorations of old persons when there is no tubercular disease of lungs; but they are forbidden in heart diseases.

The wealth and health of Sligo depend upon its industrial resources, its health-restoring mineral waters, its royalties of nature, and its attractive charms of scenery, which only require to be introduced to the outer world, when crowds from transatlantic and ultramontane lands would be drawn thereto, which would enrich the town and neighbourhood in return, and promote railway traffic to Dublin and Bundoran immensely. The wood, water, mountain, marine, lake and landscape scenery of Sligo furnish the poetic beauties of nature within the intramontane amphitheatre of this charmed spot, render it unrivalled in Ireland, and justifies the prediction of the late illustrious stateman, Lord Palmerston, "That Sligo was destined by nature to be great – to be the Liverpool of Ireland". No wonder that a county so rich in all the royalties, and industrial resources of nature, and in her beauties of scenery would be selected by the Nagnatae of Ptolemy's time to colonise and erect their ancient city thereon, called "Sligo of the Ships," and the "beautiful city of Sligo" in after ages, which was noticed in 1772 by Gabriel Beranger, a Dutchman, and Angelo Bigari, an Italian, both eminent artists, in such flattering terms, when selected by Viscount Conyngham, President of the Hibernian Antiquarian Society, to take sketches of the county of Sligo, and other parts of the province of Connaught. Lady Morgan also reflected the diamond light of her genius, in translating the poetic beauties of living nature through eloquent and patriotic sketches of Sligo scenery, about fifty years ago. The ancient city of Drumcliffe, within four miles of Sligo, once a bishop's see, remarkable for its cathedral, its monasteries, its learning and religion, its 1,500 houses, constructed of wood, deserves notice, if it were only to exhibit the remains of its former greatness – the most beautifully-sculptured stone cross in Ireland, and a round tower.

The intelligence that Her Majesty has been graciously pleased to honour this western province by creating his Royal Highness Prince Arthur, Duke of Connaught, is an important fact of incalculable advantage to the people of Sligo, better known in the annals of Ireland as North Connaught, for it is an introduction of Sligo to tourists to come to see and enjoy life and health here. His Royal Highness the Prince of Wales, in his reply to the address of the Sligo Corportion in '67, said "he hoped an opportunity might yet present itself to review the romantic scenery of Sligo". That period seems approaching. May we hope that Sligo, so rich in the surrounding royalties of nature, and the commercial capital of the province, may yet be honoured with a residence for His Royal Highness the Duke of Connaught, and that he may shortly review it's panoramic scenery from Belvoir Hill, where he could look down upon the town, sunk between the mountains, and appearing as if about to be submerged, by the meeting of the waters of the lake and sea; see towards the east Lough Gill, Hazlewood, and Holywell, surrounded by galleries of landscape, and the romantic village of Dromahair, and "the valley lay smiling before me;" towards the west Knocknarea, the hill of kings and its cleft off glen of glens; and towards the north Benbulben rise up stupendously amid the clouds, throw off his snow white cap, and being bathed in mountain dew, with a southern sunny smile, shelter the town against the northern blast; and see in the distance the intermontane lake of Glencar, its water-fall, water flight, and mineral water sulphur spa.

The following letter may have some interest:–

"Brighton, 29th May, 1874.

"Dear Dr. Tucker – I read your admirable letter on 'the Mineral Water Wealth of Sligo'. You would greatly oblige me by letting me see the analysis of Mullaghmore, if in print; some years ago I visited Bundoran, but heard nothing of Mullaghmore. I can testify to the health restoring power of your Atlantic, and only wish the landholders in Ireland would give sites for hotels and other suitable buildings. Look at Bath, Buxton, Cheltenham, Leamington, Harrowgate, all owing their position and wealth to the care taken of their healthy waters, the beautiful temples around them and over them, the intelligent servants in charge, the accomplished physicians and residents drawn thereto, not forgetting the good and wise landowners enjoying life in mansions erected in their own parks around. Do continue to point out Ireland's resources.

"Believe me your well wisher in this noble work,
R. T. MASSEY, M.D."
J. Tucker, M.D., M.R.C.S.Eng.;
Medical Officer, District of Sligo;
Medical Officer of Health, Borough of Sligo;
Medical Inspector, Port of Sligo;
Surgeon, Sligo Rifles and Royal Irish Constabulary, Sligo.

Cliffoney's Rebel Priest

Michael O'Flanagan was born on 12th August 1876 in a breac Gaeltacht at Cloontower, near Castlerea, Co. Roscommon, to parents who were native speakers of Irish. The O'Flanagans were small farmers who managed on mixed land bordering on the fertile estates of the landlords and wedged on the other side by barren bogland. Cloonboniffe N.S., where he received his primary education had been donated to the locality some time previously by the O'Connor-Don. He attended secondary school at Summerhill College, Co. Sligo and on graduating there in 1894, entered St. Patricks College, Maynooth, where he was ordained for the Diocese of Elphin in 1900. He returned to Summerhill as a priest and worked there as a teacher until 1904.

After this time, his clerical duties became interlaced with efforts to establish a viable basis for the movement towards Irish Independence, believing the Irish language, rural industry and the local Church to be vital elements in the achievement of this. He took a group to America in 1906 to promote Irish lace, an industry which was widespread in rural areas of Ireland at this time. Shortly after this, at Bishop Clark's request, he returned to America to raise funds to clear the debt on Loughlyn Convent near his home. This was entirely in line with his policy of promoting local business, as the convent had brought a new industry, cheese-making, into the area. His skills of oratory were matched by an originality and genius for fundraising; prior to one of his trips to America, he cut a sod from each of the thirty two counties of Ireland; bringing these with him, he invited Irish-Americans to walk on their native soil at a dollar a time. He also did fundraising work for Connradh na Gaeilge, raising over £3,000 for them between 1910-12. An inventor also, he brought special water goggles for underwater viewing, which he had invented, to the harbour at Mullaghmore, inviting visitors and bystanders to have a go at a shilling a time! (This was after the War of Independence when his "O'Flanagan Patent Water Goggles" were patented and on sale in the U.S.) From 1912-14 he served as Advent preacher at St. Sylvester in Rome.

On his return to Ireland in 1914 he was appointed as curate to the parish of Cliffoney late in the same year. Immediately on his arrival he commenced to encourage the people to organise, openly and in secret, in the United Irish Leagues, Sinn Fein and the Irish Volunteers.

He shortly became involved in what became known as the "Clooner-co Bog Fight" which is fully described in Chapter 5 in this book. The civil charges against Fr. O'Flanagan were dropped by the authorities but he was transferred by an angry Bishop Coyne to Crossna, near Boyle, in County Roscommon. It was in August 1915, on being selected to give an oration at the funeral of O'Donovan Rossa, that he came to national prominence and to the attention of Sinn Fein and the Republican movement. In the days and weeks following the Easter Rising, as the leaders of 1916 were imprisoned and shot, he spread the message of Easter Week at public meetings throughout the land. Fr. O'Flanagan incurred the displeasure of Bishop Coyne again when he spearheaded a campaign to have Count Plunkett, father of the executed 1916 leader, Joseph Mary Plunkett, elected in the Roscommon by-election of 1917.

The bye-election, which came to be known as, "the election of the snows", was caused by the death of the Irish Party M.P., James J. O'Kelly, who had beaten the O'Connor Don at the polls, and been the constituency's representative in the British Parliament for over thirty years. In February 1917, no transport moved as Fr. O'Flanagan motivated campaign activists, who often carried people on their backs through the drifting snow to the polling booths. The Irish Times reported that "The Rev. Michael O'Flanagan was the main driving force behind the candidate, "For twelve days and nights he was up and down the constituency like a whirlwind, talking to the people at every village, street corner and cross-roads where he could get people to listen to him." Plunkett's landslide win set the stage for the dramatic Sinn Fein victories in the General election of 1918. Bishop Coyne was not impressed and waiting his chance, eventually deprived Fr. O'Flanagan of his clerical faculties in 1918. The charge was a technicality in that he was accused of having, "adressed meetings within the boundaries of three parishes in Cavan during the by-election of East Cavan in June 1918, without first having got the permission of the respective parish priests. This was a set-up as he was unlikely to get permission in any case, as he was campaigning for Sinn Fein.

The parishioners of Crossna responded in the same way to Bishop Coyne's decision as did their counterparts in Cliffoney in similar circumstances some years before. Once again the doors of the church were locked to keep out any clerical replacement for Fr. O'Flanagan and the people gathered, as they did in Cliffoney, to say the rosary outside the

274

doors of the church. After a time Fr.O'Flanagan returned to tell his people that he wanted to leave the parish quietly and the protest ended. He was not to receive another clerical appointment for twenty years, when he was appointed chaplain to three convents in the Donnybrook area of Dublin, his suspension having been lifted by Archbishop Mc Quaid in 1939, three years before his death. However, ecclesiastical politics were not the focal point of this priests life as he was all this time growing in stature as a central figure in the emerging Irish independence movement.

At the Plunkett convention in 1917 when the Republican movement amalgamated with Griffith's Sinn Fein, Fr. O'Flanagan was elected vice-president of the new body. In 1918, in response to John Redmond's appeal for recruits for the British army, he addressed anti-conscription meetings all over Ireland. His oratorical skills were used to good effect too in the lead-up to the 1918 elections when he toured the country speaking in favour of Sinn Fein candidates. Jeremiah Mee, who was stationed with the R.I.C. in Grange, recalled later in his memoirs hearing O'Flanagan addressing a meeting in the village at this time:

"Men and women of Cliffoney and Grange, the Germans may be here any time now. You need not worry as the R.I.C. have the situation well in hand!"

He would then read a circular issued by the British government to the R.I.C. stationed along the Irish coast, which instructed them, in the event of a German landing, to get the inhabitants to move twenty miles inland with their livestock. The R.I.C. were then instructed to see that all crops in the vacated area were destroyed by fire or otherwise. Using the instructions in the circular to ridicule the British, he then said to the cheering crowd:

"We have twenty policemen in Cliffoney, Grange and Drumcliffe, who will see that your crops are all destroyed and then with their twenty rifles, they will keep back the German Army and Navy!"

It can be said that his was the first voice heard in Dail Eireann as he was invited to say the opening prayers at the opening of the First Dail in 1919. In the years following, he was a judge in the Republican courts, an executive member of the Irish Agriculture Organisation Society and vice-president of the Gaelic League. In the winter of 1920, the President of Sinn Fein, Griffith, had been arrested and de Valera was out of the country; as vice-president of Sinn Fein, Fr. O'Flanagan was now the chief executive in Ireland. This could be said to be the pinnacle of his political power and immediately he caused a political sensation by sending a telegram to the British Prime Minister, Lloyd George, which read "Ireland is willing to make peace. What first steps do you propose?" Questioned shortly before his death about this manouevre, he explained: "Lloyd George had been boasting and bragging about his desire for peace. I was the only one who called his bluff and took the wind out of his sails without doing any harm. After this, he said no more about peace!"

In the Autumn of 1921 immediately before the signing of the "Articles of Agreement", which he opposed, he was sent by Dail Eireann on a special fundraising mission to the U.S. and to promote the Irish cause. From there he was sent to Australia where he was arrested and deported to France "for some compliments paid to St.George on the occasion of his feast." Undaunted, he made his way back to America where he continued his mission until 1925 when he was invited back to Ireland by de Valera, to help with a bye-election. The Sligo/Leitrim bye election in March was brought about by the retirement of Alex McCabe and M. Carter. Fr. O'Flanagan supported the anti-treaty candidates, Samuel Holt, Carrick-on-Shannon and Francis O'Beirne, Coolaney against the Cumainn na nGaedheal candidates Martin Roddy, Breegone and Andrew Mooney, Drumshambo.[1]

This was only a short few years after the Civil War and feelings still ran high; the election was hotly contested and huge crowds attended the rallies, on both sides. Willie Devins recalled attending one of these rallies in Cliffoney where the crowd was to be addressed by Fr. Michael O'Flanagan, O'Beirne and Holt. A huge crowd had gathered, accompanied by bands from Grange and Bunduff, Volunteer units and contingents of Cumainn na mBann. Bonfires were lit in barrels and blazing, paraffin soaked turf, held aloft on pitchforks, lit up the night sky.

Willie recalls as if it were only yesterday how five car loads of pro-Treaty supporters, travelling from Sligo town, passed his unit at Ballinaphortaigh as Willie and his comrades marched to the meeting. Fighting broke out as the pro-Treatyites attempted to break up the meeting but the odds were against the intruders and very soon they were routed in disarray. They made a desperate dash for the protection of the Garda barracks but were refused entry by Sgt. Marren who, according to Willie, told them, "Ye're broke up now but ye'll be broke up better before ye get home". The road back to Sligo was blocked by a mass of Cliffoney people and the unfortunate miscreants were forced to make a retreat via Ballintrillick where they "got hammered again; some didn't get home for days". It was said later that the intruders from Sligo had been paid 5 shillings each to break up the meeting, by a named Sligo priest, whose brother, an R.I.C. man in Cork, had been shot by the I.R.A. some time previously.

1. The result of this bitterly fought contest was that Roddy and Holt were elected.

Fr. O'Flanagan stayed with Sinn Fein when de Valera left to form Fianna Fail, becoming one of his severest critics and blaming him for destroying Sinn Fein. Disillusioned with the turn of events he later resigned from Sinn Fein and took a less active role in politics for a time. When Fianna Fail came into office in 1932, Fr. O'Flanagan was appointed by de Valera to a post as researcher in the Dept. of Education. Seven of the county histories which he researched in a room provided for him in the National Library were published but he died with his work uncompleted; his work on O'Donovans letters never got past the typed script stage. During this time, he emerged from the relative security of his Civil Service post to support Republican Spain during the Spanish Civil War (1936-38), despite the Joint Irish Bishops Statement of October 12th 1936, which supported Franco. On O'Duffy's volunteers, who sailed to help Franco with the blessing of the Church he said, "the Spaniards didn't send any people to support the "Black and Tans" here and they didn't take up any collections in their churches to help the English cause in Ireland either". He continued to support the Sinn Fein cause in the thirties and went on a speaking and fund raising tour of Canada and America on their behalf and on behalf of the Spanish Republicans.

He did eventually, become estranged from the Executive of the Gaelic League, Sinn Fein and the Catholic Church, yet until his death he passionately shared the principals of those organisations.

"I am a suspended priest", he said once, "I have been disobedient and have been suspended for disobedience, but unlimited authority I am not prepared to give to any authority in the world. I am a priest, but I was an Irishman twenty years before I was a priest. Almighty God made me an Irishman and put upon me the duties of a citizen of Ireland..... no institution can take that away from me."

He became ill in 1942 but never forgot Cliffoney; in a poignant letter dated 2 August 1942, he wrote to his old friend, Bernie Conway of Cliffoney saying, "I am dying with a very special love of the people in my inmost heart. I'll be waiting in heaven to greet the Cliffoney people, especially those who prayed for me at the front door." This great patriot, the man who Cathail Brugha claimed was "the staunchest priest who ever lived" died in Sandyford, Dublin, on 7 August 1942. In two days, 21,000 people filed past Fr. Michael O'Flanagan's open coffin as it lay on a catafalque in the Rotunda at City Hall, thousands more had to be turned away. War of Independence veterans guarded the remains and as the people passed by, children were lifted up to get a glimpse of the Patriot Priest. Dev was among the host of dignitaries and members of the government and Oireachtais who attended the interment in Glasnevin cemetery where Sceilig Mr. J.J. O'Kelly delivered the oration saying that, "the manifestations of sympathy were symbolic of the place Fr. O'Flanagan held in the hearts of the Irish people."

Ireland on that day was honouring a very special man, a man who could look into the hearts of the Irish people, discern everything noble and true inside them and express their highest dreams and aspirations in his own noble language. They knew that without his eloquent speeches, hard work and ability to motivate people, Count Plunkett might not have been elected in 1917, thus setting the stage for the successes of the "risen people" and the Republican cause which followed. Without his counsel and leadership, Sinn Fein might not have emerged as the great political party which formed the first Dail; without his courage as he travelled around the country, spreading everywhere the message of Easter Week and addressing meetings in the face of Black and Tan death threats, national solidarity and the dream of freedom might never have been realised.

The freedom of Sligo was conferred on Fr. Michael O'Flanagan by Sligo Corporation in June 1918 and an illuminated scroll presented to him, on behalf of a grateful people, by Mayor Hanley. Today, this scroll gathers dust in an obscure forgotten corner of Sligo courthouse; no public building has ever been named after him (Fr. O'Flanagan Hall in Summerhill, where he taught, is named after the priest of that name in Boystown, U.S.A.); his grave in Glasnevin, until recently, lay unmarked and weed covered; no plaque or memorial has ever been erected to his memory in Sligo or in the Cliffoney that he loved so much; the holy water font at the entrance of Cliffoney Church, which was installed in his memory is still uninscribed.

How soon we forget! Some day, when we reclaim our national pride, perhaps we will give Fr.Michael O'Flanagan and his comrades their rightful place in history, and the honour they so richly deserve. Now, remembered by only a few, there is a danger that his name and his achievements and those of his comrades, will fade into obscurity. It merits a better fate!

THE REBEL COUNTESS

Constance Georgina Gore-Booth, the eldest daughter of Sir Josslyn and Lady Gore-Booth, of Lisadell, was born on February the 4th, 1868, at Buckingham Gate, close by the Royal Palace in London. Grand-daughter of Sir Robert Gore-Booth, her father was a descendant of Captain Paul Gore who came over with Essex in 1598 and was made a commander of a troop of horse. He was charged by Mountjoy with the responsibility of escorting the last two Irish chieftains (Rory ODonnell and Donough O'Connor) to submit to Queen Elizabeth, escorting them to Athlone. He was granted lands by the Queen and later by James 1st and created a Baronet of Ireland in 1621. He married Isabella, niece of Sir Thomas Wentworth, the Earl of Strafford.

Constance spent her youth at Lisadell from where she often galloped across Moffit's Burra to Classiebawn Castle, owned at that time by Evelyn Ashley. Her friend, Mary Leslie of Castle Leslie, Glaslough, who also stayed at Classiebawn, wrote of their first meeting,

> "I thought I had never seen anyone so lovely. In the evening she started off at a hand gallop over the shores as if she feared the tide would come up and stop her. Hatless, dressed in a brown carduroy frock, she was startlingly beautiful as the sun caught her fair hair".

She eventually left her beloved Sligo at the age of eighteen to study art in Paris. There she met a Polish Count, Joseph Dunin Markievicz, whom she married at St. Marylebone's Parish Church, in London in 1900. Having settled in Dublin, she met Padraic Pearse and Thomas McDonagh, and became deeply involved in the national movement. She joined James Connolly's Citizen Army and became known as "the Rebel Countess". She founded na Fianna Eireann, the national boy scout movement. In the Rising of 1916, she was Vice-Commandant to Michael Mallin in the College of Surgeons garrison at St. Stephen's Green.

On the morning of Easter Monday, 1916, clad in the green uniform and carrying a small Mauser automatic pistol, Countess Markievicz, marched at the head of a small column of Citizen Army men to St. Stephen's Green.

During the ensuing fight she served so bravely and fearlessly side by side with her male comrades in arms that her courage became a watchword and her name a legend, even in her own lifetime. She played an important role in the capture of the College of Surgeons and led several sorties into nearby buildings.

After the surrender she was sentenced to death. This was later commuted to penal servitude for life, solely on account of her sex. She was released from Aylesbury Jail in the general amnesty of 1917. She became a Catholic the same year, and was baptized at Holy Cross College. Early in 1918, when the prospect of wholesale conscription hung over the heads of thousands of Irishmen, the Countess campaigned vigorously against the implementation of this threat by the British. Her actions brought her once more into conflict with Dublin Castle, and she was eventually arrested and imprisoned in Holloway jail. It was during this time, in 1918 that she was returned as a Member of Parliament for St. Patrick's electoral division in Dublin. She created history then by being the first woman ever elected to the British House of Commons. She adopted the abstentionist policy of Sinn Féin, however, and never took her seat at Westminster. She was appointed to the Ministry of Labour when Dáil Éireann was set up in January 1919.

She continued her work for the Republic and supported the anti-Treaty side after the split, winning her seat again in the general elections of 1923. She continued to speak on behalf of the prisoners until she was arrested again on 20th November, 1923. Many prisoners from this area and all over Ireland (my father included), were on hunger strike at this time; she immediately joined the hunger strike in solidarity with the other prisoners. On her release she continued her work with de Valera and became a founder member of Fianna Fáil in 1926. Her image as a national heroine was still preserved, her personality still retained its old magnetism and in the 1927 Dáil Éireann elections she was returned for the Dublin constituency for the last time.

To the end of her life she devoted herself to the welfare of the Irish people. She dispensed so much of her wealth to the poor of Dublin, that when she died in a public ward of Sir Patrick Dun's Hospital, she was virtually penniless. She breathed her last at 1.25 a.m. on the morning of July 15th, 1927; by her bedside was her daughter Maeve. The Freestate Government refused to give the Mansion House, so her body, dressed in her Irish Citizen Army uniform was laid in state in the Rotunda Cinema.

Around her bier for two days and nights, her own boys of na Fianna Éireann stood as guard of honour. Two of their comrades, Con Colbert of Limerick and Sean Heuston of Dublin, had been executed in 1916.

Thousands came to pay homage, many in tears, not least among them were the poverty stricken people whom she had succoured so well. Freestate soldiers and Gardai lined the route to Glasnevin to prevent shots being fired at her grave but her greatest tribute came from the tens of thousands who lined the streets. Fianna Eireann, Fianna Fail, Sinn Fein, Cumainn na mBann, I.T.G.W.,U., and Irish Citizen Army marched behind her hearse. Dev gave the oration at her graveside:

> "Madame, the friend of the toiler, the lover of the poor. Ease and station she put aside and took the hard way of service with the weak and downtrodden".

Ireland mourned one of her greatest heroines. Her greatness and her deeds should not be forgotten!

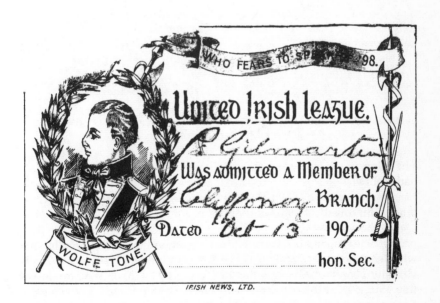

WHO FEARS TO SPEAK OF '98.

United Irish League.

Was admitted a Member of

Branch.

Dated Oct 13 1907

hon. Sec.

WOLFE TONE.

IRISH NEWS, LTD.

Specification for the work of an extension proposed for the Pier of Mulloughmore

The extension to be of the form & dimensions delineated on the plan and Crofs Section —

The foundation when it extends into a depth of water, which will render it impractable to lay the bottom stones in the usual way is to be managed as follows.

A platform is to be constructed of the entire breadth of the pier and sloping pavement, and to rise above the level of low water. The commencing Stone is to be set with a slope which will cause the succeeding stone to slide down along and rest

SPECIFICATION FOR THE WORK OF AN EXTENSION PROPOSED FOR THE PIER
OF MULLAGHMORE

The extension to be of the form and dimensions delineated on the plan and crofs section.

The foundation when it extends into a depth of water which will render it impracticable to lay the bottom stones in the usual way is to be managed as follows.

A platform is to be constructed of the entire breadth of the pier and sloping pavement, and to rise above the level of low water. The commencing stone is to be set with a slope which will cause the succeeding stone to slide down along and rest firmly on it. They will also have a face batter of 2 inches to each foot of rise. These stones will of course be progressively lengthening as the bottom deepens and to render each stone manageable, a hole must be bored with a jumper six inches deep in the upper end. Into this hole a deal plug will be driven. and then a holdfast or ironhook will be driven into the plug whereby the stone may be suspended and raised or lowered as occasion shall require until it be satisfactorily fixed in its berth, which being done, the headfast may then be extricated or broken off. This is meant as a substitute for a Leivy, the stones being too hard to admit of having regular Leivy holes cut in them.

These facing stones are to be backed by large rough blocks dropped down behind them always dropping the first stone nearest the facing and filling thence inwards to the centre which may be done with stone progressively smaller. The interstices amongst these filling stones to be made solid by means of smaller rubble shingle and gravel being progressively thrown down amongst and carefully mingled through them.

No stone in the above facing to be less than 3 feet long, 4 feet breadth of insertion into the work and 8 inches thick, moreover each stone must have sufficient length to reach above low water level.

The foundation platform being thus raised above low water level the superstructure will be executed as follows:-

The sea pavement to be of stones pitched on end, with the edges radiating in the direction of the stroke of the sea – no stone therein to be less than 3.6" long and 2.6" broad and 8 inches thick. – No facing stone in the quay wall of the jetty to have less than 3.0" of insertion into the wall, and not to be less than 14 inches on the head and 8 inches thick. No facing stone in the adjoining stretch of the quay to have less than 2.6" insertion in the wall, nor to be less than 12 inches on the head and 8 inches thick, the remainder of the quay to be similar to the part already done. The backing to be of stones, one half of which to have dimensions respectively similar to the facing, and to be carefully bonded in upon the facing stones. These facing stones to be rough hammer drefsed, but not face hammered so as to form an even surface with close and square joints without closures or filling spauls.

No stone in the coping of the jetty to be lefs than 4 feet across the wall, 3 feet in breadth and 12 inches thick, to be square jointed at least 2.6" in from the front. No stone in the coping of the adjoining stretch to be less than 3.6" across the wall, 2.6" in breath and 12 inches thick, to be square jointed at least 2 feet from the front. The remainder of the coping not to be less than 3 feet across the wall, 2 feet broad and 12 inches thick, to be square jointed at least 2 feet in.

The body of the pier to be hearted with rubble and beachstones to be rough packed and have a portion of shingle and gravel mingled through them, sufficient to fill up and colsolidate the interstices.

The parapet to be built with lime mortar, all the stones to be set on edge; no stone in the sea face to be lefs than 3 feet long, 2 feet broad and 7" thick, the coping to be of thorough stones on edge none lefs than 8 inches thick, no filling spaul or closure will be admitted in the sea face.

The return on the end of the pier to round down into the quay coping in the manner of an arch, the accommodation steps to be 3 feet wide, to be of thorough stones none lefs than 7 inches riser and 12 inches tread to bond at least 12 inches into the quay wall and 6 inches under each riser.

The pier to be built dry to within 3 feet of the top including the coping; this excepted part is to be built with lime mortar.

The mortar to consist of two parts coarse sea sand to one of hot lime and to be used fresh after mixing.

The surface of the quay to be compactly paved with refuse flag stones set on edge; no stone to have less than 12 inches of depth and all to be properly blended with gravel.

Five mooring posts and five mooring rings to be set in the quay. The mooring posts to be of stone, two of them for the pier head to be at least 16 inches in diameter and 8 feet long, the others to be at least 12 inches in diameter in the smallest part and 6 feet long, 3 feet of the length to be hammer-drefsed to a round form.

The mooring rings to be of 2 inch bolt, 8 inches diameter in the clear in eye-bolts of 2 inch bar, to be drove tailed, sunk at least 6 inches and securely leaded in stone blocks each stone to be a cube of at least two and a half feet.

All loose stones within the harbour and in the entrance to be removed.

J. Donnell CE

Specification for the Break Water

The extension to be of the form and dimensions marked on the plan and crofs section.

The interior face and end to batter one inch to the foot of rise, so as to answer for a quay, to be executed similarly to the corresponding opposite quay wall – The back of be executed similarly to the part done of this work. The surface to be coped and paved in a similar manner to the corresponding opposite quay wall. Three mooring posts to be fixed similar to the smaller clafs described for the pier. The loose stones to be cleared out of the basin and the bottom to be excavated to the level of low water spring tides.

7th July, 1826   J. Donnell C.E.

Holyhead 24th Decr. 1827

My Lord

I beg leave to Acquaint You that
the Lantern was sent to Howth by the Wizard
Steam Packet on Saturday the 15th Instant Addressed
agreeable to the instruction which You have given me.

On the Monday following I sent a Bill by Mr Williams
Steward of the Packet, he did not go himself to Dublin
but sent by the Applyer for the Packets, to Mr Kincaid —
asking his leave to hire a Carr to bring the Lantern to Dublin
the Coach had refused to take it on account of it being too
heavy. I did not hear any thing after, but I have no doubt
that either Mr Williams will soon go to Dublin or that
Mr Kincaid will send to Me

I hope My Lord when You Shall see the Lantern that
it will please You, As I have taken as much care as I could
to do it well And I believe You will see it is better and
larger than I promised it to You.

I am My Lord
Your Obedient Servant
John Jones
Brazier &c

The Bill I sent to Mr Kincaid
was as on Next Page — }

285

Holyhead 15th Decr 1827

Joseph Kincaid Esqr

Bought of John Jones

A Large Pier Lantern with a strong 3 Light } £ s d
Burner as ʃ Agreement —————————— 3 - 0 - 0

4 setts Extra Glasses Measuring 20 feet at 1/8 = 1 - 13 - 4

Package 5/. Shiping Charges 1/. —— 0 - 6 - 0

£ 4 - 19 - 4

I think it improper to trouble Your Lordship with
a Copy of the instructions sent for the Management
of the Lantern

J. J.

MULLAGHMORE REGATTA.

For the encouragement of the Fisheries.

ON MONDAY, the 11th SEPTEMBER, 1848, there will be several Sailing and Rowing Matches. The first start to take place at one o'clock.

Particulars as to entries, &c., of Boats, may be had on application to Mr. MAHON, Mullaghmore,

LIEUT. HAMILTON, R.N.
EDWARD SMYTH, } Stewards.
JOHN LYNCH,

Mullaghmore, 31st August, 1848.

NOTICE.

THE COMMISSIONERS for Improving the Town and Harbour of Sligo, will receive, at their Office, John-street, proposals for making and erecting

14 WATCH-BOXES,

for the use of the Town Watch.—Sligo, the 10th September, 1835.

By Order,
T. REED, Secretary.

TO BE LET,

LORD PALMERSTON'S

CORN-STORE AND KILN,

AT

Mulloghmore Harbour,

Capable of holding 300 Tons of Grain.

Application to be made to Mr. WALKER, Rathcarrick, Sligo.

CAUTION.

I HEREBY caution the Public not to Credit my Wife, MARY M'CARRICK, otherwise CAWLEY, as I am determined not to pay any Debts she may contract.

Given under my hand, this 9th day of September, 1835.

JAMES CAWLEY,
COOLANY.

WM. ARMSTRONG,

SURGEON AND APOTHECARY,

WANTS A RESPECTABLE

In-Door Apprentice,

WHO will have many advantages of acquiring his profession, and will be treated as one of his family.

September 3, 1835.

NOTICE.

PLACENAME TRANSLATIONS

Following are translations of some of the Irish placenames in the Parish of Ahamlish, which have come down to us through the centuries in an oral tradition. Some of these are taken from a book of translations written by O'Donovan when he recorded some of these names during the Ordnance Survey of 1838. I am indebted to Una Loftus and Proinnsíos Ó Duigneáin for helping to unravel the remainder, particularly the local placenames of rocks and points along the shore. Some names cannot be deciphered as they may have been corrupted by various influences through the years.

Spoken	Irish	Translation
Ahamlish	Rath hAmlais	Earthen fort
Ballinabrock	Baile na mBroc	Town of the badgers
Ballincastle	Baile an Caisleán	Town of the castle
Ballinfull	Baile an Phoill	Town of the hole or pit
Ballintrillick	Bealach na Trí Leice	The way of the 3 flags
Breaghwy	Breachmaigh	Wolf field
Bunduff	Bun Dubh	Mouth of the river Dubh or Niger
Carnamadow	Ceatragh na Mada	Quarter of the dogs
Carnduff	Carrn Dubh	Black Cairn or heap
Cartronkillerdoo	Cartún Coille Dubaid	Cartron of the black wood
Castlegal	Caisle Geala	White Forts
Cliffoney	Cliathmhuine	Shrubbery or brake of the hurdles
Cloghboley	Cloch Buailde	Stone booley or dairy place
Cloonerco	Cluan Erco	Erck's lawn or meadow
Cloonkeen	Cluan Caoin	Beautiful lawn or meadow
Cloontybawn	Cluainte Bána	White bawns or meadows

Clysparrow	Cloic Sparra	Stone of the spar
Creevykeel	Craoibigh Caol	Narrow creevy or bushy land
Creevymore	Craoibigh mór	Great creevy
Derry	Doire	An oak wood
Derelehan	Doire Lithean	Lyons oak wood
Doonsaskin	Dun Seascáin	Fort of the sedgy moor
Drumfad	Drum fada	Long ridge
Edenreagh	Eadan Riabh	Grey brow or front
Glengarragh	Gleann Daireach	Glen of the oak valley
Gortaderry	Gort a Doire	Field of the oak wood
Gortnaleck	Gort na Leic	Field of the flagstone
Grange*	Grainsigh	A grange.

*Note: Property of Robert Johnson esq.,contains 548 acres.
   Six forts in that townland.

Grellagh*	Greillach	A miry place.

*Note: A corn mill situated 12.5 chains north of a bridge
   and East of the Bunduff River

Grogagh	Grogach	Land producing long grass such as fiorin or sedge.
Kilcat	Coill Cait	Wood of the cat or "Cill Caoide" = St. Caoide's church.
Kilkilloge	Cill Chaolog or Cuarog	St. Caolog or Curog's church

Note: There is an old fort and schoolhouse West of Mullaghmore (O'D)

Kiltykere	Coillte Caer	Woods of the berries
Lislarry	Lios Leatrighe	Fort of the leather bags
Lyle	Leoighill	A man's name
Moneygold	Muine Dhubaltaigh	Dhubaltaigh's shrubbery
Mt. Edward	Dreangain	Small gap, breach or chasm
Mullaghmore	Mullac Mór	A great top or summit,

Note A: quarry situated near the Northern boundary of this townland. (O'D)

Rathfrask	Rath Fraisg	Frasg's Fort
Rathhugh	Rath Aodha	Hugh's fort
Silverhill	Cnoc Riabach	Grey Hill
Streedagh	Strideach	A stripe of land

Placenames in Mullaghmore

Ballintemple   Baile tSeampail   Town of the Church,
(Area near stone tower at top of Quay Road.)

Portnahoarna   Port na hEorna   Barley port,
(Area near woods at Barry's Lane. Reputed landing place for boats when Mullaghmore was an island.)

Cill na Mucan   Cill na Moghan   Church of the shifting sands
Place where unbaptized children were buried near Classiebawn

Classiebawn   Classaigh Bán   White trenches

Along the Sea shore

Alt Brischa   Alt Briste   Broken cliffs
Bailach   Bealach   A way or passageway
Beltra Rocks   Carraic Beul Traga   Rock of the strand
On the shore, West of Mullaghmore and South of Roskeeragh Point.

Bradoge   Bradogue   The neck or throat
Carraig na Cearta   Carraig na Ceardca   Rock of the forge
Carragnarone   Carraig na Ron   Rock of the Seal
Carricgarve   Carraic Garbh   Rough Rocks.
(Celebrated for being the place where a number of persons who were wrecked on the coast were washed in by the the the tide. (O'D)

Claddagh Dubh   Cladrach Dubh   Black, rough, stony place
Claddagh Geal   Cladrach Geal   Bright Stony Place
Cluckaun   Clochan   Stepping stones or stony place
Crockannatinnew   Cnocan na Tinead   Hillock of the fire
Eadar a Leac   Eadar a Leac   Between the rocks
Cruck na Gower   Cruach na Gabhair   Height of the goats
Cool a Cutch   Cul a Chait   Bank or reef of the cat
Dreimire Bui   Dreimire Buí   Yellow ladder or steps
Gubaun   Gobán   Tip or Point
Ilaunee Beg   Oileán Beg   Small Island
Illaunee More   Olleán Mór   Big Island
Illauneeroe   Oileán Roudh   Island of the roudh *(a kind of seaweed)*

Leac na Moo	Leac na mBó	Flagstone of the cow
Leac Weea	Leac Bhuí	Yellow flagstone
Lugashanny	Lug na Seannaigh	Hollow of the fox
Pollachurry	Polla Churraigh	Hole of the currach or leather boat
Poll an Uisge	Poll an Uisge	Water Hole
Poll Cotch	Poll a Chait	Hole of the cat
Pollyarry	Polla Ghearraidh	Hole of the cutting
Pollyiarmidga	Poll ui Dhiarmada	Dermot's Hole
Rinnadew	Runna Dubh	Black Point

(Situated on North west shore of Mullaghmore (O'D)

| Roskeeragh | Ros Caorach | Point or wood of the sheep |
| Runemoghan | Rinnna Moghan | Pint of the Shifting sands |

(A projecting point on the shore at the Northwest extremity of Kilkilloge townland)

| Troyare | Traigh Gearr | Short Strand |

(on West Side of Mullaghmore

Spring Wells

Tobar Geall	Tobar Geall	Clear well
Tobarnaleice	Tobar na Leice	Well of the flagstones
Tobar Watcha	Tobar Bhaidhte	Sunken Well

Some other points along the seashore

Carraig na nÉan	Carraig na Éan	Rock of the Birds
Carraig na Spáinne	Carraig na Spáinne	Rock of the Spaniards
Turgunnell	Tor Conaill	Conall's Tower

(Located North West of Dernish Island)

| Rennanough | Roinn na nÉac | Point of the horses. |

(On Conor's Island)

| Rinablinick | Roinn na Bloinice | Point of the land. |

(On the South side of Conor's Island)

| Rinadulish | Rinn a' Duibhlis | Point of the black fprt. |

On the South side of Streedagh Point (O'D)

| Teac na Shally | Teach na Sealaigh | House of the huntings or chases. |

(On the west side of Streedagh Point O'D)

| Poll Weir | Poll Weir | A hole or indent in the shore |
| Alt Duff | Alt Dubh | Black Cliff, |

(Cliff face in Moneygold, close to the shore O'D)

| Inishnagur | Inis na gGorr | Island of the cranes. |

(A small island on the shore north of Grange, on the strand. Divided from the mainland by a strand during low water . O'D)

| Troynavanogue | Traig-na bFeannog | Strand of the scald crows. |

(North of Grange. A flat strand having a narrow hrange of sandhills between it and the ocean. O'D)

| Staad | Staad | A stop, end, limit. |

(In the townland of Agharow being the place where the ancient road to Inishmurray stopped.

| Cathmelawn | Cat Maoilean | Bald or flat cat. |

(High rock which has its base surrounded at high water. In the townland of Doonsaskin.)

| Pulnalishin | Pulnalishin | St. Molaise's cove. |

(On the shore at the junction of Lislarry and Doonsaskin. O'D)

| Bellbuoy | Beal Buidhe | Yellow mouth or ford mouth. |

(A rock projection on the coast, north of Grellagh O'D)

| Skerrydoo | — |

(A projecting point on the sea- coast on the north side of Castlegal)

| Pollnadridogue | — |

(Hole of the stairs; local = drideog to mean hole of the starlings or stares. Close to the west of Skerry cove running southward into the rock from the shore for a distance of 200 feet. It is called from the stair-like appearance of the rocks inside . O'D)

*P*oets *Corner*

Most of the songs and recitations on these pages have never been written down before; many have been lost forever. These compositions often contained hidden messages and could be sharply satirical at times. They were composed by ordinary country folk in the locality who gathered into the rambling house to pass the time during the long winter nights, before the advent of television and radio. Inspiration was drawn from local events and coloured by the spiralling smoke and bright flames of a warm hearth fire. Modern times and instant entertainment, mostly foreign imports, have ensured that these modest Bards of old Ireland write no more in this ancient tradition. More's the pity.

INVER BAY DISASTER

Ye sympathisers around the border
That overlooks our Inver bay
Come join with me now for prayer and devotion
For all those brave men who were lost at sea.

'Twas the eight of December on that fateful morning
It being on the year nineteen hundred and four
When an Inver crew left their native harbour
To fish for herring on the southern shore.

They had no suspicion of not returning
And a good intention had every man
For to hoist their sails for to cross the ocean
Into a place they call Carrigan.

From Bellel to Tullan there was herring playing
To shoot their nets now commenced the crew
But they soon say now that in reality
They were capsized by some kind of whale.

They struggled hard that cold winters evening
Their precious lives they all tried to save
But no helping hand came for to aid them
They soon descended to a watery grave.

Their seven names I now will mention
I hope in heaven their souls will shine
Inoffensive Peter Kennedy, James Brown
    and his brother Patrick
With James Gallagher and Tom McSwine

Also John Gallahgher and his son Patrick
They were respected by young and old
And rich and poor as they passed their door
Prayed the Lord have mercy upon their souls

Two of those men endured great hardship
All night they struggled against the wind
And the boat was tossed as she streamed afloat
And she came broken upon the shore.

For they often sailed from the bar of Inver
From Mullaghmore to Donegal
From the rock of Strachan to Bundoran strand
But alas they are gone to return no more.

And their poor widows and orphan children
They still are weeping beyond control
God give them relief in their present grief
As those poor people we must console.

*Folklore Commision and sung by Mary Jane Brady, Feb. 1993
(Alternative third from last verse by Brady:*

"Some of those men endured great hardships
The angels met them upon the way,
They delivered their souls now unto St. Patrick
To the gates of heaven, he holds a key".

(NOTE: THIS SONG WAS WELL KNOWN THROUGHOUT DONEGAL AND
SLIGO UNTIL RECENTLY. THE DROWNING TOOK PLACE NEAR ROSNOWLAGH).

SLIGO'S NOBLE SIX

All true men of this Irish nation
Who follow the tricolour fold.
Come and join in sincere lamentation
And pray for the true and the bold.

It is but a pitiful story
Unequalled in bloodshed and tears,
As bright as the stars in their glory
Shine the names of our dead volunteers.

Then pray for Banks, Carroll and Langan
Mc Neill, Benson, Devins, T.D.
Six hearts that were true to old Ireland
And died that their land might be free.

They died on a cold autumn evening
When nature its charms did unfold
Those heroes were crossing the mountains
Their number being six we are told.

They were marching to meet their brave comrades
Of danger they were not afraid
But out for the cause of freedom
They were followed and beastly betrayed.

The mist on the mountain was falling
While the rain in its torrents did spill
The Irish green and tans they were crossing
The side of Benbulbens big hill.

The mist on the hillside was heavy
And the sound of the rifles were low
As our brave lads they were marching onwards
And surprised by the approach of the foe.

They came in their fast Crossley tenders
And many a strong armoured car,
With lewis guns, Maxims and rifles
All Englands equipment of war.

God pity those brave Irish heroes,
The steel ring was closing in fast.
Although in the prime of their manhood
This evening, it was then their last.

From out their cars the staters poured,
Like lions swooped down on the fold.
Our brave lads were quickly surrounded
And driven from their little stronghold.

They took to the hillside for cover
While the state poured its merciless rain
They shot them like partridge in clover
And six of the bravest were slain.

Then pray for Banks, Carroll and Langan
McNeill, Benson, Devins T.D.,
Six hearts that were true to old Ireland
And died that their land might be free.

Borne on the shoulders of comrades
Who mourned them silent and deep
In a republican plot in North Sligo
We laid them to take their last sleep.

Beloved, honoured, respected,
Forgotten ne'er shall they be
While the sun it shines over North Sligo
And the Shannon flows into the sea.

(GIVEN TO ME BY JOHN GILMARTIN OF CARNAMADOW MARCH 1993)

BALLAD OF SEAMUS DEVINS

You heroes bold and undaunted,
The truth I will pen down
Concerning a brave Irishman,
The pride of Sligo Town.

He was a soldier in the Rahelly camp
And he died his land to free,
But he met his fate by the accursed state
On the hills of Rahelly.

When Irelands flag was flying low
And in the dust was flung
'Twas raised by soldiers on Easter week
Which England shot and hung.

He nobly answered Pearses call
Tt the foot of the Glencar Brae
And he raised the flag of freedom
To pass the tyrant away.

His house was next surrounded
When the news was spread around
He was a soldier of the Republic
And disloyal to the crown.

They burned down the house he owned
And left it roofless too
But they did not take his life away
As the freestate hounds did do.

Farewell to you Jim Devins
Farewell to Sligo Town
For many a time you fought against
The forces of the crown.

Farewell to dear old Cliffoney
Where the foes you did subdue
For you left nine peelers bleeding
For the cause of Roisín Dubh.

May Devins's name live on in fame
And his flag may ne'er go down
A republican cross now marks the spot
Where he fell in Glencar Town.

(GIVEN TO ME BY JOHN GILMARTIN, CARNAMADOW MARCH 1993)

SUNSET O'ER ROSSCAORACH

Light was fading as dusk crept by
We sat alone ... a thrush and I
He seemed impatient and chirped away
I suppose he knew 'twas the end of day
He tilted his head and watched the sun
I watched it too, and it seemed to run
Beneath the sea and there to lie
Leaving alone the thrush and I
The sky was crimson .. no 'twas pink
It was silver and grey and white, I think
I looked at the thrush and then I knew
He found such beauty confusing too.
Waves tipped white like horses mane
Creating sounds line a prison chain
Dashing pebbles up the beach
Only to claim then out of reach.
The thrush broke out in ancient song
Some notes short and some notes long
He poked the turf and off he flew
For birds have nothing else to do.
I sat awhile and thought of the tide
Dashing Roscaorach an every side
Of colour and sun and beautiful sea
Watched in the evening by a thrush and me.

Mary Deery.

298

ST. JOHN'S BONFIRE OF MULLACH MOR

I walk. I slowly encircle
The headland at night.
Sea slowly breathes,
Liberates the scent of life.
Above slate broad ocean
Sky opens the salmon of his eye.
As aubergine isles
Emerge Donegals capes.

On the Mór suddenly glows
A silent globe of flames,
Light marine breeze,
Plays with blown smoke.
I go up as a pilgrim,
St. Johns bonfire really
Burns here on the hill,
On the way of always!

Mind breaks free
To open sea and space,
Here is the magic night
Where worlds balance.
In a silent peace
My weak eye embraces
Mullach mor's planet
With ardent fire in heart.

Fire forward throws meteors,
Golden and mauve sparks,
Flow far far away in sky;
Little girls and little boys
Around fly and shriek,
Eyes and blond manes flash.
Bonfire snaps crackling. Old kegs
Jump, and blazes up.

Three tall men calmly talk,
Standing up as dark horses
In moonlight. One listens,
bends a round fine head
As a golden pottery.
An old peasant smiles,
Women midly chatter
As birds at night.
Like free fools, youth
Springs and runs
And enlacing necks, dances.

Time turns down his hourglass.
Immense blue navy ocean
looks at the ruby on the hill.
Immense cloudy skies gaze
At the headlands fire.
Dark castle opens two brillant eyes.
Giant Ben Bulben, I would
Swear to it, smiles.
Far away, asleep, Inishmurray,
I swear it is the truth,
With us sighs for joy.

Genevieve Leforestier

A FRENCH VISITOR TO BONFIRE NIGHT 1991

THE COURTSHIP OF MISS BRADY

My name is Andrew Francis, in Raspberry Hill I dwell,
My courtship to Miss brady, to her Mother they did tell.
She is a comely damsel as you all may understand
She drives her Mothers ass and cart and she has a
      farm of land.

I being my Fathers only son; that same I can't deny,
Its with horse dealer Connolly I struck it on the sly.
Horse dealer Connolly drew a deed to which he
      signed her hand,
But her Mother then would not consent to
      give up the Breaghwy land.

My Fathers farm, it is big, he has acres by the score,
He has cattle land and horses and a black pigs meat in store.
They say he was a vagabond when he was young and bold,
He used to dance the "lions rant" in the brave days of old.

My Mother's old and quarrellsome and a promise
      she did make,
To put no sugar in my tay or currant in my cake.
"Now stop your bit of foolishness and stay at home with me,
May curses on the Pryors that brought you to the sea.

"Your old respected Father, he keeps a running dog
Now leave the wrack and famluc for Ellen Terrys bog".
When young McGowan he saw his love, he told her
      all the news,
She got a bit excited and she shivered in her shoes.

She says, "Don't heed your parents or anything they say
For I've got my name upon the receipt this very blessed day.
Now we'll conclude and finish and put an end to all
And I'll crown you King of Breaghey in the old vacated Hall".

Andrew McGowan

THE AUCTION

'Twas published on the champion and telegraphed on the poles;
For sale by public auction on Monday sharp at four.
Meadows at Mount Temple, the property of Miss Park
For the luck of all the farmers on the land commision mark.
It was under supervision, Oh, we're so glad to hear
Of Mr. Sean O'Carroll, the Sligo auctioneer.
After long consideration and a-planning for awhile
I started for the auction an acre for to buy.

Sure I thought I was back in Boston or the sidewalks of New
          York
When I came to Carns corner and heard the chitter-chatter talk.
Of the economizing farmers from Carns and Drumfad,
Moneygold and the Island boys,'twas eloquent speech they had.
Along comes Paddy Newman with his machine and his steed
To mow for Annie Meehan, way down in Finnegans field.
It was better than a picture you would see at the Savoy,
the machine and grey bay driven by this fair haired boy.

Like the train going through the tunnel near the
  town of Mullingar,
He drove them down the Quayroad as he safely crossed the tar,
Accompanied by the eager ones who came from near and far
To purchase Parks'es meadows inside the avenue pier.
All sat there so patiently, so Carroll to beguile
And Michael Joseph Healy with his roguish Irish smile.
He invited Andy Meehan the meadows to travel o'er,
So they walked it down and in and out 'till their
Shoes were nearly wore.

Well, if you would slyly watch them as they travelled all the fields,
No mistake about it but you really would believe
They were off to sign the treaty, or the estate to commandeer
With their foolscap, pen and paper and fags behind their ear.
In the gate came Patrick Branley, who has a family, four,
A qualified eye specialist, though it is an Elsinore.
Tom Gilroy, he did tell them, his tongue and teeth were wore
From giving music lessons to the Scotties by the shore.

Above between the fences, Mrs. Terry gave a shout
And up the field ran Terry with his tongue a half mile out.
Saying, "I'm your loving husband and you're my wee wife.
I have no time to court you but tonight I'll see you right".
In his private car came Carroll: poor Terry was away,
But it's not in every woman that the heart of man can stay.
Carroll addressed the audience and read the terms of sale,
To pay the purchase of meadows before the removal of hay.

The first allotment offered was an acre of ryegrass.
Then Mick the Newman bid a pound and twisted his mustache.
No other bid was offered for his value or for style
And Newman got the acre for the sum of one pound five.
Four acres more of ryegrass; 'twas then put up for sale
And the rush that they all made for it was just like Christmas mail.
The first bid put upon it was Ger Costello's of a pound
And Healy jumping on it increased by half a crown.

After the keenest revaluing to George it was struck down
And he really had some value for the figure of five pound.
Up then came Smiler Healey, he got the remaining lot
And said that he was thankful for 'twas quality that he sought.
He said he owned a stallion and Newman had two mares;
they'd fatten on the ryegrass, 'twas full of salty airs.
No matter says the Newman, 'tis me will mow some hay
with the purchase of Parkes's meadow inside the avenue pier.

Now for the upland meadow Paddy Keagan scored two quid
But sure his doughty neighbours outdone him in the bid.
Mick Burns marked it final at twenty three half crowns.
Carroll struck the hammer and to him he knocked it down.
He sang a merry chorus, he was so full of joy
That he courted the handsome owner; he was the bonny
  Drumfad boy.
"Oh, now", says Jimmy McGann, "I'm entitled to a share.
"Good enough", says Carroll, "I'll give you half the square".

He then bowed down so modestly, and Carroll he did thank
Saying "I have no fodder for my cows, and what I've bought
  is very rank"
Says Johnny Mickey Bog to Carroll,"I'm acquainted with Lemass,
  I'll have to get a portion as well as some aftergrass".
"Oh, needless for to tell you, I'm a man with no conceit,
I've had many bridal offers in this leap year '48".
Then Terry, he came running, "I haven't missed the sale,
When you go to meet a woman, you may as well be under bail".

"I meant to buy an acre, here and there and all,
I missed it all so footy while up at yonder wall"
Carroll gave a gentle laugh and said "You are not late,
There still remains an acre one side of yonder gate".
"Oh, bedad then", says Terry, "you'll give it to me and all,
Then I will take a holiday in County Donegal.
What entertainment at the auction that was held on that day;
We got cockle shells and mussells too, in the real old Irish way.

It was not the last discipline from near Mountemple school;
We came back to Carns corner and we danced the 'Foggy Dew'.

MOFFITS BURRA SONG

Come all ye lads and lassies
And listen to my lay:
I'll sing to you a melody
And a true one you may say.

It's all about the Burra's
Its known both near and far
From Mullaghmore's sweet harbour
To the weirs of Castlebar.

These lands were owned by Ashley
A few short years ago
But the land commision interfered
And claimed it was not so.

At first the grazers did not like
And would not recognise
That freestate lawyers had the right
These lands for to divide.

Says wee Pat Loughlin in a rage
"A meeting we must hold
To discuss all matters inwardly
Our plans we will unfold.

We'll advertise in the champion
That the rabbits are for sale"
"Well, if you do says Rooney,
We'll join Fianna Fail."

Says cunning Tommy Harkin,
"This pouching must be stopped
For we will all get punishment,
This pouching is a rot.

The guards they will assist us
The laws for to maintain
For we are all so loyal
Since we joined Fianna Fail."

Says Tommy Watters, "I'm not blind,
And a flashlight I will shine
To show our ways in darkness
For the cause it is sublime".

But pause awhile, there now it is,
The squeal is heard once more,
The pouchers they are at it
And the rabbits fall galore.

Says Patrick Timoney, "I am poor,
And a family I have got,
A pound to me is not too much,
But pouching is a rot."

But spare our days, it is alright,
We'll have to pouch no more
Our appetites will all be filled
With meat from Aughris shore.

"My bully man", says Dutchman,
"A lawyer we must get,
A local one if possible
We surely won't forget".

"We'll leave our case to Loughlin,
Our case he will not sell,
For O'Doherty has taught him
And taught him very well".

The Gillespies they are loyal
And will not now agree
To take a bribe thats offered
For a cow that should be free.

Our Edward says "Its just like this,
A bribe we'll never claim
And I will upset all your plans,
The rabbits will remain".

Says Henry Gallagher, "I am small
And very much afraid,
Kilfeather, he will head me
And through some blood we'll wade".

"There's ten of us to trap it
And we'll do that very soon,
For we have no need to wait
For the Rising of the Moon".

A republic we have really got
And freedom is proclaimed:
It's known as Moffits Burra
And that is why its named.

R.C. Church, Cliffoney, Co. Sligo.

THE BALLYCONNELL SCHOOL

From the rockbound coast of Cloonagh,
To the green hills of Knocklane,
From the pebbly shores of Raughley
To the far off Munianane.

The farmer folk, the fisher folk,
The foreigner and the fool:
They headed west dressed in their best
For the Ballyconnell school.

The Griffins, they are beautiful:
their faces are like the dawn.
They live down in a hollow
In a vale at Cloonaghbawn.

Another beauty is Miss Meehan
(she comes from Attyduff).
Some say she's fantastic,
I think she's plain enough.

The Corcorans from Collooney
Were of a high degree,
But whether they are high or low,
It's not to do with me.

Their father is a farmer,
He owns both sheep and cows:
His son is down in Holmes' place
To instruct the Maugherows.

When his days work is over
He goes to meet his mark,
The beautiful Miss Doherty,
From the hills of Carr na gCearc.

Now I'll quit about the teachers
And I'll turn upon the guards:
I'm sure you will excuse me,
You know I can't hit too hard.

There's Sergt. McGinty,
(He's a man of high renown)
He has bent his whole endeavour
To keep the poitin down.

He's on the tramp, both dry and damp
From morning until dawn.
And you're sure to always meet him
On the road to Cloonaghbawn.

The fairhaired Sgt. Martin, I can't say much to him,
He's lazy and he's easygoing and he's always time enough
And you're always sure to meet him
On the road to Attyduff.

BIBLIOGRAPHY

O' Rourke, T	HISTORY OF SLIGO. 2 VOLS	1898
Woodmartin W.G.	HISTORY OF SLIGO . 3 VOLS	1882-'93
Kilgannon, T	SLIGO AND ITS SURROUNDINGS	1926
Mac Manus S.	THE STORY OF THE IRISH RACE	1922
Doherty & Hickey	CHRONOLOGY OF IRISH HISTORY	1989
Gaughan, J. A.	MEMOIRS OF CONST. JEREMIAH MEE	
Lewis, S	TOPOGRAPHICAL DICTIONARY OF IRELAND 1837	
Ashley, E.	LIFE OF VISCOUNT PALMERSTON	2 vols 1897

D. Edwards & H. Williams THE GREAT FAMINE

Woodham Smith, Cecil   THE GREAT HUNGER   1962

Bourne, Kenneth	PALMERSTON: THE EARLY YEARS
Winters, Gordon.	SECRETS OF THE ROYALS
Ridley, Joseph	LORD PALMERSTON
Lambton, Anthony	THE MOUNTBATTENS
Macardle, Dorothy	THE IRISH REPUBLIC
Prendergast, John P.	THE CROMWELLIAN SETTLEMENT OF IRELAND 1870
O'Muillane, M.J.	THE CRUISE OF THE ERIN'S HOPE
Lane-Poole, Stanley	NORTH-WEST AND BY NORTH
Campbell-Foster, T	LETTERS ON CONDITION OF PEOPLE OF IRELAND 1846
O'Dowd, Mary	POWER, POLITICS AND LAND 1568 1688 (Pub.1991)
Burke, Rev. Wm. P.	IRISH PRIESTS IN THE PENAL TIMES
Allingham, Hugh	CAPT. CUELLARS ADVENTURES IN CONNAUGHT &
	ULSTER

| Martin, F.X. | THE IRISH VOLUNTEERS 1913-1915 |
| Marreco, Anne | The Rebel Countess |

Newspapers, Periodicals, Articles, Manuscripts:

THE SLIGO CHAMPION   THE SLIGO JOURNAL

THE SLIGO INDEPENDENT   AP/RN

THE IRISH PRESS   LEITRIM GUARDIAN

JOURNAL OF THE RAILWAY SOCIETY (article by Walter McGrath)

RESOURCE MAGAZINE

PAPERS RELATING TO THE RELIEF OF DISTRESS

SIXTH REPORT OF THE COMMISSIONERS

LETTERS RELATIVE TO THE ORDNANCE SURVEY OF 1836 (O'DONOVAN)

BOOKS OF SURVEY AND DISTRIBUTION c1690

TITHE APPLOTMENT BOOKS

DUBLIN CASTLE RECORDS

C.D.B. SURVEY AND VARIOUS, REGISTERED PAPERS, POLICE REPORTS.

I am grateful to the following for permission to use items of material from their collections:

Trustee's of the BROADLANDS ARCHIVES for material stored in the HARTLEY LIBRARY, UNIVERSITY OF SOUTHHAMPTON.

PUBLIC RECORDS OFFICE, KEW, London for items CO904/113, CO 904/155, ADM 175/15/16/17. Material is Crown Copyright.

ORDNANCE OFFICE DUBLIN. O.S. Maps are based on the Ordnance Survey by kind permission of the Government (permit no. 5744)

NATIONAL LIBRARY, Kildare St., Dublin

NATIONAL MUSEUM, Kildare St. Dublin

PUBLIC RECORDS OFFICE, Bishop St., Dublin.

SLIGO COUNTY LIBRARY, Courthouse, Sligo.

Verse where it is not otherwise credited is quoted from:

HUGH ALLINGHAM   PATRICK KAVANAGH

W.B. YEATS   PADRAIG H. PEARSE

SEAMUS HEANEY   AUBREY DEVERE

OLIVER GOLDSMITH   SEAMUS MAC MANUS

LADY WILDE   H. W. LONGFELLOW

CHARLES KICKHAM   T.D. SULLIVAN

311

HEARTH MONEY ROLLS

A hearth tax was introduced to Ireland in 1662 during the reign of Charles 11 by which the citizens were,"charged with the annual payment to the Kings Majefty, his heirs and fucceffors for every fire hearth, and other place ufed for firing and ftoves within every fuch houfe and edifice as aforefaid, the fum of two fhillings by the year, to ɒe paid yearly and every year at the feaft of the annunciation of the Bleffed Virgin St, Mary and the feaft of St. Michael and arch-angel, by even and equal portions......" While the tax provides an interesting record of some of the names existing in the area at the time, it is quite incomplete as some hearths would have escaped the notice of the tax collector, other families would have devised some artifice to avoid paying the tax while in other cases more than one family may have lived in the same house. Here are the names given for the Parish of Ahamlish:

Birne, James Creevymore
O'Mullvoge, Brian, Creevymore
O'Connor, Brian, Creevykeel
O'Cruelly, Donagh, Creevykeel
McGillpedder, Gillchrist, "
Luin, William, William, "
Mc Nuiske, Cormac, "
Braduaine, Hugh, Grange
O'Cunaine, Hugh, Grange
Mc Curriod, John "
Gara, Grange "
O' Harcaine, Hugh "
Connolly, Manus, Silverhill
Creane, John, Cliffoney
Creane, Nicholas, Cliffoney
Tualon, John, Cliffoney

Mr. Collins, Morish, Bunduff
O'Downy, Morish, Bunduff
McGinnly, Ambrose, Bunduff
Preston, James, Bunduff
Welsh, Michael, Bunduff
Gillaine, Donnagh, Streedagh
Liney, Geoffrey, Streedagh
Piece, Richard, Grange
Sodden, Thomas, (2) Grange
"Sodden, Thomas, Jr. "
Kelly, Myles, Grange
Gillaine, Brian, Grange
McKelly, Carne, Grange
McCurriod, James, Ballyscannell
(Cuimes, Wm. Ballygilgan)
Mc Ulbaine, Patricke, "

GRIFFITH VALUATION

It was required by the Irish poor Act of 1838 that land and property should be valued for the purpose of levying taxes to finance the relief of the poor. Today, this list provides an invaluable reference for leased and owned land and family history in the middle of the last century. The complete list, part of which is reproduced here is obtainable in Sligo County Library.

Valuation of Tenements.

ACTS 15 & 16 VIC., CAP. 63; 17 VIC., CAP. 8; AND 19 & 20 VIC., CAP. 63.

COUNTY OF SLIGO.

BARONY OF CARBURY.

UNION OF SLIGO.

PARISH OF AHAMLISH.

No. and Letters of Reference to Map	Townlands and Occupiers	Immediate Lessors	Description of Tenement	Area A. R. P.	Land £ s. d.	Buildings £ s. d.	
	BALLINPHULL. (Ord. S. 2.)						
1	George Conway,	Viscount Palmerston,	Land,	1 0 14	0 12 0	—	
2	Anthony Timmony,	Same,	Land,	4 2 13	2 15 0	—	
3	Michael Timmony,	Same,	Land,	3 2 36	2 5 0	—	
4	John Leudon,	Same,	Land,	0 3 25	0 15 0	—	
5 a	Patrick Commons,	Same,	Land and house,	6 2 6	4 0 0	1 0 0	
6 a	Patrick Timmony,	Same,	Land and house,	13 3 36	8 10 0	3 0 0	
— b	Thomas Killelen,	Patrick Timmony,	House,			1 10 0	
7 a	Terence Connolly,	Viscount Palmerston,	Land and house,	6 2 26	3 15 0	0 10 0	
8 a			Land, house, and offices,	17 1 12	13 10 0	16 0 0	
9	Mary Corrigan,	Same,	Land,	0 3 20	0 15 0	—	
8 b	Owen Dunleavy,	Same,	Garden and house,	0 1 5	0 5 0	4 0 0	
— c	Catherine M'Gunnigle,	Same,	Garden and house,	0 1 0	0 5 0	3 0 0	
— d	Unoccupied,	Same,	Old market-house,		—	3 0 0	
9 a	Mary Horgilen,	Mary Corrigan,	House,		—	0 10 0	
10 a	Robert Mahon,	Viscount Palmerston,	Land and house,	1 0 0	1 0 0	6 0 0	
11 a			Male and Female National school-ho., & gar. (see Exemptions).				
— b	Mathias Leonard,	Viscount Palmerston,	House,		—	3 0 0	
— c	Susan Tomlinson,	Same,	House,		—	3 0 0	
12 a			R. C. Chapel and yard, (see Exemptions).				
— b			Constabulary bar., off., & yd. (see Exemptions).				
		Viscount Palmerston,	Half the annual rent derived from Constabulary-bar., off., & yard,				7 0 0
13 a	Francis Commons,	Same,	Land and house,	1 1 34	1 10 0	2 5 0	
— b	Timothy Scanlan,	Francis Commons,	House,			1 15 0	
— c			Dispensary (see Exemptions).				
		Francis Commons,	Half the annual rent derived from dispensary,				
— d	Cornelius Commons,	Viscount Palmerston,	Garden and house,	0 0 26	0 5 0	3 0 0	
14 a	James M'Garrigle,	Same,	Land, house, and forge,	1 0 35	1 5 0	2 0 0	
15 a	Bridget Waters,	Same,	Land and house,	2 2 35	2 10 0	1 5 0	
16	Cornelius Commons,	Same,	Land,	3 3 28	3 10 0	—	
17 a	Malachy Conway,	Same,	Land and house,	1 3 10	1 10 0	0 10 0	
18	Patrick M'Intire, Michael M'Intire,	Same,	Land,	1 1 20	0 12 0	—	
19	Mary Corrigan,	Same,	Land,	5 3 27	5 0 0	—	
			Total of Rateable Property,	75 3 8	55 1 0	55 5 0	

PARISH OF AHAMLISH.

No. and Letters of Reference to Map.		Names.		Description of Tenement.	Area.	Rateable Annual Valuation.		Total Annual Valuation of Rateable Property.
		Townlands and Occupiers.	Immediate Lessors.			Land.	Buildings.	
					A. R. P.	£ s. d	£ s. d	£ s. d
		BALLINPHULL— *continued.*		EXEMPTIONS:				
11	a	. . . .	. . . .	Male and Female Nat. school-house & garden,	0 3 27	1 0 0	6 0 0	7 0 6
12	a			R. C. Chapel and yard,	0 2 15	0 5 0	24 0 0	24 5 0
12	b	Constabulary Force, .	Viscount Palmerston,	Barrack, off., and yard,	0 0 15	—	6 0 0	6 0 0
13	c	. . . .	Francis Commons,	Dispensary, . .	—	—	3 0 0	3 0 0
				Total of Exemptions,	1 2 17	1 5 0	39 0 0	40 5 0
				Total including Exemptions, .	77 1 25	56 6 0	94 5 0	161 1 0
		KILKILLOGE. (Ord. S. 2 & 3.)						
1		James Gorman, sen., .	Viscount Palmerston,	Land, . .	6 3 0	3 15 0		
2	a			Land and house,	0 1 25	0 5 0	1 5 0	5 5 0
3	a	Bryan Barry, .	Same,	Land, house, and office,	0 3 24	0 15 0	3 0 0	
4				Land, . .	12 2 20	5 10 0		9 5 0
	a	Peter Ravington,		Land and house,		0 10 0	2 10 0	3 0 0
	b	John Burke,		Land and house,		0 10 0	2 10 0	3 0 0
	c	Anthony Coyle,		Land and house,		0 10 0	2 10 0	3 0 0
5	d	Maurice M'Carthy,	Same, .	Land and house,	2 2 25	0 10 0	2 10 0	3 0 0
	e	John Gray,		Land and house,		0 10 0	2 10 0	3 0 0
		Unoccupied,		Land and house,		0 10 0	2 10 0	3 0 0
6	a			Land and house,	1 0 35	1 5 0	1 10 0	
7		Peter M'Cannon,	Same, .	Land, . .	3 3 5	1 15 0	—	5 5 0
8				Land, . .	1 1 5	0 15 0		
9	a	Hugh Gilmartin, sen.,	Same,	Land and house,	1 1 10	1 5 0	4 10 0	5 15 0
—	b	Unoccupied, .	Hugh Gilmartin, sen.,	House, . .	—	—	5 0 0	5 0 0
—	c	Unoccupied, .	Same, .	House and office,	—	—	5 10 0	5 10 0
—	d		Viscount Palmerston,	Coast-guard station, boat & watch houses (see Exemptions).				
			Viscount Palmerston,	*Half the annual rent derived from Coast-guard station, boat and watch houses,*		—	—	1 15 0
10		Viscount Palmerston,	In fee, . .	Land, . .	89 2 11	57 0 0	—	60 0 0
11					15 1 29	3 0 0		
	10 a	Unoccupied, .	Viscount Palmerston,	Ho., corn-stores, & offs.,			15 0 0	15 0 0
—	b		Same, .	National school-house (see Exemptions)				
—	c	James M'Glone,	Same, .	Garden, house, & office,	0 0 32	0 5 0	5 5 0	5 10 0
—	d	James Gardiner,	Same, .	House, . .	—	—	2 0 0	2 0 0
—	e	William Petrie,	Same, .	House and office,	—	—	2 10 0	2 10 0
12		Michael Kelly, sen.,	Same, .	Land, . .	1 1 0	0 10 0	—	2 15 0
13	a			Land and house,	2 1 10	1 10 0	0 15 0	
14	a	Denis M'Cannon,	Same, .	Land and house,	6 1 22	2 15 0	1 10 0	9 0 0
15				Land, . .	10 2 18	4 15 0		
16	a	Patrick Barry,	Same, .	Land and house,	1 0 25	0 8 0	0 12 0	1 0 0
	b	Peter Barry,		Land and house,		0 8 0	0 12 0	1 0 0
17	a	Patrick Barry,	Same, .	Land and office,	16 0 13	3 5 0	0 5 0	3 10 0
	b	Peter Barry,		Land and office,		3 5 0	0 5 0	3 10 0
18	a	Patrick M'Andrew,	Same,	Land and house,	9 1 17	3 15 0	1 10 0	5 5 0
19	a	Patrick M'Gooran,	Same,	Land and house,	1 1 25	0 18 0	1 2 0	2 0 0
20	a	Michael Leonard,	Same,	Land and house,	5 1 0	2 5 0	0 15 0	3 0 0
21	a	Terence Moohan,	Same,	Land and house,	0 2 5	0 8 0	1 2 0	1 10 0
22	a	Thomas M'Grath,	Same,	Land and house,	0 2 30	0 8 0	1 2 0	1 10 0
23	a	Hugh M'Cauley,	Same,	Land and house,	0 1 35	0 8 0	1 2 0	1 10 0
24	a	Thomas M'Andrew,	Same,	Land and house,	0 1 30	0 8 0	1 2 0	1 10 0
25	a	Michael Rogers,	Same,	Land and house,	0 3 10	0 13 0	1 2 0	1 15 0
26	a	Daniel M'Gowan,	Same,	Land and house,	5 0 37	2 5 0	0 15 0	3 5 0
27				Land, . .	0 1 30	0 5 0		
28		John Barry, .	Same,	Land, . .	6 0 21	2 15 0		5 0 0
29	a			Land and house,	2 2 16	1 5 0	1 0 0	
30		Hugh Gilmartin,	Same,	Land, . .	2 1 15	1 10 0		4 10 0
31	a			Land and house,	3 1 0	2 0 0	1 0 0	
—	b	Francis Gray, .	Hugh Gilmartin,	Garden, . .	0 1 20	0 5 0		0 5 0

PARISH OF AHAMLISH.

No. and Letters of Reference to Map.		Townlands and Occupiers.	Immediate Lessors.	Description of Tenement.	Area. A. R. P.	Rateable Annual Valuation. Land. £ s. d.	Rateable Annual Valuation. Buildings. £ s. d.	Total Annual Valuation of Rateable Property. £ s. d.
		KILKILLOGE—con.						
32	a	William Mulholland,	Viscount Palmerston,	Land and house,	1 0 30	0 15 0	0 5 0	1 0 0
33	a	Thomas M'Gowan,	Same,	Land and house,	0 2 10	0 8 0	1 2 0	1 10 0
34	a	Patrick Leydon,	Same,	Land and house,	0 2 25	0 8 0	1 2 0	1 10 0
35	a	James M'Gowan,	Same,	Land and house,	0 1 35	0 8 0	1 2 0	1 10 0
36	a	Charles Gallagher,	Same,	Land and house,	2 2 30	1 10 0	0 10 0	2 0 0
37	a	Thomas Gilvarry,	Same,	Land and house,	2 3 10	1 10 0	0 10 0	2 0 0
38	a	Hugh Barry,	Same,	Land and house,	3 1 14	1 15 0	0 15 0	2 10 0
39	a	Andrew Mohan,	Same,	Land and house,	1 1 7	0 18 0	1 2 0	2 0 0
40	a	Peter M'Gowan,	Same,	Land and house,	16 2 27	7 5 0	1 0 0	8 5 0
41	a	Terence Gorman,	Same,	Land and house,	1 1 11	0 18 0	1 2 0	2 0 0
42	a	Denis Rourke,	Same,	Land and house,	2 2 34	1 8 0	0 12 0	2 0 0
43	}	Owen Commins,	Same,	Land,	2 2 16	1 8 0	—	} 5 5 0
44	a }			Land and house,	6 3 37	3 2 0	0 15 0	
45	a	James Doodigan,	Same,	Land and house,	1 1 26	0 18 0	1 2 0	2 0 0
46	a	Michael Kelly,	Same,	Land and house,	3 1 34	1 10 0	0 15 0	2 5 0
47	a }			Land and house,	4 0 32	2 0 0	1 0 0	}
48	a }	Bryan Kelly (Dan),	Same,	Land and office,	5 0 30	2 10 0	0 10 0	} 15 5 0
49	a }			Land and office,	15 0 20	9 0 0	0 5 0	
50	a	Thade Duffy,	Same,	Land and house,	0 3 13	0 10 0	1 0 0	1 10 0
51	a	Patrick Commins,	Same,	Land and house,	0 3 18	0 15 0	1 0 0	1 15 0
—	b	John Commins,	Same,	House,	—	—	1 2 0	1 2 0
52		John Commins,	Same,	Land,	0 1 35	0 8 0	—	0 8 0
53	a	Hugh Kennedy,	Same,	Land and house,	0 1 35	0 8 0	1 2 0	1 10 0
54	}	Martin Boy,	Same,	Land,	0 2 10	0 10 0	—	} 3 10 0
55	a }			Land and house,	4 0 35	2 5 0	0 15 0	
56	a	Bryan Clinton,	Same,	Land and house,	0 1 35	0 8 0	1 2 0	1 10 0
57	a	John Gilmartin,	Same,	Land and house,	0 1 25	0 8 0	1 2 0	1 10 0
58	a	Patrick Gilmartin,	Same,	Land and house,	1 2 21	2 10 0	0 15 0	3 5 0
59	a	Christopher Dunleavy,	Same,	Land and house,	5 0 20	3 0 0	0 15 0	3 15 0
60	a	Thade Boy,	Same,	Land and house,	4 1 35	2 13 0	0 12 0	3 5 0
61	a	James M'Glone,	Same,	Land and office,	6 2 20	3 15 0	0 5 0	4 0 0
62		Martin Doodigan,	Same,	Land,	3 2 24	2 0 0	—	2 0 0
63	a	Patrick Rogers,	Same,	Land and house,	1 1 0	1 0 0	0 10 0	1 10 0
64	a	Martin Leonard,	Same,	Land and house,	3 0 21	1 15 0	0 10 0	2 5 0
65	a	Patrick Commins,	Same,	Land and house,	3 0 21	1 13 0	0 12 0	2 5 0
66	a	Patrick Healy,	Same,	Land and house,	3 2 20	1 15 0	0 10 0	2 5 0
67		Edward Gilmartin,	Same,	Land,	95 0 0	12 0 0	—	12 0 0
68	a	James M'Cannon,	Same,	Land and house,	5 0 26	3 10 0	1 10 0	5 0 0
69	a	John Gallagher,	Same,	Land and house,	2 3 10	0 15 0	0 10 0	1 5 0
70	a	Michael Duffy,	Same,	Land and house,	0 2 5	0 8 0	1 2 0	1 10 0
71	a	James Gorman, jun.,	Same,	Land and house,	0 2 15	0 8 0	1 2 0	1 10 0
72	a	Mary Clinton,	Same,	Land and house,	0 2 35	0 8 0	1 2 0	1 10 0
73	a	James Boy,	Same,	Land and house,	5 1 0	2 15 0	0 15 0	3 10 0
74	a	John M'Sharry,	Same,	Land and house,	0 1 25	0 5 0	1 5 0	1 10 0
75	a	James Rourke,	Same,	Land and house,	5 0 20	2 0 0	1 0 0	3 0 0
76	a	Bryan Kelly (Pat.),	Same,	Land and house.	8 1 0	3 5 0	0 15 0	4 0 0
77	a	John Gilmartin,	Same,	Land and house,	6 2 38	2 10 0	0 15 0	3 5 0
78	a	Francis Gray,	Same,	Land and house,	0 1 35	0 8 0	1 2 0	1 10 0
79	a	John Gilbarry,	Same,	Land and house,	7 3 18	3 10 0	1 0 0	8 5 0
80	a	Patrick Horkin,	Same,	Land,	12 3 27	7 5 0	1 0 0	8 5 0
81	}	Patrick Boy,	Same,	Land,	0 2 38	0 10 0	—	} 3 10 0
82	a }			Land and house,	3 3 20	2 5 0	0 15 0	
83	a	Terence Clinton,	Same,	Land and house,	0 2 0	0 8 0	1 2 0	1 10 0
				Total of Rateable Property,	486 3 8	220 8 0	115 12 0	340 15 0
				EXEMPTIONS:				
9	d	. . . .	Viscount Palmerston,	Coast-guard station, boat & watch houses,	—	—	4 0 0	4 0 0
10	b	. . . .	Same,	National school-house,	—	—	1 10 0	1 10 0
				Total of Exemptions,	—	—	5 10 0	5 10 0
				Total including Exemptions,	486 3 8	220 8 0	121 2 0	346 5 0
		ADJOINING TOWNLAND OF KILKILLOGE.						
		William Petrie,	Viscount Palmerston,	Salmon Fishery,	—	—	—	20 0 0
		Patrick M'Gloin,	Col. Hugh W. Barton,	Salmon Fishery,	—	—	—	4 0 0

VALUATION OF TENEMENTS.

PARISH OF AHAMLISH.

No. and Letters of Reference to Map.	Townlands and Occupiers.	Immediate Lessors.	Description of Tenement.	Area. A. r. p.	Rateable Annual Valuation. Land. £ s. d.	Buildings. £ s. d.	Total Annual Valuation of Rateable Property. £ s. d.
	BUNDUFF. (*Ord. S. 3 & 2.*)			A. r. p.	£ s. d.	£ s. d.	£ s. d.
1				33 0 34	0 10 0	—	
2	Viscount Palmerston,	In fee, . .	Land, . .	22 2 19	0 5 0	—	3 15 0
3				7 2 20	2 5 0	—	
4				111 1 4	0 15 0		
3 a	John Johnston,	Viscount Palmerston,	House, . .		—	1 0 0	1 0 0
— b	Bridget Sweeny,	Same, . .	House, . .		—	0 5 0	0 5 0
5 a	James Nealis, .	Same, . .	Land and house, .	7 3 34	3 15 0	0 10 0	4 5 0
6 a	James Munday, .	Same, . .	Land and house, .	5 2 11	1 17 0	0 8 0	2 5 0
7 a	Mary Carvey, .	Same, . .	Land and house, .	2 3 5	0 17 0	0 3 0	1 0 0
8 a	John Sweeny, .	Same, . .	Land and house, .	10 3 29	3 0 0	0 5 0	3 10 0
9 a	John Harris, .	Same, . .	Land and house, .	13 1 13	2 12 0	0 3 0	2 15 0
10 a	Patrick M'Govran,	Same, . .	Land and house, .	14 1 9	7 10 0	0 10 0	8 0 0
11 a	Martin M'Govran,	Same, . .	Land and house, .	11 0 28	5 10 0	0 10 0	6 0 0
12 a	John Murtagh, .	Same, . .	Land and house, .	6 0 19	2 10 0	0 10 0	3 0 0
13			Land, . .	6 3 19	3 5 0		
14 a	Bryan Barry, .	Same, . .	Land and house, .	3 3 18	2 0 0	0 15 0	6 0 0
15 a	Terence Murtagh,	Same, . .	Land and house, .	3 1 8	1 10 0	0 5 0	1 15 0
16 a	John M'Govran,	Same, . .	Land and house, .	4 2 2	1 15 0	0 10 0	2 5 0
17 a	Charles M'Quade,	Same, . .	Land and house, .	4 1 17	1 13 0	0 7 0	2 0 0
18 a	Patrick Barry, .	Same, . .	Land and house, .	10 3 20	4 15 0	0 10 0	5 5 0
19 a	Andrew Murtagh,	Same, . .	Land and house, .	7 0 10	3 12 0	0 3 0	3 15 0
20 a	Bridget M'Govran,	Same, . .	Land and house, .	19 3 32	7 15 0	1 0 0	8 15 0
21 a	Manus Waters, .	Same, . .	Land and house, .	9 1 20	3 15 0	0 10 0	4 5 0
22 a	John Wemys, .	Same, . .	Land and house, .	14 1 19	6 0 0	0 5 0	6 5 0
23 a	Patrick Barry, .	Same, . .	Land and house, . .	11 0 34	4 15 0	0 15 0	5 10 0
24 a	Bryan Harrison,	Same, . .	Land and house, .	6 1 22	2 10 0	0 10 0	3 0 0
25			Land, . .	11 1 18	4 10 0		
26 a	Martin Wemys, .	Same, . .	Land and house, .	6 3 0	3 0 0	0 15 0	8 5 0
27 a	Margaret Harrison,	Same, . .	Land and house, .	8 2 5	3 10 0	0 10 0	4 0 0
28 a	Thady Harrison,	Same, . .	Land and house, .	9 1 22	3 18 0	0 12 0	4 10 0
29 a	Michael M'Gowan,	Same, . .	Land and house, .	9 0 34	4 0 0	0 15 0	4 15 0
30 a	William Clancy,	Same, . .	Land and house, .	4 2 30	2 5 0	0 10 0	2 15 0
31 a	Francis Rourke,	Same, . .	Land and house, .	6 2 0	3 5 0	0 10 0	3 15 0
32 a	Margaret O'Neill,	Same, . .	Land and house, .	6 1 0	3 5 0	0 10 0	3 15 0
33 a	Bridget Leadon,	Same, . .	Land and house, .	5 2 20	3 0 0	0 10 0	3 10 0
34	Bridget Sweeny,	Same, . .	Land, . .	4 0 10	2 5 0	—	2 5 0
35 a	Patrick M'Gowan,	Same, . .	Land and house, .	10 1 23	6 5 0	0 10 0	6 15 0
36 a	Patrick M'Govran,	Same, . .	Land and house, .	3 0 0	1 18 0	0 7 0	2 5 0
37 a	Daniel M'Sharry,	Same, . .	Land and house, .	6 3 10	4 0 0	0 10 0	4 10 0
38 a	Andrew Rourke,	Same, . .	Land and house, .	4 1 25	2 0 0	0 15 0	2 15 0
39	Thady Higgins,	Same, . .	Land, . .	0 3 30	0 5 0	—	0 5 0
40 a	Thady Harrison,	Same, . .	Land and house, .	6 0 6	4 8 0	0 12 0	5 0 0
— b	Michael Higgins,	Same, . .	Garden, . .	0 0 25	0 2 0	—	0 2 0
41 a	Mary Gilmartin,	Same, . .	Land and house, .	6 2 30	0 12 0	0 8 0	1 0 0
42 a	Patrick M'Glone,	Same, . .	Land and house, .	5 3 4	4 0 0	0 10 0	4 10 0
43 a	Denis Gilmartin,	Same, . .	Land and house, .	11 2 37	6 10 0	1 0 0	7 10 0
44	John Johnston, .	Same, . .	Land, . .	6 1 6	3 5 0	—	3 5 0
45 a	Andrew Harrison,	Same, . .	Land and house, .	8 0 17	3 17 0	0 8 0	4 5 0
46 a	Thomas Gilmartin,	Same, . .	Land and house, .	15 0 25	8 0 0	0 15 0	8 15 0
47 a	John M'Govran,	Same, . .	Land and house, .	7 3 37	4 0 0	0 10 0	4 10 0
48 a	Arthur Million, .	Same, . .	Land and house, .	4 0 5	2 0 0	0 5 0	2 5 0
49 a			Land, house, and office,	4 3 14	2 10 0	1 5 0	
50	Patrick O'Connor,	Same, . .	Land, . .	38 0 30	9 0 0	—	16 0 0
51			Land, . .	12 3 12	3 5 0		
52 a	Thomas Gardner,	Same, . .	Land and house, .	7 0 36	4 5 0	1 0 0	7 10 0
53			Land, . .	8 1 23	2 5 0		
54 a	Patrick Hannon,	Same, . .	Land and forge, .	4 3 23	3 0 0	0 5 0	8 5 0
55 a			Land and house, .	7 2 22	4 5 0	0 15 0	
56 a	Thomas M'Andrew,	Same, . .	Land and house, .	16 0 0	8 10 0	0 10 0	9 0 0
57 a	Mary Gilmartin,	Same, . .	Land and house, .	5 2 30	3 5 0	0 10 0	3 15 0
58 a	Terence M'Gowan,	Same, . .	Land and house, .	4 0 15	2 0 0	0 10 0	2 10 0
59 a	Thomas M'Cahill,	Same, . .	Land and house, .	5 2 14	2 18 0	0 12 0	3 10 0
60	George M'Loughlin,	Same, . .	Land, . .	5 1 31	3 0 0	—	3 0 0
61 a	Terence M'Garrigle,	Same, . .	Land and house, .	7 3 15	4 15 0	0 10 0	5 5 0
— b	Cormack M'Garrigle,	Same, . .	House, . .		—	0 10 0	0 10 0
62 a	Owen Leonard,	Same, . .	Land and house, .	5 1 32	3 7 0	0 18 0	4 5 0
63 a	John Leonard, .	Same, . .	Land and house, .	5 0 26	3 5 0	0 15 0	4 0 0
64 a	Patrick Kelly, .	Same, . .	Land and house, .	14 1 31	3 10 0	0 10 0	4 0 0
65 a	James M'Glone,	Same, . .	Land and house, .	5 1 39	0 15 0	0 5 0	1 0 0

PARISH OF AHAMLISH.

No. and Letters of Reference to Map.		Names.		Description of Tenement.	Area.			Rateable Annual Valuation.		Total Annual Valuation of Rateable Property.
		Townlands and Occupiers.	Immediate Lessors.					Land.	Buildings.	
					A. R. P.			£ s. d.	£ s. d.	£ s. d.
		BUNDUFF— *continued.*								
66	a	Alice Daly, . .	Viscount Palmerston, .	Land and house, .	3 3 28			0 7 0	0 3 0	0 10 0
67	a	Patrick Currid, .	Same, . .	Land and house, .	4 3 10			0 12 0	0 3 0	0 15 0
68	a	Edward Gallagher, .	Same, . .	Land and house, .	17 2 6			4 5 0	0 15 0	5 0 0
69	a	Patrick Murtagh, .	Same, . .	Land and house, .	14 0 13			1 12 0	0 3 0	1 15 0
70	a	Peter Murtagh, .	Same, . .	Land and house, .	10 1 30			3 2 0	0 8 0	3 10 0
71	a	Hugh Murtagh, .	Same, . .	Land and house, .	9 3 3			3 0 0	0 5 0	3 5 0
72	a	Thomas Wemys, .	Same, . .	Land and house, .	16 1 35			4 10 0	0 15 0	5 5 0
73	a	Patrick Wemys, .	Same, . .	Land and house, .	19 3 15			4 15 0	0 15 0	5 10 0
74	a	Bryan Oates, .	Same, . .	Land and house, .	4 2 4			0 12 0	0 3 0	0 15 0
75	a	John M'Sharry, .	Same, . .	Land and house, .	5 2 10			0 7 0	0 3 0	0 10 0
76	a	Charles Lynch, .	Same, . .	Land and house, .	3 1 30			0 7 0	0 3 0	0 10 0
77	a	Matthew Flannagan, .	Same, . .	Land and house, .	3 3 20			0 12 0	0 3 0	0 15 0
78	a	Martin Oates, .	Same, . .	Land and house, .	9 0 13			2 10 0	0 10 0	3 0 0
79	a	Hugh M'Glone, .	Same, . .	Land and house, .	19 2 4			4 10 0	1 5 0	5 15 0
—	b	Catherine M'Glone, .	Hugh M'Glone, .	House, . .	—			—	0 10 0	0 10 0
80		Anne Gardiner, .	Viscount Palmerston, .	Land, . .	2 3 0			0 10 0	—	0 10 0
81	a	Edward Murtagh, .	Same, . .	Land and house, .	10 1 7			3 12 0	0 8 0	4 0 0
82	a	John Gilmartin, .	Same, . .	Land and house, .	6 1 14			2 15 0	0 10 0	3 5 0
83	a	Sibby Murtagh, .	Same, . .	Land and house, .	4 0 6			1 13 0	0 7 0	2 0 0
84	a	Mary M'Nulty, .	Same, . .	Land and house, .	5 0 27			2 10 0	0 5 0	2 15 0
85		John Harrison, .	Same, . .	Land, . .	8 1 2			3 10 0	—	3 10 0
86	a	Bridget Wemys, .	Same, . .	Land and house, .	4 2 5			2 10 0	0 10 0	3 0 0
87	a	Patrick Neary, .	Same, . .	Land and house, .	7 3 16			4 10 0	0 10 0	5 0 0
88	a }	Edward Burke, .	Same, . .	{ Land and house, .	6 2 18			3 17 0	0 18 0	} 7 0 0
89				{	8 2 0			2 5 0	—	
90	a	Bryan Judge, . .	Same, . .	Land and house, .	8 1 16			5 0 0	1 0 0	6 0 0
				Total, .	893 2 0			286 4 0	40 3 0	326 7 0
		CARTRONPLANK. *(Ord. S. 2 & 3.)*								
1		Mary Corrigan, . .	Viscount Palmerston, {	{ Land, . .	0 2 30			0 13 0	—	} 3 10 0
2	a }			{ Land and house, .	8 3 10			2 12 0	0 5 0	
3		Denis M'Cannon, .	Same, . .	Land, . .	14 1 13			6 5 0	—	6 5 0
—	a	John M'Cannon, .	Same, . .	Land (severance), .	0 0 24			0 1 0	—	0 1 0
4				{	4 2 35			3 5 0	—	
5	}	Robert Mahon, . .	Same, . .	Land, . .	0 3 0			0 5 0	—	} 4 5 0
6					2 0 6			0 15 0	—	
7	a	Michael Loughlin, sen.,	Same, . .	Land and house, .	6 3 26			3 0 0	0 10 0	3 10 0
8	a	Michael Loughlin, jun.,	Same, . .	Land and house, .	11 1 16			4 10 0	0 10 0	5 0 0
9	{ a	James Loughlin, .	Same, . .	Land and house, . }	16 0 31			{ 3 7 0	0 8 0	3 15 0
	{ b	Catherine Loughlin, .	Same, . .	Land and house, . }				{ 3 8 0	0 7 0	3 15 0
10	a	Bryan Oates, .	Same, . .	Land and house, .	5 0 20			4 0 0	1 0 0	5 0 0
11	a	Patrick Conway, .	Same, . .	Land and house, .	3 1 29			2 15 0	1 0 0	3 15 0
12	a	Jeremiah Commons, .	Same, . .	Land and house, .	3 1 29			2 15 0	1 0 0	3 15 0
13		Patrick M'Intire, jun.,	Same, . .	Land, . .	5 2 39			3 5 0	—	3 5 0
14	a	Robert Moore, .	Same, . .	Land and house, .	8 3 30			5 5 0	0 15 0	6 0 0
15	a }	Phelim Gallagher, .	Same, . .	{ Land and house, .	8 0 23			4 5 0	0 5 0	} 9 0 0
16				{ Land, . .	16 2 27			4 10 0	—	
	15 b	John Costello, .	Same, . .	House, . .	—			—	0 5 0	0 5 0
—	c	Patrick Feeny, .	Same, . .	House, .	—			—	0 5 0	0 5 0
17	a	Eliza M'Garrahy, .	Same, . .	Land and house, .	9 0 8			4 0 0	0 15 0	4 15 0
—	b	Hugh Gilmartin, .	Same, . .	House, . .	—			—	0 5 0	0 5 0
18	a	James Langan, .	Same, . .	Land and house, .	4 0 19			2 0 0	0 15 0	2 15 0
19		James M'Garrigle, .	Same, . .	Land, . .	14 1 20			4 5 0	—	4 5 0
20		Matthias Leonard, .	Same, . .	Land, . . }	17 3 30			{ 3 0 0	—	3 0 0
		Thomas Higgins, .	Same, . .	Land, . . }				{ 1 10 0	—	1 10 0
21		Patrick M'Intire, sen.,	Same, . .	Land, . . }	0 1 0			{ 0 3 0	—	0 3 0
		Michael M'Intire, .	Same, . .	}				{ 0 3 0	—	0 3 0
22		Viscount Palmerston, .	In fee, . .	Land (plantation), .	5 2 20			0 15 0	—	0 15 0
23		Martin Warnick, .	Viscount Palmerston, .	Land (severance), .	0 2 25			0 3 0	—	0 3 0
24	a	Thade Kennedy, .	Same, . .	Land and house, .	4 2 30			2 0 0	0 10 0	2 10 0
25	a	Patrick M'Sharry, .	Same, . .	Land and house, .	4 3 39			2 0 0	0 10 0	2 10 0
26	a	Patrick Barry, .	Same, . .	Land and house, .	8 0 32			3 15 0	0 15 0	4 10 0
27		Phelim O'Neill, .	Same, . .	Land, . .	0 3 16			0 5 0	—	0 5 0
				Total, . .	188 0 27			78 15 0	10 0 0	88 15 0

3

VALUATION OF TENEMENTS.

PARISH OF AHAMLISH.

No. and Letters of Reference to Map.	Townlands and Occupiers.	Immediate Lessors.	Description of Tenement.	Area. A. R. P.	Rateable Annual Valuation. Land. £ s. d.	Buildings. £ s. d.	Total Annual Valuation of Rateable Property. £ s. d.
	CARTRON-KILLERDOO. *(Ord. S. 2 & 3.)*						
1 a	James Clancy, . .	Viscount Palmerston,	Land and house,	15 0 30	11 0 0	1 10 0	12 10 0
— b	Mary Clancy, . .	James Clancy, . .	House,	—		0 10 0	0 10 0
2 a	Thomas Horkin, .	Viscount Palmerston,	Land and house,	3 0 0	1 10 0	0 10 0	2 0 0
3 a	Mary Kilbride, . .	Same, .	Land and house,	10 0 11	8 0 0	0 10 0	8 10 0
4 a	Thomas Higgins, jun.,	Same, .	Land and house,	6 3 20	5 15 0	1 10 0	7 5 0
— b	Denis M'Cannon,	Same, .	Garden and house,	0 1 25	0 5 0	3 0 0	} 3 10 0
— c			Garden,	0 1 25	0 5 0		
— a	Mary Kilbride, . .	Thomas Higgins, jun.,	House,	—		0 10 0	0 10 0
5	John Foley, . .	Viscount Palmerston,	Land, house, and office,	0 2 10	0 10 0	3 10 0	4 0 0
6 a	Nicholas Gunnigle, .	Same, .	Land, house, and office,	0 2 15	0 10 0	1 5 0	1 15 0
7 a	Paul Higgins, .	Same, .	Land and house,	3 2 25	2 15 0	1 0 0	3 15 0
8 a			Land and house,	3 3 0	2 10 0	3 10 0	} 11 10 0
9	Thomas Higgins, sen.,	Same, .	Land,	3 1 10	2 10 0	—	
10			Land,	4 1 24	1 15 0	—	
11			Land,	5 0 0	1 5 0	—	
12 a	Andrew Harrison,	Same, .	Land and house,	2 0 0	1 10 0	0 10 0	2 0 0
13 a	Gilbert Higgins,	Same, .	Land and house,	3 0 2	2 0 0	0 10 0	2 10 0
14 a	Thomas Kennedy,	Same, .	Land and house,	3 2 31	2 5 0	0 10 0	2 15 0
15 a	Daniel Gallagher,	Same, .	Land and house,	3 2 5	1 5 0	0 10 0	1 15 0
16 a	Patrick Harrison,	Same, .	Land and house,	3 3 32	1 10 0	0 10 0	2 0 0
17 a	Mary Loughnan,	Same, .	Land and house,	8 1 18	3 10 0	0 10 0	4 0 0
18 a	Daniel Loughnan,	Same, .	Land and house,	2 1 10	1 10 0	0 5 0	1 15 0
19	Denis M'Cannon,	Same, .	Land,	15 0 6	6 15 0	—	6 15 0
20	James M'Cannon,	Same, .	Land *(severance).*	0 0 30	0 1 0	—	0 1 0
21	Edward Gallagher, .	Same, .	Land *(severance),*	0 1 20	0 3 0	—	0 3 0
			Total, .	99 2 19	58 19 0	20 10 0	79 9 0
	CREEVYKEEL. *(Ord. S. 3 & 2.)*						
1 a	Patrick Frehely, sen.,	Viscount Palmerston, .	Land and house,	4 0 17	2 7 0	0 10 0	2 17 0
— b	Patrick Mullany,	Same, .	Land,	0 2 0	0 7 0	—	0 7 0
2 a	John Gallagher,	Same, .	Land and house,	4 0 35	2 10 0	0 10 0	3 0 0
3 a	Denis M'Cannon,	Same, .	Land and office,	3 1 25	2 5 0	0 5 0	2 10 0
4 a	Michael Christal,	Same, .	Land and house,	2 2 10	1 12 0	0 8 0	2 0 0
5 a	Phelim Gallagher,	Same, .	Land and office,	2 3 5	1 17 0	0 3 0	} 4 15 0
6 a			Land and house,	3 3 33	1 15 0	1 0 0	
5 b	Patrick Gallagher,	Same, .	House,	—		0 7 0	0 7 0
7	Patrick Gallagher,	Same, .	Land,	3 1 20	2 8 0	—	2 8 0
8 a	Mary Nealis, .	Same, .	Land and house,	4 0 19	2 17 0	0 8 0	3 5 0
— b	William Connelly,	Same, .	House,	—		0 8 0	0 8 0
9	William Connelly,	Same, .	Land,	4 2 38	3 7 0	—	3 7 0
10 a	John Hannon, . .	Same, .	Land and house,	15 1 22	10 15 0	2 0 0	} 16 5 0
11			Land,	8 1 36	3 10 0	—	
12 a	Denis Gilmartin,	Same, .	Land and house,	8 3 36	6 0 0	0 10 0	6 10 0
13 a	Anne M'Garrigle,	Same, .	Land and house,	4 3 4	3 0 0	0 15 0	3 15 0
14 a	Malachy Henly, .	Same, .	Land and house,	3 0 22	1 10 0	0 15 0	2 5 0
15 a	Francis M'Sharry,	Same, .	Land and house,	3 1 20	2 5 0	0 15 0	3 0 0
16 a	William Nicholson,	Same, .	Land and house,	3 3 0	2 15 0	0 15 0	3 10 0
17 a	Michael Gunnigle,	Same, .	Land and house,	4 1 2	3 5 0	0 15 0	4 0 0
18 a	Bryan Meehan, .	Same, .	Land and house,	3 0 34	2 8 0	0 12 0	3 0 0
19 a	Thomas Loughlin,	Same, .	Land and house,	3 2 12	2 15 0	0 15 0	3 10 0
20 a	Michael Rooney,	Same, .	Land and house,	3 1 14	2 10 0	0 10 0	3 0 0
21 a	Hugh O'Neill, .	Same, .	Land, house, and office,	30 2 27	18 0 0	1 0 0	19 0 0
22 a	Roger Connolly,	Same, .	Land and house,	12 0 20	7 0 0	1 0 0	8 0 0
23 a	John Gilmartin,	Same, .	Land and house,	3 2 15	2 17 0	0 8 0	} 5 5 0
24			Land, .	6 1 20	2 0 0	—	
25 a	James O'Hara, .	Same, .	Land and house,	0 2 10	0 6 0	0 9 0	0 15 0
26 a	Andrew Rourke,	Same, .	Land and house,	1 1 10	0 15 0	0 15 0	1 10 0
27 a	John Connolly, .	Same, .	Land and house,	1 0 20	0 12 0	0 15 0	} 2 10 0
28			Land, .	4 1 35	1 3 0	—	
29 a	Patrick M'Loughlin,	Same, .	Land and house,	3 1 15	2 15 0	0 15 0	3 10 0
30 a	Patrick Leonard,	Same, .	Land and house,	3 3 27	3 0 0	0 15 0	} 5 15 0
31			Land, .	7 0 12	2 0 0	—	
32 a	John Leonard, jun.,	Same, .	Land and house,	8 3 10	4 15 0	0 15 0	5 10 0
33 a	Mary Meehan, .	Same, .	Land and house,	6 0 4	2 15 0	0 15 0	3 10 0
34	John Leonard (*Waters*),	Same, .	Land, .	2 1 24	1 0 0	—	1 0 0
35 a	Daniel M'Hugh,	Same, .	Land and house,	6 2 10	2 5 0	0 10 0	2 15 0
36 a	Francis O'Neill, .	Same, .	Land and house,	6 0 34	0 12 0	0 3 0	0 15 0

PARISH OF AHAMLISH.

No. and Letters of Reference to Map.	Townlands and Occupiers.	Immediate Lessors.	Description of Tenement.	Area. A. R. P.	Rateable Annual Valuation. Land. £ s. d.	Buildings. £ s. d.	Total Annual Valuation of Rateable Property. £ s. d.
	CREEVYMORE— *continued.*						
34	Robert Mahon, .	Viscount Palmerston, .	Land, . . .	13 2 10	3 10 0	—	3 10 0
— a	Michael Loughlin, jun.,	Same, .	Land (*severance*),	0 0 15	0 1 0	—	0 1 0
35 a	John Commons, .	Same, .	Land and house,	4 0 12	0 12 0	0 8 0	1 0 0
36 a	Phelim Gallagher, .	Same, .	Land and house,	8 0 12	1 0 0	0 5 0	1 5 0
37 a } 38	Francis Dunleavy, .	Same, .	Land, house, & office, {	13 2 20 18 3 22	5 10 0 3 5 0	1 0 0	} 9 15 0
39 a	Patrick O'Neill, .	Same, .	Land and house,	6 3 30	2 10 0	0 10 0	3 0 0
40 a	John M'Cannon, .	Same, .	Land and house,	6 3 7	2 10 0	0 10 0	3 0 0
41 a	James M'Cannon, .	Same, .	Land, house, and office,	6 3 11	2 10 0	0 15 0	3 5 0
42 a	James Mullany, .	Same, .	Land and house,	6 2 26	2 8 0	0 12 0	3 0 0
— b	Denis M'Cannon, .	Same, .	Land (*severance*),	0 0 20	0 1 0	—	0 1 0
43 a	Daniel Harrison, .	Same, .	Land and house,	6 3 25	2 15 0	0 15 0	3 10 0
44 a	Michael Oates, .	Same, .	Land and house,	6 0 31	2 5 0	0 10 0	2 15 0
45 a	Patrick Hargiden, .	Same, .	Land and house,	2 3 37	1 2 0	0 8 0	1 10 0
46 a	Hugh Farrell, .	Same, .	Land and house,	7 3 34	3 5 0	0 10 0	3 15 0
47 a } 48	Hugh Gilmartin, .	Same, . {	Land and house, Land, . .	10 0 20 9 0 10	4 0 0 1 10 0	1 0 0	} 6 10 0
49 a	Thomas Hennigan, .	Same, .	Land and house,	15 2 27	5 10 0	0 10 0	6 0 0
50 a	Terence Roneen, .	Same, .	Land and house,	3 3 0	0 7 0	0 3 0	0 10 0
51 a	Bryan Roneen, .	Same, .	Land and house,	3 1 20	0 7 0	0 5 0	0 12 0
52 a	Francis Gilgar, .	Same, .	Land and house,	5 3 10	0 12 0	0 3 0	0 15 0
53 a	James M'Canty, .	Same, .	Land and house,	2 1 0	0 3 0	0 2 0	0 5 0
54	Michael M'Cabe, .	Same, .	Land, . .	2 0 10	0 7 0	—	0 7 0
55 a } 56 57 58	Viscount Palmerston, .	In fee, . . {	Land, agriculturist's house, and offices,	16 1 39 3 3 0 20 3 38 71 2 6	16 0 0 0 5 0 0 5 0 0 15 0	8 10 0	} 25 15 0
59	Patrick Harrison, .	Viscount Palmerston, .	Land, . .	1 0 30	0 5 0	—	0 5 0
60	Daniel Gallagher, .	Same, .	Land, . .	1 0 10	0 5 0	—	0 5 0
61 a	Martin Warnick, .	Same, .	Land and house,	7 2 0	2 10 0	0 10 0	3 0 0
62 a	Mary Wemys, .	Same, .	Land and house,	33 0 20	9 15 0	1 0 0	10 15 0
63	. . . .	. . .	Cloonty Lough (*pt. of*),	18 2 31	—	—	—
			Total, .	598 3 33	215 18 0	47 4 0	263 2 0
	MULLAGHMORE. (*Ord. S. 2 & 3.*)						
1 a	Alexander Lockhart, .	Viscount Palmerston, .	Land, house, and offices,	56 1 27	28 0 0	4 0 0	32 0 0
2 a	Patrick Gunnigle, .	Same, .	Land and house,	2 2 10	1 10 0	0 10 0	2 0 0
3 a	Anne Clinton, .	Same, .	Land and house,	1 2 30	1 0 0	0 10 0	1 10 0
4 a	Edward Gilmartin, .	Same, .	Land and house,	8 0 24	4 15 0	0 15 0	5 10 0
5	John Gilmartin, .	Same, .	Land, . .	2 0 30	1 5 0	—	1 5 0
6 a	Patrick Gilmartin, .	Same, .	Land and house,	2 2 20	1 10 0	0 10 0	2 0 0
7 a	Mary M'Gowan, .	Same, .	Land and house,	2 3 15	1 10 0	0 5 0	1 15 0
8 a	John M'Hugh, .	Same, .	Land and house,	1 3 30	1 2 0	0 8 0	1 10 0
9 a	Michael Bruen, .	Same, .	Land and house,	2 2 5	1 2 0	0 8 0	1 10 0
10 a	Viscount Palmerston, .	In fee, .	Land and office,	780 2 38	102 10 0	1 10 0	104 0 0
— b	John Donohoe, .	Viscount Palmerston, .	House & small garden,	—	—	0 10 0	0 10 0
— c	Thomas Donohoe, .	Same, .	House, .	—	—	0 10 0	0 10 0
11	John Lynch, .	Same, .	Land, .	17 2 38	3 15 0	—	3 15 0
12	Thady Hargidan, .	Same, .	Land, .	2 1 30	0 10 0	—	0 10 0
13	Bryan M'Loughlin, .	Same, .	Land, .	4 2 0	1 0 0	—	1 0 0
			Total, .	886 1 17	149 9 0	9 16 0	159 5 0
	CASTLEGAL. (*Ord. S. 3.*)						
1 a	Connor Higgins, .	Viscount Palmerston,	Land and house,	10 0 0	3 15 0	0 15 0	4 10 0
2 a	Michael Higgins, .	Same, .	Land and house,	11 0 21	4 10 0	1 0 0	5 10 0
3 a	Mary Higgins (*John*),	Same, .	Land and house,	10 0 11	4 0 0	0 10 0	4 10 0
4 a	Mary Higgins (*Wm.*),	Same, .	Land and house,	9 3 28	4 0 0	0 10 0	4 10 0
5	Peter M'Hugh, .	Same, .	Land and house,	8 2 30	3 5 0	0 10 0	3 15 0
6 a	Margaret M'Sharry, .	Same, .	Land and house,	14 2 27	5 15 0	0 15 0	6 10 0
7 a	James M'Cormack, .	Same, .	Land and house,	8 2 5	2 15 0	0 15 0	3 10 0
8 a	Michael Burke, .	Same, .	Land and house,	16 0 15	4 15 0	0 10 0	5 5 0
9 a	Bryan Higgins, (*Tim*),	Same, .	Land and house,	18 3 1	5 10 0	0 15 0	6 5 0
10 a	Patrick Higgins, .	Same, .	Land and house,	14 1 23	4 0 0	0 15 0	4 15 0
11 a	James Burke, .	Same, .	Land and house,	10 1 35	3 0 0	0 10 0	3 10 0
12 13 a }	Timothy Connolly, .	Same, . {	Land, . . Land and house,	13 2 1 5 0 25	3 15 0 2 15 0	0 15 0	} 7 5 0
14 a	Bryan Higgins (*Pat.*),	Same, .	Land and house,	36 0 2	4 5 0	0 10 0	4 15 0

PARISH OF AHAMLISH.

No. and Letters of Reference to Map.		Names.		Description of Tenement.	Area.			Rateable Annual Valuation.		Total Annual Valuation of Rateable Property.
		Townlands and Occupiers.	Immediate Lessors.					Land.	Buildings.	
					A.	R.	P.	£ s. d.	£ s. d.	£ s. d.
		GRELLAGH— *continued.*								
23	a	Charles M'Gowan,	Viscount Palmerston,	Land and house,	8	0	30	4 5 0	0 10 0	4 15 0
24					55	1	5	8 10 0	—	
25		Viscount Palmerston,	In fee,	Land (*plantation*),	4	1	6	1 0 0	—	10 0 0
26					3	3	19	0 10 0	—	
27	a	Patrick Gilmartin,	Viscount Palmerston,	Land and house,	7	1	0	2 15 0	1 0 0	4 15 0
28				Land,	3	1	29	1 0 0	—	
29	a	Thomas Gilmartin,	Same,	Land and house,	14	3	30	5 0 0	0 15 0	5 15 0
30	a	Ellen Oates,	Same,	Land and house,	1	1	10	0 10 0	0 5 0	0 15 0
31	a	Patrick Gibbons,	Same,	Land and house,	3	2	5	1 5 0	0 5 0	1 10 0
		Bartholomew Burke,	Same,	Land,	2	0	20	0 10 0	—	0 10 0
				Total,	418	0	13	126 0 0	16 5 0	142 5 0
		ADJOINING TOWNLAND OF GRELLAGH.								
		Hugh M'Intire,	Viscount Palmerston,	Salmon fishery,	—			—	—	10 0 0
		BALLINCASTLE. (Ord. S. 2.)								
		Matthias Leonard,	Viscount Palmerston,	Land,	1	2	10	1 10 0	—	1 10 0
	a	Patk. M'Intire, sen.,	Same,	Land and house,	40	3	2	13 0 0	1 0 0	14 0 0
	b	Michael M'Intire,	Same,	Land and house,				13 0 0	1 0 0	14 0 0
	c	Patrick M'Intire, jun.,	Same,	House & small garden,	—				1 0 0	1 0 0
		Patrick M'Intire, jun.,	Same,	Land,	8	1	8	3 5 0	—	3 5 0
	c	Phelim O'Neill,	Same,	Land and house,	7	1	28	2 0 0	0 15 0	2 15 0
		James Langan,	Same,	Land,	3	3	13	0 10 0	—	0 10 0
	a	Eliza Garrahy,	Same,	Garden,	0	0	24	0 1 0	—	0 1 0
		Roger Gilgan,	Same,	Land,	6	3	14	1 5 0	—	1 5 0
	a	Robert Moore,	Same,	House,	—				0 5 0	0 5 0
		Edward Gillespy,	Same,	Land,	8	2	27	1 10 0	—	1 10 0
		Catherine Gillespy,	Same,	Land,	8	1	37	1 10 0	—	1 10 0
		John Costello,	Same,	Land,	5	2	0	0 15 0	—	0 15 0
		Denis Kelly,	Same,	Land,	5	3	2	1 0 0	—	1 0 0
		John White,	Same,	Land,	5	1	0	1 0 0	—	1 0 0
		Patrick Waters,	Same,	Land,	5	0	22	0 10 0	—	0 10 0
		Patrick Feeny,	Same,	Land,	7	3	34	0 15 0	—	0 15 0
		Viscount Palmerston,	In fee,	Land (*bog*),	25	2	10	0 5 0	—	0 5 0
				Total,	141	0	31	41 16 0	4 0 0	45 16 0
		BALLYNABROCK. (Ord. S. 2.)								
1	a	Patrick Waters,	Viscount Palmerston,	Land and house,	12	1	22	2 10 0	0 10 0	3 0 0
		James Waters,		Land,				3 15 0	—	3 15 0
2	a	Mary Loughlin,	Same,	Land and house,	5	0	35	2 12 0	0 18 0	3 10 0
3	a	Mary Gilgar,	Same,	Land and house,	12	2	15	6 10 0	0 15 0	7 5 0
4	a	John M'Morrow,	Same,	Land and house,	8	1	9	4 0 0	0 15 0	4 15 0
5				Land,	3	3	28	2 2 0	—	4 5 0
6	a	Michael Timmony,	Same,	Land and house,	0	3	0	0 13 0	1 10 0	
7	a	Patrick Commons,	Same,	Land and house,	5	0	4	2 15 0	1 0 0	3 15 0
8	a	Manus Conway,	Same,	Land and house,	5	0	2	2 15 0	0 15 0	3 10 0
9	a	George Conway,	Same,	Land and house,	2	3	16	1 15 0	1 0 0	2 15 0
10	a	Anthony Timmony,	Same,	Land and house,	2	1	0	1 15 0	1 5 0	3 0 0
11	a	John Leydon,	Same,	Land and house,	1	0	37	1 0 0	1 0 0	2 0 0
12		Patrick Commins,	Same,	Land,	0	1	20	0 5 0	—	0 5 0
13	a	Andrew M'Loughlin,	Same,	Land and house,	4	0	33	2 10 0	0 10 0	3 0 0
				Total,	64	0	21	34 17 0	9 18 0	44 15 0
		EDENREAGH. (Ord. S. 2.)								
1	a	Bryan Feeny,	Viscount Palmerston,	Land and house,	4	0	20	2 0 0	0 5 0	2 5 0
2	a	James Gardiner,	Same,	Land and house,	13	2	10	6 18 0	0 12 0	7 10 0
3		William Gillespy,	Same,	Land,	10	3	34	2 10 0	—	2 10 0
4		Roger Finnigan,	Same,	Land,	7	1	11	1 15 0	—	7 0 0
5	a			Land and house,	9	2	25	4 15 0	0 10 0	
6		Patrick Gunnigle,	Same,	Land,	6	2	37	2 0 0	—	6 10 0
7	a			Land and house,	7	2	30	3 15 0	0 15 0	
8		Malachy Conway,	Same,	Land,	8	1	26	2 10 0	—	6 5 0
9	a			Land, house, and office,	5	2	0	2 15 0	1 0 0	

PARISH OF AHAMLISH.

No. and Letters of Reference to Map.	Names.		Description of Tenement.	Area.			Rateable Annual Valuation.						Total Annual Valuation of Rateable Property.		
	Townlands and Occupiers.	Immediate Lessors.					Land.			Buildings.					
				A.	R.	P.	£	s.	d.	£	s.	d.	£	s.	d.
	EDENREAGH— *continued.*														
10	a	James Conway, .	Viscount Palmerston,	Land and house,	10	0	10	4	15	0	0	15	0	5	10	0
11	a	John Gallagher,	Same,	Land and house,	5	0	37	1	10	0	0	5	0	1	15	0
12	a	Michael Horkin,	Same,	Land and house,	4	2	36	1	10	0	0	10	0	2	0	0
13	a	John Horkin,	Same,	Land and house.	5	2	10	2	0	0	0	10	0	2	10	0
14	a	Michael Burne,	Same,	Land and house,	12	3	4	5	10	0	0	15	0	6	5	0
15	}	Viscount Palmerston,	In fee, . .	Land (bog),	14	0	15	0	5	0	—			} 5	5	0
16				Land (sand-hills),	99	3	37	5	0	0						
17	a	Patrick M'Gowan, .	Viscount Palmerston,	Land and house,	4	3	30	2	10	0	0	10	0	3	0	0
18	a	James M'Gowan, .	Same,	Land and house,	7	1	0	3	10	0	0	10	0	4	0	0
19	a	Thomas Finnigan,	Same,	Land and office,	8	0	15	2	10	0	0	5	0	2	15	0
				Total, .	246	2	27	57	18	0	7	2	0	65	0	0
	MULLAGHMORE, WEST. (Ord. S. 2.)														
1	Viscount Palmerston,	In fee, ...	Land, . .	133	3	1	6	10	0	—			6	10	0
				Total, .	133	3	1	6	10	0	—			6	10	0
	NEWTOWNCLIF- FONY. (Ord. S. 2.)														
1	a	Viscount Palmerston,	In fee, . .	Land and herd's house,	28	2	29	2	15	0	0	15	0	3	10	0
2	} a	James Gilmartin,	Viscount Palmerston, {	Land, .	6	3	21	3	10	0	—			} 9	5	0
3	a }			Land and house,	9	2	17	4	15	0	1	0	0			
4	a	William Gillespy, .	Same,	Land and house,	0	3	13	0	8	0	0	17	0	1	5	0
5	a	Catherine Gillespy, .	Same,	Land and house,	2	0	6	1	0	0	1	0	0	2	0	0
6	a }	Mary Gillespy, .	Same,	Land and house,	8	0	37	4	5	0	0	15	0	} 6	0	0
7				Land, .	2	0	26	1	0	0	—					
8	a	Daniel Conway,	Same,	Land and house,	4	0	5	2	5	0	0	15	0	3	0	0
9	a	Edward Gillespy, jun.,	Same,	Land and house,	5	2	20	2	10	0	1	0	0	3	10	0
10	a	Andrew Gillespy,	Same,	Land and house,	15	2	28	7	15	0	1	0	0	8	15	0
11	a	John Gallagher,	Same,	Land and house,	3	3	0	2	0	0	1	0	0	3	0	0
12	a	Edward Gillespy,	Same,	Land and house,	6	1	33	3	10	0	1	0	0	4	10	0
13	a	Patrick Cullen,	Same,	Land and house.	7	3	27	3	15	0	0	15	0	4	10	0
14		Patrick Conway,	Same,	Land, . .	3	1	8	1	10	0	—			1	10	0
				Total, .	105	0	30	40	18	0	9	17	0	50	15	0
	ISLANDS. No. 1, INISHMURRAY ISLAND. (Ord. S. 1.)														
1	{ a	John Waters, .	Viscount Palmerston, {	Land and house,	57	1	0	8	0	0	0	15	0	8	15	0
	{ b	Martin Heraghty,		Land and house,				4	0	0	0	10	0	4	10	0
2	{ a	James Heraghty,	Same, .	Land and house,	49	2	10	7	2	0	0	8	0	7	10	0
	{ b	Henry Hart, .		Land and house,				2	7	0	0	3	0	2	10	0
3	{ a	John Boyle, .	Same, .	Land and house,	45	0	26	5	2	0	0	8	0	5	10	0
	{ b	Bridget Brady, .		Land and house,				3	8	0	0	7	0	3	15	0
4	{	Bridget Brady, .	Same, .	Land, . . .	38	0	5	0	15	0	—			0	15	0
	{	Patrick Brady, .						1	2	0	—			1	2	0
	{	Thomas Hoy, .						1	3	0	—			1	3	0
	{	William Brady, .						0	15	0	—			0	15	0
	{	Bridget Heraghty,						0	15	0	—			0	15	0
5	{ a	Bridget Heraghty,	Same, .	Land and house,	19	0	2	0	15	0	0	2	0	0	17	0
	{ b	William Brady, .		Land and house,				0	15	0	0	2	0	0	17	0
	{ c	Thomas Hoy, .		Land and house,				1	10	0	0	5	0	1	15	0
	{	Patrick Brady, .		Land, . .				1	10	0	—			1	10	0
—		John Waters and the other Tenants of this Townland, . .	Same, .	Right of seaweed,	—			—			—			10	0	0
				Total, .	209	0	5	38	19	0	3	0	0	51	19	0
	No. 2, CONOR'S ISLAND. (Ord. S. 2 & 5.)														
1	a	James O'Connor, .	Ormsby Jones, . {	Land, house, and office,	111	0	30	21	0	0	1	0	0	22	0	0
				Right of seaweed,	—			—			—			20	0	0
				Total, .	111	0	30	21	0	0	1	0	0	42	0	0

PARISH OF AHAMLISH.

No. of Ref. to map	Letters of Reference to map	Names. Townlands and Occupiers.	Immediate Lessors.	Description of Tenement.	Area. A. R. P.	Rateable Annual Valuation. Land. £ s. d.	Buildings. £ s. d.	Total Annual Valuation of Rateable Property. £ s. d.
		ISLANDS—*continued.* No. 3, DERNISH ISLAND. (Ord S. 2.)						
1				Land,	11 1 13	4 5 0	—	
2	a	John Gillen, . .	Viscount Palmerston,	Land and house,	0 3 10	0 10 0	1 0 0	5 15 0
—				Right of seaweed,	—	—		4 0 0
3				Land, . .	5 0 0	2 10 0	—	
4		Margaret Gillen, .	Same, .	Land, . .	5 0 0	2 5 0	—	4 15 0
—				Right of seaweed,	—	—		4 0 0
5				Land, . .	5 0 0	2 5 0	—	
6	a	Peter Mulligan, .	Same, .	Land, house, and office,	5 0 20	3 0 0	2 5 0	7 10 0
—				Right of seaweed,	—	—		4 0 0
7		Viscount Palmerston,	In fee, .	Land (*plantation*),	19 0 15	5 15 0	—	5 15 0
—	a	Margaret Gillen, .	Viscount Palmerston,	Garden, house, & office,	0 0 33	0 3 0	0 12 0	0 15 0
8		John Gillen. . William Mulligan, Margaret Gillen, James Mulligan, Peter Mulligan, . Michael Gillen, .	Same, .	Land, . .	3 2 32	0 2 0 0 2 0 0 2 0 0 2 0 0 2 0 0 2 0	— — — — — —	0 2 0 0 2 0 0 2 0 0 2 0 0 2 0 0 2 0
9		John Gillen. . William Mulligan, Margaret Gillen, James Mulligan, Peter Mulligan, . Michael Gillen, .	Same, .	Land, . .	9 1 23	0 4 0 0 4 0 0 4 0 0 4 0 0 4 0 0 4 0	— — — — — —	0 4 0 0 4 0 0 4 0 0 4 0 0 4 0 0 4 0
10	a			Land, house, and office,	4 2 10	1 15 0	1 5 0	
11		William Mulligan, .	Same, .	Land, . .	5 3 0	2 10 0	—	5 10 0
—				Right of seaweed,	—	—		4 0 0
12	a			Land and house,	5 2 30	2 10 0	0 5 0	
13		James Mulligan, .	Same, .	Land, . .	6 3 0	4 0 0		6 15 0
—				Right of seaweed,	—	—		4 0 0
14	a	Michael Gillen, . .	Same, .	Land, house, and office,	10 3 30	6 5 0	2 5 0	8 10 0
—				Right of seaweed,	—	—		4 0 0
				Total, .	103 1 16	39 9 0	7 12 0	71 1 0
		CLOYSPARRA. (Ord. S. 2 & 5.)						
1		Viscount Palmerston,	In fee, .	Land (*sand-hills*),	11 2 8	0 15 0	—	1 0 0
2				Land (*bog*),	13 0 21	0 5 0	—	
3	a	Thomas Finnigan,	Viscount Palmerston,	Land and house,	20 1 8	11 5 0	0 15 0	12 0 0
4	a	Matthew M'Hugh,	Same, .	Land and house,	13 3 13	5 10 0	0 15 0	6 5 0
5	a	John M'Hugh, .	Matthew M'Hugh,	Land and house,	2 3 35	1 5 0	0 5 0	2 5 0
6					5 0 0	0 15 0		
7	a	Peter Waters, .	Viscount Palmerston,	Land and house,	28 0 25	11 0 0	1 0 0	12 0 0
8	a	Luke Gilmartin,	Same, .	Land and house,	22 3 36	3 0 0	0 10 0	3 10 0
	b	Daniel Gilmartin,	Same, .	Land and house,		3 0 0	0 10 0	3 10 0
9		James Evans,	Same, .	Land and house,	5 0 20	1 2 0	0 3 0	1 5 0
10		Patrick Finnigan,	Same, .	Land, .	4 1 20	0 5 0	—	0 5 0
—	a	John Finnigan, .	Same, .	Land (*severance*),	0 0 20	—	—	
11	a	Cormack Waters,	Same, .	Land and house,	7 2 16	4 0 0	0 15 0	4 15 0
12	a	Henry Gallagher,	Same, .	Land and house,	19 0 25	8 0 0	1 0 0	9 0 0
13		John O'Neill, .	Same, .	Land, .	9 2 8	3 15 0	—	3 15 0
14	a	Terence Waters, jun.,	Same, .	Land and house,	11 2 12	3 5 0	0 10 0	3 15 0
15	a	Phelim Gallagher,	Same, .	Land and house,	8 2 10	4 0 0	0 15 0	4 15 0
16	a	Terence Waters, sen.,	Same, .	Land and house,	18 3 36	9 5 0	0 15 0	10 0 0
				Total, .	202 3 33	70 7 0	7 13 0	78 0 0
		DRUMFAD. (Ord. S. 5, 6, 2, & 3.)						
1	a b	Luke Gilmartin, John Gilmartin,	Viscount Palmerston,	Land and house, Land and house,	22 0 12	5 13 0 2 17 0	0 12 0 0 8 0	6 5 0 3 5 0
2	a	John Moffit, .	Same, .	Land and house,	5 3 1	2 10 0	0 10 0	3 0 0
3	a	Patrick Moffit, jun.,	Same, .	Land and house,	19 2 5	9 10 0	0 15 0	10 5 0
4	a	Michael Gilmartin, .	Same, .	Land and house,	6 3 2	3 5 0	0 15 0	4 0 0
5	a	Peter Gilmartin, .	Same, .	Land and house,	9 1 12	3 15 0	0 15 0	4 10 0
6	a	Anne Feeny, .	Same, .	Land and house,	4 2 9	1 13 0	0 12 0	2 5 0
7 8	a	Patrick Gilmartin, jun.	Same, .	Land and house, Land, . .	4 2 0 1 2 30	1 12 0 1 0 0	1 0 0	3 12 0

PARISH OF AHAMLISH.

No. and Letters of Reference to Map.		Names.		Description of Tenement.	Area.			Rateable Annual Valuation.		Total Annual Valuation of Rateable Property.
		Townlands and Occupiers.	Immediate Lessors.					Land.	Buildings.	

		Names	Lessors	Description	A.	R.	P.	£ s. d.	£ s. d.	£ s. d.
		DRUMFAD— *continued.*								
9	a	Mary Gilmartin,	Viscount Palmerston,	Land and house,	14	3	4	7 10 0	1 0 0	8 10 0
10	a	Mary Healy,	Same,	Land and house,	4	3	15	2 10 0	0 15 0	5 15 0
11			Same,	Land,	·5	1	26	2 10 0	—	
12	a	Patrick Moore,	Same,	Land and house,	9	2	10	4 5 0	0 10 0	4 15 0
13	a	Bryan Hargiden,	Same,	Land and house,	9	0	10	4 0 0	0 10 0	4 10 0
14	a	Patrick Kelly,	Same,	Land and house,	11	0	32	3 15 0	0 10 0	4 5 0
15		James Horan,	Same,	Land,	1	1	0	0 15 0	—	4 10 0
16	a			Land and house,	18	0	0	3 10 0	0 5 0	
17	a	Patrick Gilmartin, sen.	Same,	Land and house,	16	0	20	7 15 0	0 15 0	8 10 0
18	a	James Moore, Sr	Same,	Land and house,	11	2	30	4 5 0	0 10 0	4 15 0
19	a	William Nicholson,	Same,	Land and house,	25	2	39	6 15 0	0 15 0	7 10 0
20	a	Denis Kerigan,	Same,	Land and house,	15	0	10	3 13 0	0 12 0	4 5 0
21	a	John Finnigan,	Same,	Land and herd's house,	36	2	35	11 0 0	0 5 0	11 5 0
—	b	Patrick Finnigan,	Same,	Land (bog),	1	1	20	—	—	—
22	a	John Gilmartin, jun.,	Same,	Land and house,	45	2	6	8 10 0	1 5 0	9 15 0
23	a	Mary Bower,	Same,	Land and house,	1	0	35	0 12 0	0 8 0	1 0 0
24	a	Patk. Gilmartin (John),	Same,	Land and house,	25	0	30	3 5 0	0 10 0	3 15 0
25	a	Patrick Finnigan,	Same,	Land and house,	14	0	39	2 5 0	0 10 0	2 15 0
	b	Francis Commons,						1 15 0	0 10 0	2 5 0
26	a	Hugh Gaffney,	Same,	Land and house,	1	2	30	0 7 0	0 3 0	0 10 0
27	a	Patrick M'Gowan,	Same,	Land and house,	23	3	30	2 15 0	0 15 0	3 10 0
28	a	Patrick Higgins,	Same,	Land and house,	25	1	32	3 5 0	0 10 0	3 15 0
29	a	Thomas Moore,	Same,	Land and house,	18	0	20	2 5 0	0 15 0	5 15 0
30			Same,	Land,	37	0	22	2 15 0		
31		Viscount Palmerston,	In fee,	Land (bog),	125	2	6	0 10 0	—	0 10 0
		Martin M'Garrahy,	Same,	Land (severance),	0	2	30	0 2 0	—	0 3 0
32		Patrick M'Garrahy,	Viscount Palmerston,	Land (severance),	1	0	10	0 7 0	—	0 3 0
33		James M'Garrahy,	Same,	Land (severance),					—	0 3 0
34		Patrick Gilmartin, jun.	Same,	Land (severance),	1	2	20	0 9 0	—	0 9 0
35		Peter Feeny,	Same,	Land,	2	0	20	0 5 0	—	0 5 0
36		Hugh Prior,	Same,	Land,	2	3	20	0 5 0	—	0 5 0
37	a	Patrick Moffit, sen.,	Same,	Land and house,	10	1	18	4 10 0	0 15 0	5 5 0
38	a	Martin Healy,	Same,	Land and house,	9	3	2	4 5 0	0 15 0	5 0 0
39	a	Peter M'Cann,	Same,	Land and house,	19	2	2	6 0 0	1 0 0	7 0 0
40	a	John Gilmartin sen.,	Same,	Land and house,	19	3	2	3 0 0	0 15 0	3 15 0
				Total,	640	3	25	141 5 0	20 5 0	161 10 0
		MOUNT TEMPLE. *(Ord. S. 5 & 2.)*								
1	a	John O'Neill,	Viscount Palmerston,	Land and house,	6	1	11	3 10 0	0 15 0	4 5 0
2		Matthew M'Hugh,	Same,	Land,	2	1	20	1 5 0	—	1 5 0
3	a	Thomas M'Cann,	Same,	Land and house,	5	2	31	3 5 0	0 15 0	4 0 0
4	a	Arthur Sweeny,	Same,	Land and house,	6	3	12	3 10 0	0 18 0	5 0 0
5			Same,	Land,	1	3	20	0 12 0	—	
6	a	Daniel Conway,	Same,	Land and house,	17	1	10	9 15 0	1 0 0	10 15 0
7	a	Thomas Langan,	Same,	Land and house,	15	1	6	7 10 0	0 15 0	8 5 0
8		John Gunnigle,	Same,	Land,	12	1	10	3 0 0	—	7 10 0
9	a			Land and house,	5	3	11	3 10 0	1 0 0	
10	a	Bridget Conway,	Same,	Land and house,	6	1	28	3 10 0	0 15 0	5 5 0
11			Same,	Land,	3	2	20	1 0 0	—	
12	a	Bryan Conway,	Same,	Land and house,	6	3	2	3 15 0	0 15 0	5 10 0
13			Same,	Land,	3	2	0	1 0 0	—	
	a	Cornick Gilmartin,		Land and house,				6 10 0	1 0 0	7 10 0
	b	John Finnigan, sen.,		Land and office,				2 10 0	0 5 0	2 15 0
	c	Phelim Gallagher,		Land and house,				2 0 0	0 10 0	2 10 0
	d	Patrick Gillen,		Land and house,				1 10 0	0 10 0	2 0 0
	e	Bridget Martin,		Land and house,				1 13 0	0 7 0	2 0 0
	f	Owen M'Gann,		Land and house,				0 10 0	0 10 0	1 0 0
	g	Thomas M'Gann,		Land and house,				1 0 0	0 10 0	1 10 0
	h	Catherine Finnigan,		Land and house,				2 6 0	0 9 0	2 15 0
14	i	Winifred Judge,	Same,	Land and house,	103	3	31	2 7 0	0 8 0	2 15 0
	j	James Quinn,		Land and house,				1 7 0	0 8 0	1 15 0
	k	Patrick Finnigan,		Land and house,				3 0 0	0 15 0	3 15 0
	l	John Finnigan, jun.,		Land, house, & office,				10 12 0	1 13 0	12 5 0
	m	Patrick Feeny,		Land and house,				6 10 0	0 15 0	7 5 0
	n	Bridget Finnigan,		Land and house,				2 5 0	1 0 0	3 5 0
	o	Patk. Finnigan, sen.,		Land and house,				3 5 0	2 0 0	5 5 0

PARISH OF AHAMLISH.

No. and Letters of Reference to Map.	Townlands and Occupiers.	Immediate Lessors.	Description of Tenement.	Area. A. R. P.	Rateable Annual Valuation. Land. £ s. d.	Rateable Annual Valuation. Buildings. £ s. d.	Total Annual Valuation of Rateable Property. £ s. d.
	MOUNT TEMPLE— *continued.*						
p {	Peter M'Gann,		Land and house, }		3 0 0	0 10 0	3 10 0
	John Gillin,		Land, }		1 10 0	—	1 10 0
	James M'Garrigle,		Land, }		2 5 0	—	2 5 0
— q	Dolly Judge,	Free,	Garden and house,	0 0 16	0 2 0	0 3 0	0 5 0
— r	Bridget Commins,	Free,	House,		—	0 3 0	0 3 0
— s	Honoria Fox,	Free,	House,		—	0 3 0	0 3 0
— t	Honoria M'Gann,	Viscount Palmerston,	House,		—	0 15 0	0 15 0
— u	Unoccupied,	John Finnigan, jun.,	House,		—	0 5 0	0 5 0
— v	Unoccupied,	Same,	House,		—	0 5 0	0 5 0
— w	William Irwin,	Free,	House,		—	0 5 0	0 5 0
— x	Mary Tucker,	John Finnigan, sen.,	House,		—	0 5 0	0 5 0
— y	Patrick Sweeny,	Same,	House,		—	0 5 0	0 5 0
— z	Margaret Gilligan,	John Gilligan,	House,		—	0 5 0	0 5 0
— a²	Thady M'Glone,	Same,	House,		—	0 5 0	0 5 0
15	Patrick Feeny,	Viscount Palmerston,	Land,	4 1 30	3 0 0	—	3 0 0
16 a	Phelim Gallagher,	Same,	Land and house,	1 2 5	1 5 0	0 15 0	2 0 0
17 a	John Gallagher,	Same,	Land and house,	2 3 10	2 5 0	0 15 0	3 0 0
18 }	Patrick M'Gowan,	Same,	{ Land,	1 3 0	1 0 0	—	} 4 0 0
19 a }			Land and house,	3 0 14	2 0 0	1 0 0	
20 a }	Edward Parke,	Same,	{ Land, house, and office,	35 1 10	25 0 0	3 15 0	} 40 0 0
21 }			Land,	16 0 0	11 5 0	—	
22 a	James M'Sharry,	Same,	Land, house, and office,	2 0 24	1 5 0	2 5 0	3 10 0
23	Roger Finnigan,	James M'Sharry,	Land,	7 1 30	3 5 0	—	3 5 0
24 a	John M'Gowan,	Viscount Palmerston,	Land and house,	4 2 28	2 10 0	1 0 0	3 10 0
25 a	Michael M'Gowan,	Same,	Land and house,	4 0 8	2 0 0	0 15 0	2 15 0
26 a	Patrick Quinn,	Same,	Land and house,	3 2 33	2 0 0	0 10 0	2 10 0
27 a	James Mangan,	Same,	Land and house,	4 0 10	1 15 0	0 5 0	2 0 0
28 a	James M'Gowan,	Same,	Land and house,	6 3 2	4 15 0	1 0 0	5 15 0
29 a	Owen Quinn,	Same,	Land and house,	3 0 14	2 0 0	0 10 0	2 10 0
30 a	Bridget M'Gowan,	Same,	Land and house,	7 0 28	3 3 0	0 7 0	3 10 0
— b			National school-house (see Exemptions).				
		Bridget M'Gawan,	Half the annual rent derived from National school-house,		—	—	0 10 0
31	John M'Hugh,	Matthew M'Hugh,	Land,	3 2 0	1 10 0	—	1 10 0
32 a }	Denis Sweeny,	Viscount Palmerston,	{ Land and house,	7 3 23	4 0 0	1 0 0	} 5 15 0
33 }			Land,	2 0 20	0 15 0	—	
34 a	Mary Conway,	Same,	Land and house,	3 1 34	2 0 0	0 10 0	2 10 0
35 a	Charles Higgins,	Same,	Land, house, and office,	57 0 16	17 15 0	1 5 0	19 0 0
36 a	Patrick Commons,	Same,	Land and house,	20 0 3	11 15 0	1 0 0	12 15 0
37 a	John Gillin,	Same,	Land and house,	3 2 30	2 10 0	1 0 0	3 10 0
38	Viscount Palmerston,	In fee,	Land (plantation),	6 1 27	3 10 0	—	3 10 0
			Total of Rateable Property,	410 1 27	211 7 0	38 14 0	250 11 0
			EXEMPTIONS:				
30 b			National school-house,	—	—	1 0 0	1 0 0
			Total, including Exemptions,	410 1 27	211 7 0	39 14 0	251 11 0
	DERRY. (Ord. S. 5.)						
a	Michael M'Sharry,	Viscount Palmerston,	Land and house,	15 0 24	4 0 0	0 15 0	4 15 0
a	James Gillen,	Same,	Land and house,	15 0 20	6 15 0	1 0 0	7 15 0
a	John Gilmartin,	Same,	Land and house,	6 1 20	3 0 0	0 15 0	3 15 0
a	Bridget Waters,	Same,	Land and house,	15 1 34	6 10 0	0 15 0	7 5 0
5 a }	Peter M'Sharry,	Same,	{ Land and house,	13 2 30	6 0 0	0 15 0	} 12 5 0
6 }			Land,	13 1 2	5 10 0	—	
— a	James M'Gowan,	Peter M'Sharry,	House,		—	0 5 0	0 5 0
7 a	Charles Finnigan,	Viscount Palmerston,	Land and house,	19 2 0	8 0 0	0 15 0	8 15 0
8 a	Patrick Hoy,	Same,	Land and house,	10 1 10	5 15 0	0 15 0	6 10 0
9	Patrick Horkin,	Same,	Land,	7 3 14	4 5 0	—	4 5 0
10	Euphemia Munds,	Same,	Land,	50 3 24	10 15 0	—	10 15 0
	James Mulligan,	Same,	Land,	0 1 0	0 2 0	—	0 2 0
11 a	Michael Kilfeather,	Same,	Land and house,	8 3 10	4 0 0	0 15 0	4 15 0
			Total,	176 2 28	64 12 0	6 10 0	71 2 0

PARISH OF AHAMLISH.

No. and Letters of Reference to Map		Names.		Description of Tenement.	Area.	Rateable Annual Valuation.		Total Annual Valuation of Rateable Property.
		Townlands and Occupiers.	Immediate Lessors.			Land.	Buildings.	
					A. R. P.	£ s. d.	£ s. d.	£ s. d.
		KILCAT.						
		(Ord. S. 5.)	*Geo. Le Noel 1875*					
1	a	Matthew Walsh,	Viscount Palmerston,	Land, house, and offices,	100 3 34	45 0 0	5 0 0	50 0 0
2	a	John Gilmartin,	Same,	Land and office,	56 0 31	21 0 0	0 15 0	21 15 0
–	b	Francis Roony,	Same,	Land,	0 2 0	0 1 0	—	0 1 0
3	a	Patrick Kearns,	Same,	Land, house, and office,	51 1 14	17 10 0	1 0 0	18 10 0
4	a	Thomas Kearns,	Same,	Land, house, and office,	39 1 0	19 0 0	1 5 0	20 5 0
5		Thady Roony,	Same,	Land,	1 0 30	0 10 0	—	0 10 0
				Total,	249 1 29	103 1 0	8 0 0	111 1 0
		KILTYKERE.						
		(Ord. S. 5.)						
1		Matthew Leonard,	Viscount Palmerston,	Land,	10 1 0	4 0 0	—	4 0 0
2	a	Michl. Cunningham,	Same,	Land and house,	17 0 16	3 10 0	0 15 0	4 5 0
	b	Charles Gilmartin,		Land and house,		3 10 0	0 15 0	4 5 0
3	a	Mary Currid,	Same,	Land and house,	16 3 22	7 15 0	1 0 0	8 15 0
4	a	Anne Currid,	Same,	Land and house,	14 3 33	7 10 0	0 15 0	8 5 0
5	a	Patrick Kilfeather,	Same,	Land and house,	19 3 34	9 15 0	1 0 0	10 15 0
6	a	Daniel Kilfeather,	Same,	Land and house,	11 0 29	5 15 0	1 0 0	6 15 0
7	a	John Leyden,	Same,	Land and house,	18 2 6	9 0 0	1 5 0	10 5 0
8	a			Land & Nat. school-ho. (see Exemptions).				
9	a	Roger Connolly,	Viscount Palmerston,	Land and house,	17 0 34	8 5 0	1 0 0	9 5 0
10	a	Mary Connolly,	Same,	Land and house,	15 3 30	7 15 0	1 0 0	8 15 0
11		James Mulligan,	Same,	Land,	1 2 10	0 10 0	—	0 10 0
12	a	John Gilmartin,	Same,	Land, house, and offices,	14 2 37	7 5 0	1 0 0	8 5 0
–	b	James Kilfeather,	Same,	House,			0 15 0	0 15 0
13		James Kilfeather,	Same,	Land,	15 3 37	7 10 0	—	7 10 0
				Total of Rateable Property,	174 1 8	82 0 0	10 5 0	92 5 0
				Exemptions:				
8				Land & Nat. school-ho.	1 2 34	1 0 0	5 0 0	6 0 0
				Total, including Exemptions,	176 0 2	83 0 0	15 5 0	98 5 0
		MONEYGOLD.						
		(Ord. S. 5.)						
1	a	Patrick M'Glone,	Viscount Palmerston,	Land and house,	9 3 0	4 15 0	1 0 0	5 15 0
2	a	Michael Cunnane,	Same,	Land and house,	8 0 2	4 15 0	0 15 0	5 10 0
3	a	Patrick Gilmartin,	Same,	Land and house,	7 3 20	4 0 0	0 10 0	4 10 0
4	a	Bryan M'Glone,	Same,	Land and house,	4 2 10	2 15 0	0 5 0	3 0 0
5	a	Patrick Mechan,	Same,	Land and house,	5 0 20	3 10 0	0 15 0	4 5 0
6	a	Moun Foley,	Same,	Land and house,	3 2 20	2 5 0	0 5 0	2 10 0
7	a	Patrick Burns,	Same,	Land and house,	10 0 20	5 5 0	0 15 0	6 0 0
8	a	Thomas Currid,	Same,	Land and house,	3 2 10	2 5 0	0 10 0	2 15 0
9	a	Charles Costello,	Same,	Land and house,	8 2 30	3 15 0	0 15 0	4 10 0
10	a	Patrick Harrison,	Same,	Land and house,	2 3 20	1 15 0	0 10 0	2 5 0
11		— Fawcett,	Same,	Land, house, and offices,	161 3 14	135 0 0	13 0 0	148 0 0
12		Isabella Soden,	Same,	Land,	1 0 36	0 15 0	—	0 15 0
13				Church and grave-yard (see Exemptions.)				
14	a	Roger Keragan,	Viscount Palmerston,	Land and house,	7 0 30	4 15 0	0 15 0	5 10 0
15	a	John Hog.	Same,	Land and house,	5 3 10	3 10 0	1 0 0	4 10 0
16	a	James Horigan,	Same,	Land and house,	3 1 20	2 2 0	0 8 0	2 10 0
17		Bartholomew M'Glone,	Same,	Land and house,	4 0 20	2 10 0	0 15 0	3 5 0
18	a	John Currid,	Same,	Land and house,	1 2 30	1 0 0	0 10 0	1 10 0
19	a	Bartholomew Hart,	Same,	Land and house,	10 2 20	5 15 0	0 15 0	6 10 0
20	a	Patrick Leyden,	Same,	Land and house,	5 1 0	2 10 0	0 10 0	3 0 0
21	a	Eliza Burns,	Same,	Land and house,	10 0 0	4 17 0	0 8 0	5 5 0
22	a	Patrick Horkin,	Same,	Land and house,	19 1 9	7 10 0	1 0 0	8 10 0
23	a	John Gillen,	Same,	Land and house,	3 1 10	2 0 0	1 0 0	3 0 0
24	a	Thomas Currid,	Same,	Land and house,	4 0 10	2 5 0	0 10 0	2 15 0
25	a	Denis Loughlin,	Same,	Land and house,	9 0 0	4 10 0	0 10 0	5 0 0
26	a	Bernard Mohan,	Same,	Land and house,	12 0 3	6 5 0	1 0 0	7 5 0
27	a	Euphemia Munds,	Same,	Land, house, and office,	33 1 22	14 0 0	3 10 0	17 10 0
28		James M'Sharry,	Same,	Land,	17 0 17	8 0 0	—	8 0 0

PARISH OF AHAMLISH.

No. and Letters of Reference to Map.		Names.		Description of Tenement.	Area.			Rateable Annual Valuation.		Total Annual Valuation of Rateable Property.
		Townlands and Occupiers.	Immediate Lessors.					Land.	Buildings.	
					A.	R.	P.	£ s. d.	£ s. d.	£ s. d
		BALLYSCANNEL—*continued.*								
4	a	John Brennan, .	Capt. James Jones,	Land and house,	8	2	9	4 10 0	1 10 0	
4	a			Land and office,	21	2	8	12 0 0	0 5 0	19 10 0
4				Land, .	3	1	10	1 5 0	—	
46 a		Denis Mulligan,	John Brennan, .	House, .	—			—	0 5 0	0 5 0
47 b		. . . .	Captain James Jones,	National school-house (*see Exemptions*).	—			—	—	
		John Young and the other Tenants of this Townland, . .	Same, .	Right of seaweed, .	—			—	—	5 0 0
		Captain James Jones,	Charles Tottenham, .	Right of seaweed, .	—			—	—	5 0 0
				Total of Rateable Property,	423	3	11	206 19 0	22 15 0	239 14 0
				EXEMPTIONS:						
4	b	. . . .	. . . .	National school-house,	—			—	1 0 0	1 0 0
				Total, including Exemptions, .	423	3	11	206 19 0	23 15 0	240 14 0
		CLOONTYPROCK-LIS. (*Ord. S. 5.*)								
	a	James Waters, .	Viscount Palmerston,	Land and house, .	2	0	0	1 5 0	0 10 0	1 15 0
	a	James Foran, .	Same, .	Land and house, .	4	2	11	2 10 0	0 10 0	3 0 0
	a	Bridget Foran, .	Same, .	Land and house, .	2	2	20	1 10 0	0 10 0	2 0 0
	a	Patrick Gillen, .	Same, .	Land and house, .	5	0	30	2 5 0	0 15 0	3 0 0
	a	Patrick Waters, .	Same, .	Land and house, .	6	3	20	3 5 0	0 15 0	4 0 0
	a	Thomas Gillen, .	Same, .	Land and house, .	9	3	0	4 0 0	0 15 0	4 15 0
	a	Martin Waters, .	Same, .	Land and house, .	8	0	10	3 10 0	0 10 0	4 0 0
	a	Daniel Gilmartin, .	Same, .	Land and house, .	6	3	10	2 15 0	0 15 0	3 10 0
	a	Thomas Feeny, .	Same, .	Land and house, .	6	2	10	2 10 0	0 15 0	3 5 0
10	a	Roger Byrne, .	Same, .	Land and house, .	7	0	10	2 15 0	0 15 0	3 10 0
11	a	Michael Waters, .	Same, .	Land and house, .	9	1	30	4 5 0	0 10 0	4 15 0
12	a	James Currid, .	Same, .	Land and house, .	4	3	0	2 5 0	0 5 0	2 10 0
13	a	Michael Woods, .	Same, .	Land and house, .	7	1	0	3 15 0	0 15 0	4 10 0
14	a	James Devins, .	Same, .	Land and house, .	5	1	0	2 5 0	0 10 0	2 15 0
15	a	James O'Connor, .	Same, .	Land, house, and office,	10	1	20	5 5 0	1 5 0	6 10 0
—	b	George Cocheran, .	James O'Connor,	Garden, house, & office,	0	1	20	0 10 0	3 15 0	4 5 0
16	a	James Hoy, .	Viscount Palmerston,	Land and house, .	3	1	18	1 15 0	0 10 0	2 5 0
17	a	John Woods, .	Same, .	Land and house, .	5	1	10	3 5 0	0 15 0	4 0 0
18	a	Mary Horne, .	Same, .	Land and house, .	1	2	20	1 0 0	0 10 0	1 10 0
19	a	Matthew M'Sharry, .	Same, .	Land and house, .	7	0	20	5 0 0	0 15 0	5 15 0
20	a	Robert Moore, .	Same, .	Land and house, .	9	0	16	5 10 0	1 0 0	6 10 0
—	b	. . . .	. . . .	Petty Sessions-house (*see Exemptions*).						
		. . . .	Robert Moore, .	*Half the annual rent derived from Petty Sessions-house,*	—			—	—	4 0 0
				Total of Rateable Property,	123	1	35	61 0 0	17 0 0	82 0 0
				EXEMPTIONS:						
20	b	. . . .	. . . .	Petty Sessions-house,	—			—	1 0 0	1 0 0
				Total, including Exemptions,	123	1	35	61 0 0	18 0 0	83 0 0
		DRANGAN, OR MOUNT EDWARD. (*Ord. S. 5.*)								
1		John Healy, .	Captain James Jones,	Land, . .	1	3	20	1 0 0	—	1 0 0
2	a	Bartholomew Dyer, .	Same, .	Land and house, .	6	0	30	3 2 0	0 8 0	3 10 0
3	a	Patrick Currid, .	Same, .	Land and house, .	18	3	7	6 0 0	0 15 0	6 15 0
4	a	John Leonard, .	Same, .	Land and house, .	7	3	20	3 15 0	1 0 0	4 15 0
5	a	Dominick Brennan, .	Same, .	Land and office, .	21	1	20	5 5 0	0 5 0	5 10 0
6		Dominick Brennan, ⎫ Patrick Currid, . ⎬ John Leonard, . ⎭	Same, .	Land, . .	6	1	5	1 10 0 ⎱ 1 10 0 ⎰ 0 15 0	—	1 10 0 1 10 0 0 15 0
—	a	Terence Boyle, .	Same, .	House, . .	—			—	0 5 0	0 5 0
7	a	Patrick Hennigan, .	Same, .	Land and house, .	3	2	30	1 10 0	0 15 0	2 5 0

PARISH OF AHAMLISH.

No. and Letters of Reference to Map.	Names.		Description of Tenement.	Area.			Rateable Annual Valuation.		Total Annual Valuation of Rateable Property.
	Townlands and Occupiers.	Immediate Lessors.		A.	R.	P.	Land. £ s. d.	Buildings. £ s. d.	£ s. d.
	DRANGAN, OR MOUNT EDWARD—*continued.*								
8	Terence Cleary,	Capt. James Jones,	Land, . .	5	0	10	3 5 0	—	} 5 10 0
9 *a*			Land and house,	2	1	30	1 15 0	0 10 0	
10	Patrick Carway,	Same,	Land, . .	1	1	30	1 0 0	—	} 9 0 0
11 *a*			Land and office,	9	3	0	7 10 0	0 10 0	
12 *a*	John M'Govern,	Same,	Land and house,	13	3	34	10 5 0	0 10 0	10 15 0
- *b*	Bridget Leonard,	Same,	House, . .	—			—	0 10 0	0 10 0
- *c*	Mary M'Cauly,	Same,	House, . .	—			—	0 8 0	0 8 0
13	Captain James Jones,	Charles Tottenham,	Land (*bog*), .	12	1	28	0 5 0	—	} 0 10 0
14				16	3	0	0 5 0	—	
15	Owen Leonard, .	Captain James Jones,	Land, . .	12	3	9	5 10 0	—	5 10 0
16 *a*	Patrick Mulligan,	Same,	Land and house,	39	0	30	11 15 0	1 0 0	12 15 0
- *b*	Sarah Hart, .	Patrick Mulligan,	House, . .	—			—	0 5 0	0 5 0
17 *a*	James Waters, .	Captain James Jones,	Land and house,	6	2	0	2 10 0	0 15 0	3 5 0
18 *a*	William Hood, .	Same,	Land, house, and office,	65	1	23	33 10 0	2 10 0	36 0 0
- *b*	John Hoey, .	William Hood,	House, . .	—			—	0 .5 0	0 5 0
- *c*	James Meehan, .	Same,	House, . .	—			—	0 5 0	0 5 0
19 *a*	Paul Cunningham,	Captain James Jones,	Land and house,	9	1	35	4 0 0	0 15 0	4 15 0
20 *a*	Michael Brennan,	Same,	Land, house, and forge,	10	2	10	6 0 0	1 10 0	7 10 0
21 *a*	Patrick Gilmartin,	Same,	Land and house,	3	0	20	2 0 0	0 10 0	2 10 0
22 *a*	Daniel Jones, .	Same,	Land and house,	4	2	10	3 5 0	0 10 0	3 15 0
23 *a*	James Gilmartin,	Same,	{ Land and house, Land, . .	1 11	1 1	10 0	0 15 0 5 0 0	0 10 0 —	} 6 5 0
24									
25 *a*	Mary M'Cauly, .	Same,	Land and office,	9	2	20	4 10 0	0 5 0	4 15 0
26 *a*	Michael Gilmartin,	Same,	Land and house,	5	1	35	3 5 0	0 15 0	4 0 0
			Total, .	307	0	26	130 12 0	15 11 0	146 3 0
	GRANGE. (*Ord. S.* 5.)								
1 *a*	James Hart, .	William Johnston,	Land, house, and offices,	64	2	36	57 10 0	5 10 0	63 0 0
- *b*			R. C. Chapel (*see Exemptions*).						
2 *a*	Roger Gillen, .	William Johnston,	Land and house,	10	0	10	11 10 0	0 15 0	12 5 0
3 *a*	James Finnigan,	Same,	Land and house,	13	1	37	9 5 0	1 0 0	10 5 0
4 *a*	Patrick Waters,	Same,	Land and house,	9	1	0	5 10 0	0 15 0	6 5 0
5 *a*	James Gorivan, .	Same,	Land and house,	10	0	10	5 10 0	1 0 0	6 10 0
6 { *a* *b* *c*	James Bore, . . Thomas Bore, . Daniel Bore, . William Bore, .	} Same,	{ Land and house, Land and house, Land and house, Land, . .	} 16	3	10	{ 3 12 0 1 4 0 3 4 0 1 5 0	{ 0 8 0 0 8 0 0 8 0 —	4 0 0 1 12 0 3 12 0 1 5 0
7 *a*	Peter Gillen, .	Same,	Land and house,	4	3	20	3 0 0	0 10 0	3 10 0
8 *a*	Anne Leydon, .	Same,	Land, house, and offices,	30	1	37	16 10 0	3 10 0	20 0 0
9 *a*	Peter Barry, .	Same,	Land and house,	4	0	30	2 5 0	0 15 0	3 0 0
- *b*	John Barry, .	Peter Barry,	Garden and house,	0	1	30	0 5 0	0 5 0	0 10 0
- *c*	Michael Hart, .	Same,	House, . .	—			—	0 5 0	0 5 0
10 11 *a* 12 13	Thomas Loughlin,	William Johnston,	{ Land, . . Land and house, Land, . . Land, . .	2 0 1 13	2 2 2 0	30 20 30 25	1 15 0 0 10 0 0 10 0 6 10 0	— 0 5 0 — —	} 3 0 0
14 *a* 15	Rebecca Allen, .	Same,	{ Land, house, and offices, Land, . .	21 0	3 2	26 30	17 0 0 0 5 0	4 10 0 —	} 28 5 0
13 *a*	Owen Grimes, .	Rebecca Allen, .	House, . .	—			—	0 5 0	0 5 0
- *b*	James Tully, .	Same,	House, . .	—			—	0 5 0	0 5 0
14 *b*	. . .	. . .	National school-house (*see Exemptions*).						
		Rebecca Allen, .	Half the annual rent derived from National school house, . .	—			—	—	0 15 0
- *c*	Susan Allen, .	William Johnston,	House, . .	—			—	3 0 0	3 0 0
- *d*	. . .	. . .	Revenue police-barrack, office and garden (*see Exemptions*).						
		Rebecca Allen, .	Half the annual rent derived from Revenue police-barrack, office, and garden, . .	—			—	—	7 10 0
- *e*	Ellen Cunningham, .	Same,	House, . .	—			—	0 5 0	0 5 0

PARISH OF AHAMLISH.

No. and Letters of Reference to Map.	Townlands and Occupiers.	Immediate Lessors.	Description of Tenement.	Area. A. R. P.	Rateable Annual Valuation. Land. £ s. d.	Buildings. £ s. d.	Total An. Value of Rat. Property. £ s.
	GRANGE— *continued.*						
– f	Michael Frael,	William Johnston,	Garden and house,	0 0 24	0 5 0	1 0 0	1 5
– g	Mary Gilmartin,	Same,	House,	—	—	0 5 0	0 5
– h	Timothy Scanlan,	Same,	Garden and house,	0 0 6	0 1 6	1 4 0	1 5
– i	Owen Waters,	Rebecca Allen,	House & small garden,	—	—	0 5 0	0 5
– j	Bryan Roony,	Same,	House & small garden,	—	—	0 5 0	0 5
– k	Mary Feeny,	Same,	House & small garden,	—	—	0 5 0	0 5
– l	Michael M'Keon,	William Johnston,	Garden and house,	0 0 5	0 1 0	1 9 0	1 10
– m	Michael Gilmartin,	Same,	Garden and house,	0 0 5	0 1 0	3 11 0	3 15
– n	Margaret Boyle,	Same,	Garden and house,	0 0 5	0 1 0	0 11 0	0 15
– o	Mary Kerngan,	Rebecca Allen,	Garden and house,	0 0 8	0 1 0	0 4 0	0 5
– p	Dorothea Rooney,	Same,	House,	—	—	0 3 0	0 3
– q	Catherine M'Dermot,	Same,	House,	—	—	0 3 0	0 3
16	Michael Frael,	William Johnston,	Land,	0 3 0	0 2 0	—	0 2
17 a	John Branley,	Same,	Land and house,	0 2 10	0 4 0	0 8 0	0 12
18	Michael Gilmartin,	Same,	Land,	3 3 10	1 15 0	—	1 15
19 20 21 {20 a	Mary Loughlin,	Same,	Land and house,	2 2 20 / 4 3 36	1 0 0 / 2 15 0	0 15 0	3 15
– b}	John Loughlin,	Same,	Land and house,	3 0 30	2 5 0	0 15 0	3 15
– c	Patrick Gillen,	Same,	Garden and house,	0 0 24	0 2 0	0 8 0	0 10
– d	John Pie,	Same,	House,	—	—	0 10 0	0 10
– e	Martin Gillen,	Same,	House & small garden,	—	—	0 10 0	0 10
– f	Mary Gillen,	Same,	House,	—	—	0 10 0	0 10
22 25 {a	Patrick Gillen (*Martin*),	Same,	Land and house, / Land,	1 3 0 / 2 0 20	1 5 0 / 0 15 0	0 5 0	2 5
24	Rev. Patrick Noone,	Same,	Land,	0 3 0	0 10 0	—	0 10
25 {a	Michael Gillen,		Land, house, & office,		1 5 0	5 10 0	6 15
b	Dominick Gillen,	Same,	Land and house,	2 1 10	0 10 0	1 5 0	1 15
c	Martin Waters,		Land, house, & office,		0 5 0	4 10 0	4 15
d'	Hugh Gallagher,		Land, house, & office,		0 10 0	3 10 0	4 0
– e	Owen M'Gowan,	Same,	House,	—	—	0 5 0	0 5
– f	John Brennan,	Same,	House and forge,	—	—	0 5 0	0 5
– g	Thomas M'Garrigle,	Same,	House and forge,	—	—	0 10 0	0 10
26 a	Michael Kilroy,	Same,	Land, house, and office,	1 0 13	1 4 0	1 16 0	3 0
– b	Patrick Brenly,	Same,	House & small garden,	—	—	0 10 0	0 10
– c	Bryan Hart,	Same,	Garden and house,	0 0 8	0 1 0	0 11 0	0 15
– d	Michael Gorivan,	Same,	House & small garden,	—	—	0 5 0	0 5
– e	Bryan Horne,	Same,	Garden and house,	0 0 9	0 1 0	0 14 0	0 15
– f	Bridget M'Gann,	Susan Allen,	House,	—	—	0 10 0	0 10
27 {	William Johnston, Elizabeth Palmer.	In fee,	Land (*bog*),	12 3 5	0 10 0 / 0 10 0	—	0 10 / 0 10
– a	Patrick Gillen, sen.,	Elizabeth Palmer,	Garden and house,	0 0 30	0 2 0	0 5 0	0 7
1	Patrick Gillen,		Land and house,		12 0 0	0 15 0	12 15
2	Thomas Gillen,		Land and house,		6 18 0	0 15 0	7 13
3	Malachy Waters,		Land and house,		3 8 0	0 15 0	4 3
4	Charles Waters,		Land and house,		6 15 0	0 15 0	7 10
5	John Rooneyan,		Land and house,		3 15 0	0 10 0	4 5
6	John Waters, sen.,		Land and house,		9 10 0	0 15 0	10 5
7	James Waters, sen.,		Land and house,		8 12 0	0 15 0	9 7
8	Patrick Gilmartin,		Land and house,		4 11 0	0 12 0	5 6
9	Martin Waters,		Land and house,		5 16 0	0 12 0	6 8
10	Daniel Waters,		Land and house,		3 7 0	0 15 0	4 2
11	James Waters, jun.,		Land and house,		4 4 0	0 16 0	5 0
12	Bridget Haran,		Land and house,		2 9 0	0 15 0	3 4
13	Patrick Burnes,		Land and house,		4 7 0	0 15 0	5 2
14	Mary Kilroy,		Land and house,		4 9 0	0 11 0	5 0
15	Michael Burnes,		Land and house,		4 0 0	0 10 0	4 10
16	John Waters, jun.,		Land and house,		4 18 0	0 15 0	5 13
17	Bryan Waters,		Land and house,		2 3 0	0 5 0	2 8
18	James Mullany,		Land and house,		6 15 0	0 15 0	7 10
19	James Currid,		Land and house,		6 12 0	0 15 0	7 7
28 {20	Jas. Waters (*Charles*),	Same,	Land and house,	262 0 1	6 18 0	0 15 0	7 13
21	Patrick Gillen, jun.,		Land and house,		8 12 0	1 5 0	9 17
22	Martin Feeny,		Land and house,		3 0 0	0 15 0	3 15
23	Bryan Currid,		Land and house,		4 12 0	0 15 0	5 7
24	Thaddeus Currid,		Land and house,		5 16 0	0 15 0	6 11
25	Peter Gillen,		Land and house,		2 5 0	0 10 0	2 15

PARISH OF AHAMLISH.

No.	Townlands and Occupiers.	Immediate Lessors.	Description of Tenement.	Area. A. R. P.	Rateable Annual Valuation. Land. £ s. d.	Buildings. £ s. d.	Total Annual Valuation of Rateable Property. £ s. d.
	GRANGE— *continued.*						
26	Denis Gillen, .		Land and house,		6 2 0	0 10 0	6 12 0
27	Peter M'Hugh, .		Land and house,		2 15 0	0 10 0	3 5 0
28	Michael Waters,		Land and house,		4 6 0	0 14 0	5 0 0
29	Charles M'Morrow,		Land and house,		1 4 0	0 10 0	1 14 0
30	Hugh Kerigan, .		Land and house,		4 10 0	0 8 0	4 18 0
31	Patrick Waters, .		Land and house,		4 6 0	0 10 0	4 16 0
32	Michael Rooneyan,		Land and house,		4 18 0	0 10 0	5 8 0
	Daniel Gilmartin,		Land, . .		2 17 0	—	2 17 0
	Thomas Feeny,		Land, . .		2 6 0	—	2 6 0
	Michael Woods,		Land, . .		3 18 0	—	3 18 0
	James Devins,		Land, . .		0 9 0	—	0 9 0
	Roger Gillen,		Land, . .		1 4 0	—	1 4 0
	James Gorivan,		Land, . .		0 2 0	—	0 2 0
	James Finnigan,		Land, . .		0 2 0	—	0 2 0
33	Mary Waters, . .	Elizabeth Palmer, .	House, . . .	—	—	0 5 0	0 5 0
	Malachy Waters,				0 6 0	—	0 6 0
	Daniel Waters,				0 6 0	—	0 6 0
	Charles Waters,				0 6 0	—	0 6 0
	James Waters, sen.,				0 9 0	—	0 9 0
11	Martin Waters,	Same, . .	Land, . . .	17 2 6	0 9 0	—	0 9 0
	Thomas Feeny,				0 9 0	—	0 9 0
	Mary Kilroy,				0 9 0	—	0 9 0
	Patrick Burnes,				0 18 0	—	0 18 0
a	John Currid, .	William Johnston, .	Land, house, and forge,	1 1 10	0 16 0	0 9 0	1 5 0
	James Tully, . .	Rebecca Allen, .	Land, . .	1 0 0	0 10 0	—	0 10 0
				3 2 30	2 0 0	—	
	Hugh Gallagher,	William Johnston, .	Land, . .	1 3 0	0 12 0	—	3 0 0
				1 0 20	0 8 0	—	
	Martin Waters,		Land, . .		0 7 0	—	0 7 0
a	John M'Gowan,		Land and house,		0 7 0	0 15 0	1 2 0
	Hugh Gallagher,	Same, .	Land, . .	7 0 9	3 7 0	—	3 7 0
	Rebecca Allen,		Land, . .		0 17 0	—	0 17 0
	Michael Frael,		Land, . .		1 7 0	—	1 7 0
24	Patrick Gillen (*Mason*),	Same, . .	Land, . .	2 0 0	1 0 0	—	1 0 0
25 a	Martin Gillen, . .	Same, . .	Land and house,	3 3 20	2 7 0	0 8 0	2 15 0
29 a	Martin Waters, .	Same, .	Land and office,	3 3 1	2 1 0	0 5 0	4 15 0
			Land, . .	2 2 0	2 9 0	—	
			Total of Rateable Property, .	550 0 36	377 15 0	81 5 0	467 5 0
			EXEMPTIONS :				
	. . . . . .	. . .	R. C. Chapel, . .	—	—	25 0 0	25 0 0
	. . . . . .	. . .	National school-house, .	—	—	0 10 0	0 10 0
	. . . . . .	. . .	Revenue police-barrack, office, and garden, .	0 1 0	0 7 0	6 3 0	6 10 0
			Total of Exemptions,	0 1 0	0 7 0	31 13 0	32 0 0
			Total, including Exemptions, .	550 1 36	378 2 0	112 18 0	499 5 0
	ISLANDS. No. 1. INISHNAGOR ISLAND. (*Ord. S. 5.*)						
	Denis Gillen,	Elizabeth Palmer, .	Land, . . .	5 0 16	1 8 0	—	1 8 0
	Charles M'Morrow,				1 8 0	—	1 8 0
			Total, . .	5 0 16	2 16 0	—	2 16 0
	SILVERHILL. (*Ord. S. 5.*)						
	Thomas Devins, .	Captain James Jones,	Land, . . .	10 2 0	3 0 0	—	3 0 0
	Captain James Jones,	Charles Tottenham,	Land, . .	50 1 17	10 0 0	—	10 5 0
			Land (*bog*), .	22 3 23	0 5 0	—	
	Hugh Hart, .	Capt. James Jones,	Land and house,	4 1 0	1 5 0	0 5 0	1 15 0
			Land, . .	0 2 10	0 5 0	—	
	Dominick Hoey, .	Same, . .	Land and house,	13 2 8	5 15 0	0 15 0	6 10 0
	James Meehan, .	Same, . .	Land, house, and office,	8 1 10	1 15 0	0 15 0	2 10 0

9

O.S. MAP C. 1837 SHOWING GRANGE AS IT WAS

Revenue Police
Barrack
C K L I S

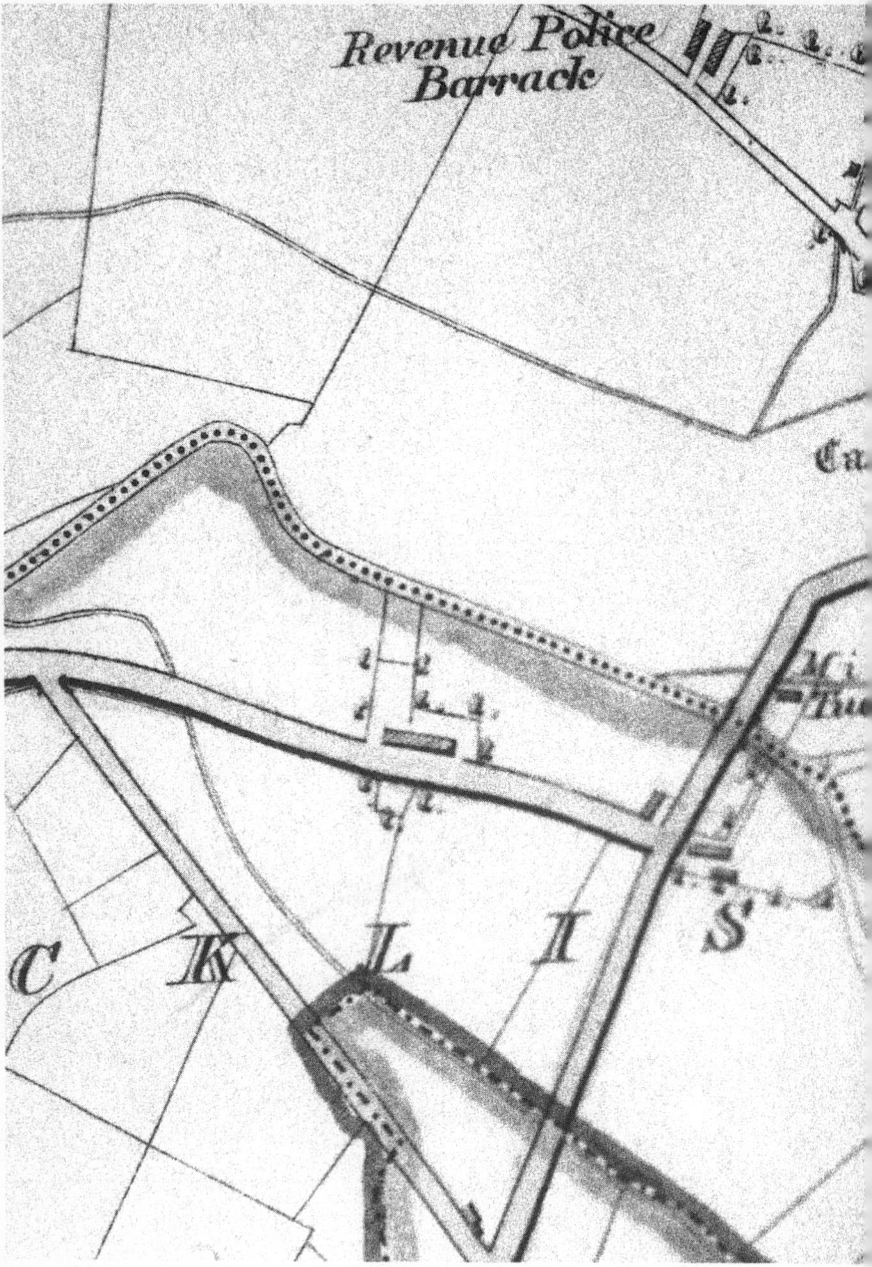

R.C.Chapel

Grange

Mill

Race

Pound

N

E

54

58

Corn Mill

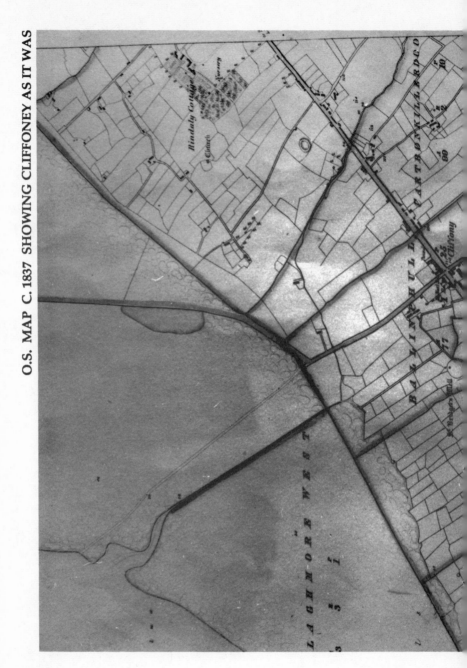

O.S. MAP C. 1837 SHOWING CLIFFONEY AS IT WAS

332

333

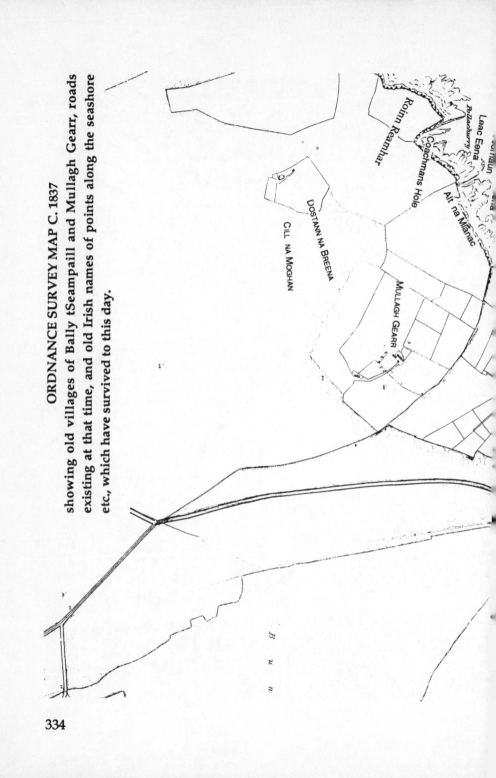

ORDNANCE SURVEY MAP C. 1837

showing old villages of Bally tSeampaill and Mullagh Gearr, roads existing at that time, and old Irish names of points along the seashore etc., which have survived to this day.

Leac Eena

Pollacharry

Coachmans Hole

Roinn Reamhar

Alt na Mìanac

DOSTANN NA BREENA

CILL NA MOGHAN

MULLAGH GEARR

Oilean Eamonn

Cockannatinnow
Cruach na Gabhair
Lugnashanag
Dreimire Buidhe
Cule a Cutch
Illaunes beg
Mill Island
Illaunes more

Leac Fada

Cromadac

Leac Ailsie

Leac Cam

Leac a Beaga

Leac Bhuidhea
Alt Briste

Oilean na Crugadaí

Poll an Uisge

Carraig Mac Gabhann

Carraig na Pisheen

Dunlevy's Island

Pig's Hole

Leac Coradha

Poll Ui Dhiarmuide

Leac Fionn Roidh

Eadear a Leic

Leac na Meala

Poll Eibhlin

Poll Glas

Poll Garu

Poll Chait
Carrickgarve
Claddagh Geal

Leac na gCaoileac

Gubaun

Pigeon Cove

Poll a Fibia

Poll Domhain
Poll Fionn

Thomas's Rock
Coast Guard Station
CLADDAGH HARBOUR

Mullaghmore

BALLY TSEAMPAILL

K I L L I L O G H E R

Hughes' Island

Yellow Rock

Bally

Sheet 2

335

THE AUTHOR

The author, Joe McGowan, is a native of Mullaghmore. He worked the family farm, where he was born, until 1961, when he emigrated to the U.S.A. In 1962 he was drafted into the U.S. army and served there for two years during the 'Cuban Crisis' and the early years of the Vietnam era. After discharge he lived and worked in America for many years, married and returned to Ireland in 1976 with his wife Antoinette, three daughters and one son.

Keenly aware of the great changes in rural Ireland he decided to record the old lore before it disappeared altogether. This book is the result of many nights spent visiting the older men and women of North Sligo and listening to their stories. Another facet of this research eventually led to many hours being spent in Sligo Library, the National Library, National Museum and Public Records Office in Dublin. Old estate and R.I.C. records had to be researched in England, at the P.R.O in Kew, London and the Hartley Library in Southampton.

The days of the story-tellers are gone, but their stories and lore will, happi'

336

CHICAGO PUBLIC LIBRARY
BEVERLY BRANCH
1962 W. 95th STREET
CHICAGO, IL   60643

CHICAGO PUBLIC LIBRARY
BEVERLY BRANCH
1962 W. 95th STREET
CHICAGO, IL   60643

CHICAGO PUBLIC LIBRARY
BEVERLY BRANCH
1962 W. 95th STREET
CHICAGO, IL   60643